W9-BFU-130

DISCARDED:
OUTDATED, REDUNDANT
MATERIAL

Date: 5/20/19

**PALM BEACH COUNTY
LIBRARY SYSTEM**

**3650 Summit Boulevard
West Palm Beach, FL 33406**

PALM BEACH COUNTY
LIBRARY SYSTEM
3650 SUMMIT BLVD.
WEST PALM BEACH, FL 33406

Gender Roles in American Life

Gender Roles in American Life

A Documentary History of Political, Social, and Economic Changes

Volume 2: 1955–Present

CONSTANCE L. SHEHAN, EDITOR

 ABC-CLIO™

An Imprint of ABC-CLIO, LLC
Santa Barbara, California • Denver, Colorado

Copyright © 2018 by ABC-CLIO, LLC

All rights reserved. No part of this publication may be reproduced, stored in a retrieval system, or transmitted, in any form or by any means, electronic, mechanical, photocopying, recording, or otherwise, except for the inclusion of brief quotations in a review, without prior permission in writing from the publisher.

Library of Congress Cataloging-in-Publication Data

Names: Shehan, Constance L., editor.
Title: Gender roles in American life : a documentary history of political, social, and economic changes / Constance L. Shehan, editor.
Description: Santa Barbara, California : ABC-CLIO, [2018] | Includes bibliographical references and index.
Identifiers: LCCN 2017039203 (print) | LCCN 2017049486 (ebook) | ISBN 9781440859595 (eBook) | ISBN 9781440859588 (set : alk. paper) | ISBN 9781440859601 (volume 1) | ISBN 9781440859618 (volume 2)
Subjects: LCSH: Sex role—United States—History. | Sex role—United States—History—Sources. | United States—Politics and government—Sources. | United States—History—Sources.
Classification: LCC HQ1075.5.U6 (ebook) | LCC HQ1075.5.U6 G4674 2018 (print) | DDC 305.30973—dc23
LC record available at https://lccn.loc.gov/2017039203

ISBN: 978-1-4408-5958-8 (set)
        978-1-4408-5960-1 (vol. 1)
        978-1-4408-5961-8 (vol. 2)
        978-1-4408-5959-5 (ebook)

22 21 20 19   2 3 4 5

This book is also available as an eBook.

ABC-CLIO
An Imprint of ABC-CLIO, LLC

ABC-CLIO, LLC
130 Cremona Drive, P.O. Box 1911
Santa Barbara, California 93116-1911
www.abc-clio.com

This book is printed on acid-free paper ∞

Manufactured in the United States of America

Contents

Chapter 5: 1955–1975: Pushing Gender Boundaries

In the mid-1950s and early 1960s, technological developments pushed the US into a new age—actually two: the Space Age and, with the introduction of the birth control pill, the Sexual Revolution. The creation of NASA and the selection of the first crew of astronauts demonstrated—unintentionally, perhaps—that women had the "right stuff" to be astronauts, just as men did. But that did not provide them entrance into the space program, at least not until two decades later. The Sexual Revolution changed the nature of relationships between women and men, insofar as it made it possible to separate sexuality from reproduction and from marriage.

The period from 1955 to 1975 was characterized by extensive social action on behalf of civil rights, women's rights, peace, and sexual minority rights. Many people were members of several, if not all, of these social movements. The civil rights movement and the women's liberation movement were closely aligned, just as they had been in the 19th century when the abolitionist movement and the woman suffrage movement combined efforts to address their causes. The peace (or anti-war) movement was closely aligned with the student movement, as Americans increasingly opposed the U.S. involvement in Vietnam. The gay rights movement exploded into national consciousness with the Stonewall Riots in 1969, but its roots were firmly planted in the 1950s. In 1950, the Mattachine Society, one of the first gay rights organizations, was founded in Chicago. In 1955, the Daughters of Bilitis (DOB), the first lesbian organization in the United States, was founded. Although DOB originated as a social group, it later developed into a political organization to win basic acceptance for lesbians in the United States.

The environmental movement also began during this period of time. Rachel Carson (1907–1964) was a marine biologist. In 1936, she became only the second woman the Bureau of Fisheries hired for a full-time professional position, as a biologist. Much of her work at the Bureau of Fisheries involved writing publications to educate the public about the agency's work. She wrote her first book, *Under the Sea*, in 1941, and her second, *The Sea Around Us*, in 1951. In the 1950s, Carson began to focus on conservation, particularly on biological problems caused by synthetic pesticides. In 1962, she published a groundbreaking book, *Silent Spring*, which described the harmful effects of pesticides on the environment. The book reached a wide audience and inspired an environmental movement that eventually led to a national ban on DDT and other pesticides. In 1970, President Richard Nixon created the Environmental Protection Agency. Carson was posthumously awarded the Presidential Medal of Freedom, the highest civilian honor in the United States. On April 22, 1970, the first Earth Day was celebrated.

In response to—or alongside—these social movements was the passage of major pieces of federal legislation that substantially changed the legal rights, and thus the gender roles, of many Americans. Unprecedented changes in political administrations also happened during this time, with the assassination of President John F. Kennedy (in 1963); the appointment and then election of then Vice President Lyndon Johnson as his successor (in 1964) and Johnson's decision not to run for reelection in 1968 due to the conflict in Vietnam; the election of Richard Nixon (in 1968) and his reelection in 1972, followed by the Watergate scandal and Nixon's resignation in 1974; and the ascendency of Vice President Gerald Ford to the presidency after Nixon's resignation (1974). Each change in presidential administration (with the possible exception of the transition from Kennedy to Johnson) was marked by changes in political priorities.

1955 to 1960: Manly Men and Adoring Wives: The Early Space Program in the United States

In 1957, the Cold War was intensifying. Russia launched Sputnik 1 (the first artificial satellite) into Earth's orbit. The U.S. government feared that the Russians would put nuclear weapons in space and use them to attack America. As a result, the United States decided to combine its existing military and civilian space efforts into one program, the National Aeronautics and Space Administration (NASA). The goal of NASA programs was to beat the Russians to manned space flight, setting 1961 as the targeted flight time.

In 1959, NASA began an extensive search for the first astronauts. The records of over 500 military test pilots were screened, with the first round of selection resulting in 110 candidates, all men. The 67 men who volunteered were subjected to a number of written tests and interviews, and their medical histories were scrutinized. Of the candidates who were selected, four dropped out of consideration because of the intensity of the additional testing that they would have to undergo. The 32 remaining candidates were taken to the Lovelace Clinic in Albuquerque, New Mexico, where they were subjected to exhausting physical and psychological tests. All but one of these men went on to the next round of testing, which was held in the Wright Aeromedical Laboratory in Dayton, Ohio.

The tests at the Wright Laboratory went on for six days. They were designed to test the men's tolerance of extreme physical and psychological stress. One experience they were exposed to was spending an hour in a pressure chamber that simulated an altitude of 65,000 feet. Another had them spend two hours in a chamber that was heated to a temperature of 130 degrees. At the end of the week, only 18 candidates remained.

At the same time that men were being tested for space flight, a parallel but unofficial screening of women pilots was being conducted at the Lovelace Clinic. Dr. William Lovelace and Brigadier General Donald Flickinger were interested in investigating women's capabilities for space flight, because they thought that their smaller average size would fit better in the cramped space capsules. The first woman that Lovelace and Flickinger tested was Jerrie Cobb, an award-winning pilot who actually had more flight hours than John Glenn, one of the original Mercury astronauts. Cobb passed all of the stringent tests that she was asked to undergo. Lovelace and Flickinger then invited other women pilots to New Mexico to be tested. Included in the tests were a four-hour eye exam and riding a weighted stationary bike that pushed the rider to exhaustion while testing respiration. Cobb and other women who were tested had to swallow a rubber tube so that Lovelace could measure their stomach acids, and ice water was shot into their ears to induce vertigo so that their recovery time could be measured. At the end of the testing program, 13 women had passed all of the tests that Lovelace had used for NASA's selection process for male astronauts. Cobb and two other women were scheduled to take additional tests at the Naval School of Aviation Medicine in Pensacola, Florida. But a few days before they were to begin, the Navy revoked their permission to use the facilities for unofficial tests (Weitekamp, n.d.).

Cobb flew to Washington to try to have the test program resumed. Jane Hart, another of the women who had been tested, talked to Vice President Lyndon Johnson. In July, a public hearing was held before the House Committee on Science and Astronautics. The hearings were essentially investigating sex discrimination before the 1964 Civil Rights Act made it illegal. A NASA representative and astronauts John Glenn and Scott Carpenter testified that women could not qualify as astronauts because they were not graduates of military jet pilot training and did not have engineering degrees. In 1962, women were not permitted to have military jet pilot experience, which was a prerequisite for entrance into the astronaut ranks. The subcommittee was sympathetic to the women's argument, according to NASA publications, but no further action was taken. Not until 1978, when the first class of space shuttle astronauts was selected, would a woman, Sally Ride, became the first American woman in space. Interestingly, in 1963, Valentina Tereshkova, a Russian astronaut, because the first woman in space (Weitekamp, n.d.).

The Astronaut Wives

Several women did become very visible members of the astronaut family—the women who were married to the original Mercury 7 astronauts and, later, the wives of the Gemini and Apollo mission astronauts. Sociologist Helena Papanek has used the term "the two-person career" to refer to men whose jobs are so demanding and, typically, so socially visible that they require their wives to devote their time and energy to promoting their husbands' careers. Politicians' wives, for instance, often spend considerable time accompanying their husbands to fund-raising events and making frequent public appearances while maintaining the home front by performing all of the domestic labor and child care. In addition to the enormous time commitment, women married to men who hold this type of position are also held to strict standards of appearance and comportment, and they are continually scrutinized. This happened to the women married to the Mercury 7. Their husbands were hailed as all-American heroes, and the wives were viewed as the "women behind the successful men." They were featured in numerous women's magazines and television interviews, always looking flawless and talking about their husbands in glowing terms. They represented, in many respects, the quintessential American wife and mother of the 1950s and early 1960s. Their husbands, on the other hand, represented the "man's man"—that is, the risk-taking, hard-driving men who devoted their time to their male-dominated careers and colleagues.

The 1960s: Civil Rights and the Sexual Revolution

The 1960s began with the election of John F. Kennedy as president of the United States in 1960. (This was also the year when the birth control pill was approved by the Food and Drug Administration). Kennedy was hailed as the first president born in the 20th century; as such, he offered the promise of youth, vigor, and fresh ideas. One of Kennedy's lesser known legacies was providing support for the beginning of the modern women's movement (Shames and O'Leary 2013). In December 1961, after considerable prodding by several influential women, Kennedy established a Presidential Commission on the Status of Women, whose members included women who had long been involved in politics and the labor movement. Former First Lady Eleanor Roosevelt was selected as its chair. The next year, at the urging of the commission, Kennedy ordered federal agencies to end sex discrimination in hiring. In 1963, he signed into law the historic Equal Pay Act, which prohibited "discrimination on account of sex in the payment of wages by employers."[1] The next day he proposed civil rights legislation (Green 2017).

The Commission on the Status of Women issued a report entitled "American Women" in 1963, just months before President Kennedy was assassinated. The report called attention to the needs of poor women, women of color (particularly African Americans), rural as well as urban women, migrants, and women in different regions and occupations (Green 2017). It highlighted the need to draft legislation on pay equity, maternity leave, child care, and other needs of women workers. As Laurie Green, professor of history at the University of Texas notes,

> "American Women" (the Commission's report) began to introduce a new paradigm, setting the intention to dismantle disadvantage at the interconnected levels of women's identities, such as race, class and gender (Green 2017).

Lyndon B. Johnson's Support of Civil Rights

Just days after becoming president, Lyndon Johnson decided to take up the civil rights legislation that Kennedy had proposed. His experience in the Senate enabled him to get the bill through Congress. Johnson signed it into law on July 2, 1964. Title II, which outlawed segregation in public accommodations, was soon reviewed by the Supreme Court, which ruled in its favor. Title II essentially destroyed the foundation on which Jim Crow and segregation were based.

---

1. In 1942, Republican representative Winifred Stanley from New York introduced H.R. 5056, "Prohibiting Discrimination in Pay on Account of Sex," which did not pass at the time.

Title VII of the Civil Rights Act barred discrimination in employment on the basis of race and sex. It also established what became the Equal Employment Opportunity Commission (EEOC) to investigate discrimination complaints and impose penalties on employers who were found guilty. The EEOC began to take cases in 1965. Title VII is the basis on which women's rights have been established in the more than 50 years since it was founded. In 1967, President Johnson included sex discrimination in the list of employment acts that were prohibited by Title VII. Johnson's action directed federal agencies and contractors to take proactive measures (i.e., affirmative action) to ensure that women and minorities would have the same educational and employment opportunities as white men. The law did recognize that in very limited circumstances, a protected characteristic (e.g., sex) is a bona fide occupational qualification (BFOQ).[2] The BFOQ defense is never available in race discrimination cases, however. In the eyes of the law, there is no legitimate, nondiscriminatory reason for only hiring people of a particular race. In 1968, the EEOC ruled that sex-segregated help-wanted ads in newspapers were illegal. This was later upheld by the Supreme Court.

The Beginning of the Second Women's Rights Movement

The Publication of The Feminine Mystique and the Creation of NOW

During the early 1960s, when Kennedy and Johnson were moving toward civil rights legislation, a grassroots women's movement was developing. In 1963, Betty Friedan (1921–2006) published *The Feminine Mystique*, which describes the dissatisfaction felt by middle-class American housewives with the limited domestic role imposed on them by society. Friedan was a graduate of Smith College (an elite Ivy League school in the Northeast). After graduating from Smith in 1942, she went to Berkeley to get the training necessary to become a psychologist. Instead of establishing a career in psychology, however, she got married and became a suburban housewife and mother in New York, occasionally writing articles for women's magazines. At her 15th Smith College class reunion, Friedan conducted a survey of her classmates and found that many were dissatisfied with their lives as housewives. This piqued her interest, because she too was experiencing dissatisfaction with her life, even though she supposedly "had it all." She and her classmates had the education and skills to pursue careers, but instead they were living in a period when women were supposed to find their entire fulfillment in domesticity. The average age at marriage for women in the late 1950s was between 19 and 20, and the majority of women college students dropped out before graduating. Friedan and her colleagues completed college but still found themselves in a situation where their intellectual curiosity was being thwarted. After supplementing her interviews with additional research, Friedan wrote and published *The Feminine Mystique* in 1963.

---

2. An example of a BFOQ involved the restaurant chain Hooters, which claimed that only women could be "Hooters Girls." The court agreed with the restaurant.

The Feminine Mystique became a bestseller, and it is considered one of the most influential nonfiction books of the 20th century. In 1963, the rights of women in the United States were limited. They could not get financial credit without having a man co-sign the loan. In some states, married women's husbands had control over their earnings and property. Newspapers were allowed to divide their help-wanted ads into categories for men and women, and it was perfectly legal for an employer to announce that certain jobs were for men only. Because of the legal status of women in 1963, the book found an audience and became a rallying call for 28 other feminist leaders, who joined with Friedan (who became the president of the new organization) to found the National Organization for Women in 1966, at the third National Conference of the Commission on the Status of Women. "The [original] purpose of NOW is to take action to bring women into full participation in the mainstream of American society now, exercising all privileges and responsibilities thereof in truly equal partnership with men" (NOW, n.d). Friedan and others in the women's movement helped change laws that disadvantaged women in the workplace. Their primary strategies were legislative lobbying, litigation, and public demonstrations. In 1968, for instance, NOW formed a special committee to launch a major campaign to pass the Equal Rights Amendment. (As mentioned earlier, Alice Paul first introduced the Equal Rights Amendment in 1923.) In 1972, it passed in Congress and was sent to the individual states for ratification.

Friedan and NOW were, and still are, criticized for focusing on the needs of white, upper-middle-class women to the exclusion of women of other racial and ethnic groups, social classes, and sexual identities.[3] Other feminist groups with different philosophies and strategies emerged to advocate for the concerns of women who were excluded from NOW's focus.[4] Feminists of color were essential to the creation of a broader, more inclusive form of feminism. Their writings continue to have influence today.

In the 1960s, access to safe and legal abortion was a major concern of women. In 1968, the National Abortion Rights Action League (NARAL) was founded. It is still active today. The radical feminist group Redstockings began in New York. Members staged an abortion speak-out (i.e., a public rally), arguing that women, rather than male legislators, should have authority in making laws and policies about women's reproductive rights. Feminist activity flourished during the late 1960s and into the 1970s. Different feminist groups used different tactics. In 1969, the New York Radical Women organization protested at the Miss America pageant. NOW activists marched in Washington, DC, for Mother's Day, demanding "Rights, Not Roses." In 1972, the first issue of the magazine *Ms.* was published by Gloria Steinem.

---

3. Today, this period of feminism characterized by Betty Friedan and NOW is often referred to as "second wave" feminism. A "third wave" of feminism, which focuses on the intersectionality of people's social statuses (e.g., race, ethnicity, gender, social class, sexual identity), is considered more inclusive and thus more acceptable than "second wave" feminism.

4. For instance, the Women's Equity Action League broke off from NOW to avoid the "controversial" issues of sexuality, reproductive choice, and the Equal Rights Amendment.

Legal Developments for Women's Rights in the 1970s

In 1972, Title IX of the Education Amendments banned sex discrimination in schools. It states, "No person in the United States shall, *on the basis of sex*, be excluded from participation in, be denied the benefits of, or be subjected to discrimination under any educational program or activity receiving federal financial assistance" (emphasis added). As a result of Title IX, the enrollment of women in athletics programs and professional schools increased dramatically. In 1974, the Equal Credit Opportunity Act was passed. It prohibited discrimination in consumer credit practices on the basis of sex, race, marital status, religion, national origin, age, or receipt of public assistance. In *Corning Glass Works v. Brennan*, the U.S. Supreme Court ruled that employers could not pay women lower wages because that is what they traditionally received under the "going market rate." A wage differential occurring "simply because men would not work at the low rates paid women" was ruled unacceptable.

This was also a period of significant "firsts" when it came to women in political office. For instance, in 1968 Shirley Chisholm became the first black woman elected to the U.S. Congress. She represented New York's 12th Congressional District for seven terms, from 1969 to 1983. In 1972, she became the first black candidate nominated by a major party for president of the United States and the first woman to receive the Democratic Party's presidential nomination.

The Sexual Revolution

The approval of the first oral contraceptive, known as "the Pill," in 1960 opened the door for major changes in sexual behavior. With the possibility to engage in (hetero)sexual relationships with a reduced risk of pregnancy, sexuality became increasingly detached from marriage. Because many states had laws restricting access to contraception, the Supreme Court heard many cases that involved state restriction. For instance, in 1965, in *Griswold v. Connecticut*, the Supreme Court struck down a law that restricted married couples' access to contraception. By 1970, 12 million women were taking "the Pill," and the use of other means of birth control, such as diaphragms and IUDs, also increased. In 1972, in *Eisenstadt v. Baird*, the Supreme Court extended to unmarried couples the right to use contraceptives . Then in 1973, in a landmark decision, the Court (in *Roe v. Wade*) established a woman's right to safe and legal abortion. Prior to this decision, which was based on the right to privacy guaranteed by the 14th Amendment, some states did allow women to terminate pregnancies, but others did not.

References and Further Reading

Ackmann, Martha, and Lynn Scherr. *The* Mercury 13: *The True Story of Thirteen Women and the Dream of Space Flight.* New York: Random House, 2003.

Carson, Rachel. *The Sea Around Us*, Special Edition. New York: Oxford University Press, 1991.

Carson, Rachel. *Silent Spring*, Anniversary Edition. New York: Houghton Mifflin, 2002.

Carson, Rachel. *Under the Sea Wind.* Rev. ed. New York: Oxford University Press, 1952.

Chisholm, Shirley. *Unbought and Unbossed*, Expanded 40th Anniversary Edition. New York: Take Root Media.

Davis, Angela Y. *Women, Race, and Class*, First Vintage Books Edition. New York: Vintage Books, 2011.

Eig, Jonathan. *The Birth of the Pill: How Four Crusaders Reinvented Sex and Launched a Revolution.* New York: W. W. Norton, 2015.

Friedan, Betty, and Gail Collins. *The Feminine Mystique*, 50th Anniversary Edition. New York: W. W. Norton, 2013.

Green, Laurie. "On JFK's 100th Birthday, We Should Celebrate a Women's Rights Legacy." UT News, University of Texas, May 31, 2017. https://news.utexas.edu/2017/05/31/on -jfk-s-100th-birthday-we-should-celebrate-women-s-rights.

Hite, Shere. *The Hite Report: A Nationwide Study of Female Sexuality.* New York: Macmillan, 1976.

Hite, Shere. *The Hite Report on Male Sexuality.* New York: Ballantine Books, 1987.

Imbornoni, Ann-Marie. "Women's Rights Movements in the U.S.: Timeline of Key Events in the American Women's Rights Movement, 1921–1979." https://www.infoplease.com /spot/womens-rights-movement-us-0.

Koppel, Lily. *The Astronaut Wives' Club.* New York: Grand Central Publishing, 2013.

Mann, Susan Archer. *Doing Feminist Theory: From Modernity to Postmodernity.* New York: Oxford University Press, 2012.

NOW (National Organization of Women). "When and How Was NOW Founded?" http:// now.org/faq/when-and-how-was-now-founded.

Shames, Shauna, and Pamela O'Leary. "JFK, a Pioneer in the Women's Movement." *Los Angeles Times,* November 23, 2013. http://articles.latimes.com/2013/nov/22/opinion /la-oe-shames-kennedy-women-20131122.

Weitekamp, Margaret A. "Lovelace's Woman in Space Program." National Aeronautics and Space Administration. https://history.nasa.gov/flats.html.

Wolfe, Tom, *The Right Stuff*, 2nd ed. New York: Farrar, Straus and Giroux, 2004.

PRESIDENT EISENHOWER URGES WORKING MOTHERS TO RETURN TO THE HOME, 1958

During the 1950s the United States experienced a cultural retrenchment of sorts when it came to gender roles and responsibilities. During a sustained postwar economic expansion that saw accelerating development of both the American suburbs and infrastructure (ranging from new highways to new water treatment and electric plants) capable of supporting those suburbs, women were on the receiving end of a steady drumbeat of messages urging them to embrace domestic life and turn away from careers outside the home. Television programming, popular magazines, and community organizations all painted the "all-American" home as one in which the husband provided economic support for his family and the wife took primary responsibility for the house and children. Women who dared to pursue careers or passions that might interfere with their duties of raising the kids, preparing tasty meals, and keeping the house neat and tidy were subjected to negative attention ranging from raised eyebrows to outright condemnation. This message of subordination to traditional gender roles even came from the White House, as this excerpt from President Dwight D. Eisenhower's December 1958 speech to the National Committee for the 1960 White House Conference on Children and Youth shows.

I assure you first of all it is a privilege and a great honor to welcome you here to this convocation—those who have been appointed to this traditional Committee, started fifty years ago by Theodore Roosevelt and which meets every ten years. It has become something that I believe we can now classify as a permanent part of our educational process, at least so far as youth and children are concerned.

Certainly they had a great effect because President Theodore Roosevelt was gravely concerned about infant mortality and children's health. And now I am informed that the percentage for reaching adult life for a child born today is five times better than it was fifty years ago. If a Committee such as this were responsible even for part of that progress, then indeed it is worthwhile. Such a record as that—and it has been repeated in different forms in 1920, 1930, 1940 and 1950—is always a continuing challenge to your understanding and your energy. As a matter of fact, your dedication to America's welfare is exactly what your concern about children means.

Before such a group as this I am not going to be bold enough to make any very ponderous statements or any that are by any stretch of the imagination to be interpreted as erudite. But I do like children—I have some grandchildren—and so I think I can talk a little bit before we disperse.

I am concerned about the opportunity that is put before every child from the day of his or her birth until certainly he or she gets through high school. And of course, this starts at the home.

Today there are 22 million working women. Of that 22 million, 7 and a half million are working mothers, and unquestionably a great number of that 7 and a half million are working because they have to help keep the wolf from the door.

They work because they have to work. But if there is only a tiny percentage doing this because they prefer a career to an active career of real motherhood and care for the little child, I should think they would have to consider what is the price they are paying in terms of the opportunities that child has been denied. Certainly no one can do quite as much in molding the child's habit of thinking and implanting certain standards as can the mother.

Source: Eisenhower, Dwight D. "Remarks to the National Committee for the 1960 White House Conference on Children and Youth," December 16, 1958. *Public Papers of the Presidents, Dwight D. Eisenhower: 1958.* Washington, DC: Government Printing Office, 1958.

KENNEDY ADVISER RECALLS THE WORK OF THE PRESIDENT'S COMMISSION ON THE STATUS OF WOMEN, 1961–1963

Richard A. Lester (1908–1997) was a prominent economist and labor expert who was appointed by President Kennedy to serve as vice chairman of the President's Commission on the Status of Women in 1961. Lester became chairman of the Commission following the death of former First Lady Eleanor Roosevelt in November 1962. In the following excerpt from a December 24, 1970, interview that Lester gave to Ann M. Campbell for the John F. Kennedy Library Oral History Program, he discusses the goals of the Commission, Roosevelt's leadership, the contributions of several other members, and the way in which an opponent of women's rights actually paved the way for increased civil rights protections for women.

CAMPBELL: Let's talk about the President's Commission on the Status of Women. I wonder if you were consulted very early about this. Were you involved in the early planning, the idea itself through the commission?

LESTER: It must've been either November or December when this first was brought to my attention. I was asked if I would be willing to go on it. And Esther Peterson [Esther E. Peterson], whom I had known a little bit but not well, talked with me. I guess it was fairly early because she and I went to see Mrs. Roosevelt [Eleanor R. Roosevelt] in her apartment in New York. It must've been about December sixty...

CAMPBELL: '61.

LESTER: . . . '61. Right. It may have been even before that because I guess by then Mrs. Roosevelt had practically agreed, if not agreed, to be chairman. And I remember we talked about the work the commission would do. We talked about people. I'm pretty sure that at that time the commission had not been appointed. And Mrs. Roosevelt, of course, was acquainted with a great many of these people, much more so than I was. And she had some very acute things to say.

CAMPBELL: She then was actively interested and involved in the selection process.

LESTER: She was. She was tremendously so. We spent, we had lunch there and spent, I would say, at least two hours, maybe even a little longer.

CAMPBELL: At that stage, do you recall what your expectations were, and the expectations of Mrs. Roosevelt for the accomplishments of the group? Did you hope to sort of pinpoint the problem and highlight the problem? Or did you really hope to generate specific legislation?

LESTER: I don't think we talked about the legislation quite so much then. We had talked about the areas where work needed to be done and the way the commission ought to operate in terms of committees, something on the timing, and heavily of people. And question of the Equal Rights Amendment and the influence that the proponents could or should have. And of course we got a great deal into the economic aspects, equal pay and, of course, equal rights, too. But at that point we were talking pretty heavily about people.

CAMPBELL: I have a list here of the commission members. I suppose the members of the Cabinet are easily understood, but it was interesting, for example, that Senator Aiken [George D. Aiken] was chosen as a commission member.

LESTER: Well, I think President Kennedy was fairly close to Aiken. And we wanted a Republican. We wanted it bipartisan. And, Aiken actually turned out to be quite good. He had a person on his staff whom we dealt with mostly. But he attended meetings. And we found Aiken quite good. He really went along in the end more readily than one might have expected. And I think he understood some of the issues all right.
[. . .]

CAMPBELL: What do you recall about how Mrs. Boddy [Sarabeth Boddy] who was on the commission?

LESTER: Well, that was a very interesting. . . . She was Lyndon Johnson's person, Mrs. Roosevelt handled her quite well. When Boddy first came on the commission, she had all the prejudices of a Texan who comes from a fairly well-to-do environment. She used to get up and give examples of people who were, you know, getting more than they deserved from government and the ill effects of the minimum wage and other labor legislation. Mrs. Roosevelt handled her quite well. She let her talk some. And then I think Mrs. Roosevelt actually told Johnson of the troubles that we were having with her. And I think maybe Johnson said something to Mrs. Boddy.

I remember we went to Vice President Johnson's house. He invited the commission members out to his house—Lady Bird [Claudia Alta—Lady Bird Johnson] was there—to a kind of cocktail party or reception. I was there with Mrs. Roosevelt when we shook hands with Vice President Johnson and Mrs. Johnson. We talked a bit about the commission and something was said about Mrs. Boddy and Mrs. Roosevelt said something like,—Well, I think she's learning things. We've had some problems. But I think she's coming along. It may have been a little more cutting than that, but I'm sure Vice President Johnson got the point.

Subsequently we arranged for a conference in a large room in the building next to the Department of Labor building. We arranged to have Johnson, Robert Kennedy [Robert F. Kennedy] and Bill Wirtz on the panel of speakers. We had people in from industry and from the unions. The room was filled. There must've been two hundred and fifty representatives there. We had them all in for a one day conference on what we were doing and getting their advice.

For some reason or other Mrs. Roosevelt could not be there to serve as chairman so I served as chairman. And Lyndon Johnson had flown up all that night to be present there to give a talk. As I said, we had Lyndon; Bobby Kennedy; and Bill Wirtz; and, perhaps, a fourth. And Lyndon was really quite good. I think Liz Carpenter [Elizabeth S. Carpenter] had kept him in touch with what the commission was doing. He gave a very good talk, made it rather personal because he referred a couple of times to his daughters, to the extent to which he tied up the questions of equal opportunity and ability to work out a career or whatever other type of life a young lady might wish to engage in without being restricted by outmoded traditions or legal holdovers and so on. That meeting went much better than we had anticipated, partly because of what Johnson said. Even at that time, I think he had influence with the business people and with the people, the southern representatives that it was helpful for us to have.

[. . .]

CAMPBELL: Who of the commission members did turn out to be most active in commission affairs?

LESTER: Of the Cabinet people and the Congress people. . . . It's hard to say because they had their staff people. Now the staff person for Robert Kennedy was quite effective. The staff person for Orville Freeman [Orville L. Freeman] was quite effective also. We didn't get so much from the staff person for Hodges [Luther H. Hodges]. Of course, Willard Wirtz had Esther Peterson there. HEW [Department of Health, Education, and Welfare] wasn't so influential. Senator Aiken's man did more behind the scenes.

Now, Senator Neuberger [Maurine B. Neuberger] did participate a great deal. She was quite effective. Edith Green [Edith S. Green] was too. She was a person that you felt you had to cater to a bit. She had her own views that she asserted very vigorously. John Macy [John W. Macy Jr.] did participate a great deal, as did the people he had in the civil service commission whose names I can't all remember now. One was Catherine East [Catherine Shipe East]. But there were people over there that did work very closely with us.

CAMPBELL: A lady named Harrison [Evelyn Harrison], I believe.
LESTER: Yes.
CAMPBELL: Evelyn Harrison.
LESTER: Evelyn Harrison was probably the one we worked the most with. Mary Bunting [Mary Ingraham Bunting] was a very effective person. She did a great deal. At meetings she was very effective. Mary Callahan was all right too. She represented her point of view. But I wouldn't say she was highly effective. Henry David, in his own way, was quite effective. Henry was quite willing to assert himself and was very effective in bringing people together. Dorothy Height [Dorothy I. Height], I think we all had a considerable respect for her. She was very effective in presenting the problems of the people that she represented. Margaret Hickey, of course, was really one of the outstanding people in her participation, her interest, and her ability to work things out. Viola Hymes [Viola Hoffman Hymes] was quite good. On the whole, she was active and had a great deal of knowledge. And could present her point of view fairly effectively. Margaret Mealey [Margaret J. Mealey] was not one of the most influential members. Norm Nicholson, he didn't have much to say. But he went along and was helpful. Marguerite Rawalt in terms of her special interests which were legal, was quite insistent. In that sense she had quite an influence. William Schnitzler [William F. Schnitzler], whom I had known slightly before this, with the trade unions movement back of him had significant influence. I don't think it was so much in terms of his own thought-out views as what he represented. He had staff people who worked with us further down the line. Caroline Ware [Caroline F. Ware] certainly asserted herself. I think she had, if anything, the problems of a person who had made up her mind some time ago and was asserting those opinions now. She was quite able and persuasive. Cynthia Wedel [Cynthia Clark Wedel] was good and she represented a group that was quite important. All of the commission members, I would have to say, did work fairly hard, did the best they could. I think they all deserve a great deal of credit for the way things worked out.

Mrs. Roosevelt was a remarkable person. She could conduct those meetings very effectively. She knew in advance where the problems were. She could work around them, get by them pretty effectively. And I think she had the respect of all and, particularly, the ladies on that group. If it was necessary to get an agreement on something or to get people to move along and cease pursuing a special point of view which really didn't have much support, Mrs. Roosevelt was very effective in handling the situation with grace. She really was exceedingly effective in chairing the meetings in view of the time she could give to working on the problems of the commission.

Esther, of course, gained the affection and goodwill and respect of pretty much everybody there. She worked very hard. They knew that her heart was in the right place. She was, of course, in contact with many people and she really did a great deal in the way of managing things.

CAMPBELL: Did you feel that the support from the administration was adequate?

LESTER: Yes, it was. There was no doubt about that. I think the President gave us all the support we needed. He had a great deal of respect for Mrs. Roosevelt. And when I went over to the White House with Esther Peterson, I think there was a great deal of respect there for Esther Peterson. Presumably the President felt that this was something that was highly desirable to do from the point of view of the problems that the government would face. Problems that he and his administration would face politically if the commission was not successful.

CAMPBELL: There was some movement during the time the commission sat. There was a decision by the Attorney General and a subsequent order by the President to enlarge employment opportunities for women in the federal service. And then in June of 1963, the equal pay bill passed. But also during those years the President issued an executive order on equal employment opportunity and managed to leave out the question of sex.

LESTER: Yes. Well, I think some of the staff people like Miss Harrison and others working with John Macy were able to have the commission contribute quite a bit in the area of federal employment. Commission members were also influential in working out and passing the Equal Pay Act.

CAMPBELL: You chaired, I think, one of the committees, the committee on private employment. And in your recommendations, the committee recommendations, recommended an executive order putting the good faith of the government or something behind equal employment opportunity for women. . . .

LESTER: That was about as far as we thought we could go then.

CAMPBELL: Well, you've anticipated my question. It was a mild proposal, I thought.

LESTER: Yes. Looking back, it was. That was about as far as we thought we could go at that time. Now you see, looking back, it does look too mild. But even to go that far was difficult in some cases because we had a lot of discussion with the people in the trade union movement. They had agreements which were in violation of that. There were others who were worried about any weakening or repealing of state protective legislation and what any attempt at movement for equal employment opportunities would do where you had state weightlifting legislation; where you have hours legislation, which the trade union movement had supported and had gotten built into these laws. Of course, some of the state protective laws, such as house legislation, included men in the coverage.

In 1964, much to our amazement, a congressman on the rules committee [Senate Committee on Rules and Administration] from Virginia, included women in a civil rights bill.

CAMPBELL: Judge Smith [Howard W. Smith].

LESTER: Yes, Judge Smith put that into the civil rights bill in '64 on the assumption that that would sink the bill, that it would get so much opposition then by putting that equal rights in, equal employment opportunities by putting sex in there, that the trade union movement and others would secretly lobby against it. It didn't work out that way. And that was a tremendous advantage. We didn't dream that we could get anything like that in legislation at that time.

CAMPBELL: Do you have memories of the back and forth that might have gone on when your . . . [Interruption] . . . if you recalled serious negotiations about this report.

LESTER: There were a lot of controversies, you know. But I suppose memory is good at separating out and neglecting the problems and recalling the gains and satisfactions. We had some difficulties in my committee, on the matter of equal work rights and also on state protective legislation. And we had controversy on the Equal Rights Amendment. For practical and other reasons, many members of the commission were opposed to pressing for an equal rights amendment to the Constitution. You will note that the report is silent on that subject.
           [. . .]

CAMPBELL: Do you recall—I believe it was in October of 1963 that the report was issued—at that time were you generally satisfied with what the Commission had accomplished?

LESTER: Yes. I think we felt that we'd accomplished quite a bit. Perhaps, it was about as far as we could go at that time. I was a little surprised actually that, in the end we had no dissenting opinion. I had a suspicion that Mrs. Boddy would come along in the end, which she did.
           [. . .]

I think there were people, certainly many people on the commission who felt that this was a start, but you needed to have a kind of continuing oversight of the developments, and that things in the report wouldn't get adopted unless you had people who were continually raising the questions with the President and with people in Congress and in the states. I believe that Henry David wanted to continue it, and Marguerite Rawalt, I'm sure, did. Mary Bunting, I presume did.

I felt at this stage—I didn't have a great deal more to contribute. And I couldn't follow things very closely because I had other interests and was heavily occupied here in the University. There was need for some follow up, but I wasn't sure that it should be done by much the same group. Many states had already established commissions on the status of women. I had been asked to go on the one here in New Jersey. I decided that I shouldn't really, even though I was close to people in the state government. I felt that at this point the effort ought to be largely in the hands of women, that they ought to keep pushing. I didn't really represent any constituency. At this stage, it was really political pressure and other kinds of pressure that needed to be brought to bear.

Source: Lester, Richard A. Recorded interview by Ann M. Campbell, December 24, 1970, pp. 16–25, John F. Kennedy Library Oral History Program. Available online at https://www.jfklibrary.org/Asset-Viewer/Archives/JFKOH-RAL-01.aspx.

REPORT OF THE PRESIDENT'S COMMISSION ON THE STATUS OF WOMEN, 1963

On December 14, 1961, President John F. Kennedy signed an executive order authorizing the creation of the President's Commission on the Status of Women. The Commission was charged with examining the employment, educational, and legal environments facing American women, with special focus on discriminatory practices in the workplace. Following is the first section of the final 1963 report, which made wide-ranging recommendations for making American laws and society more gender-equitable. The report, however, avoided taking an explicit stand on a proposed "equal rights amendment" to the U.S. Constitution. Leery of antagonizing the anti-ERA organized labor movement, a key constituency for Kennedy and other Democrats, the Kennedy administration hoped instead that the Supreme Court would enshrine gender equality by explicitly extending the 14th Amendment's equal protection clause to women.

Invitation to Action

This report is an invitation to action. When President John F. Kennedy appointed our Commission, he said: . . . *we have by no means done enough to strengthen family life and at the same time encourage women to make their full contribution as citizens. . . . It is appropriate at this time . . . to review recent accomplishments, and to acknowledge frankly the further steps that must be taken. This is a task for the entire Nation.*

The 96 million American women and girls include a range from infant to octogenarian, from migrant farm mother to suburban homemaker, from file clerk to research scientist, from Olympic athlete to college president. Greater development of women's potential and fuller use of their present abilities can greatly enhance the quality of American life. We have made recommendations to this end.

We invite response to our recommendations by citizen initiative exercised in many ways—through individual inventiveness, voluntary agencies, community cooperation, commercial enterprise, corporate policy, foundation support, governmental action at various levels. In making our proposals, we have had in mind the well-being of the entire society; their adoption would in many cases be of direct benefit to men as well as women.

Certain tenets have guided our thinking.

Respect for the worth and dignity of every individual and conviction that every American should have a chance to achieve the best of which he—or she—is capable are basic to the meaning of both freedom and equality in this democracy. They have been, and now are, great levers for constructive social change, here and around the world. We have not hesitated to measure the present shape of things against our convictions regarding a good society and to note discrepancies between American life as it is in 1963 and as it might become through informed and intelligent action.

The human and national costs of social lag are heavy; for the most part, they are also avoidable. That is why we urge changes, many of them long overdue, in the conditions of women's opportunity in the United States.

Responsible Choice

We believe that one of the greatest freedoms of the individual in a democratic society is the freedom to choose among different life patterns. Innumerable private solutions found by different individuals in search of the good life provide society with basic strength far beyond the possibilities of a dictated plan.

Illumined by values transmitted through home and school and church, society and heritage, and informed by present and past experience, each woman must arrive at her contemporary expression of purpose, whether as a center of home and family, a participant in the community, a contributor to the economy, a creative artist or thinker or scientist, a citizen engaged in politics and public service. Part and parcel of this freedom is the obligation to assume corresponding responsibility.

Yet there are social as well as individual determinants of freedom of choice; for example, the city slum and the poor rural crossroad frustrate natural gifts and innate human powers. It is a bitter fact that for millions of men and women economic stringency all but eliminates choice among alternatives.

In a progress report to the President in August 1962, the Commission's Chairman, Eleanor Roosevelt, said: *A rapidly rising national output is the strongest weapon against substandard jobs, poverty-stricken homes, and barren lives.*

In the same vein, Secretary of Labor W. Willard Wirtz has warned: *There is not going to be much in the way of expanding opportunities for women unless we are ready and able to assure the jobs which the economy as a whole requires.*

Growth and Opportunity

Unless the economy grows at a substantially faster rate than at present, oncoming generations will not find work commensurate with their skills. The number of new entrants of all ages into the labor force was about 2 million a year in 1960. By 1970, it will be 3 million.

Much of the work offered by a modern economy demands types of skill requiring levels of education that only a nation with abundant resources can supply; if such skills, when acquired, are not used because the economy is lagging, the resulting human frustrations and material waste are very costly indeed.

Economic expansion is of particular significance to women. One of the ironies of history is that war has brought American women their greatest economic opportunities. In establishing this Commission, the President noted: *In every period of national emergency, women have served with distinction in widely varied capacities but thereafter have been subject to treatment as a marginal group whose skills have been inadequately utilized.*

Comparable opportunity—and far more varied choice—could be provided by full employment in a period without war.

The Council of Economic Advisers has estimated that between 1958 and 1962 the country's productive capacity exceeded its actual output by some $170 billion, or almost $1,000 per person in the United States. Had this potential been realized, lower rates of unemployment and an impressive supply of additional goods and services would have contributed to national well-being. The currently unused resources of the American economy include much work that could be done by women.

Higher Expectations

But while freedom of choice for many American women, as for men, is limited by economic considerations, one of the most pervasive limitations is the social climate in which women choose what they prepare themselves to do. Too many plans recommended to young women reaching maturity are only partially suited to the second half of the 20th century. Such advice is correspondingly confusing to them.

Even the role most generally approved by counselors, parents, and friends—the making of a home, the rearing of children, and the transmission to them in their earliest years of the values of the American heritage—is frequently presented as it is thought to have been in an earlier and simpler society. Women's ancient function of providing love and nurture stands. But for entry into modern life, today's children need a preparation far more diversified than that of their predecessors.

Similarly, women's participation in such traditional occupations as teaching, nursing, and social work is generally approved, with current shortages underscoring the Nation's need for such personnel. But means for keeping up to date the skills of women who continue in such professions are few. So, too, are those for bringing up to date the skills of women who withdraw in order to raise families but return after their families are grown.

Commendation of women's entry into certain other occupations is less general, even though some of them are equally in need of trained people. Girls hearing that most women find mathematics and science difficult, or that engineering and architecture are unusual occupations for a woman, are not led to test their interest by activity in these fields.

Because too little is expected of them, many girls who graduate from high school intellectually able to do good college work do not go to college. Both they as individuals and the Nation as a society are thereby made losers.

The subtle limitations imposed by custom are, upon occasion, reinforced by specific barriers. In the course of the 20th century many bars against women that were firmly in place in 1900 have been lowered or dropped. But certain restrictions remain.

Discriminations and Disadvantages

Some of these discriminatory provisions are contained in the common law. Some are written into statute. Some are upheld by court decisions. Others take the form of practices of industrial, labor, professional, or governmental organizations that discriminate against women in apprenticeship, training, hiring, wages, and promotion. We have identified a number of outmoded and prejudicial attitudes and practices.

Throughout its deliberations, the Commission has kept in mind certain women who have special disadvantages. Among heads of families in the United States, 1 in 10 is a woman. At least half of them are carrying responsibility for both earning the family's living and making the family's home. Their problems are correspondingly greater; their resources are usually less.

Seven million nonwhite women and girls belong to minority racial groups. Discrimination based on color is morally wrong and a source of national weakness. Such discrimination currently places an oppressive dual burden on millions of Negro women. The consultation held by the Commission on the situation of Negro women emphasized that in too many families lack of opportunity for men as well as women, linked to racial discrimination, has forced the women to assume too large a share of the family responsibility. Such women are twice as likely as other women to have to seek employment while they have preschool children at home; they are just beginning to gain entrance to the expanding fields of clerical and commercial employment; except for the few who can qualify as teachers or other professionals, they are forced into low-paid service occupations.

Hundreds of thousands of other women face somewhat similar situations: American Indians, for instance; and Spanish-Americans, many of whom live in urban centers hut are new to urban life and burdened with language problems.

While there are highly skilled members of all of these groups, in many of the families of these women the unbroken cycle of deprivation and retardation repeats itself from generation to generation, compounding its individual cost in human indignity and unhappiness and its social cost in incapacity and delinquency. This cycle must be broken, swiftly and at as many points as possible. The Commission strongly urges that in the carrying out of its recommendations, special attention he given to difficulties that are wholly or largely the products of this kind of discrimination.

Lengthening Life Spans

The Commission has also been impressed with the extent to which lengthening life spans are causing changes in women's occupations and preoccupations from decade to decade of their adult experience. The life expectancy of a girl baby is now 73 years; it was 48 years in 1900. In comparison with her own grandmother, today's young woman has a quarter century of additional life with abundant new choices to plan for. It is essential that the counseling of girls enable them to foresee the later as well as the earlier phases of their adulthood.

Eight out of ten women are in paid employment outside the home at some time during their lives, and many of these, and others as well, engage in unpaid work as volunteers.

The population contains 13 million single girls and women 14 and over. A 20-year-old girl, if she remains single, will spend some 40 years in the labor force. If after working for a few years, she marries and has a family, and then goes back into the labor force at 30, she is likely to work for some 23 more years. Particularly during the years when her children are in school but have not yet left home permanently, the work she seeks is apt to be part time. Inflexibility with regard to part-time employment in most current hiring systems, alike in government and in private enterprise, excludes the use of much able and available trained womanpower; practices should be altered to permit it.

Women's greater longevity as compared with men makes them the predominant group in the final age brackets. There are almost 800,000 more women than men 75 and over. The number of such women grew from slightly over 2 million in 1950 to more than 3 million in 1960. To most, this is a period of economic dependency which often ends in a need for terminal care.

Areas of Special Attention

With such facts in view, the Commission has considered developments in American institutions which might usefully be coupled to the long series of historic changes that have increased women's opportunities and security. We were directed to review progress and make recommendations as needed for constructive action in six areas:

- Employment policies and practices, including those on wages, under Federal contracts.
- Federal social insurance and tax laws as they affect the net earnings and other income of women.
- Federal and State labor laws dealing with such matters as hours, nightwork, and wages, to determine whether they are accomplishing the purposes for

which they were established and whether they should be adapted to changing technological, economic, and social conditions.

- Differences in legal treatment of men and women in regard to political and
civil rights, property rights, and family relations.
- New and expanded services that may be required for women as wives, mothers, and workers, including education, counseling, training, home services,
and arrangements for care of children during the working day.
- The employment policies and practices of the Government of the United
States with reference to additional affirmative steps which should be taken
through legislation, executive, or administrative action to assure nondiscrimination on the basis of sex and to enhance constructive employment opportunities for women.

As our work progressed, we became convinced that greater public understanding
of the value of continuing education for all mature Americans is perhaps the highest priority item on the American agenda. And it is one of particular importance
to women.

In the past, Americans have regarded education as something for the young. It
is true that over recent decades the age at which a person's education was generally
held to be completed has moved up. When a majority of the population went to
work at 14, much used to be made of closing exercises for the eighth grade. Such
ceremonies are now commonly reserved for high school graduation; to a rising
proportion of the population, commencement means the award of college diplo-
mas. But even so, education continues to be thought of as a preparation for life that
ends when adult life begins. Recognition of the necessity of education during adult
life has still to be established.

Yet today, abilities must be constantly sharpened, knowledge and skills kept up
to date. Continuing opportunities to do this must be widely available and broad
enough to include both the person who did not finish elementary school and the
highly gifted specialist who must follow the frontiers of learning as they move;
both the person whose skill has been superseded by automation and the person
(usually a woman) who has been out of the labor market for a time but can, with
preparation, go back in and make effective use of her talents. Formal and informal
adult education can enable women of all ages both to fit themselves for what they
do next and to experience the satisfactions that come from learning for its own
sake.

Source: President's Commission on the Status of Women, *American Women.* Washington, DC: U.S. Department of Labor, 1963, pp. 1–8.

THE NATIONAL ORGANIZATION FOR WOMEN'S STATEMENT OF PURPOSE, 1966

*In October 1966 a new feminist group called the National Organization for Women, or
NOW, was founded in Washington, DC. Creation of the group was inspired in part by*

the civil rights movement. But it also stemmed from feminist anger over a 1965 ruling by the Equal Employment Opportunity Commission (EEOC)—an agency specifically founded to enforce Title VII of the 1964 Civil Rights Act, which among other things outlawed sex discrimination—that sex segregation in job advertising was legally permissible.

The following Statement of Purpose unveiled by NOW at the organization's first national conference was written by Betty Friedan (1921–2006), author of The Feminine Mystique *and NOW's first president.*

We, men and women who hereby constitute ourselves as the National Organization for Women, believe that the time has come for a new movement toward true equality for all women in America, and toward a fully equal partnership of the sexes, as part of the world-wide revolution of human rights now taking place within and beyond our national borders.

The purpose of NOW is to take action to bring women into full participation in the mainstream of American society now, exercising all the privileges and responsibilities thereof in truly equal partnership with men.

We believe the time has come to move beyond the abstract argument, discussion and symposia over the status and special nature of women which has raged in America in recent years; the time has come to confront, with concrete action, the conditions that now prevent women from enjoying the equality of opportunity and freedom of choice which is their right, as individual Americans, and as human beings.

NOW is dedicated to the proposition that women, first and foremost, are human beings, who, like all other people in our society, must have the chance to develop their fullest human potential. We believe that women can achieve such equality only by accepting to the full the challenges and responsibilities they share with all other people in our society, as part of the decision-making mainstream of American political, economic and social life.

We organize to initiate or support action, nationally, or in any part of this nation, by individuals or organizations, to break through the silken curtain of prejudice and discrimination against women in government, industry, the professions, the churches, the political parties, the judiciary, the labor unions, in education, science, medicine, law, religion and every other field of importance in American society.

Enormous changes taking place in our society make it both possible and urgently necessary to advance the unfinished revolution of women toward true equality, now. With a life span lengthened to nearly 75 years it is no longer either necessary or possible for women to devote the greater part of their lives to child-rearing; yet childbearing and rearing—which continues to be a most important part of most women's lives—still is used to justify barring women from equal professional and economic participation and advance.

Today's technology has reduced most of the productive chores which women once performed in the home and in mass-production industries based upon routine unskilled labor. This same technology has virtually eliminated the quality of muscular strength as a criterion for filling most jobs, while intensifying American industry's need for creative intelligence. In view of this new industrial revolution created by automation in the mid-twentieth century, women can and must participate in old and new fields of society in full equality—or become permanent outsiders.

Despite all the talk about the status of American women in recent years, the actual position of women in the United States has declined, and is declining, to an alarming degree throughout the 1950's and 60's. Although 46.4% of all American women between the ages of 18 and 65 now work outside the home, the overwhelming majority—75%—are in routine clerical, sales, or factory jobs, or they are household workers, cleaning women, hospital attendants. About two-thirds of Negro women workers are in the lowest paid service occupations. Working women are becoming increasingly—not less—concentrated on the bottom of the job ladder. As a consequence full-time women workers today earn on the average only 60% of what men earn, and that wage gap has been increasing over the past twenty-five years in every major industry group. In 1964, of all women with a yearly income, 89% earned under $5,000 a year; half of all full-time year round women workers earned less than $3,690; only 1.4% of full-time year round women workers had an annual income of $10,000 or more.

Further, with higher education increasingly essential in today's society, too few women are entering and finishing college or going on to graduate or professional school. Today, women earn only one in three of the B.A.'s and M.A.'s granted, and one in ten of the Ph.D.'s.

In all the professions considered of importance to society, and in the executive ranks of industry and government, women are losing ground. Where they are present it is only a token handful. Women comprise less than 1% of federal judges; less than 4% of all lawyers; 7% of doctors. Yet women represent 51% of the U.S. population. And, increasingly, men are replacing women in the top positions in secondary and elementary schools, in social work, and in libraries—once thought to be women's fields.

Official pronouncements of the advance in the status of women hide not only the reality of this dangerous decline, but the fact that nothing is being done to stop it. The excellent reports of the President's Commission on the Status of Women and of the State Commissions have not been fully implemented. Such Commissions have power only to advise. They have no power to enforce their recommendation; nor have they the freedom to organize American women and men to press for action on them. The reports of these commissions have, however, created a basis upon which it is now possible to build. Discrimination in employment on the basis of sex is now prohibited by federal law, in Title VII of the Civil Rights Act of 1964. But although nearly one-third of the cases brought before the Equal Employment Opportunity Commission during the first year dealt with sex discrimination and the proportion is increasing dramatically, the Commission has not made clear its intention to enforce the law with the same seriousness on behalf of women as of other victims of discrimination. Many of these cases were Negro women, who are the victims of double discrimination of race and sex. Until now, too few women's organizations and official spokesmen have been willing to speak out against these dangers facing women. Too many women have been restrained by the fear of being called "feminist." There is no civil rights movement to speak for women, as there has been for Negroes and other victims of discrimination. The National Organization for Women must therefore begin to speak.

WE BELIEVE that the power of American law, and the protection guaranteed by the U.S. Constitution to the civil rights of all individuals, must be effectively applied and enforced to isolate and remove patterns of sex discrimination, to ensure equality of opportunity in employment and education, and equality of civil and political rights and responsibilities on behalf of women, as well as for Negroes and other deprived groups.

We realize that women's problems are linked to many broader questions of social justice; their solution will require concerted action by many groups. Therefore, convinced that human rights for all are indivisible, we expect to give active support to the common cause of equal rights for all those who suffer discrimination and deprivation, and we call upon other organizations committed to such goals to support our efforts toward equality for women.

WE DO NOT ACCEPT the token appointment of a few women to high-level positions in government and industry as a substitute for serious continuing effort to recruit and advance women according to their individual abilities. To this end, we urge American government and industry to mobilize the same resources of ingenuity and command with which they have solved problems of far greater difficulty than those now impeding the progress of women.

WE BELIEVE that this nation has a capacity at least as great as other nations, to innovate new social institutions which will enable women to enjoy the true equality of opportunity and responsibility in society, without conflict with their responsibilities as mothers and homemakers. In such innovations, America does not lead the Western world, but lags by decades behind many European countries. We do not accept the traditional assumption that a woman has to choose between marriage and motherhood, on the one hand, and serious participation in industry or the professions on the other. We question the present expectation that all normal women will retire from job or profession for 10 or 15 years, to devote their full time to raising children, only to reenter the job market at a relatively minor level. This, in itself, is a deterrent to the aspirations of women, to their acceptance into management or professional training courses, and to the very possibility of equality of opportunity or real choice, for all but a few women. Above all, we reject the assumption that these problems are the unique responsibility of each individual woman, rather than a basic social dilemma which society must solve. True equality of opportunity and freedom of choice for women requires such practical, and possible innovations as a nationwide network of child-care centers, which will make it unnecessary for women to retire completely from society until their children are grown, and national programs to provide retraining for women who have chosen to care for their children full-time.

WE BELIEVE that it is as essential for every girl to be educated to her full potential of human ability as it is for every boy—with the knowledge that such education is the key to effective participation in today's economy and that, for a girl as for a boy, education can only be serious where there is expectation that it will be used in society. We believe that American educators are capable of devising means of imparting such expectations to girl students. Moreover, we consider the decline in the proportion of women receiving higher and professional education to be evidence of discrimination. This discrimination may take the form of quotas against the admission of women to colleges, and professional schools; lack of encouragement by parents, counselors and educators; denial of loans or fellowships; or the traditional or arbitrary procedures in graduate and professional training geared in terms of men, which inadvertently discriminate against women. We believe that the same serious attention must be given to high school dropouts who are girls as to boys.

WE REJECT the current assumptions that a man must carry the sole burden of supporting himself, his wife, and family, and that a woman is automatically entitled to lifelong support by a man upon her marriage, or that marriage, home and family are primarily woman's world and responsibility—hers, to dominate—his to support. We believe that a true partnership between the sexes demands a different concept of marriage, an equitable sharing of the responsibilities of home and children and of the economic burdens of their support. We believe that proper recognition should be given to the economic and social value of homemaking and child-care. To these ends, we will seek to open a reexamination of laws and mores governing marriage and divorce, for we believe that the current state of "half-equity" between the sexes discriminates against both men and women, and is the cause of much unnecessary hostility between the sexes.

WE BELIEVE that women must now exercise their political rights and responsibilities as American citizens. They must refuse to be segregated on the basis of sex into separate-and-not-equal ladies' auxiliaries in the political parties, and they must demand representation according to their numbers in the regularly constituted party committees—at local, state, and national levels—and in the informal power structure, participating fully in the selection of candidates and political decision-making, and running for office themselves.

IN THE INTERESTS OF THE HUMAN DIGNITY OF WOMEN, we will protest, and endeavor to change, the false image of women now prevalent in the mass media, and in the texts, ceremonies, laws, and practices of our major social institutions. Such images perpetuate contempt for women by society and by women for themselves. We are similarly opposed to all policies and practices—in church, state, college, factory, or office—which, in the guise of protectiveness, not only deny opportunities but also foster in women self-denigration, dependence, and evasion of responsibility, undermine their confidence in their own abilities and foster contempt for women.

NOW WILL HOLD ITSELF INDEPENDENT OF ANY POLITICAL PARTY in order to mobilize the political power of all women and men intent on our goals.

We will strive to ensure that no party, candidate, president, senator, governor, congressman, or any public official who betrays or ignores the principle of full equality between the sexes is elected or appointed to office. If it is necessary to mobilize the votes of men and women who believe in our cause, in order to win for women the final right to be fully free and equal human beings, we so commit ourselves.

WE BELIEVE THAT women will do most to create a new image of women by acting now, and by speaking out in behalf of their own equality, freedom, and human dignity—not in pleas for special privilege, nor in enmity toward men, who are also victims of the current, half-equality between the sexes—but in an active, self-respecting partnership with men. By so doing, women will develop confidence in their own ability to determine actively, in partnership with men, the conditions of their life, their choices, their future and their society.

Source: National Organization of Women Statement of Purpose (1966). Available online at http://now.org/about/history/statement-of-purpose. Used by permission of the National Organization for Women. This is a historical document and may not reflect the current language or priorities of the organization.

PRESIDENT JOHNSON BANS SEX DISCRIMINATION IN FEDERAL HIRING, 1967

During the mid-1960s, the Johnson administration came under sustained pressure from feminist women's groups and allied lawmakers to close loopholes in American law that permitted continued discrimination against women in the workplace. On October 13, 1967, President Johnson responded with Executive Order 11375, which added "sex" to the forms of discrimination that the U.S. government would not tolerate, either within its own agencies or by private employers doing business with the U.S. government. Following is the full text of that executive order.

It is the policy of the United States Government to provide equal opportunity in Federal employment and in employment by Federal contractors on the basis of merit and without discrimination because of race, color, religion, sex or national origin.

The Congress, by enacting Title VII of the Civil Rights Act of 1964, enunciated a national policy of equal employment opportunity in private employment, without discrimination because of race, color, religion, sex or national origin.

Executive Order No. 11246 of September 24, 1965, carried forward a program of equal employment opportunity in Government employment, employment by Federal contractors and subcontractors and employment under Federally assisted construction contracts regardless of race, creed, color or national origin.

It is desirable that the equal employment opportunity programs provided for in Executive Order No. 11246 expressly embrace discrimination on account of sex.

Now, THEREFORE, by virtue of the authority vested in me as President of the United States by the Constitution and statutes of the United States, it is ordered that Executive Order No. 11246 of September 24, 1965, be amended as follows:

(1) Section 101 of Part I, concerning nondiscrimination in Government employment, is revised to read as follows:

"SECTION 101. It is the policy of the Government of the United States to provide equal opportunity in Federal employment for all qualified persons, to prohibit discrimination in employment because of race, color, religion, sex or national origin, and to promote the full realization of equal employment opportunity through a positive, continuing program in each executive department and agency. The policy of equal opportunity applies to every aspect of Federal employment policy and practice."

(2) Section 104 of Part I is revised to read as follows:

"SECTION 104. The Civil Service Commission shall provide for the prompt, fair, and impartial consideration of all complaints of discrimination in Federal employment on the basis of race, color, religion, sex or national origin. Procedures for the consideration of complaints shall include at least one impartial review within the executive department or agency and shall provide for appeal to the Civil Service Commission."

(3) Paragraphs (1) and (2) of the quoted required contract provisions in section 202 of Part II, concerning nondiscrimination in employment by Government contractors and subcontractors, are revised to read as follows:

"(1) The contractor will not discriminate against any employee or applicant for employment because of race, color, religion, sex, or national origin. The contractor will take affirmative action to ensure that applicants are employed, and that employees are treated during employment, without regard to their race, color, religion, sex or national origin. Such action shall include, but not be limited to the following: employment, upgrading, demotion, or transfer; recruitment or recruitment advertising; layoff or termination; rates of pay or other forms of compensation; and selection for training, including apprenticeship. The contractor agrees to post in conspicuous places, available to employees and applicants for employment, notices to be provided by the contracting officer setting forth the provisions of this nondiscrimination clause.

"(2) The contractor will, in all solicitations or advertisements for employees placed by or on behalf of the contractor, state that all qualified applicants will receive consideration for employment without regard to race, color, religion, sex or national origin."

(4) Section 203 (d) of Part II is revised to read as follows:

"(d) The contracting agency or the Secretary of Labor may direct that any bidder or prospective contractor or subcontractor shall submit, as part of his Compliance Report, a statement in writing, signed by an authorized officer or agent on behalf of any labor union or any agency referring workers or providing or supervising apprenticeship or other training, with which the bidder or prospective contractor deals, with supporting information, to the effect that the signer's practices and policies do not discriminate on the grounds of race, color, religion, sex or national origin, and that the signer either will affirmatively cooperate in the implementation of the policy and provisions of this order or that it consents and agrees that recruitment, employment, and the terms and conditions of employment under the proposed contract shall be in accordance with the purposes and provisions of the order. In the event that the union, or the agency shall refuse to execute such a statement, the Compliance Report shall so certify and set forth what efforts have been made to secure such a statement and such additional factual material as the contracting agency or the Secretary of Labor may require."

The amendments to Part I shall be effective 30 days after the date of this order. The amendments to Part II shall be effective one year after the date of this order.

LYNDON B. JOHNSON
The White House
October 13, 1967

Source: Executive Order 11375. Amending Executive Order No. 11246, Relating to Equal Employment Opportunity, October 13, 1967. 32 Federal Register 14303; October 17, 1967.

SHIRLEY CHISHOLM SPEAKS OUT FOR EQUAL RIGHTS FOR WOMEN, 1969

When Shirley Chisholm (1921–2005) won election to the House of Representatives in 1968 as representative of a newly created New York district that included Brooklyn and surrounding parts of the city, she became America's first-ever African American congresswoman. From then until 1982, when she declined to seek reelection for an eighth term (she also made an unsuccessful bid for the 1972 Democratic presidential nomination), Chisholm was one of the House's most outspoken liberal voices on women's rights, racial equality, and the Vietnam War. One of her most famous speeches came on May 21, 1969, when she took to the floor of the House of Representatives to deliver an impassioned plea for passage of the Equal Rights Amendment. Her remarks from that day are reprinted below.

After leaving Congress, Chisholm returned to her first love, teaching, though she remained active in Democratic Party politics. In 2015, 10 years after she died at the age of 80, she was posthumously awarded the Presidential Medal of Freedom by President Barack Obama. "There are people in our country's history who don't look left or right—they just look straight ahead," said Obama. "Shirley Chisholm was one of those people. . . . Shirley Chisholm's example transcends her life. And when asked how she'd like to be remembered, she had an answer: 'I'd like them to say that Shirley Chisholm had guts.' And I'm proud to say it: Shirley Chisholm had guts."

Mr. Speaker, when a young woman graduates from college and starts looking for a job, she is likely to have a frustrating and even demeaning experience ahead of her. If she walks into an office for an interview, the first question she will be asked is, "Do you type?"

There is a calculated system of prejudice that lies unspoken behind that question. Why is it acceptable for women to be secretaries, librarians, and teachers, but totally unacceptable for them to be managers, administrators, doctors, lawyers, and Members of Congress.

The unspoken assumption is that women are different. They do not have executive ability, orderly minds, stability, leadership skills, and they are too emotional.

It has been observed before, that society for a long time, discriminated against another minority, the blacks, on the same basis—that they were different and inferior. The happy little homemaker and the contented "old darkey" on the plantation were both produced by prejudice.

As a black person, I am no stranger to race prejudice. But the truth is that in the political world I have been far oftener discriminated against because I am a woman than because I am black.

Prejudice against blacks is becoming unacceptable although it will take years to eliminate it. But it is doomed because, slowly, white America is beginning to admit that it exists. Prejudice against women is still acceptable. There is very little understanding yet of the immorality involved in double pay scales and the classification of most of the better jobs as "for men only."

More than half of the population of the United States is female. But women occupy only 2 percent of the managerial positions. They have not even reached the level of tokenism yet. No women sit on the AFL-CIO council or Supreme Court. There have been only two women who have held Cabinet rank, and at present there are none. Only two women now hold ambassadorial rank in the diplomatic corps. In Congress, we are down to one Senator and 10 Representatives.

Considering that there are about 3 1/2 million more women in the United States than men, this situation is outrageous.

It is true that part of the problem has been that women have not been aggressive in demanding their rights. This was also true of the black population for many years. They submitted to oppression and even cooperated with it. Women have done the same thing. But now there is an awareness of this situation particularly among the younger segment of the population.

As in the field of equal rights for blacks, Spanish-Americans, the Indians, and other groups, laws will not change such deep-seated problems overnight. But they can be used to provide protection for those who are most abused, and to begin the process of evolutionary change by compelling the insensitive majority to reexamine it's [sic] unconscious attitudes.

It is for this reason that I wish to introduce today a proposal that has been before every Congress for the last 40 years and that sooner or later must become part of the basic law of the land—the equal rights amendment.

Let me note and try to refute two of the commonest arguments that are offered against this amendment. One is that women are already protected under the law and do not need legislation. Existing laws are not adequate to secure equal rights for women. Sufficient proof of this is the concentration of women in lower paying, menial, unrewarding jobs and their incredible scarcity in the upper level jobs. If women are already equal, why is it such an event whenever one happens to be elected to Congress?

It is obvious that discrimination exists. Women do not have the opportunities that men do. And women that do not conform to the system, who try to break with the accepted patterns, are stigmatized as "odd" and "unfeminine." The fact is that a woman who aspires to be chairman of the board, or a Member of the House, does so for exactly the same reasons as any man. Basically, these are that she thinks she can do the job and she wants to try.

A second argument often heard against the equal rights amendment is that is [sic] would eliminate legislation that many States and the Federal Government have enacted giving special protection to women and that it would throw the marriage and divorce laws into chaos.

As for the marriage laws, they are due for a sweeping reform, and an excellent beginning would be to wipe the existing ones off the books. Regarding special protection for working women, I cannot understand why it should be needed. Women need no protection that men do not need. What we need are laws to protect working people, to guarantee them fair pay, safe working conditions, protection against sickness and layoffs, and provision for dignified, comfortable retirement. Men and women need these things equally. That one sex needs protection more than the other is a male supremacist myth as ridiculous and unworthy of respect as the white supremacist myths that society is trying to cure itself of at this time.

Source: Chisholm, Shirley. "Address to the U.S. House of Representatives," Washington, DC, May 21, 1969. *Congressional Record*, Extension of Remarks E4165–E4166.

FEMINIST AUTHOR CAROLINE BIRD EXPRESSES SUPPORT FOR THE EQUAL RIGHTS AMENDMENT, 1970

Caroline Bird (1915–2011) was an American author and outspoken feminist whose 1968 book Born Female: The High Cost of Keeping Women Down *established her as an influential voice in the fast-growing women's movement of the 1960s. In 1970 she was invited to Washington, DC, to testify at special congressional hearings on the proposed Equal Rights Amendment. Following are excerpts from her remarks at the hearing, in which she discusses her own experiences of sex-based discrimination in the workplace, lauds young women for taking themselves "seriously" as people, and describes passage of the ERA as both "needed and politically feasible."*

[Miss Bird.] We have never added the guarantee of equal rights to our Constitution the way it has appeared in other constitutions, I think, because our legislators have made two assumptions about American women.

One. We don't need any more rights. We have got everything. We are happy, or at least we are quiet.

Two. If we do not like our lot, it is something that laws cannot change. If there are inequities, they are based on the sex role of women, and that is too deep for the law. We have made the assumption that laws cannot change morals, laws cannot change customs.

Now, I used to believe both of these assumptions, as recently as 1966, but things have changed in the past few years. In 1970 neither assumption is a safe premise for ignoring the equal rights amendment once again.

First, women do care—all women. We have all been mistaken about the apathy of women about their legal rights. That includes women themselves. Most women shrug off or smile at talk about their rights. They say they don't care.

But hidden deep in every woman there is a well of anger. Women don't like to think of all the little slights, putdowns, and limitations they have learned to accept under the name of being a woman. It makes them too angry. They fear that this anger will damage their relations with the men on whom they depend, so they repress it.

But when a woman is forced to take a situation seriously, to look at all those slights, limitations, putdowns, and restrictions that other witnesses have documented, then she cannot contain her anger. Once she admits to herself that she is a victim, she can never go back to the Garden of Eden. When one woman admits it, she makes it harder for the woman next to her to ignore it.

That is why you find most ardent opposition to equal rights from women themselves.

Now, in 1970 the lid is off the volcano. All over the country women are gathering in each other's living rooms to tell each other about the way they really feel about their vaunted role. They are saying out loud to each other things they never said out loud before, that they do not like losing their names when they marry, for instance, that they do care about getting promoted at work, that sometimes they really don't like children or don't want to have children. They don't like being put down. They don't like being used.

I think it is very significant that women's liberation girls do not smile: they do not have these little feminine characteristics. They look you straight in the face like Gloria Steinem, and tell you just as it is.

Senator Bayh. I noticed Miss Steinem smiling right now. I think it adds a great deal.

Miss Bird. But she doesn't sort of giggle and use feminine smiles in an artificial way to put over points, and I think that is a big change in mood.

Miss Steinem. That is Uncle Tomming.

Miss Bird. It means taking yourself seriously as a person. I think that is really happening, and this is the important thing that is happening, the big change in young women, and I think it is important for men to realize this.

As for the rest of us, like me, who have been around for a while, I am astounded to discover how strongly I actually feel about this matter. So what I want to say today, there is all sorts of evidence about how women are discriminated against. All these putdowns are well documented. They have been around for a long time. But what I think you should know is the way women really feel about them. This is what is so mysterious to men. They say, "What do women really want?"

It seems to me what they really want is to be taken seriously. They keep saying this but nobody seems to believe it.

So let me tell you a little bit about how I got liberated by recognizing some of these things.

In 1966, after I did that article on the draft, an editor of the *Saturday Evening Post* asked me to find out whether women were really discriminated against. And I will never forget the moment. I said, "Gee, I guess they are discriminated against, but I have never really had any trouble, you know. I have just gone as far as my own talents could carry me."

But I said, "Sure, I will go out and find out." I was very cool and professional about this, and I tackled it by doing more work than necessary, which I still do. And I think that women probably are good at detail because they do not have the self-confidence to ignore it.

But I got a little Russell Sage grant, and I went tearing around the country and I talked to women in a dozen cities who had succeeded by earning $10,000 a year or more. I discovered that none of them were very angry about their lot. They all started out by saying what I said, that they really had no trouble. Many of them begged me not to stir men up. "Don't talk rights. Don't talk like Betty Friedan because it will just make it harder for women to get ahead. We want to forget about this whole women's rights business."

When I asked, "Why don't more women get ahead," they'd answer, "Because most women won't work hard enough and long enough. Sure there is discrimination. But I am sick and tired of hearing about it, because you can get around it."

They told me about all sorts of ploys and situations that made it easier for a woman to do something than if she were a man. I concluded that the women who have succeeded in this country have taken advantage of their sex in many of the same ways that Negroes have used their subservience to get into policymaking places.

But then even as I interviewed these women a very funny thing happened. The more they talked about their careers the more you could see resentment beginning to dawn. A woman stockbroker would say, "Well, now, of course, I don't earn as much as the men, but, you see, I run the office. The men are all too busy out selling clients." She would start out as if it were a plausible explanation, but by the time she heard what she said you could see she was wondering, "Why am I not out making money, too?"

I would ask a woman why she couldn't be president of her company and she would say, "Well, you see, my work has been on the inside. I just don't know all the big customers." I did not have to ask her, "How come your work was all on the inside?"

Women generally have taken their situation for granted.

When I got two or three of these women together they reminded each other of the little things they usually put out of mind. One would say, "They don't invite me to the meetings," and another would say, "Come to think of it, they don't invite me either." One would say, "I never thought of asking for a business card. I suppose I really do need one, don't I."

After sessions like this, women sometimes called me up the next morning to say "I had never thought of it that way before, and please don't use my name."

I must have gone through this in two or three cities before it dawned on me that I had been discriminated against myself. I began as a researcher at Newsweek and

Fortune, and I spent World War II putting red dots over names and dates on copy written by men to be sure in their great creativity they had not spelled the name wrong. At the end of World War II I was fired for incompetence, and I believed it. I believed I was incompetent. It never occurred to me to question that verdict. And I was sort of crushed and just wished I was better qualified. But I luckily had a father who said, "You know, Caroline, I think you can write." And I said, "Oh, go on." But I tried it and I have earned a living ever since at writing.

A couple of years ago there was a Fortune editor who said I made Caroline Bird a writer by getting her fired from Fortune magazine.

Now, the point of this story is not that I made it. The real point is that 20 years later in 1966 I could say in all honesty that I had never suffered any discrimination. Women get so used to their role that they don't question it. But once you do, once you see it, you can never go back to that state of innocence in which you can put up with all this stuff.

So on that story I began to question this whole situation, and my report was a resounding "yes," women are discriminated against, and I likened the role of women in business to the role of Negroes.

It was soon very clear that this was not what the *Saturday Evening Post* wanted. They wrote long memos about my piece. They questioned my facts, my logic, my style. Editors said women don't get ahead because it's only the dregs who are in offices working. Some editors thought women didn't get ahead because the best ones were hauled off to the suburbs to have babies, so only the inferior women were left working. And they said, "Of course, now, Miss Bird doesn't understand how hard it is for a man to sit next to a woman in an office, and women really don't understand how it is to be men." My editor kept saying, "We are not questioning your conclusions. We are not questioning your data. It's just the way you say it. If you could only say it better."

And once again I accepted this verdict—if only I could write better; if I were more clever; if only I were more graceful in the way I said it, then I could put the point across.

I rewrote that piece three times. When it was turned down, I was crushed. I was also furious by this time, absolutely furious. And when I went to bed, I don't mind telling you for a week I was just unable to move.

Finally I looked at this material and I said something has to be done with it. Luckily I had just done a book "The Invisible Scar" that was well received, so I had a sympathetic publisher and editor in Eleanor Rawson of David McKay, but some of the people around the office said, "Well, you know, women don't really care about getting ahead in business. However, if Caroline really wants to do this book." So I did it.

In 1967 women's liberation was a kaffeeklatch of women in the radical movement who claimed that they hadn't joined the revolution to tote coffee.

In 1967, airline stewardesses could be fired for getting married or for attaining the great age of 30, and if you suggested that they fire the stewards for getting married or attaining the great age of 30, people just giggled and laughed at you.

In 1967, women were excluded from some of the best colleges and professional schools. The sex provision of Title VII of the Civil Rights Act of 1964 was widely regarded as a joke.

Now 3 short years have passed and things have changed. You can get an abortion on demand in New York State. You can get a divorce practically on demand in California. Women are now on every major college campus in the country, not on an equal basis with men but some arrangement has been made so that they are not totally excluded by virtue of sex. The pay gap between the starting salary of men and women college graduates is narrowing, and the percentage of Ph.D.'s awarded to women is rising. I rather imagine that when the 1970 census is in it will show that women have made some progress over 1960. While there was a decline between 1950 and 1960, I think the economic outlook for women is improving.

I am not about to say that discrimination has ended, but I think that we have turned the corner, and it's fair to ask: How did it happen? Why do we have women's liberation in every single city of this country? Why do we have people more aware of the plight of women? So I go around asking the sociologists: "How did this come about?" And they say, "It started with this law—this law against discrimination—back in 1964."

Well, now, you and I know that Title VII was just about the weakest law that you could possibly imagine. You remember that it was added to the Civil Rights Act of 1964 as a joke. The people who put it in hoped it would serve to laugh the whole idea of a law against discrimination out of court. Many who voted for it thought it would never be applied. The EEOC charged with enforcing it publicly said it was embarrassing. Lawyers said it was as full of holes as a sieve. Personnel people said women don't care. There is one thing women don't care about—their jobs. They said they will never complain. They are too timid to complain. They don't want to assert themselves. The newspapers had a wonderful time laughing at Title VII. But it was the law of the land. Some women did complain, and then others complained. In some times and places there were almost as many complaints on the basis of sex as of race. There were no real teeth in Title VII but it was a law and it had an enormous effect. It got people to thinking, both employers and women. Sometimes that is all that is needed. I do not believe that men are trying to hold women down. I do not think that there is a real hostility. We are just brought up in a culture that makes this difference. Everybody accepts it. Both men and women accept it. And so when discrimination is inadvertent and covert, it just rankles along inside, poisoning the relations of men and women and undermining the confidence of women.

I do not want to imply that Title VII has ended discrimination, but it has begun the fight and it shows that laws do matter even in this day and age in which we assume that there is no respect for law. I believe that a law that states a high moral purpose, especially one that most people deep down can agree with, starts thought, makes people recognize inequities that they have passed over in silence, and ultimately will do more good toward equalizing the roles of men and women in this country than any specific correction of a specific disability.

Even if the equal rights amendment did nothing but state the principle, it would be worth it. I think the time has come when this equal rights amendment is both needed and politically feasible. Women are beginning to see their situation. They can never go back so we must all go forward. To paraphrase a great magazine: "Never underestimate the anger of a woman."

Thank you.

Source: Bird, Caroline. "Testimony at Hearings before the Subcommittee on Constitutional Amendments, 91st Congress, 2nd Session, S.J. Res. 61: To Amend the Constitution so as to Provide Equal Rights for Men and Women." May 5, 6, and 7, 1970. Washington, DC: Government Printing Office, 1970, pp. 343–347.

SENATOR SAM ERVIN FRAMES THE EQUAL RIGHTS AMENDMENT AS DAMAGING TO WOMEN, 1970

Sam Ervin (1896–1985) was a Democrat who represented the state of North Carolina in the U.S. Senate from 1954 to 1974. He is best known for his truth-seeking efforts as chairman of the Senate Watergate Committee in the early 1970s, but while historians praise him for his leadership in investigating the Nixon administration, he also strongly opposed civil rights and women's rights legislation in the 1960s and early 1970s. The following is a speech that Ervin delivered in Congress on August 21, 1970, denouncing the Equal Rights Amendment legislation recently passed in the House as a misbegotten bill that would worsen the lives of American women and families.

THE HOUSE-PASSED EQUAL RIGHTS AMENDMENT: A POTENTIALLY DESTRUCTIVE AND SELF-DEFEATING BLUNDERBUSS

UNFAIR LEGAL DISCRIMINATIONS AGAINST WOMEN

Mr. ERVIN. Mr. President, the objective of those who advocate the adoption of the House-passed equal rights amendment is a worthy one. It is to abolish unfair discriminations which society makes against women in certain areas of life. No one believes more strongly than I that discriminations of this character ought to be abolished, and that they ought to be abolished by law in every case where they are created by law.

Any rational consideration of the advisability of adopting the House-passed equal rights amendment raises these questions:

First. What is the character of the unfair discriminations which society makes women?

Second. Does it require an amendment to the Constitution of the United States to invalidate them?

Third. If so, would the House-passed equal rights amendment constitute an effective means to that end?

It is the better part of wisdom to recognize that discriminations not created by law cannot be abolished by law. They must be abolished by changed attitudes in the society which imposes them.

From the many conversations I have had with advocates of the House-passed equal rights amendment since coming to the Senate, I am convinced that many of their just grievances are founded upon discriminations not created by law, and that for this reason the equal rights amendment will have no effect whatsoever in respect to them.

When I have sought to ascertain from them the specific laws of which they complain, the advocates of the equal rights amendment have cited certain State statutes, such as those which impose weight-lifting restrictions on women, or bar women from operating saloons, or acting as bartenders, or engaging in professional wrestling. Like them, I think these laws ought to be abolished. I respectfully submit, however, that resorting to an amendment to the Constitution to effect this purpose is about as wise as using an atomic bomb to exterminate a few mice.

From the information given me by many advocates of the equal rights amendment and from my study of the discriminations which society makes against women. I am convinced that most of the unfair discriminations against them arise out of the different treatment given men and women in the employment sphere. No one can gainsay the fact that women suffer many discriminations in this sphere, both in respect to the compensation they receive and the promotional opportunities available to them. Some of these discriminations arise out of law and others arise out of the practices of society.

Let me point out that Congress has done much in recent years to abolish discriminations of this character insofar as they can be abolished at the Federal level. It has amended the Fair Labor Standards Act to make it obligatory for employers to pay men and women engaged in interstate commerce or in the production of goods for interstate commerce equal pay for equal work, irrespective of the number of persons they employ.

Congress has also decreed by the equal employment provisions of the Civil Rights Act of 1964 that there can be no discrimination whatever against women in employment in industries employing 25 or more persons, whose business affects interstate commerce, except in those instances where sex is a bona fide occupational qualification reasonably necessary to the normal operation of the enterprise. Furthermore, it is to be noted that the President and virtually all of the departments and agencies of the Federal Government have issued orders prohibiting discrimination against women in Federal employment.

Moreover, State legislatures have adopted many enlightened statutes in recent years prohibiting discrimination against women in employment.

If women are not enjoying the full benefit of this Federal and State legislation and these Executive orders of the Federal Government, it is due to a defect in enforcement rather than a want of fair laws and regulations.

A good case can be made for the proposition that it is not necessary to resort to a constitutional amendment to abolish State laws which make unfair discriminations between men and women in employment or any other sphere of life. This argument rests upon the equal protection clause of the 14th amendment which prohibits States from treating differently persons similarly situated, and is now being interpreted by the courts to invalidate State laws, which single out women for different treatment not based on some reasonable classification.

To be sure, the equal protection clause may not satisfy the extreme demands of a few advocates of the equal rights amendment who would convert men and women into beings not only equal but alike, and grant them identical rights and impose upon them identical duties in all the relationships and undertakings of life.

It cannot be gainsaid, however, that the equal protection clause, properly interpreted, nullifies every State law lacking a rational basis, which seems to make rights and responsibilities turn upon sex.

My view is shared by legal scholars. Their views on this subject are succinctly expressed by Bernard Schwartz in his recent commentary on the Constitution of the United States which declares "that a law based upon sexual classification will normally be deemed inherently unreasonable unless it is intended for the protection of the female sex."

As I pointed out later, the House-passed equal rights amendment is shrouded in obscurity, and no one has sufficient prophetic power to predict with accuracy what interpretation the Supreme Court will place upon it. One possible interpretation is that it will nullify every existing Federal and State law making any distinction whatever between men and women, no matter how reasonable the distinction may be, and rob Congress and the legislatures of the 50 States of the legislative power to enact any future laws making any distinction between men and women, no matter how reasonable the distinction may be.

If it should be adopted and this interpretation should be placed upon it by the Supreme Court, the House-passed equal rights amendment would produce constitutional and legal chaos, and would not accomplish the objective of any of its advocates. This is so because under this interpretation the equal rights amendment would merely abolish all laws making any distinctions between men and women. It would not bring into existence any new laws giving us a discrimination-free society, and those who desire such a society would have to implore Congress and the legislatures of the 50 States to enact new laws creating the kind of society they seek, insofar as such a society can be established by law.

Consequently, those who seek a discrimination-free society should seek to persuade Congress and the legislatures of the various States initially to enact suitable legislation to accomplish their purpose insofar as such purpose can be accomplished by law without first invalidating all laws making distinctions between men and women and plunging society into constitutional and legal chaos.

For these reasons, the House-passed equal rights amendment represents a potentially destructive and self-defeating blunderbuss approach to the problem of abolishing unfair discriminations against women.

What has been said makes it manifest, I think, that society does make unfair discriminations against women, and that the House-passed equal rights amendment does not constitute a sensible approach to their abolition.

This brings us to the questions whether Congress should consider the submission to the States of a constitutional amendment to deal with the matter, and whether such amendment should permit Congress and the States acting within their respective jurisdictions to make reasonable distinctions between the rights and responsibilities of men and women in appropriate areas of life.

I honestly believe that the equal protection clause, properly interpreted, is sufficient to abolish all unfair legal discriminations made against women by State law.

Nevertheless, I am constrained to favor a constitutional amendment which will abolish all unfair legal discriminations against women without robbing them of necessary legal protections and without imprisoning the legislative powers of Congress and the States in a constitutional straitjacket.

My reasons for so doing are twofold. First, some advocates of the House-passed equal rights amendment do not share my opinion of the efficacy of the equal protection clause; and, second, the equal protection clause does not apply to Congress, and it is problematical whether the Supreme Court will hold in this instance, as it did in *Bolling v. Sharp*, 347 U.S. 497, that the due process clause of the fifth amendment imposes the same prohibitions on the Federal Government that the equal protection clause does on the States.

While I believe that any unfair discriminations which the law makes against women should be abolished by law, I have the abiding conviction that the law should make such distinctions between the sexes as are reasonably necessary for the protection of women and the existence and development of the race.

I share completely this recent observation of a legal scholar:

"Use of the law in an attempt to conjure away all the differences which do exist between the sexes is both an insult to the law itself and a complete disregard of fact."

Let us consider for a moment whether there be a rational basis for reasonable distinctions between men and women in any of the relationships or undertakings of life.

FUNCTIONAL DIFFERENCES BETWEEN MEN AND WOMEN

When He created them, God made physiological and functional differences between men and women. These differences confer upon men a greater capacity *to* perform arduous and hazardous physical tasks. Some wise people even profess the belief that there may be psychological differences between men and women. To justify their belief, they assert that women possess an intuitive power to distinguish between wisdom and folly, good and evil.

To say these things is not to imply that either sex is superior to the other. It is simply to state the all-important truth that men and women complement each other in the relationships and undertakings on which the existence and development of the race depend.

The physiological and functional differences between men and women empower men to beget and women to bear children, who enter life in a state of utter helplessness and ignorance, and who must receive nurture, care, and training at the hands of adults throughout their early years if they and the race are to survive, and if they are to grow mentally and spiritually. From time whereof the memory of mankind runneth not to the contrary, custom and law have imposed upon men the primary responsibility for providing a habitation and a livelihood for their wives and children to enable their wives to make the habitations homes, and to furnish nurture, care, and training to their children during their early years.

In this respect, custom and law reflect the wisdom embodied in the ancient Yiddish proverb that God could not be everywhere, so he made mothers.

The physiological and functional differences between men and women constitute earth's important reality. Without them human life could not exist.

For this reason, any country which ignores these differences when it fashions its institutions and makes its law is woefully lacking in rationality.

Our country has not thus far committed this grievous error. As a consequence, it has established by law the institutions of marriage, the home, and the family, and has adopted some laws making rational distinctions between the respective rights and responsibilities of men and women to make these institutions contribute to the existence and advancement of the race.

OBSCURITY OF THE HOUSE-PASSED EQUAL RIGHTS AMENDMENT

In the nature of things, lawmakers use words to express their purpose and courts must ascertain their purpose from their words.

In his famous opinion in *Towne v. Eisner,* 245 U.S. 418, 425, Justice Oliver Wendell Holmes made this trenchant observation:

"A word is not a crystal, transparent and unchanged; it is the skin of a living thought and may vary greatly in color and content according to the circumstances and the time in which it is used."

During my many years as a lawyer, a judge, and a legislator, I have discovered that many words have many meanings, and that the purpose they are intended to express must be gathered from the context in which they are used. I have also learned that the most difficult task which ever confronts a court is determining the meaning of imprecise words used in a scrimpy context.

The word "sex" is imprecise in exact meaning, and no proposed constitutional amendment ever drafted exceeds the House-passed equal rights amendment in scrimpiness of context. The amendment contains no language to elucidate its meaning to legislators or to guide courts in interpreting it. When all is said, the House-passed equal rights amendment, if adopted, will place upon the Supreme Court the obligation to sail upon most tumultuous constitutional seas without chart or compass in quest of an undefined and unknown port.

The imprecision of the word "sex" as used in the proposed amendment is clearly revealed by these definitions set forth in the recently published "American Heritage Dictionary of the English Language":

"1.a. The property or quality by which organisms are classified according to their reproductive functions. b. Either of two divisions, designated male and female, of this classification. 2. Males or females collectively. 3. The condition or character of being male or female; the physiological, functional, and psychological differences that distinguish the male and the female. 4. The sexual urge or instinct as it manifests itself in behavior. 5. Sexual intercourse."

When one undertakes to ascertain the obscure meaning of the ambiguous House-passed equal rights amendment in an impartial, intellectual and unemotional manner, he is inevitably impelled to the conclusion that it is susceptible of several different and discordant interpretations.

If it should accept the fourth and fifth definitions of the term "sex" as set forth in the dictionary, the Supreme Court could reach the conclusion that the House-passed equal rights amendment merely annuls existing and future laws visiting upon the adulterous acts of women different legal consequences from those it visits upon such acts of men.

If it should accept the first, fourth, and fifth definitions of "sex" as set forth in the dictionary, the Supreme Court could reach the conclusion that the amendment is only concerned with sex per se, and has no application whatever to legal distinctions made between men and women on the basis of their respective functions in the relationships and undertakings on which the existence and development of the race depend.

A learned student of the constitutional aspects of sex-based discrimination in American law, Prof. Leo Kanowitz, accepts this interpretation. He had this to say in a Law Review article on the subject:

"It is submitted that the adoption of the Equal Rights Amendment would not fundamentally change the picture. While the proposed amendment states that equality of rights shall not be abridged on account of sex, sex classification could continue if it can be demonstrated that though they are expressed in terms of sex, they are in reality based upon function."

If it should accept the third definition of "sex" as set out in the dictionary, the Supreme Court could reach the conclusion that the House-passed equal rights amendment annuls every existing Federal and State law making any distinction between men and women, however reasonable such distinction might be in particular cases, and forever robs Congress and the legislatures of the 50 States, of the constitutional power to enact any such laws at any time in the future.

This is the interpretation which I fear the Supreme Court may feel itself obliged to place upon the House-passed equal rights amendment. I am not alone in entertaining this fear.

Source: Ervin, Sam. "The House-Passed Equal Rights Amendment: A Potentially Destructive and Self-Defeating Blunderbuss." Testimony of Senator Sam J. Ervin Jr., North Carolina, Equal Rights 1970: Hearings, 91st Cong., 2d sess., on S.J. Res. 61 and S.J. Res. 231 [before the Senate Comm. on the Judiciary]. Washington, DC: U.S. Government Printing Office, 1970.

BETTY FRIEDAN TESTIFIES ABOUT THE "SEX PLUS" DOCTRINE, 1970

In 1969 U.S. Supreme Court justice Abraham "Abe" Fortas resigned from the Court under a cloud of scandal. When President Richard M. Nixon's first choice to replace Fortas, Clement Haynsworth, failed to secure Senate approval, Nixon turned to federal appeals court judge G. Harrold Carswell. But Carswell was a controversial choice as well, with a history of rulings and opinions that women's rights advocates, civil rights groups, and others found troubling. One of Carswell's critics was famed feminist Betty Friedan (1921–2006), whose Senate testimony against Carswell's nomination from January 29, 1970, is excerpted below. Much of Friedan's criticism of Carswell focused on a "pernicious" judicial decision that she described as blatantly discriminatory against mothers in the workplace and defiant of established federal civil rights law.

Carswell's nomination ultimately fell apart after reports came out that he had explicitly endorsed segregation and white supremacy during an unsuccessful 1948 Georgia legislative campaign. As a result, for the first time since 1894, two nominees for a Supreme Court vacancy had been turned down. The Senate, however, then approved Nixon's third choice, Harry A. Blackmun of Minnesota, who served on the Court from 1970 to 1994.

I am here to testify before this committee to oppose Judge Carswell's appointment to Supreme Court Justice on the basis of his proven insensitivity to the problems of the 53 percent of United States citizens who are women, and specifically on the basis of his explicit discrimination in a circuit court decision in 1969 against working mothers.

I speak in my capacity as national president of the National Organization for Women, which has led the exploding new movement in this country for "full equality for women in truly equal partnership with men," and which was organized in 1966 to take action to break through discrimination against women in employment, education, government and in all fields of American life.

On October 13, 1969, in the Fifth Circuit Court of Appeals, Judge Carswell was party to a most unusual judiciary action which would permit employers, in defiance of the law of the land as embodied in Title VII of the 1964 Civil Rights Act, to refuse to hire women who have children.

The case involved Mrs. Ida Phillips, who was refused employment by Martin Marietta Corporation as an aircraft assembler because she had pre-school aged children, although the company said it would hire a man with pre-school aged children. This case was considered a clear-cut violation of the law which forbids job discrimination on the grounds of sex as well as race. The E.E.O.C., empowered to administer Title VII, filed an amicus brief on behalf of Mrs. Phillips; an earlier opinion of the Fifth Circuit filed in May upholding the company was considered such a clear violation of the Civil Rights Act by Chief Judge John Brown that he vacated the opinion and asked to convene the full court to consider the case.

Judge Carswell voted to deny a rehearing of the case, an action which in effect would have permitted employers to fire the 4.1 million working mothers in the U.S. today who have children under six. They comprise 38.9 percent of the nearly 10.6 million mothers in the labor force today.

In his dissent to this ruling in which Judge Carswell claimed no sex discrimination was involved, Chief Judge Brown said: "The case is simple. A woman with pre-school aged children may not be employed, a man with pre-school children may. The distinguishing factor seems to be motherhood versus fatherhood. The question then arises: Is this sex related? To the simple query, the answer is just as simple: Nobody—and this includes judges, Solomonic or life-tenured—has yet seen a male mother. A mother, to over-simplify the simplest biology, must then be a woman.

"It is the fact of the person being a mother—i.e., a woman—not the age of the children, which denies employment opportunity to a woman which is open to men."

It is important for this committee to understand the dangerous insensitivity of Judge Carswell to sex discrimination, when the desire and indeed the necessity of women to take a fully equal place in American society has already emerged as one of the most explosive issues in the 1970's, entailing many new problems which will ultimately have to be decided by the Supreme Court.

According to government figures, over 25 percent of mothers who have children under six are in the labor force today. Over 85 percent of them work for economic reasons. Over half a million are widowed, divorced or separated. Their incomes are vitally important to their children. Perhaps even more important, as a portent of the future, is the fact that there has been an astronomical increase in the last three decades in the number of working mothers. Between 1950 and the most recent compilation of government statistics, the number of working mothers in the United States nearly doubled. For every mother of children who worked in 1940, ten mothers are working today, an increase from slightly over 1.5 million to nearly 11 million.

In his pernicious action, Judge Carswell not only flouted the Civil Rights Act, designed to end the job discrimination which denied women, along with other minority groups, equal opportunity in employment, but specifically defied the policy of this administration to encourage women in poverty, who have children, to work by expanding day-care centers, rather than having them depend on the current medieval welfare system which perpetuates the cycle of poverty from generation to generation. Mothers and children today comprise 80 percent of the welfare load in major cities.

Judge Carswell justified discrimination against such women by a peculiar doctrine of "sex plus," which claimed that discrimination which did not apply to all women but only to women who did not meet special standards—standards not applied to men—was not sex discrimination.

In his dissent, Chief Judge Brown said, "The sex plus rule in this case sows the seed for future discrimination against black workers through making them meet extra standards not imposed on whites." The "sex plus" doctrine would also penalize the very women who most need jobs.

Chief Judge Brown said, "Even if the 'sex plus' rule is not expanded, in its application to mothers of pre-school children, it will deal a serious blow to the objectives of Title VII. If the law against sex discrimination means anything, it must protect employment opportunities for those groups of women who most need jobs because of economic necessity. Working mothers of pre-schoolers are such a group. Studies show that, as compared to women with older children or no children, these mothers of pre-school children were much more likely to have gone to work because of pressing need . . . because of financial necessity and because their husbands are unable to work. Frequently, these women are a key or only source of income for their families. Sixty-eight percent of working women do not have husbands present in the household, and two-thirds of these women are raising children in poverty. Moreover, a barrier to jobs for mothers of pre-schoolers tends to harm non-white mothers more then white mothers."

I am not a lawyer, but the wording of Title VII of the Civil Rights Act so clearly conveys its intention to provide equal job opportunity to all oppressed groups, including women—who today in America earn on the average less than half the earnings of men—that only outright sex discrimination or sexism, as we new feminists call it, can explain Judge Carswell's ruling.

Human rights are indivisible, and I, and those for whom I speak, would oppose equally the appointment to the Supreme Court of a racist judge who had been totally blind to the humanity of black men and women since 1948, as the appointment of a sexist judge totally blind to the humanity of women in 1969.

To countenance outright sexism, not only in words, but by judicial flaunting of the law in an appointee to the Supreme Court in 1970, when American women—not in the hundreds or thousands but in the millions—are finally beginning to assert their human rights, is unconscionable.

I trust that you gentlemen of the committee do not share Judge Carswell's inability to see women as human beings, too. I will, however, put these questions to you.

How would you feel if in the event you were not reelected, you applied for a job at some company or law firm or university, and were told you weren't eligible because you had a child?

How would you feel if your sons were told explicitly or implicitly that they could not get or keep certain jobs if they had children?

Then how do you feel about appointing to the Supreme Court a man who has said your daughters may not hold a job if they have children?

The economic misery and psychological conflicts entailed for untold numbers of American women, and their children and husbands, by Judge Carswell's denial of the protection of a law that was enacted for their benefit suggest only a faint hint of the harm that would be done in appointing such a sexually backward judge to the Supreme Court. For during the next decade I can assure you that the emerging revolution of the no-longer-quite-so-silent majority will pose many pressing new problems to our society, problems which will inevitably come before the courts and which indeed will probably preoccupy the Supreme Court of the 1970's as did questions arising from the civil rights movement in the 1960's.

It is already apparent from decisions made by judges in other circuit courts that Judge Carswell is unusually blind in the matter of sex prejudice and that his blindness will make it impossible for him to judge fairly the cases of sex prejudice that will surely come up.

Recently, courts have begun to outlaw forms of discrimination against women long accepted in society. The Fifth Circuit Court of Appeals (convened as a three-judge court without Judge Carswell), on March 4, 1969, in *Weeks v. Southern Bell Telephone* ruled that weight-lifting limitations barring women, but not men, from jobs, were illegal under Title VII. The Seventh Circuit Court of Appeals, on September 26, 1969, in *Bowe v. Colgate Palmolive Co.* ruled that, if retained, a weight-lifting test must apply to ALL employees, male and female, and that each individual must be permitted to "bid on and fill any job which his or her seniority entitled him or her." Separate seniority lists for men and women were forbidden.

Here are a few existing instances of discrimination against women, that are or will be before the courts:

1. In New York City, male, but not female, teachers are paid for their time spent on jury duty.
2. In Syracuse, New York, male, but not female, teachers are paid for athletic coaching.
3. In Syracuse, an employer wants to challenge the rule that forbids her to hire female employees at night in violation of New York State restrictive laws.
4. In Pennsylvania, a woman has requested help in obtaining a tax deduction for household help necessary for her to work.
5. In Arizona, a female law professor is fighting a rule that forbids her to be hired by the same university that employs her husband in another department.
6. In California, a wife is challenging a community property law which makes it obligatory for a husband to control their joint property.
7. And all over the country the E.E.O.C. regulation, which made it illegal to have separate want ads for males and females, have not been followed by most newspapers.

The Honorable Shirley Chisholm, a national board member of NOW, has summed it all up in her statement that she has been more discriminated against as a woman than as a black.

It would show enormous contempt for every woman of this country and contempt for every black American, as well as contempt for the Supreme Court itself, if you confirm Judge Carswell's appointment.

Source: Friedan, Betty. "Testimony. Nomination of George Harrold Carswell of Florida, Hearings before the Committee on the Judiciary, U.S. Senate, 91st Congress, 2d session, January 27, 28, 29, and February 2 and 3, 1970." Washington, DC: Government Printing Office, 1970, pp. 88–101.

GLORIA STEINEM CALLS FOR PASSAGE OF THE EQUAL RIGHTS AMENDMENT, 1970

Gloria Steinem (1934–) was one of the most visible and influential members of the "second wave" feminist movement during the 1960s and 1970s. Her work as a journalist, political activist, and cofounder of Ms. magazine had a significant impact on both women's rights advocacy and public perceptions of the wider movement. Not surprisingly, Steinem was an outspoken proponent of the Equal Rights Amendment and actively worked to drum up public support for the amendment in her speeches, writings, and organizational activities. She also appeared before Congress to defend the ERA from its critics. Following is an excerpt from 1970 testimony that she gave before a Senate subcommittee in which she talked about the traditional roles occupied by men and women in American society and the need for women to take a more active role in shaping U.S. culture and politics.

My name is Gloria Steinem. I am a writer and editor, and I am currently a member of the policy council of the Democratic committee. And I work regularly with the lowest-paid workers in the country, the migrant workers, men, women, and children both in California and in my own State of New York. . . .

During 12 years of working for a living, I have experienced much of the legal and social discrimination reserved for women in this country. I have been refused service in public restaurants, ordered out of public gathering places, and turned away from apartment rentals; all for the clearly-stated, sole reason that I am a woman. And all without the legal remedies available to blacks and other minorities. I have been excluded from professional groups, writing assignments on so-called "unfeminine" subjects such as politics, full participation in the Democratic Party, jury duty, and even from such small male privileges as discounts on airline fares. Most important to me, I have been denied a society in which women are encouraged, or even allowed to think of themselves as first-class citizens and responsible human beings.

However, after 2 years of researching the status of American women, I have discovered that in reality, I am very, very lucky. Most women, both wage-earners and housewives, routinely suffer more humiliation and injustice than I do.

As a freelance writer, I don't work in the male-dominated hierarchy of an office. (Women, like blacks and other visibly different minorities, do better in individual professions such as the arts, sports, or domestic work; anything in which they don't have authority over white males.) I am not one of the millions of women who must support a family. Therefore, I haven't had to go on welfare because there are no day-care centers for my children while I work, and I haven't had to submit to the humiliating welfare inquiries about my private and sexual life, inquiries from which men are exempt. I haven't had to brave the sex bias of labor unions and employers, only to see my family subsist on a median salary 40 percent less than the male median salary.

I hope this committee will hear the personal, daily injustices suffered by many women—professionals and day laborers, women housebound by welfare as well as by suburbia. We have all been silent for too long. But we won't be silent anymore.

The truth is that all our problems stem from the same sex based myths. We may appear before you as white radicals or the middle-aged middle class or black soul sisters, but we are all sisters in fighting against these outdated myths. Like racial myths, they have been reflected in our laws. Let me list a few.

That woman are biologically inferior to men. In fact, an equally good case can be made for the reverse. Women live longer than men, even when the men are not subject to business pressures. Women survived Nazi concentration camps better, keep cooler heads in emergencies currently studied by disaster-researchers, are protected against heart attacks by their female sex hormones, and are so much more durable at every stage of life that nature must conceive 20 to 50 percent more males in order to keep the balance going.

Man's hunting activities are forever being pointed to as tribal proof of superiority. But while he was hunting, women built houses, tilled the fields, developed animal husbandry, and perfected language. Men, being all alone in the bush, often developed into a creature as strong as women, fleeter of foot, but not very bright.

However, I don't want to prove the superiority of one sex to another. That would only be repeating a male mistake. English scientists once definitively proved, after all, that the English were descended from the angels, while the Irish were descended from the apes; it was the rationale for England's domination of Ireland for more than a century. The point is that science is used to support current myth and economics almost as much as the church was.

What we do know is that the difference between two races or two sexes is much smaller than the differences to be found within each group. Therefore, in spite of the slide show on female inferiorities that I understand was shown to you yesterday, the law makes much more sense when it treats individuals, not groups bundled together by some condition of birth. . . .

Another myth, that women are already treated equally in this society. I am sure there has been ample testimony to prove that equal pay for equal work, equal chance for advancement, and equal training or encouragement is obscenely scarce in every field, even those—like food and fashion industries—that are supposedly "feminine."

A deeper result of social and legal injustice, however, is what sociologists refer to as "Internalized Aggression." Victims of aggression absorb the myth of their own inferiority, and come to believe that their group is in fact second class. Even when they themselves realize they are not second class, they may still think their group is, thus the tendency to be the only Jew in the club, the only black woman on the block, the only woman in the office.

Women suffer this second class treatment from the moment they are born. They are expected to be, rather than achieve, to function biologically rather than learn. A brother, whatever his intellect, is more likely to get the family's encouragement and education money, while girls are often pressured to conceal ambition and intelligence, to "Uncle Tom."

I interviewed a New York public school teacher who told me about a black teenager's desire to be a doctor. With all the barriers in mind, she suggested kindly that he be a veterinarian instead.

The same day, a high school teacher mentioned a girl who wanted to be a doctor. The teacher said, "How about a nurse?"

Teachers, parents, and the Supreme Court may exude a protective, well-meaning rationale, but limiting the individual's ambition is doing no one a favor. Certainly not this country; it needs all the talent it can get.

Another myth, that American women hold great economic power. Fifty-one percent of all shareholders in this country are women. That is a favorite male-chauvinist statistic. However, the number of shares they hold is so small that the total is only 18 percent of all the shares. Even those holdings are often controlled by men.

Similarly, only 5 percent of all the people in the country who receive $10,000 a year or more, earned or otherwise, are women. And that includes the famous rich widows.

The constantly repeated myth of our economic power seems less testimony to our real power than to the resentment of what little power we do have.

Another myth, that children must have full-time mothers. American mothers spend more time with their homes and children than those of any other society we know about. In the past, joint families, servants, a prevalent system in which grandparents raised the children, or family field work in the agrarian systems—all these factors contributed more to child care than the labor-saving devices of which we are so proud.

The truth is that most American children seem to be suffering from too much mother, and too little father. Part of the program of Women's Liberation is a return of fathers to their children. If laws permit women equal work and pay opportunities, men will then be relieved of their role as sole breadwinner. Fewer ulcers, fewer hours of meaningless work, equal responsibility for his own children: these are a few of the reasons that Women's Liberation is Men's Liberation too.

As for psychic health of the children, studies show that the quality of time spent by parents is more important than the quantity. The most damaged children were not those whose mothers worked, but those whose mothers preferred to work but stayed home out of the role-playing desire to be a "good mother."

Another myth, that the women's movement is not political, won't last, or is somehow not "serious."

When black people leave their 19th century roles, they are feared. When women dare to leave theirs, they are ridiculed. We understand this; we accept the burden of ridicule. It won't keep us quiet anymore.

Similarly, it shouldn't deceive male observers into thinking that this is somehow a joke. We are 51 percent of the population; we are essentially united on these issues across boundaries of class or race or age; and we may well end by changing this society more than the civil rights movement. That is an apt parallel. We, too, have our right wing and left wing, our separatists, gradualists, and Uncle Toms. But we are changing our own consciousness, and that of the country. Engels noted the relationship of the authoritarian, nuclear family to capitalism: the father as capitalist, the mother as means of production, and the children as labor. He said the family would change as the economic system did, and that seems to have happened, whether we want to admit it or not. Women's bodies will no longer be owned by the state for the production of workers and soldiers; birth control and abortion are facts of everyday life. The new family is an egalitarian family.

Gunnar Myrdal noted 30 years ago the parallel between women and Negroes in this country. Both suffered from such restricting social myths as: smaller brains, passive natures, inability to govern themselves (and certainly not white men), sex objects only, childlike natures, special skills, and the like. When evaluating a general statement about women, it might be valuable to substitute "black people" for "women"—just to test the prejudice at work.

And it might be valuable to do this constitutionally as well. Neither group is going to be content as a cheap labor pool anymore. And neither is going to be content without full constitutional rights.

Finally, I would like to say one thing about this time in which I am testifying.

I had deep misgivings about discussing this topic when National Guardsmen are occupying our campuses, the country is being turned against itself in a terrible polarization, and America is enlarging an already inhuman and unjustifiable war. But it seems to me that much of the trouble in this country has to do with the "masculine mystique"; with the myth that masculinity somehow depends on the subjugation of other people. It is a bipartisan problem; both our past and current Presidents seem to be victims of this myth, and to behave accordingly.

Women are not more moral than men. We are only uncorrupted by power. But we do not want to imitate men, to join this country as it is, and I think our very participation will change it. Perhaps women elected leaders—and there will be many of them—will not be so likely to dominate black people or yellow people or men; anybody who looks different from us.

After all, we won't have our masculinity to prove.

Source: Steinem, Gloria. Testimony, Senate Committee on the Judiciary, *The "Equal Rights" Amendment: Hearings before the Subcommittee on Constitutional Amendments of the Committee on the Judiciary*, 91st Cong., 2d sess., May 5, 6, and 7, 1970. Washington, DC: Government Printing Office, 1970, pp. 331–334.

A WOMAN LABOR UNION OFFICIAL DECLARES OPPOSITION TO THE ERA, 1970

On May 6, 1970, Myra Wolfgang, an official with the AFL-CIO's Hotel and Restaurant Employees and Bartenders International Union, appeared before a Senate subcommittee studying a proposed Equal Rights Amendment, to declare her opposition to such an amendment. As Wolfgang's testimony shows, not all American women supported the ERA. Some thought that the amendment (and its supporters) diminished the contributions made by women who supported their families as wives and mothers, others objected to the societal chaos that would be unleashed by dramatic realignments of traditional gender roles, and still others argued that the ERA would jeopardize legal protections that already existed for women workers.

My name is Myra K. Wolfgang. I reside in the City of Detroit, State of Michigan, and am represented in this body by Senator Philip Hart. I am the Vice President of the Hotel and Restaurant Employees and Bartenders International Union AFL-CIO and Secretary-Treasurer of its Detroit Local, No. 705. I am a member of the Michigan State Minimum Wage Board and I have served on the Mayor's Committee of Human Relations. I am presently a member of the Michigan Women's Commission (the Governor's Commission on the Status of Women).

I am opposed to the enactment of the Equal Rights Amendment to our Constitution. I state my position after long and careful consideration in spite of the fact that we find sex prejudice parading in the cloth of tradition everywhere. We are aware that it is tailored to the patterns of ignorance and special interest.

The principle of equal pay for equal work is being violated throughout the breadth and length of this nation. Women are being discriminated against unjustly in hiring and in promotion. Our social security laws remain discriminatory. Equal access to our educational institutions is still denied women. Qualified women are, in the main, excluded from the policy making bodies of this nation from the Cabinet down to our County institutions.

Fully aware of all of the inequities visited upon the women of America, I still appear here today to oppose the Equal Rights Amendment. I believe that the amendment is not only undemocratic and its effects will bring frustration and tragedy, but that it will accomplish the exact opposite its proponents claim it will do. . . .

Until last week, I had many grave misgivings about the outcome of this legislation. I had seen the Equal Rights Amendment run through the House of Representatives like a herd of stampeded cattle on a discharge petition maneuver. Never have so few business and professional women been so effective and done such harm. The hysteria created by bra-burning and other freak antics is not a justification for the action taken by the House of Representatives, nor is the fear of political reprisal. Let me assure you the threat is not borne of reality. It must have been this same type of hysteria that created the conditions for the passage of the Volstead Act. But now that the dust has settled and we begin to look around at the damaged past, the damaged present and the damaged future, more seasoned hands seem to be in the saddle.

Even though I appear here before you in my various capacities, capacities not usually associated by chauvinistic males with philosophical legislative considerations, I want you to know the women of America are not unaware of what government is, what it means and what it should mean. We grow more aware daily. We know the theory around which our Constitution was conceived. Abigail Adams is not the only woman who had or has ideas about its structure, or about man's predilection for tyranny in designing laws. Molly Pitcher knew that we threw off the yoke of oppression with these words "we hold these truths to be self evident that all men are created equal" comma, not period, for she knew that the Declaration of Independence continued on to further define equal with "that they are endowed by their creator with certain unalienable rights, that among these are life, liberty and the pursuit of happiness." And Martha Wayles Jefferson knew that her husband in penning the Virginia Declaration of Rights, had written "that all men are by nature equally free and independent and have certain inherent rights, namely the enjoyment of life and liberty, with the means of acquiring *safety*."

Yes, Dolly Madison knew, as I know, that our Constitution was based upon the best of man's thinking down through the ages. We know that the very foundation of all government worth having, is predicted upon laws designed to protect the unequal, those who are smaller and less strong from those who are larger and stronger.

We know that this concept is as American as squash and chitlins. . . .

Now, if one of the major and fundamental roles of government is this equalizing one, then the adoption of the so-called Equal Rights Amendment will negate this same equalizing function under the guise of broadening it. The Equal Rights Amendment will invalidate all the legislation, hundreds of pieces of it, which has been adopted over the last 100 years which were passed to permit a semblance of equality which had been denied women down through the ages.

There are various kinds of protection for women workers provided by State laws and regulations (1) minimum wage; (2) overtime compensation; (3) hours of work, meal and rest period; (4) equal pay; (5) industrial homework; (6) employment before and after childbirth; (7) occupational limitations; and (8) other standards, such as seating and washroom facilities and weightlifting limitations. It would be desirable for some of these laws to be extended to men, but the practical fact is that an Equal Rights Amendment is likely to destroy the laws altogether rather than bring about coverage for both sexes. Those State laws that are outmoded or discriminatory, should be repealed or amended and should be handled on a "case by case" basis.

I am appalled by leaders of social institutions working hand in glove with industry leaders who wish to repeal the above mentioned laws. I warn the women of America who seek equality without repression to reject the old saw "you can't have your cake and eat it too." That admonition comes with a hollow ring, especially from those who enjoy their having a housekeeper, wife-mother, and breadwinner combined at their disposal.

The chief conflict between those who support the Equal Rights Amendment and those of us who oppose it, is not whether women should be discriminated against, but what constitutes a discrimination. We, who want equal opportunities, equal pay for equal work and equal status for women, know that frequently we obtain real equality through a difference in treatment, rather than identity in treatment. We think that democratic concept is an important part of our Constitution.

We believe that orderly legislative revision is the practical way to erase such "specific bills for specific ills." I oppose adoption of the Equal Rights Amendment since I believe that the adoption of the amendment would jeopardize existing labor laws and standards that apply to women. That it would create endless confusion in the wide field of laws relating to property, personal status and marriage. This will adversely affect the women of America and their families.

Equality of opportunity for men and women must be achieved without impairing the social legislation which promotes true equality for safeguarding the health, safety and economic welfare of all.

For an example, the passage of an hours limitation law for women provided them with a shield against obligatory overtime to permit them to carry on their life at home as wives and mothers. While all overtime should be optional for both men and women, it is absolutely mandatory that overtime for women be regulated because of her double role in our society.

At the time that State protective legislation was initiated, there were relatively few women in the labor force, yet, society recognized the need to protect women workers. At present, there are more than 30,000,000 women in the labor force. Almost 60% of them are married and living with their husbands. Working mothers constitute 38% of all working women. Obviously, the majority of women workers have domestic responsibilities, and a very substantial number of them, almost 11,000,000, have children under the age of 18 years. Even with the 40 hour work week, such women (between their paid employment and their many hours of cooking, cleaning, shopping, child-care and other household duties) work arduously long hours. While "the double income economy" has forced millions of women into the labor force, millions more the sole or major breadwinners for their families, it has not released them from home and family responsibilities.

To deprive women of protective legislation, for as long as one second, frustrates their basic constitutional right to safety and the pursuit of happiness and denies to them the fundamental reason for their participation in a government of law.

You must understand that the overwhelming portion of women who work, need to work. They need their job and the income it produces. Where women are unorganized, and that means 85% or more of them, they depend solely upon their employers' understanding of their home responsibilities. In most cases, he is a man more concerned with meeting production standards than he is for his female workers' children's safety and well-being. . . .

Those of us in the struggle for the advancement of women prefer to fight for positive measures such as equal pay for equal work and equal employment opportunities. We fought for the Civil Rights Act of 1964. We fought for and got Title VII to the Civil Rights Act. In its positive application, Title VII can be an effective instrument for overcoming discrimination against women in employment and can contribute substantially to their progress. However, some of the guidelines established by the Equal Employment Opportunity Commission, unfortunately, have invited an assault upon State protective legislation, without distinguishing between those provisions which might be viewed as discriminatory and those which are not, in fact, discriminatory. The result of such sweeping guidelines has made the equality that many have sought, an equality of mistreatment.

In Detroit, six Penn Central System office women were assigned to jobs as checkers of freight cars at the Detroit-area railroad yards, after they complained about sex discrimination to the Michigan Civil Rights Commission. The women had been employed as clerks and typists. Climbing in and out of box cars as railroad checkers is a back-breaking job, but a company executive said, "They asked for equal rights, so what are they complaining about?"

Eleanor Hannon, 51, a widow with five children, said, "I can't afford to quit, but I don't know how long I can last on this job, particularly if I have to work a night shift." The transfer from the office pool to the freight docks was within the scope of the railroad's contract with the Brotherhood of Railway Clerks. . . .

Do we discard protective legislation for women, if we are unable to get such legislation for men? The passage of the Equal Rights Amendment would do this, and it is wrong. Ironically, many of the Business and Professional Women, most vocal in advocating the overthrow of hour limitations, would not be affected at all, since many of the States with hours limitations already exempt them from these restrictions. I must remind those who are influenced by the Business and Professional Women that the Equal Rights Amendment does not require equal pay for equal work, nor does it require promotion of women to better or "decision making jobs." It does not elect more women to public office. It does not convince men to help with the housework.

The Federation of Business and Professional Women would do well to legislate for their own inclusion into the equal pay for equal work provision of our law rather than seek repeal of protective legislation for others as they do in a booklet published by them entitled "How to Repeal Protective Legislation." Their booklet states "the days of sweat shops and intolerable working conditions, in which exploitation of women workers went rampant, are largely passed. The notion that women are frail and require special protection is obsolete."

The days of exploitation are not over for thousands of women workers, among them the domestics who work in the homes of many of the Business and Professional Women!! . . .

Many of today's feminists oppose and resent protective legislation for women since they postulate that such legislation treats them as children whose lives have to be regulated by other adults. Yet the Women's Liberation groups wish to regulate the lives of other women and treat them as children, telling them that the job of wife and mother is unfulfilling and unsatisfying. Should the woman, so being lectured, disagree, she is immediately charged with having been brainwashed!

Feminists, assuredly, do not represent the majority of women and do not correctly relate their needs and feelings. For the most part, women who join "liberation groups" are white, middle-class and college-oriented. The most active of these women, who do the work of the organizations, are those with no or grown children. Working women, like the mothers of young children, are too busy to be liberated.

The National Organization of Women (N.O.W.), one of the most vocal supporters of the Equal Rights Amendment, claim to have about 3,000 members. They speak of the discontent of wives and mothers. They speak for a small minority when they urge passage of the Equal Rights Amendment. They do not speak for Mary Dennison of the Congress of Racial Equality, who is quoted as saying, "The Women's Liberation Movement is a luxury that only bored white women can afford." They do not speak for the divorced, separated or abandoned mother when they urge passage of the Equal Rights Amendment which will weaken the husband and father obligation for child support. Divorced, separated and deserted wives struggling to support themselves and their children may find their claims to support even harder to enforce than they are right now.

The Equal Rights Amendment could create new obligations for women to support their husbands and children. Wives and mothers who are not in the labor force (and they are a substantial majority) may find they can no longer choose to stay out of the labor force. Under the Equal Rights Amendment, they might become obligated for furnishing half the family support. The right of choice for these women should be protected. For many American women, particularly for those in the lower brackets, losing that choice is a heavy and undemocratic price to pay for an illogical theory of equality.

Women's Liberation is the most misused and abused phrase in the English Language. To some, the word means—liberation from marriage—liberation from housework—liberation from bearing and rearing children—liberation from all forms of social responsibility—copping out. To others, not so.

I believe women should be a part of a social movement dedicated to reforming our social structure to permit true equality between the sexes. It should accomplish for all women, young and old, married and single, housewives and breadwinners, mothers and the childless, wives and widows; their goals and aspirations. It should improve their life, gain recognition for their double role in society and the recognition of that responsibility. It should broaden the fruits of science to lessen the drudgery of our housework and to making clothing functional, yet enhancing. It should bring peace to the world and bring our teenagers home, going to colleges or learning a trade rather than working towards expanding the draft by including women to kill and destroy. It should fight to maintain the right to stay home as a housewife and mother, if circumstances permit, and that be the preference of the individual woman. It should fight to have an economy that's free from hunger and privation, that affords freedom from want and need in a society that promises every man and woman equal pay for equal work. That's the kind of liberation I'm interested in.

Not everyone agrees with me, I am sure, for there is no more unanimity of opinion among women than among men. The plight of the black woman forced to leave her children untended as she goes off to clean the home of the rich women is unbridgeable. Both may be wives and mothers, both are women, but they have little in common to cause them to be of one opinion.

We live in a world of socially prescribed differences, of fashion prejudices, of customs relating to masculinity and femininity. To achieve equality, we must start equal by recognizing physical and biological differences. We are different, and remember, different does not mean deficient. . . .

No, gentlemen, women receive nothing, absolutely nothing, from the Equal Rights Amendment except a vague male guilt freeing generality about "Pie in the sky, bye and bye." What we lose may not be all we hope to get, but it's the fruit of our 100 years' effort and we have it now today, we need it now today, and we don't propose giving it up today or in the immediate or even distant future.

I have attempted to convey to you my opposition to the Equal Rights Amendment as a citizen, woman, widow, mother, worker and union official representing thousands of women (and men). I have tried to prove that women (and men, as well) will suffer adversely, socially, politically and economically. I have endeavored to prove to you that the action before you is based upon an undemocratic concept contrary to the philosophy embodied in our Constitution.

I urge you oppose S.J. Res. 61. The legislative process of enacting "specific bills for specific ills" must be invoked to correct the inequities in our society today.

The differences between men and women cannot be changed by an Act of Congress—or by a Constitutional Amendment. . . .

Source: Wolfgang, Myra. Testimony. Senate Committee on the Judiciary, *Equal Rights 1970: Hearings before the Committee on the Judiciary*, 91st Cong., 2d sess., September 9, 10, 11, and 15, 1970. Washington, DC: U.S. Government Printing Office, 1970.

PHYLLIS SCHLAFLY CONDEMNS THE EQUAL RIGHTS AMENDMENT, 1972

Phyllis Schlafly (1924–2016) was a lawyer who became one of America's most famous conservative social activists during the 1970s. Alarmed by the forward momentum for rat-ification that the proposed Equal Rights Amendment (ERA) was gathering in the individual states, she spearheaded the creation of a vast opposition movement that attacked the ERA as both anti-family and anti-American. Her organization, first known as Stop ERA and later renamed Eagle Forum, did not become active until more than 30 of the necessary 38 states had already ratified the bill. But Schlafly and likeminded religious and social conservatives helped construct a legislative firewall against ratification, and by 1982, the deadline for ratification, it was still three states short of passage.

After the defeat of the ERA, Schlafly and Eagle Forum remained influential voices in Republican conservative politics. But she will always be best known for her role in defeat-ing the Equal Rights Amendment. When Schlafly died in 2016, in fact, her obituary in the Washington Post *stated that Schlafly "is credited with almost single-handedly stopping the passage of the Equal Rights Amendment in the 1970s," while Eleanor Clift wrote in a post on the Daily Beast that "Phyllis Schlafly is the reason why we don't have an Equal Rights Amendment today." The following is a 1972 article that Schlafly wrote for her own* Phyllis Schlafly Report *that lays out some of her arguments for opposing the ERA.*

Of all the classes of people who ever lived, the American woman is the most priv-ileged. We have the most rights and rewards, and the fewest duties. Our unique status is the result of a fortunate combination of circumstances.

We have the immense good fortune to live in a civilization which respects the family as the basic unit of society. This respect is part and parcel of our laws and our customs. It is based on the fact of life—which no legislation or agitation can erase—that women have babies and men don't.

If you don't like this fundamental difference, you will have to take up your complaint with God because He created us this way. That fact that women, not men have babies is not the fault of selfish and domineering men, or of the estab-lishment, or of any clique of conspirators who want to oppress women. It's simply the way God made us.

Our Judeo-Christian civilization has developed the law and custom that, since women must be required to bear the physical consequences of the sex act, men must be required to bear the other consequences and pay in other ways. These laws and customs decree that a man must carry his share by physical protection and financial support of his children and of the woman who bears his children, and also by a code of behavior which benefits and protects both the woman and the children.

The Greatest Achievement of Women's Rights

. . . The institution of the family . . . assures a woman the most precious and important right of all—the right to keep her own baby and to be supported and protected in the enjoyment of watching her baby grow and develop.

The institution of the family is advantageous for women for many reasons. . . . Children are a woman's best social security—her best guarantee of social benefits such as old age pension, unemployment compensation, workman's compensation, and sick leave. The family gives a woman the physical, financial and emotional security of the home—for all her life.

The Financial Benefits of Chivalry

The second reason why American women are a privileged group is that we are the beneficiaries of a tradition of special respect for women which dates from the Christian Age of Chivalry. The honor and respect paid to Mary, the Mother of Christ, resulted in all women, in effect, being put on a pedestal. . . .

In other civilizations, such as the African and the American Indian, the men strut around wearing feathers and beads and hunting and fishing (great sport for men!), while the women do all the hard, tiresome drudgery including the tilling of the soil (if any is done), the hewing of wood, the making of fires, the carrying of water, as well as the cooking, sewing, and caring for babies.

This is not the American way because we were lucky enough to inherit the traditions of the Age of Chivalry. In America, a man's first significant purchase is a diamond for his bride, and the largest financial investment of his life is a home for her to live in. . . .

The Real Liberation of Women

The third reason why American women are so well off is that the great American free enterprise system has produced remarkable inventors who have lifted the backbreaking "women's work" from our shoulders.

In other countries and in other eras, it was truly said that "Man may work from sun to sun, but woman's work is never done." . . .

The real liberation of women from the backbreaking drudgery of centuries is the American free enterprise system which stimulated inventive geniuses to pursue their talents—and we all reap the profits. The great heroes of women's liberation are not the straggly-haired women on television talk shows and picket lines, but

Thomas Edison who brought the miracle of electricity to our homes to give light and to run all those labor-saving devices. . . .

The Fraud of the Equal Rights Amendment

In the last couple of years, a noisy movement has sprung up agitating for "women's rights." Suddenly, everywhere we are afflicted with aggressive females on television talk shows yapping about how mistreated American women are, suggesting that marriage has put us in some kind of "slavery," that housework is menial and degrading, and—perish the thought—that women are discriminated against. New "women's liberation" organizations are popping up . . . and purporting to speak for some 100,000,000 American women.

It's time to set the record straight. The claim that American women are downtrodden and unfairly treated is the fraud of the century. The truth is that American women never had it so good. Why should we lower ourselves to "equal rights" when we already have the status of special privilege?

The proposed Equal Rights Amendment states: "Equality of rights under the law shall not be denied or abridged by the United States or by any state on account of sex." So what's wrong with that? Well, here are a few examples of what's wrong with it.

This Amendment will absolutely and positively make women subject to the draft. . . .

Another bad effect of the Equal Rights Amendment is that it will abolish a woman's right to child support and alimony. . . .

By law and custom in America, in case of divorce, the mother always is given custody of her children unless there is overwhelming evidence of mistreatment, neglect or bad character. This is our special privilege because of the high rank that is placed on motherhood in our society. Do women really want to give up this special privilege and lower themselves to "equal rights" . . . ? I think not.

Women's Libbers do NOT Speak for Us

The "women's lib" movement is *not* an honest effort to secure better jobs for women who want or need to work outside the home. This is just the superficial sweet-talk to win broad support for a radical "movement." Women's lib is a total assault on the role of the American woman as wife and mother, and on the family as the basic unity of society.

Women's libbers are trying to make wives and mothers unhappy with their career, make them feel that they are "second-class citizens" and "abject slaves." Women's libbers are promoting free sex instead of the "slavery" of marriage. They are promoting Federal "day-care centers" for babies instead of homes. They are promoting abortions instead of families. . . .

If the women's libbers want to reject marriage and motherhood, it's a free country and that is their choice. But let's not permit these women's libbers to get away with pretending to speak for the rest of us. Let's not permit this tiny minority to degrade the role that most women prefer. Let's not let these women's libbers deprive wives and mothers of the rights we now possess.

Tell your Senators NOW that you want them to vote NO on the Equal Rights Amendment. Tell your television and radio stations that you want equal time to present the case FOR marriage and motherhood.

Source: Schlafly, Phyllis."What's Wrong with 'Equal Rights' for Women?" *Phyllis Schlafly Report* 5, no. 7 (February 1972): 1–4. Used by permission of the Phyllis Schlafly Center.

MARABEL MORGAN DESCRIBES *THE TOTAL WOMAN,* 1973

Marabel Morgan (1937–) rose to prominence in the 1970s with The Total Woman, *a book that offered wives guidance for building happier marriages through a program of bible-based submission to the psychological and physical desires and needs of their husbands. Morgan and her* Total Woman *book were mocked and condemned by the feminist movement for proposing chauvinistic and retrograde solutions to issues of marriage and gender, but the self-help book was the top-selling nonfiction title in the United States in 1974 and has sold millions of copies since its initial 1973 publication. Following is an excerpt from Morgan's bestselling book.*

Psychiatrists tell us that a man's most basic needs, outside of warm sexual love, are approval and admiration. Women need to be loved; men need to be admired. We women would do well to remember this one important difference between us and the other half.

Just the other day a woman told me, "My husband doesn't fulfill me. He never tells me his real feelings; he never expresses his love. He's about as warm as a cold fish!"

Your man, like so many American males, may be like an empty cup emotionally. He may seem void of emotions, unable to properly express his real feelings to you. Why is this? Remember that he grew up in a culture that taught him not to cry when he scratched his leg. Instead of hugging Uncle Jack, he shook hands. Grown-ups were generally unavailable to listen, so he learned to keep his feelings to himself.

We girls, on the other hand, were allowed to cry and throw temper tantrums. We were encouraged to kiss baby dolls, Aunt Susie, and the baby-sitter. We grew up full of emotions and knew basically how to express love. Then one day the fun began. Mr. Cool married Miss Passion. Is it any wonder that she felt unfulfilled because he never showed her any emotion?

Have you ever wondered why your husband doesn't just melt when you tell him how much you love him? But try saying, "I admire you," and see what happens. If you want to free him to express his thoughts and emotions, begin by filling up his empty cup with admiration. He must be filled first, for he has nothing to give until this need is met. And when his cup runs over, guess who lives in the overflow? Why, the very one who has been filling up the cup—you!

Love your husband and hold him in reverence, it says in the Bible. That means admire him. *Reverence,* according to the dictionary, means "To respect, honor, esteem, adore, praise, enjoy, and admire."

As a woman, you yearn to be loved by that man, right? He, being a man, yearns to be admired by you. And he needs it first. This irritates some women until they see that they have certain strengths that a man doesn't have. It's a great strength, not a weakness, to give for the sheer sake of giving. It is your nature to give. Calvin Coolidge once said, "No person was ever honored for what he received. Honor has been the reward for what he gave."

You are the one person your husband needs to make him feel special. He married you because he thought you were the most enchanting girl of all. The world may bestow awards on him, but above all others, he needs your admiration. He needs it to live. Without it his motivation is gone.

A young executive was literally starved for admiration from his wife. She wanted him to fulfill her before she met his needs. She explained, "Why should I give in first? Marriage is a fifty-fifty deal. I'm not about to give everything." Her husband threw himself into his business, working extra-long hours. He hoped his work would fill up that inner emptiness.

During a Total Woman class, this wife realized that she had the power to pour into him the admiration he needed. She began to admire him. Their relationship began to change. One evening he told her, "Something beautiful is happening. I don't know what it is, but it's great. You seem more alive for some reason."

Hero Worship

Try this test for a week. Starting tonight determine that you will admire your husband. By an act of your will, determine to fill up his cup, which may be bone dry. Be positive. Remember that compliments will encourage him to talk.

Admire him as he talks to you. Concentrate on what he's saying. Let him know you care. Put your magazine down and look at him. Even if you don't care who won yesterday's football game, your attention is important to him and he needs you. Let him know he's your hero.

Don't interrupt or be preoccupied. A pilot told me, "When my wife is indifferent and doesn't respond to what I'm saying, it shatters me for two or three days. Indifference is the worst pain of all."

Another woman called me the night she was sued for divorce. When she asked her husband why, she was shocked at his reply: "You've always been completely indifferent to my life. You never cared what I did or thought."

Every marriage needs tact—that special ability to describe another person as he sees himself. Your husband needs you to see him as he sees himself. For example, take a good look at him. He happens to love his body. It's the only one he has and he lives in there. He wants you to love it too. The only way he'll ever know that you do is for you to tell him.

Perhaps this sounds very foreign to you. You may even think it vulgar. If so, your husband is probably long overdue for some badly needed praise. It is your highest privilege to assure him that he is as special as he hoped he was.

Tonight when he comes home, concentrate on his body. Look at him, really observe him. It may have been years since you actually looked at him with eyes that see. Try looking at him through another woman's eyes—his secretary's or your neighbor's. That might help bring him into focus.

Tell him you love his body. If you choke on that phrase, practice until it comes out naturally. If you haven't admired him lately, he's probably starving emotionally. He can't take too much at once, so start slowly. Give him one good compliment a day and watch him blossom right before your eyes.

Look for his admirable qualities. Even the ugliest man has certain qualities worth admiring, but we're talking about the dream man you married. Compliment that one who used to make your heart pound and make your lips stammer. Admire that one who stood far above the crowd of common men.

Pick out his most masculine characteristics and let him know they please you. His whiskers, for instance. The day he shaved for the first time was a milestone in his life. But have you ever complained with irritation, "Ouch, why don't you shave once in awhile? You're rubbing my face raw"? Instead, try telling him nicely, "Honey, your scratchy beard is too strong for my tender skin." You can compliment your husband into shaving off his weekend whiskers by reinforcing his masculine image.

Thin Arms, Full Heart

Admire him *personally*. This is what he is yearning for. When he comes home tonight, would you rather have him admire your newly waxed floor, or tell you how great you look? In the same way, he'd rather hear how handsome he is, than how great his corporation is.

Tomorrow morning watch your husband when he looks in the mirror. He sees an eighteen-year-old youth, with firm stomach muscles and a full head of hair. No matter what his age, he doesn't see his pouch or receding hairline. He sees what he wants to see, and wants you to see that eighteen-year-old, too. Of course, this isn't really so strange. What age girl do you see in the mirror? My own grandmother admitted to feeling that she was not much past twenty-one.

A dentist's wife told me she had blurted out one night, "Look, you're getting fat and bald. It's disgusting. Why don't you just face the truth? You're not a kid anymore." The first shot had been fired. Her husband felt devastated and to protect himself, he lashed out at her weaknesses in a brutal way that only he could do. He could not rationally answer her comment but instead struck out at her personally.

In class one day, I gave the assignment for the girls to admire their husband's body that night. One girl went right to work on her homework. Her husband was shorter than she, but quite handsome. In all their years together she had never put her admiration into words. It was a big step for her. She didn't quite know how to start, even though it was her own husband. That evening while he was reading the paper, she sat down next to him on the sofa and began stroking his arm. After a bit, she stopped at the bicep and squeezed. He unconsciously flexed his muscle and she said, "Oh, I never knew you were so muscular!" He put down the paper, looked at her, and inquired, "What else?" He was so starved for admiration, he wanted to hear more!

The next day, she told this to her girl friend, who also decided to try it. Her husband had thin arms, but she admired his muscles anyway. Two nights later she couldn't find him at dinner time. He was out lifting his new set of weights in the garage! He wanted to build more muscles for her to admire.

By the way, admiration can also work wonders for your children. For example, one mother always nagged her son to hop out of the car to open the garage door. One afternoon she said, "Tommy, I'll bet a boy with muscles like yours could flip that garage door up in nothing flat." That's all she said, and that's all he needed. She never again had to ask him to open the door.

Your husband won't mind helping you either, if he's approached in the proper way. Instead of struggling with a jar and breaking a fingernail, ask him to loan you his strong hands for a minute. He derives pleasure from showing off his strength, even on a little old jar.

I know of only one case where this principle backfired. One wife asked her husband, one of the Miami Dolphin football players, to give her a muscular hand with the jars. Finally he asked, "Say, what's with you? You've been opening these baby food jars for five months and now all of a sudden you can't seem to manage them." So don't overdo it. Give him only the jars you really can't handle.

Rebuilding a Partial Man

I heard one wife say, "I feel guilty using feminine wiles on my husband. It seems dishonest. Anyway, his ego is so big, it doesn't need expanding. His body is not all that great. Why should I lie to build him up? I want to be honest, but still meet his needs."

If you're secure within yourself, you won't be afraid to give your husband credit. Instead of feeling threatened, you will feel joy in meeting his needs. As you know, you cannot express love to your husband until you really love yourself. But once you do, you can give with abandon. In fact, you can give with no thought of what you'll receive in return.

I am not advocating that you lie to give your husband a superficial ego boost; even a fool will see through flattery. But I am saying he has a deep need for sincere admiration. Look for new parts to compliment as you see him with new eyes.

Consider his weaknesses and things about which he may be self-conscious. Larry had a nasty scar on his neck as the result of an accident. His wife knew that it upset him and saw that he kept rubbing it. She said, "I really love your scar, honey.

It makes you look so rugged." Her admiration made him feel relieved inside and less self-conscious.

If you haven't been communicating much lately with your husband, you may have trouble finding something to compliment. If that's your case, think back to those days when you were first convinced that he was the one. What did you love about him then?

An older couple was so estranged that the wife could not see anything to admire about her husband. She forced herself to think back, all the way to the Depression days, when he frugally kept the family together with shrewd business management. Now, nearly forty years later, she shyly mentioned how she had admired his financial leadership during that time. Those were the first appreciative words he had heard in years, and his reaction was pitiful. He looked at her with disbelieving eyes, tears welled up, and though he found no way of verbally expressing his appreciation, he was very tender that evening. The wife was amazed that such a little remark from the distant past could cause this behavior. It was a turning point in their marriage.

A marriage must not remain stagnant. You can keep yours exciting and growing, and in order to succeed, you must. At the end of a long day, your husband especially needs your compliments. One husband called his wife just before quitting time to say, "This is a partial man looking for a Total Woman; be prepared!"

Put your husband's tattered ego back together again at the end of each day. That's not using feminine wiles; that is the very nature of love. If you fulfill his needs, he won't have to escape some other way.

On the other hand, you may have a husband who does not do anything but stay home drinking beer in his underwear. The responsibility of the family may rest on your back because somewhere along the line you usurped his role. Your nagging may have taken the wind out of his sails and now he has no desire to keep working for you. If so, he needs your compliments to restart his engine, regardless of the distance or bitterness between you.

Life is made up of seemingly inconsequential things, but often it's a little thing that can turn the tide. Behind every great man is a great woman, loving him and meeting his needs. There are some exceptions to this, but very few.

Self cries, "Love me, meet my needs." Love says, "Allow me to meet your needs." Dish out some sincere compliments to your man tonight, and watch his cup fill up and overflow. What nagging cannot do, admiration will!

[. . .]

One Monday morning Bobbie Evans, the wife of Miami Dolphins tackle Norm Evans, arrived at my doorstep fed up and resentful. The football team was flying in at noon and she was picking up Norm at the airport. Bobbie needed to talk out her anger to a buddy before she unloaded it on her husband. She was tired of Norm's neverending football schedule, his endless appearances and speaking engagements, and her having to bear sole responsibility for disciplining the children. In fact, the heartbreaking question of her little boy, "Isn't Daddy ever coming home for dinner again?" prompted her to seek a solution.

She felt lonely, neglected, and unloved. The situation didn't look good. I wondered what to tell her—put her foot down? insist that he quit football? demand that he spend more time at home? threaten him? She had already tried that for two years, but of course nothing had changed. Should I tell her *to* withhold her love? make him come begging to her? play the martyr? She had tried that too. Result? No change.

What I told her, she didn't like. Later she admitted, "I was so mad, I almost got up and walked out. I certainly hadn't come over to hear that *I* should adapt to *Norm's* life."

Adapting was the only thing I knew that would work. "Bobbie," I told her, "adapt to his way of life wholeheartedly, even if he doesn't come home for weeks. When he is home, make life so attractive he won't want to leave. Don't make him feel guilty and don't complain. Instead, treat him like a king and cater to his needs."

Bobbie cried a little, but finally dried her eyes and smiled. "I'm going to do it," she said. The first thing Norm said when he got off the plane and saw her radiant face was, "Hey, what's happened to you?" Nothing had changed except Bobbie's attitude. The unreal schedule was still the same, but Bobbie had determined to adapt.

Two years later, Norm told her one night during sweet communion, "I love you so much right now that if you asked me to quit playing football, I'd do it." She wouldn't ask him to; she has adapted to his way of life. By the way, he has become an All-Pro NFL player, a Total Tackle, and she, a Total Woman teacher. They've never been happier together.

My Way

What causes most of the problems in your marriage? I find that the conflict between two separate egos is usually the culprit—your viewpoint versus his viewpoint. If they happen to be the same, fine. If not, as so often is the case, conflict results.

For instance, your weary man comes home from the office longing for a quiet evening. You've been cooped up in the house all day and want to get out. There's instant conflict with two egos, each shouting, "Me, me, me."

Or you have a little extra money. He wants that new car and you have your heart set on new carpeting. Conflict. He wants to go to the game Saturday and you want to go shopping. And so it goes.

Every couple has this problem. How can two different egos fuse their two different opinions into one? Some don't. Often these conflicts are "resolved" when the parties go their separate ways, instead of growing together.

The biblical remedy for marital conflict is stated, "You wives must submit to your husbands' leadership in the same way you submit to the Lord." God planned for woman to be under her husband's rule.

Now before you scream and throw this book away, hear me out. First of all, no one says you have to get married. If you do not wish to adapt to a man, the negative implication is to stay single. If you are married but not adapting, you probably already know that marriage isn't the glorious experience you anticipated.

Secondly, you may think, "That's not fair. I have my rights. Why shouldn't he adapt to my way first, and then maybe I'll consider doing something to please him?" I have seen many couples try this new arrangement, unsuccessfully. Unless the wife adapts to his way of life, there's no way to avoid the conflict that is certain to occur.

Thirdly, please note that I did not say a woman is inferior to man, or even that a woman should be subservient to all men, but that a wife should be under her own husband's leadership.

Fourthly, another little phrase may cause some consternation: ". . . in the same way you submit to the Lord." Perhaps you are thinking, "I don't submit to the Lord. I don't even know Him. How archaic can you get? Even if you believe in Him, who submits to Him?"

The fact is that God originally ordained marriage. He gave certain ground rules and if they are applied, a marriage will work. Otherwise, the marriage cannot be closely knit because of the inherent conflict between your husband's will and yours. The evidence is all too clearly visible. In some cities there are now more people getting divorced each day than getting married.

Man and woman, although equal in status, are different in function. God ordained man to be the head of the family, its president, and his wife to be the executive vice-president. Every organization has a leader and the family unit is no exception. There is no way you can alter or improve this arrangement. On occasion, families have tried to reverse this and have elected a woman as president. When this order is turned around, the family is upside down. The system usually breaks down within a short period of time. Allowing your husband to be your family president is just good business.

Oh, King, Live Forever

I have been asked if this process of adapting places a woman on a slave–master basis with her husband. A Total Woman is not a slave. She graciously chooses to adapt to her husband's way, even though at times she desperately may not want to. He in turn will gratefully respond by trying to make it up to her and grant her desires. He may even want to spoil her with goodies.

Marriage has also been likened to a monarchy, where the husband is king, and his wife is queen. In a royal marriage, the king's decision is the final word, for his country and his queen alike. The queen is certainly not his slave, for she knows where her powers lie. She is queen. She, too, sits on a throne. She has the right, and in fact, the responsibility to express her feelings, but of course, she does so in a regal way. Though the king relies heavily on her judgment, if there is a difference of opinion, it is the king who makes the final decision.

Now hold on, I know just what you're thinking; remember, I've been through all of this, too. What if the king makes the wrong decision? Oh, that's a hard one, especially when you *know* you're right, and there are times when that is the case. The queen is still to follow him, forthwith. A queen shall not nag or buck her king's decision after it is decreed. Remember those speedy trials, gals!

In so many marriages today, the woman rules the roost.

Source: Morgan, Marabel. *The Total Woman.* Grand Rapids, MI: Fleming H. Revell Company, 1973. Used by permission of Charles Morgan.

ALICE PAUL REFLECTS ON A HALF CENTURY OF CRUSADING FOR GENDER EQUALITY, 1974

Alice Paul (1885–1977) was one of the giants of the women's suffrage movement in America. During the 1910s she stood at the vanguard of dramatic and confrontational activities and strategies to demand gender equality in the United States. In 1916 she left the National American Women's Suffrage Association (NAWSA) to lead a new organization called the National Woman's Party (NWP) that picketed the White House, demanding that President Woodrow Wilson throw his support behind the suffrage movement. Paul and other protesters were eventually arrested and subjected to such brutal treatment that when word of their plight became known, public support for suffrage actually increased. Paul and the others were eventually released, and Wilson eventually committed to supporting women's right to the voting franchise.

After the passage of the 19th Amendment, Paul remained deeply committed to securing gender equality in aspects of American society outside of the voting booth. She wrote the first equal rights amendment introduced in Congress in 1923 (the ERA was introduced every year after that until it finally passed Congress in 1972) and helped in getting a sexual discrimination clause added to Title VII of the Civil Rights Act of 1964. After Congress passed the ERA in 1972 and sent it to the states for ratification, Paul added her voice to those of other men and women supporting the amendment. The following is a 1974 interview that Paul conducted with American Heritage *in which she looked back on her years with the suffrage movement and her many decades of women's rights activism.*

How did you first become interested in woman suffrage?
It wasn't something I had to think about. When the Quakers were founded in England in the 1600's, one of their principles was and is equality of the sexes. So I never had any other idea. And long before my time the Yearly Meeting in Philadelphia, which I still belong to, formed a committee to work for votes for women. The principle was always there. . . .

Were you a good speaker?
Not particularly. Some people enjoyed getting up in public like that, but I didn't. I did it, though. On the other hand, Lucy Burns was a very good speaker—she had what you call that gift of the Irish—and she was extremely courageous, a thousand times more courageous than I was. I was the timid type, and she was just naturally valiant. Lucy became one of the pillars of our movement. We never, never, never could have had such a campaign in this country without her. . . .

*In her book about the suffrage movement Inez Haynes Irwin tells about your hiding over-
night on the roof of St. Andrew's Hall in Glasgow, Scotland, in order to break up a political
rally the next day.*
Did Mrs. Irwin say that? Oh, no. I never hid on any roof in my life. In Glasgow I
was arrested, but it was at a street meeting we organized there. Maybe Mrs. Irwin
was referring to the Lord Mayor's banquet in London. I think it was in December
of 1909, and Miss Burns and I were asked to interrupt the Lord Mayor. I went into
the hall, not the night before but early in the morning when the charwomen went
to work, and I waited up in the gallery all day. That night Lucy went in down below
with the banquet guests. I don't remember whether she got up and interrupted the
mayor. I only remember that I did.

What happened?
I was arrested, of course.

*Was this the time you were imprisoned for thirty days and forcibly fed to break your
hunger strike?*
I can't remember how long I was in jail that time. I was arrested a number of times.
As for forcible feeding, I'm certainly not going to describe that.

The whole concept of forcible feeding sounds shocking.
Well, to me it was shocking that a government of men could look with such extreme
contempt on a movement that was asking nothing except such a simple little thing
as the right to vote. Seems almost unthinkable now, doesn't it? With all these millions and millions of women going out happily to work today, and nobody, as far
as I can see, thinking there's anything unusual about it. But, of course, in some
countries woman suffrage is still something that has to be won.

*Do you credit Mrs. Pankhurst with having trained you in the militant tactics you subse-
quently introduced into the American campaign?*
That wasn't the way the movement was, you know. Nobody was being trained. We
were just going in and doing the simplest little things that we were asked to do.
You see, the movement was very small in England, and small in this country, and
small everywhere, I suppose. So I got to know Mrs. Pankhurst and her daughter,
Christabel, quite well. I had, of course, a great veneration and admiration for Mrs.
Pankhurst, but I wouldn't say that I was very much trained by her. What happened was that when Lucy Burns and I came back, having both been imprisoned
in England, we were invited to take part in the campaign over here; otherwise
nobody would have ever paid any attention to us.

That was in 1913?
I came back in 1910. It was in 1912 that I was appointed by the National American Woman Suffrage Association to the chairmanship of their Congressional Committee in Washington, which was to work for the passage of the amendment that

Susan B. Anthony had helped draw up. And Lucy Burns was asked to go with me. Miss Jane Addams, who was on the national board, made the motion for our appointments. They didn't take the work at all seriously, or else they wouldn't have entrusted it to us, two young girls. They did make one condition, and that was that we should never send them any bills, for as much as one dollar. Everything we did, we must raise the money ourselves. My predecessor, Mrs. William Kent, the wife of the congressman from California, told me that she had been given ten dollars the previous year by the national association, and at the end of her term she gave back some change.

Weren't you discouraged by the national association's attitude?
Well, when we came along, we tried to do the work on a scale which we thought, in our great ignorance, might bring some success. I had an idea that it might be a one year's campaign. We would explain it to every congressman, and the amendment would go through. It was so clear. But it took us seven years. When you're young, when you've never done anything very much on your own, you imagine that it won't be so hard. We probably wouldn't have undertaken it if we had known the difficulties. . . .

A few weeks after Mr. [Woodrow] Wilson became President, four of us went to see him. And the President, of course, was polite and as much of a gentleman as he always was. He told of his own support, when he had been governor of New Jersey, of a state referendum on suffrage, which had failed. He said that he thought this was the way suffrage should come, through state referendums, not through Congress. That's all we accomplished. We said we were going to try and get it through Congress, that we would like to have his help and needed his support very much. And then we sent him another delegation and another and another and another and another and another and another—every type of women's group we could get. We did this until 1917, when the war started and the President said he couldn't see any more delegations.

So you began picketing the White House?
We said we would have a perpetual delegation right in front of the White House, so he wouldn't forget. Then they called it picketing. We didn't know enough to know what picketing was, I guess.

How did you finance all this work?
Well, as I mentioned, we were instructed not to submit any bills to the National American. Anything we did, we had to raise the money for it ourselves. So to avoid any conflict with them we decided to form a group that would work exclusively on the Susan B. Anthony amendment. We called it the Congressional Union for Woman's Suffrage. You see, the Congressional Committee was a tiny group, so the Congressional Union was set up to help with the lobbying, to help with the speech-making, and especially to help in raising money. The first year we raised $27,000. It just came from anybody who wanted to help. Mostly small contributions. John

McLean, the owner of the Washington Post, I think, gave us a thousand dollars. That was the first big gift we ever got.

The records indicate that you raised more than $750,000 over the first eight years. Did your amazing fund-raising efforts cause you any difficulties with the National American?
I know that at the end of our first year, at the annual convention of the National American, the treasurer got up—and I suppose this would be the same with any society in the world—she got up and made a speech, saying, "Well, this group of women has raised a tremendous sum of money, and none of it has come to my treasury," and she was very displeased with this. Then I remember that Jane Addams stood up and reminded the convention that we had been instructed to pay our own debts, and so that was all there was to it. Incidentally, the Congressional Union paid all the bills of that national convention, which was held in Washington that year. I remember we paid a thousand dollars for the rent of the hall. If you spend a hard time raising the money, you remember about it. . . .

You didn't have much faith in state referendums?
The first thing I ever did—after I graduated from Swarthmore, I did some social work in New York City—one of the suffragists there asked me to go with her to get signatures for a suffrage referendum in New York State. So I went with her, and she was a great deal older and much more experienced than I was. I remember going into a little tenement room with her, and a man there spoke almost no English, but he could vote. Well, we went in and tried to talk to this man and ask him to vote for equality for women. And almost invariably these men said, "No, we don't think that it is the right thing. We don't do that in Italy, women don't vote in Italy." You can hardly go through one of those referendum campaigns and not think what a waste of the strength of women to try and convert a majority of men in the state. From that day on I was convinced that the way to do it was through Congress, where there was a smaller group of people to work with.

Then the National Woman's Party was formed to continue the work on the federal amendment?
We changed our name from the Congressional Union to the National Woman's Party in 1916, when we began to get so many new members and branches. Mainly people who disagreed with the National American's support of the Shafroth-Palmer. And the person who got us to change our name was Mrs. [Alva E.] Belmont. . . .

Did Mrs. Belmont have something to do with the decision to campaign against the Democrats in the November, 1914, elections?
Yes. You see, here we had an extremely powerful and wonderful man—I thought Woodrow Wilson was a very wonderful man—the leader of his party, in complete control of Congress. But when the Democrats in Congress caucused, they voted against suffrage. You just naturally felt that the Democratic Party was responsible. Of course, in England they were up against the same thing. They couldn't get this

measure through Parliament without getting the support of the party that was in complete control.

Didn't this new policy of holding the party in power responsible represent a drastic change in the strategy of the suffrage movement?
Up to this point the suffrage movement in the United States had regarded each congressman, each senator, as a friend or a foe. It hadn't linked them together. And maybe these men were individual friends or foes in the past. But we deliberately asked the Democrats to bring it up in their caucus, and they did caucus against us. So you couldn't regard them as your allies anymore. I reported all this to the National American convention in 1913, and I said that it seemed to us that we must begin to hold this party responsible. And nobody objected to my report. But when we began to put it into operation, there was tremendous opposition, because people said that this or that man has been our great friend, and here you are campaigning against him.

Would you have taken the same position against the Republicans if that party had been in power in 1914?
Of course. You see, we tried very hard in 1916—wasn't it [Charles Evans] Hughes running against Wilson that year?—to get the Republicans to put federal suffrage in their platform, and we failed. We also failed with the Democrats. Then we tried to get the support of Mr. Hughes himself. Our New York State committee worked very hard on Mr. Hughes, and they couldn't budge him. So we went to see former President [Theodore] Roosevelt at his home at Oyster Bay to see if he could influence Mr. Hughes. And I remember so vividly what Mr. Roosevelt said. He said, "You know, in political life you must always remember that you not only must be on the right side of a measure, but you must be on the right side at the right time." He told us that that was the great trouble with Mr. Hughes, that Mr. Hughes is certainly for suffrage, but he can't seem to know that he must do it in time. So Mr. Hughes started on his campaign around the country, and when he came to Wyoming, where women were already voting, he wouldn't say he was for the suffrage amendment. And he went on and on, all around the country. Finally, when he came to make his final speech of the campaign in New York, he had made up his mind, and he came out strongly for the federal suffrage amendment. So it was true what Mr. Roosevelt had said about him.

Do you think Hughes might have beaten Wilson in 1916 if he had come out for suffrage at the beginning of his campaign?
Oh, I don't know about that. I was just trying to show you that we were always trying to get the support of both parties.

You were once quoted to the effect that in picking volunteers you preferred enthusiasm to experience.
Yes. Well, wouldn't you? I think everybody would. I think every reform movement needs people who are full of enthusiasm. It's the first thing you need. I was full of enthusiasm, and I didn't want any lukewarm person around. I still am, of course.

One of your most enthusiastic volunteers was Inez Milholland Boissevain, wasn't she?
Inez Milholland actually gave her life for the women's movement. I think Inez was our most beautiful member. We always had her on horseback at the head of our processions. You've probably read about this, but when Inez was a student at Vassar, she tried to get up a suffrage meeting, and the college president refused to let her hold the meeting. So she organized a little group, and they jumped over a wall at the edge of the college and held the first suffrage meeting at Vassar in a cemetery. Imagine such a thing happening at a women's college so short a time ago. You can hardly believe such things occurred. But they did.

How did Miss Milholland give her life for the movement?
After college Inez wanted to study law, but every prominent law school refused to admit a girl. She finally went to New York University, which wasn't considered much of a university then, and got her law degree. Then she threw her whole soul into the suffrage movement and really did nothing else but that. Well, in 1916, when we were trying to prevent the re-election of Woodrow Wilson, we sent speakers to all the suffrage states, asking people not to vote for Wilson, because he was opposing the suffrage which they already had. Inez and her sister, Vita, who was a beautiful singer, toured the suffrage states as a team. Vita would sing songs about the women's movement, and then Inez would speak. Their father, John Milholland, paid all the expenses for their tour, which began in Wyoming. Well, when they got to Los Angeles, Inez had just started to make her speech when she suddenly collapsed and fell to the floor, just from complete exhaustion. Her last words were "Mr. President, how long must women wait for liberty?" We used her words on picket banners outside the White House. I think she was about twenty-eight or twenty-nine. . . .

Do you think that the President's daughters, Jessie and Margaret, who were strong supporters of the suffrage movement, exerted any pressure on the President?
Well, I think if you live in a home and have two able daughters—the third daughter was younger, and I didn't know much about what she was doing—it would almost be inevitable that the father would be influenced. Also, I think the first Mrs. Wilson was very sympathetic to us, but we never knew Mrs. Gait, his second wife. Someone told me that she wrote a book recently about her life in the White House in which she spoke in the most derogatory terms about the suffragists.

Do you want to talk about the violence that occurred on the White House picket line?
Not particularly. It is true that after the United States entered the war [April 6, 1917], there was some hostility, and some of the pickets were attacked and had their banners ripped out of their hands. The feeling was—and some of our own members shared this and left the movement—that the cause of suffrage should be abandoned during wartime, that we should work instead for peace. But this was the same argument used during the Civil War, after which they wrote the word "male" into the Constitution. Did you know that "male" appears three times in the Fourteenth Amendment? Well, it does. So we agreed that suffrage came before war.

Indeed, if we had universal suffrage throughout the world, we might not even have wars. So we continued picketing the White House, even though we were called traitors and pro-German and all that.

Mrs. Irwin wrote in her book that on one occasion a sailor tried to steal your suffrage sash on the picket line and that you were dragged along the sidewalk and badly cut.
Oh, no. She wrote that? No, that never happened. You know, when people become involved in a glorious cause, there is always a tendency, perhaps, to enlarge on the circumstances, to magnify situations and incidents.

And is there, perhaps, on your part a tendency to be overmodest about your activities?
I wouldn't know about that. All this seems so long ago and so unimportant now, I don't think you should be taking your precious lifetime over it. I try always, you know, to vanquish the past and try to be a new person.

But it is true, isn't it, that you were arrested outside the White House on October 20, 1917, and sentenced to seven months in the District of Columbia jail?
Yes.

And that when you were taken to the cell-block where the other suffragists were being held, you were so appalled by the stale air that you broke a window with a volume of Robert Browning's poetry you had brought along to read?
No. I think Florence Boeckel, our publicity girl, invented that business about the volume of Browning's poetry. What I actually broke the window with was a bowl I found in my cell.

Was this the reason you were transferred to solitary confinement in the jail's psychopathic ward?
I think the government's strategy was to discredit me. That the other leaders of the Woman's Party would say, well, we had better sort of disown this crazy person. But they didn't.

During the next three or four weeks you maintained your hunger strike. Was this the second or third time you underwent forcible feeding?
Probably, but I'm not sure how many times.

Is this done with liquids poured through a tube put down through your mouth?
I think it was through the nose, if I remember right. And they didn't use the soft tubing that is available today. . . .

And on January 9, 1918, President Wilson formally declared for federal suffrage. The next day the House passed the amendment 274–136, and the really critical phase of the legislative struggle began.
Yes. Well, when we began, Maud Younger, our congressional chairman, got up this card catalogue, which is now on loan to the Library of Congress. We had little

leaflets printed, and each person who interviewed a congressman would write a little report on where this or that man stood. We knew we had the task of winning them over, man by man, and it was important to know what our actual strength was in Congress at all times. These records showed how, with each Congress, we were getting stronger and stronger, until we finally thought we were at the point of putting the Anthony amendment to a vote. And of course this information was very helpful to our supporters in Congress.

Yet when the Senate finally voted on October 1, 1918, the amendment failed by two votes of the necessary two thirds. What happened?
We realized that we were going to lose a few days before the vote. We sat there in the Senate gallery, and they talked on and on and on, and finally Maud Younger and I went down to see what was going on, why they wouldn't vote. People from all over the country had come. The galleries were filled with suffragists. We went to see Senator Curtis, the Republican whip, and the Republican leader, Senator Gallinger. It was then a Republican Senate. And there they stood, each with a tally list in their hands. So we said, why don't you call the roll. And they said, well, Senator Borah has deserted us, he has decided to oppose the amendment, and there is no way on earth we can change his mind.

You thought Borah was on your side?
Oh, yes. He wanted our support for his re-election campaign that year out in Idaho, and our organizer out there, Margaret Whittemore, had a statement signed by him that he would vote for the suffrage amendment. But then he changed. He never gave any reason for changing.

Did you then oppose him in the November election?
We opposed him, yes. We cut his majority, but he was reelected, and from a suffrage state.

Was it about this time that your members began burning the President's statements in public?
I'm not sure when it started. We had a sort of perpetual flame going in an urn outside our headquarters in Lafayette Square. I think we used rags soaked in kerosene. It was really very dramatic, because when President Wilson went to Paris for the peace conference, he was always issuing some wonderful, idealistic statement that was impossible to reconcile with what he was doing at home. And we had an enormous bell—I don't recall how we ever got such an enormous bell—and every time Wilson would make one of these speeches, we would toll this great bell, and then somebody would go outside with the President's speech and, with great dignity, burn it in our little caldron. I remember that Senator Medill McCormick lived just down the street from us, and we were constantly getting phone calls from him saying they couldn't sleep or conduct social affairs because our bell was always tolling away.

You had better results from the next Congress, the Sixty-sixth, didn't you?
Yes. President Wilson made a magnificent speech calling for the amendment as a war measure back in October, 1918, and on May 20, 1919, the House passed the amendment. Then on June 4 the Senate finally passed it. . . .

Were you relieved when the Anthony amendment finally passed?
Yes, for many reasons. But we still had to get it ratified. We went to work on that right away and worked continuously for the fourteen months it took. But that last state . . . we thought we never would get that last state. And, you know, President Wilson really got it for us. What happened was that Wilson went to the governor of Tennessee, who was a Democrat. The President asked him to call a special session of the state legislature so the amendment could be ratified in time for women to vote in the 1920 Presidential election. . . .

Do you think the progress of the equal-rights amendment has been helped by the women's liberation movement?
I feel very strongly that if you are going to do anything, you have to take one thing and do it. You can't try lots and lots of reforms and get them all mixed up together. Now, I think the liberation movement has been a good thing, because it has aroused lots of women from their self-interest, and it has made everyone more aware of the inequalities that exist. But the ratification of the equal-rights amendment has been made a bit harder by these people who run around advocating, for instance, abortion. As far as I can see, E.R.A. has nothing whatsoever to do with abortion.

How did abortion become involved with equal rights?
At the 1968 Republican convention our representative went before the platform committee to present our request for a plank on equal rights, and as soon as she finished, up came one of the liberation ladies, a well-known feminist, who made a great speech on abortion. So then all the women on the platform committee said, well, we're not going to have the Republican Party campaigning for abortion. So they voted not to put anything in the party platform about women's rights. That was the first time since 1940 that we didn't get an equal-rights plank in the Republican platform. And then that feminist showed up at the Democratic convention, and the same thing happened with their platform. It was almost the same story at the 1972 conventions, but this time we managed to get equal rights back into the platforms.

It's really the principle of equal rights that you're concerned with, isn't it, not the specific applications?
I have never doubted that equal rights was the right direction. Most reforms, most problems are complicated. But to me there is nothing complicated about ordinary equality. Which is a nice thing about our campaign. It really is true, at least to my mind, that only good will come to everybody with equality. If we get to the point

where everyone has equality of opportunity—and I don't expect to see it, we have such a long, long way ahead of us—then it seems to me it is not our problem how women use their equality or how men use their equality.

Miss Paul, how would you describe your contribution to the struggle for women's rights? I always feel . . . the movement is a sort of mosaic. Each of us puts in one little stone, and then you get a great mosaic at the end.

Source: Gallagher, Robert. "'I Was Arrested, of Course . . .': An Interview with the Famed Suffragette, Alice Paul." *American Heritage* 25, no. 2 (February 1974). Used by permission of *American Heritage* via the Copyright Clearance Center.

Chapter 6: 1975–1990: Accelerating Gender Role Changes at Work and at Home

Republican Gerald Ford was president of the United States in 1975. He had become president when Richard Nixon resigned in 1974 due to the Watergate scandal, and he served out Nixon's second term. He ran for president in 1976, losing to Democrat Jimmy Carter. Carter was subsequently defeated in 1980, by Republican Ronald Reagan, who served two terms in office. He was succeeded by George H. W. Bush, who had been his vice president.

In the 1970s, the Religious Right (a coalition of Christian political factions that are characterized by their strong support of socially conservative policies) began to actively try to influence the outcome of elections. Some people believe the Religious Right's involvement was motivated by the Supreme Court's upholding of *Roe v. Wade*, in 1973, which permitted abortion on demand through the second trimester of pregnancy. One of the primary objectives of the Religious Right is to elect Republican presidents who will appoint conservative, anti-choice justices to the Supreme Court. While former president Jimmy Carter is a devout Christian who could have received strong support from the Religious Right, his liberal policies conflicted with those of the right.[1] The election of Ronald Reagan in 1980, on the other hand, is widely believed to have been made possible by the support of the Religious Right due to Reagan's conservatism. The impact of the Religious Right continues today.

The years between 1975 and 1990 were marked by a number of significant changes regarding childbirth and family life, including the passage of the Pregnancy Discrimination Act (1978), a decline in the fertility rate, a substantial increase in the number of employed mothers of preschool children, the successful use of in vitro fertilization, and the introduction of no-fault divorce laws. There were also a number of significant "firsts" for women: the appointment of Sandra Day O'Connor to the U.S. Supreme Court (1981), the Democratic presidential candidate Walter Mondale's selection of a woman running mate (Geraldine Ferraro), the first U.S. woman in space (Sally Ride), and the first teacher in space (Christa McAuliffe).

---

1. In 2000, President Carter announced that he and his wife, Rosalynn, would leave the Southern Baptist Convention after 70 years of membership because it had adopted a stance on women that didn't match his own Christian beliefs. Carter referred to the Southern Baptist Convention's statement that women are inferior to men and don't have leadership roles in the convention. Carter said, "I believe that the most serious violation of human rights on Earth is the abuse of women and girls."

Changes in Family-Related Patterns and Gender Roles, 1975 to 1990

There were several very significant family-related changes in the 1970s. First, the birth rate reached an all-time low for the 20th century. Second, women's participation in the labor force increased substantially. Even mothers of preschool children entered the labor force in large numbers every year during the decade. Finally, a change in divorce laws from adversarial (i.e., one spouse has to prove that the other has committed an act considered sufficiently grievous to allow the court to terminate the marriage) to "no-fault" divorce (where a divorce can be granted whenever both spouses consent) was accompanied by a doubling of the divorce rate between 1965 and 1980.

Declining birth rates. In the second half of the 20th century, the birth rate reached a peak in 1957 (in the middle of the baby boom) and then began a long-term decline throughout the rest of the century, hitting a low point in the mid-1970s. Several factors are associated with this decline: availability of "the "Pill" starting in 1960 and the legal access to contraception provided to married couples and single individuals; the legal access to medical abortion that resulted from the 1973 Supreme Court decision in *Roe v. Wade*; and the increased economic opportunities for women.

Women's participation in the paid labor force.[2] There has been a long-term increase in women's participation in the labor force over the past hundred years in terms of the number of women in the labor force, the proportion of the labor force that is composed of women workers, and the proportion of women who are in the labor force. From 1890 to the 1990s, the number of women in the labor force increased from 4 million to over 58 million. Of course, over this period of time, the population, and the economy, of the United States increased as well. Data provided by the Bureau of Labor Statistics (in the U.S. Department of Labor) show that the growth in women's paid labor-force participation more than kept up with the expansion of the total labor force, which increased from 23.3 million in 1890 to 128 million in the early 1990s. In 1890, fewer than one-fifth of all paid workers (17 percent) were women. By 1993, almost half were women. Another way to look at this is to examine change in the percentage of all women of working age who were in the labor force over the period. In 1890, 17 percent of women were in the labor force. By 1990, the rate was nearly 58 percent. Thus, it is clear that women's paid labor has become a significant component of the U.S. economy. Moreover, it has become a typical part of a woman's life. Once, women dropped out of the paid labor force when they married, never to return. Today, women are likely to leave the labor force for only short periods of time (typically to care for a newborn), if they leave at all.

---

2. The term "labor force" includes people who are employed as well as those who are looking for employment.

Throughout much of the 20th century, Americans were most resistant to wives and mothers working outside the home. Yet between 1960 and 1993, the paid labor force participation of wives nearly doubled, from 30 percent to 59 percent. There was, in fact, a steady increase in labor force activity among women in all categories. The rates of married women with school-age children nearly doubled in this time period, from 39 percent to 75 percent. It is the employment of mothers of preschool children that has been of greatest concern to policy makers, as well as the general public. By the early 1990s, the majority of women who were mothers to children under age six were in the labor force. In 1960, fewer than one in every five were.

It was the change from a manufacturing-based economy to a service economy that drew so many women into the labor force. Manufacturing jobs were long regarded as "men's work," while service jobs (e.g., secretarial work, sales, serving in restaurants, and providing personal services such as hairdressing and domestic labor) have long been regarded as "women's work." As a result, when the service economy expanded, it increased the demand for women workers. As the demand for women workers outpaced the supply of "traditional" working women, other women were pulled in: first, married women with no dependent children; then women whose children were of school age; and finally, women with very young children. This shift started in the 1950s and gained momentum in the 1960s and 1970s, when a million women with preschool-age children entered the labor force each year.

As a result of the increasing number of mothers in the workforce, many families experienced conflict between work and family roles, which was considered a "woman's problem," since housework and child care were still the responsibility of women. In a published study that used data collected in the late 1970s, researchers examined differences in the amount of time women and men spent working each week (including paid employment, housework, and children). They focused on married couples with children at different stages in the family life cycle. In every stage, women spent more time in housework than their husbands did. Once the first child was born, women spent considerably more time in child care than their husbands. Even though mothers spent fewer hours in the paid labor force, their total time working each week was 24 hours greater than men's in the first stage of parenting.[3] They were working the equivalent of one whole day more than men in a similar situation (Rexroat and Shehan 1987). Researchers began to refer to the work that employed women did at home as the "second shift" (Hochschild 1983).

The divorce revolution. Until the 1960s, the only way to get a divorce in any state in the United States was through an adversarial process requiring one spouse to

---

3. An interesting study that used census data to count the number of men who were stay-at-home fathers found that only six men in the entire United States identified themselves as such in the 1970s (Peck 2015).

file a complaint of wrongdoing against the other.[4] This had to be done even if both spouses wanted to divorce. Under this system, many couples had to exaggerate their complaints or even commit perjury in order to obtain a divorce. Until 1966, for instance, adultery was the only ground for divorce in New York, which caused some couples to stage adulterous scenes that could be used as "evidence" that one spouse was guilty of adultery. Because of the lengths couples had to go to in order to get a divorce, there was increasing pressure during the 1960s for reform in divorce laws. Oklahoma and Maryland were the first states to adopt what were known as "no-fault divorce" laws. These laws typically grant divorces on the basis of irreconcilable differences, irretrievable breakdown of the marriage, or incompatibility. No-fault divorce removes legal obstacles to divorce and reduce economic costs. In 1970, the state of California eliminated all types of marital misconduct as grounds for divorce. Today, all states have some form of no-fault divorce (Shehan and Kammeyer 1997, p. 319).

Sociologist Lenore Weitzman studied the unintended consequences of no-fault divorce for women and their children and found that divorced men's standard of living increased substantially while that of divorced women and their children decreased. While the exact amount of change has been debated, the general pattern has been supported. The decrease in women's standard of living typically occurred because the jobs they held paid significantly less than those of their ex-husbands and because divorced fathers didn't always pay the child support they were required to pay in full or on time. The term "deadbeat dads" became a popular way to refer to these fathers.

Two additional developments in regard to childbearing occurred during the 1970s. First, the Pregnancy Discrimination Act of 1978 was amended to Title VII of the Civil Rights Act of 1964. It prohibits employers from discriminating against workers based on pregnancy, childbirth, or related medical conditions. In the same year, Louise Joy Brown was born in Great Britain. She was the world's first successful "test-tube baby." Although the technology that made her conception possible was heralded as a triumph for medicine and science, it also caused many to consider the ethical issues associated with the practice. Over the next 40 years, a number of advances in providing help to infertile couples were developed.

Equality Issues during President Carter's Administration

James (Jimmy) Earl Carter (born 1924), who served as governor of Georgia from 1971 through 1975, ran on a centrist Democratic agenda, based in large part on the social upheaval of the 1960s and on distrust of the federal government following the Watergate debacle. He argued that because he was a Washington outsider, he would be able to reform the federal government, to make it competent and compassionate. Unfortunately, the economy at the time worked against his goal.

---

4. In the United States, laws regarding families (including marriage, divorce, and parenting) are governed by individual states.

The United States was in the middle of an economic crisis produced by increasing energy prices and a prolonged period of slow economic growth accompanied by high unemployment. At the end of his administration, Carter had seen a substantial decrease in unemployment and a partial reduction of the deficit, but the recession ultimately continued.

During Carter's administration, women's programs were strengthened and greater priority was given to major health problems. Carter named more blacks, Latinos, and women to the federal judiciary than all previous administrations combined. In fact, he appointed the first black division head at the Department of Justice, the first black female cabinet member, and the first black ambassador to the United Nations. Carter was the first president to address the topic of gay rights. He opposed a California ballot measure that would have banned gays (and lesbians) and supporters of gay rights from being public school teachers. His administration was the first to meet with a group of gay rights activists. In the years following his administration, he has acted in favor of civil unions and ending the ban on gays in the military. He has stated that he opposes "all forms of discrimination on the basis of sexual orientation and believes there should be equal protection under the law for people who not heterosexual." Carter was awarded the 2002 Nobel Peace Prize for his efforts to find peaceful solutions to international conflicts, to advance democracy and human rights, and to promote economic and social development.

The 1980s: A Time of "Firsts" for Women and a Backlash against Women's Progress

The election of Republican Ronald Reagan to the presidency in 1980 is generally regarded as the beginning of a conservative revolution in U.S. politics. It is regarded as a difficult period for women because it centered on a backlash against the progress women made in the 1960s and 1970s (Faludi 2006). Reagan's own life experiences created and reinforced a rather traditional, white middle-class view of "women's place" that dominated the United States after World War II. In this worldview, women and men had clearly defined roles that were mutually exclusive but equally important. Men were solely responsible for wage earning in the public sphere, and women belonged to the domestic realm, caring for children. With this perspective on gender roles, Reagan was at odds with the feminist movement that had developed in the 1960s. Demands for equal opportunities in the workplace (with equal pay), reproductive rights (in terms of access to contraception and legalized abortion), and political participation contradicted his ideology of women's place. Reagan's 1980 campaign highlighted his anti-feminist stance (Coste 2016).

Reagan's campaign was bolstered by the support of conservative religious groups such as the Moral Majority, which was the main evangelical lobby of the time (with over half a million members). The Religious Right had three priorities that were directly related to the sexual revolution of the 1960s and women's rights. They wanted to denounce homosexuality, take back the legalization of abortion, and prevent the Equal Rights Amendment from becoming the law of the land. Reagan frequently talked about his own belief that the excesses of the 1960s were an aberration and said that he wanted to get the country back to a more traditional way of life (Coste 2016). Reagan's agenda included backing a constitutional amendment that would ban abortion in every state. His second moral priority included defeating the Equal Rights Amendment (ERA), which said, "Equality of rights under the law shall not be denied or abridged by the United States or any state on account of sex." Congress had voted in favor of the ERA in 1972. The next step in the process was having it ratified by three-quarters of the states. Many conservative groups were actively trying to prevent this, with Reagan's enthusiastic endorsement in 1980. Reagan was careful to say that he was not opposed to gender equality; he simply thought the ERA was the wrong way to achieve it. He feared that it would lead to drafting women into the military, which would lower the standards for serving, and the quality of the military would deteriorate. Another concern he had about the ERA was that it would force divorced women into the labor market, something that had been happening for years.

Women, and women's rights groups, were very critical of Reagan's candidacy and later his presidency. His election led to a new phenomenon in political elections: a gender gap. For the first time since women were granted the right to vote in 1920, the voting pattern of women differed dramatically from men's. The majority of women voters chose the pro–women's rights candidate, Jimmy Carter. As it turns out, many of the economic reforms Reagan pushed, though theoretically gender-neutral, targeted social programs that were of most help to women, especially single mothers and poor women. These programs included food stamps, Medicaid, Aid to Families with Dependent Children, energy assistance payments in the winter, federal subsidies to school lunches, and training programs for the unemployed. By the end of his first term, the amount of money allotted to social programs had declined by 25 percent, on average. And approximately one million people who had previously been helped by the federal government had lost their benefits. The number of children living in poverty started to increase again, for the first time since the 1960s (Coste 2016).

Reagan did not fully support the employment of women, so a relatively small (8 percent) percentage of his nominees to federal positions were women. Most of these women were appointed to areas regarded as aligned with women's true roles in the home. Women's groups in the 1980s were focusing their legislative efforts on the Women's Economic Equity Act (WEAA), which addressed pay discrimination and the shortage of child care facilities. Reagan and his administrative team opposed this proposed act because, in their eyes, it undermined the basis of the traditional American family with its clearly defined gender roles. Consideration of the WEEA occurred in 1982 and 1983. Without Reagan's support, the act failed to pass in Congress. However, Reagan did appoint Sandra Day O'Connor to the Supreme Court in 1981. O'Connor was a Republican judge from Arizona. During her time on the Court, her positions did not support an increase in the number of women in the highest ranks of government. As a state senator in Arizona, she had supported ratification of the Equal Rights Amendment and twice voted down anti-abortion laws in the state. When Reagan approached her about his interest in appointing her to the Supreme Court, she convinced him that these votes did not represent her personal views. This satisfied Reagan but failed to win over the Religious Right.

At the end of Reagan's second term, women had retained their right to abortion and had entered universities and the professions in record numbers, despite the defeat of the Equal Rights Amendment. In spite of Reagan's strong belief in traditional gender roles, change continued throughout his presidency,

Women in Politics

Until Reagan appointed Sandra Day O'Connor, no woman had sat on the Supreme Court. Only three women have been appointed since O'Connor: Ruth Bader Ginsburg, appointed by President Clinton (1993–present); and Sonia Sotomayor (2009–present) and Elena Kagan (2010–present), both appointed by President Obama.

It was also during this period of U.S. history that the first woman ran as a vice presidential candidate for a major party. Geraldine Anne Ferraro (1935–2011) was an American attorney, a Democratic Party politician, and a member of the U.S. House of Representatives. Before becoming an attorney, she was a teacher. After getting her law degree, Ferraro joined the Queens County District Attorney's Office in 1974, heading the new Special Victims Bureau that dealt with sex crimes, child abuse, and domestic violence. In 1978, she was elected to the U.S. House of Representatives, where she rose rapidly in the party hierarchy while focusing on legislation to bring equity for women in the areas of wages, pensions, and retirement plans. In 1984, she was selected by Democrat Walter Mondale to be his running mate in the presidential election. The Mondale–Ferraro ticket lost to incumbent president Ronald Reagan.

Sally Ride: First American Woman in Space

NASA was founded in 1958, but no U.S. woman flew in space until 1983. Physicist and astronaut Sally Ride (1951–2012), who joined NASA in 1978 with five other women, was the first, flying on the space shuttle *Challenger* in June of 1983. In the extensive media attention she received before her first shuttle mission, she was asked many gendered questions that focused on her reproductive system and her emotions. Ride asked why none of the male astronauts were asked the same type of questions. Ride played a vital role in helping the crew deploy communications satellites, conduct experiments, and make use of the first shuttle pallet satellite (NASA 2013). After flying on *Challenger* twice, she left NASA in 1987. She worked for two years at Stanford University's Center for International Security and Arms Control, then at the University of California, San Diego, as a professor of physics, primarily researching nonlinear optics and Thomson scattering. She served on the committees that investigated the *Challenger* and *Columbia* space shuttle disasters. She died in 2012 of pancreatic cancer.

References and Further Reading

Coste, Françoise. "'Women, Ladies, Girls, Gals . . .': Ronald Reagan and the Evolution of Gender Roles in the United States." *Miranda* 12 (2016).

Faludi, Susan. *Backlash: The Undeclared War against American Women*, 15th anniversary ed. New York: Broadway Books, 2006.

Hochschild, Arlie R., with Anne Machung. *The Second Shift.* New York: Viking Press, 1983.

NASA. "Sally Ride and Valentina Tereshkova: Changing the Course of Human Space Exploration." https://www.nasa.gov/topics/history/features/ride_anniversary.html.

Peck, Emily. "Only 6 American Men Identified as Stay-at-Home Dads in the 1970s: Today, It's a Different Story." Huffington Post, 2015.

Rexroat, Cynthia A., and Constance L. Shehan. "The Family Life Cycle and Spouses' Time in Housework." *Journal of Marriage and the Family* 49 (1987): 737–750.

Shehan, Constance L., and Kenneth Kammeyer. *Marriages and Families: Reflections of a Gendered Society.* Boston: Allyn and Bacon, 1997.

Weitzman, Lenore J. *The Divorce Revolution: The Unexpected Social and Economic Consequences for Women and Children in America.* New York: Free Press, 1985.

White House. "Biography of Jimmy Carter." Whitehouse.gov.

ALAN ALDA URGES MEN TO SUPPORT THE EQUAL RIGHTS AMENDMENT, 1976

As the debate over the Equal Rights Amendment raged across the United States in the 1970s, Alan Alda (1936–) was becoming one of America's best-known actors. He was the biggest star of the comedy-drama M*A*S*H, set in a U.S. Army field hospital during the Korean War. Alda played the role of "Hawkeye" Pierce, a talented, wisecracking surgeon with a progressive political sensibility and a disdain for political authority. During his rise to stardom, Alda emerged as a full-throated supporter of women's rights in general and the Equal Rights Amendment in particular. To that end, he contributed the following essay to Ms. *magazine asserting that both women and men would benefit in important and enduring ways from passage of the EPA.*

Yes, men will benefit from the Equal Rights Amendment. But not at the expense of women—as some opponents would have us believe. The ERA would simply be a sex-blind leveler of laws which discriminate against or favor either women or men. All our lives will be improved both legally and personally. The legal benefits will be strong, clear protections under the Constitution, and the personal benefits will reach us as the "cultural fallout" from the amendment.

Most of the time, of course, the sex differential in our society discriminates against women, but in the case of wives who work outside the home, their husbands very often suffer right along with them.

In these hard times, a lot of men must depend, at least in part, on whatever inflated dollars their wives can bring into the family. According to the Department of Labor's *1975 Handbook on Women Workers,* 53 percent of all husband-wife families in 1973 had earning wives whose contribution averaged about 25 percent of the family income. It's likely that many men whose consciousness has been raised by the economy will be glad to see working wives afforded the same opportunities and rewards as working husbands.

"The entire family unit is injured when the wife fails to receive fair compensation because of her sex," says Kathleen Willert Peratis, a lawyer and director of the Women's Rights Project of the American Civil Liberties Union. "A husband may also suffer if his working wife is denied mortgage insurance, because if she should die, he would have neither her economic contribution toward the family's support nor any insurance to replace it. A bank's refusal to acknowledge a married woman's income for purposes of making a joint loan plainly hurts both spouses."

Many practices of this nature are already outlawed, but enforcement is something else again. "The ERA," Peratis says, "would put the moral force of our highest form of lawmaking—constitutional amendment—behind the equality principle so that statutes outlawing such discrimination are given added enforcement impetus."

It may surprise some men to realize that there are many laws that now deny them the same rights and privileges that women enjoy. Men whose wives work are excluded from retirement benefits that are received as a matter of course by women whose husbands work. Says Peratis, "Social Security laws deny certain retirement benefits to husbands and surviving husbands of working women unless they can show that their wives supported the family unit by earning at least 75 percent of the family's total income. Wives of working men receive the benefit automatically, whether or not their husbands supported them."

Former Congresswoman Martha Griffiths, cosponsor of the ERA and longtime proponent of Social Security reform, has pointed out the practical effect of this injustice. "'If a husband doesn't work under covered employment—if he works for the government, for instance—and his wife *does* work under covered employment, the amount they can draw on retirement is reduced by one third. If the situation were reversed, if *she* were the one not covered, he'd be able to give her one half of his benefits." Several federal courts have found this scheme unconstitutional and have held that husbands are entitled to benefits on the same basis as wives. The government has appealed and the United States Supreme Court has agreed to hear the case. But, as Peratis remarks, "if there were an ERA, the eradication of the sex differential would be a certainty. Without it, we have high hopes but a big question mark."

The effect of the ERA on divorce and child-custody settlements has been the subject of great controversy. Because women have been denied equality in so many ways, some people fear that supporting rights that might also accrue to men in the domestic area may erode the few advantages that women now possess. In fact, the new fairness principle will give a winning edge neither to men nor to women, but to fairness itself. Each case will be determined according to the special factors in that case. And when parents dissolve their marriage, the fairness principle will look to the children's needs in rendering justice, not to the gender of the parents.

Peratis explains: "Matrimonial laws, including child custody, alimony, and child support, are more encrusted with sexual stereotypes and overbroad generalizations based on sex than any other area of the law. These outmoded laws hurt men, women and children—the human wreckage in family courts is a bitter reality for too many people." Some custody disputes can be especially painful partly because of an old-fashioned bias against men as parents. It is still common for judges to presume that fathers, simply because they are men, are either not interested in nurturing their children, or automatically incapable of rearing children responsibly and lovingly. It is unfair to make this assumption of all men. Furthermore, a woman who does not feel herself to be the ideal custodian of her children is often viewed as an evil or unnatural person, which may coerce her to fight for total custody even if she feels the father is better suited.

Because of the prejudice against the male parent, a man who sues for custody of his children often must take part in a discouraging, debasing, and costly battle.

Martha Griffiths tells of a custody case in one of the western states: a father felt he could provide a better home for his children than his former wife, who had enrolled the children in nine different schools in nine months. In order to counteract the normal bias favoring mothers in child-custody situations, the man found that he would have to present evidence in court that detailed the worst possible picture of the children's mother. He would have had to expose her as alcoholic and involved in prostitution. "Now of course," Griffiths says, "no one wants to bring all that out in court. He didn't, and he lost the children. And he should have had them. If the case were being decided on an equal basis, it would have been enough to point out that they had changed schools so often and that he had the ability to give them an uninterrupted education."

In some cases, men feel that for the welfare of the children they have no choice but to expose the mother's serious shortcomings. "I not only wanted them," said a Maryland father after a five-year battle for custody of his children, "but I felt they were endangered with their mother, and that made me fight hard."

"And you really have to fight," he said in an interview in the *Washingtonian*, "it's not pleasant. Evidence in this state has to be overwhelming for a man to prove his wife unfit. It took me three years to accumulate the evidence . . . we had detectives for adultery charges, we had alcohol and drug-abuse evidence. I had the backing of neighbors; the court-appointed social worker sided with me. The children wrote the judge letters; they told him they wanted to go with me."

He felt that although character assassination was not in his nature, he was forced to fight dirty because of the lesser status of the male parent. Nevertheless, he lost in court.

It wasn't until a year later, when she became involved with another man, that the mother decided to give her former husband legal custody of the children, now teenagers.

"The best interests of the children" is supposed to be the guiding principle in these cases, but when judges attempt to meet those interests by relying on sex-based bias and subjecting the entire family to unnecessary pain, then something is wrong.

This is far from saying that men should have an advantage in custody suits, or that they *would* have under the ERA. "The real beneficiaries," says Catherine East of the International Women's Year Commission, "will be the children."

The irony now is that forcing a husband to win custody by proving adultery on the part of the wife, plays into another kind of sexual bias: if she were to prove the same charge against him, it would carry far less weight against a man.

How great an effect will the ERA have in these sensitive matrimonial areas? Kathleen Peratis answers that "The ERA is not a cureall, but it will go some distance to infusing sanity into these terribly painful proceedings. The principle is plain— people must be treated according to their *actual* capacities, abilities, and functions, not according to a sexual stereotype which has nothing to do with the real-live people before the court."

In a larger sense the problems for male parents go beyond custody. Any law which presumes that all men are indifferent fathers can make it difficult for men who are single parents to function at all.

Consider, for instance, the difficulty Basil Archey had when he was called to jury duty in San Antonio, Texas. Archey, who has legal custody of his two young sons, asked for the same consideration that is given to women in Texas. (Mothers of children under 10 are automatically exempt from jury duty.)

Since Archey has no one to help him care for his sons, who are both under 10, he was concerned about how he would manage. "It's one thing," he said, "to tell your boss you have to take the day off to take the kids to the doctor—but what do you do if you're in a sequestered jury?"

The judge—unimpressed with Archey's problem—charged him with being absent from jury duty without a reasonable excuse.

At one point during his legal battles, Archey was so frustrated that he considered dropping by the judge's house with his children to see if the judge would like to sit with them while Archey sat on the jury.

The fact is there are men who do care about their children. They diaper them, feed them, walk with them in their arms in the middle of the night, worry about their physical development and emotional growth.

They side with them against unreasonable teachers and struggle through homework with them when it increases at a geometric rate. They put Band-Aids on their cuts and suffer with them the emotional bruises that will take no bandaging. They hug their children when they cry, and their own eyes can get wet at the sight of their kids growing into strength and grace and independence.

Certainly, there is the stereotype of the absent father who is absorbed in his work, cool and detached, and available only for the rewards but not the pain of parenting. But those men who do not conform to this unfortunate stereotype should certainly not be made to suffer for it, and those who *do* conform should not be reinforced in their behavior by laws and practices that accept this spiritual impoverishment as normal.

Ruth Bader Ginsburg, Professor of Law at Columbia University, feels that the greatest benefit a man will receive from the ERA will be a recognition of "his role in the family and his rights in relation to his children."

Ginsburg emphasizes that a man's relationship with his children can be warm and close rather than "just a question of laying out money for them."

However, men at every economic level are affected by laws that regard fathers simply as the ones who lay out the money.

Where men are too poor to fit that role different problems arise. Terrible indignities have been suffered by women whose personal lives are monitored by welfare investigators. In addition, Martha Griffiths has pointed out that welfare laws also discriminate against the father (and therefore against the whole family) by driving jobless men out of their homes: under current law in many states, mothers and children can collect welfare payments only if there is an absent father. This requirement institutionalizes broken families.

An additional, but optional program, Aid to Dependent Children–Unemployed Father (ADC–UF), is available in less than half the states. Here the family qualifies for welfare if the father is a temporarily unemployed breadwinner who is seeking work. But the family cannot qualify if the father is the homemaker/child-care parent and the mother is the unemployed potential breadwinner. The ERA would alter the "unemployed father" phrase to read unemployed *parent*—and doesn't that make sense when the welfare of dependent children is the key issue, not the sex of the breadwinner?

Whatever else the amendment does, of course, it will give all fathers, rich and poor, single and married, the satisfaction of seeing their daughters and sons enjoying the benefits of full citizenship and equal opportunities.

In addition to putting to rest certain myths about the parenting of children, there is the hope that the ERA will also revise some of the more rigid and unfair ideas about alimony.

For instance, men will not and *should* not escape the responsibility of continuing to support their families after divorce, ERA or not, if that was the economic basis of the marriage. Some husbands though, such as disabled men, have been dependent on their wives for support during the marriage. In many states, these dependent men are denied the right to alimony after a divorce. "The men affected are a minority," Catherine East says, "but still a significant number." More importantly, she says the automatic disqualification from alimony "indicates a basic attitude about men that puts an unfair pressure on them. It denies men the right to be dependent or in need of help. And they *are* in some cases—particularly if they're ill."

[. . .]

Kathleen Peratis believes the amendment will force some legislatures to rethink the whole notion of support in a more rational and commonsense way: "Under the ERA, state laws would have to provide that support runs from the spouse who can afford it (the one who has been gainfully employed) to the spouse who needs it (the one who has stayed at home to care for house and family). Many states already mandate this kind of functional approach to support laws. The ERA would make it universal."

Other laws under which men suffer inequality are surprisingly varied. Young girls, for instance, are protected against sexual exploitation to a greater extent than are young boys. Protection against statutory rape often doesn't extend to males. "Legislators make a big joke of it," says Ginsburg. "They say, 'Do fourteen-year-old boys really need to be protected from twenty-five-year-old women?' People have thought for so long of men exploiting girls—but it can work the other way around as well. Lives can be damaged."

Frequently, laws governing the age of majority are also sex-biased. In some states, women may marry at an earlier age than men. Although a recent Supreme Court decision "has probably rendered such statutes unconstitutional," according to *IMPACT ERA: Limitations and Possibilities,* the Equal Rights Amendment Project of the California Commission on the Status of Women, "the Equal Rights Amendment will certainly have that effect."

Meanwhile, Oklahoma still says males cannot buy 3.2 beers until they are 21, although females can start at 18.

While it may seem frivolous to want the right at 18 to drink beer and get married, especially in that order, there is something basic going on here. Inequality under the law, even in small doses, is a reminder that we have not yet decided to provide for all people in this country the protection of equal laws.

These are some of the areas in which men as well as women will benefit legally after full ratification of the ERA. Important as they are, the strictly legal benefits may not influence us as strongly as what I've called the "cultural fallout" from the amendment—benefits of a personal nature that may be even more far-reaching. While it's true that the amendment is essentially a legal instrument and not one that will mandate a cultural revolution, there are surely going to be some very important changes in our lives after ratification. Some are very broad and may go unnoticed for a while, such as the fact that there will be an influx of new talent, energy, and insight in our work force. Sexual segregation in our society has been costly. How much closer might the moon have seemed if all of us were reaching for it together?

A more immediate benefit will be that men's working conditions will probably improve when there are more women on the job. Without ascribing to women any mystical and unattainable qualities of gentleness and wisdom, I think I have observed that where men work without women there is just a little less warmth, a little less laughter, and a little less relaxation. There seem to be culturally "feminine" qualities that have for too long been absent from our working environments. It is a small but significant point that men, with all their bravado, have seldom had the courage to stick a flower on their desk.

A longer-range benefit, but one that comes even closer to home, is the pleasure we will derive from the companionship of women who finally have the ability to make free choices in their lives and to develop themselves to their fullest potential. A number of men have noticed that those women who have spent years fulfilling the approved submissive role can make men pay for that dependence. (The clinging vine can be a Venus's flytrap.) Women's independence will set those men free.

Some of the most personal benefits to men may be changes in the way we think, in the shifting of our expectations, the relinquishing of our stereotypes. The use of Title VII of the Civil Rights Act to prohibit sex discrimination in employment has already begun this process for us, but the ERA will carry it forward and will finally commit the country fully and publicly to equality under the law. As men increasingly fill jobs as secretaries, airline flight attendants, telephone operators, and receptionists we may find ourselves less likely to presume that people who fill these jobs are supposed to be servile, anonymous, and eager to fulfill our sexual fantasies. Similarly, as women fill traditionally male roles as police chiefs, gas station attendants, baseball players, and bankers, we may also begin to realize that wisdom, aggressiveness, and physical courage are not solely male attributes. The pressure to provide these qualities all by ourselves will be taken from men's shoulders. We can still be strong and brave, but we won't have to feel we're the only ones who are.

Finally, there's something at the very core of us that will benefit from the passage of the Equal Rights Amendment. It is our conscience.

How long can we live with a Constitution that is ambiguous about equality for every citizen, when the simple addition of a few words will put things right?

How long can we stand by and watch qualified people excluded from jobs or denied fair payment for their labor? How long can we do nothing while people are shut out from their fair share of economic and political power merely because they're women?

With your vote you have an opportunity to pass on to future generations the same kind of shelter for human dignity that the men who voted for the first 10 amendments passed on to us. Perhaps not every one of those men benefited personally from the Bill of Rights, but they all had one great overriding benefit—they had the knowledge that they did what was right.

Source: Alda, Alan. "Alan Alda on the ERA: Why Should Men Care," *Ms.* 5, no. 1 (July 1976). Used by permission of Alan Alda.

REPUBLICAN CONGRESSMAN DESCRIBES THE ERA AS "AN ATTACK ON MOTHERHOOD," 1978

When the Equal Rights Amendment (ERA) was approved by Congress in 1972, opponents of the amendment led by Democratic senator Sam Ervin (NC) and Democratic representative Emanuel Celler (NY) managed to attach a time limit of seven years for ratification. At first it seemed that the time limit would not matter, since dozens of states ratified the amendment in the first three years. But at that point, the drive to reach the magic threshold of approval from 38 states—the number needed to make the ERA part of the U.S. Constitution— became enormously difficult, as right-wing opponents worked to halt the amendment. In 1978 Democratic representative Elizabeth Holtzman (NY) introduced a bill granting an extension of the ERA deadline. Both the House and the Senate subsequently held hearings in August 1978 to consider the proposed extension.

Following are remarks from Republican congressman Henry Hyde of Illinois, a social conservative, at the hearings that were held in the House. He strongly criticized the proposed extension and argued that the ERA would have a calamitous social and economic impact on women.

Mr. Speaker, Ladies and Gentlemen of the House, they say that diamonds are a girl's best friend. You know what man's best friend is, don't you? It's his dog. And, I think that indicates in some manner the disparity that nature and society in custom has built up in the essential differences between man and woman. However, . . . and may I say "vive la difference." This Amendment, however, is really not anything to be treated frivolously if we care about our Constitution and if we care about the English language meaning what it says. And, I would like to read *very* briefly from a letter from Phillip Kerwin from the University of Chicago, one of the outstanding authorities on Constitutional Law, and his letter, sent to Senator Ervin in Congress, a noted Constitutional Lawyer, says, "That I'm still of the opinion that a constitutional Amendment to afford equal rights for women is both unnecessary and undesirable. I'm also of the view that a sound program of Legislative Reforms would do more, especially under the mandate now received from the Supreme Court in *Reid vs. Reid*, to eliminate more of the grievances that women have against their roles frequently imposed of them in our Society. Legislation can get at specific problems in a way that no Constitutional provision can." May I say that Paul A. Freund of the Law School of Harvard University, who said, and I quote, "In view of the Reid decision, I believe more strongly than ever that our subjects should be left to be worked out under the Equal Protection clause as the other questions of group classification. The Equal Protection guarantee together with the ample Legislative Powers of Congress is the best avenue to achieve meaningful equality of the sexes under Law. This approach is greatly to be preferred to one that for all of the manifold legal relationships of men and women from coverage under selective service to the obligation of family support mold them into mechanical unity." Now, we've heard Birch Bayh cited here as an authority. Senator Bayh inserted into the Congressional Record an Article by Tommy Emmerson, a Professor of Law, at Yale and this Article appeared in the *Yale Law Journal* in April of 1971. And this Article really tells you what this is all about because Professor Emmerson is all for this and he tells the congress and he tells us that the object of the militant supporters of the Equal Rights Amendment is to nullify every existing Federal and State Law making any distinction whatever between men and women, no matter how reasonable the distinction may be and to rob Congress and the Legislators of the 50 States of the power to enact any future Laws making any distinction between men and women, no matter how reasonable the distinction may be. Now, this Amendment means nothing if it doesn't mean that all distinctions that are reasonable that now exist under the 14th Amendment, which provides for equal protection of the Laws, but do make reasonable distinctions of the biological facts of life, are to be null and void.

Now, if you don't think that your daughter can be drafted if this becomes constitutional Law, let me cite the Chief Counsel, the Department of Defense of the United States who wrote Senator Bayh on February 24th of this year, Mr. Jay Fred Bussard. The question here is whether congress would be required, either to draft both men and woman, or to draft no one. A closely related question is whether Congress must permit women to volunteer on an equal basis for all sorts of military service including combat duty. We believe that the likely result of passage of the Equal Rights Amendment is to require both of these results. If this Amendment allows no discrimination upon the basis of sex, even for the sake of privacy, we believe that the resulting sharing of facilities and living quarters would be contrary to prevailing American standards. Even if segregation of living quarters and facilities were allowed under the Amendment during combat duty in the field, there often [are] in effect, no facilities at all. And, privacy for both sexes might be impossible to provide or enforce. And, I, again ask you if you want your daughter submitted to this sort of situation. . . .

Let's look at the Military. Here's what Professor Emmerson says and he's for this. "Women will serve in all kinds of units and they will be eligible for combat duty." Such obvious differential treatment for women as exemption from the draft, exclusion from the Service Academies and more restrictive standards for enlistment will have to be brought into conformity with the Amendment's basic prohibition of sex discrimination. A woman who will register for the draft at the age of eighteen as a man does. Under the Equal Rights Amendment, the Woman's Army Corps will be abolished. There is no reason to prevent women from doing these jobs in combat zone[s]. Look at Criminal Law, Statutory Rape Law will go out the window. The courts may be expected to hold that Laws which confine liability for prostitution to women are invalid, under this Amendment. Of course, we'll legalize pimping because the Pandering Statute will again will become, of course, unconstitutional. The Equal Rights Amendment would invalidate Prostitution laws.

Let's look at domestic relations. 90 percent of the custody cases, the Mother is awarded the custody of her child. The Equal Rights Amendment would prohibit any statutory or common law presumptions about which parent was the proper guardian based on the sex of the parent. In all states, Husbands are primarily liable for the support of their Wives and Children. Child-support Sections of the Criminal Non-support Laws could not be sustained where only the male is liable for support. How about the protective labor Legislation? Under the Equal Rights Amendment, Courts are not likely to find any justification for the continuance of Laws which exclude women from certain occupations. And, in Illinois, women aren't supposed to work in the Coal Mines. But, I guess that they want the right to do that. Now, there will be no discrimination in schools, in public schools. There will be no more girls' schools. The House of the Good Shepherd for wayward girls, I suppose can be inhabited by anybody looking for a room for the night. Convents, I don't what will become of them, but they'll be unconstitutional, I suppose. States which grant jury service exemptions to women with children will either extend the exemption to men with children or abolish the exemption altogether. So, try and get a jury sometime. They'll be composed of bachelors, I suppose, and not if they tell the truth. The YWCA and the Girl Scouts, of course, will have no meaning and the League of Women Voters will have to tear up its charter. . . . Divorced, separated and deserted wives, struggling to support themselves and their children through whatever work they can get, may find their claims of support from the Father harder to enforce than they do right now.

Now, to talk to the Women's Lib types, that's alright with them. But, I've talk[ed] to some married women who aren't trained to make a living in the world. They're housewives. They don't know shorthand. They don't know typing. They don't know structural engineering. And, to say to them that you have rights to support for you or your children, superior to man. That's just what this Amendment is going to do. Most sex discrimination is a matter of private practice, not public Law. Now we have the 14th Amendment in the Supreme Court in the Reid case has said that, "Women may not be discriminated against invidiously," but at the same time, there are discriminations in favor of women that are very important. This is really an attack on the home. It's an attack on Motherhood. It says that for a woman to have to be a Mother and have to be a housewife is somehow degrading. I submit that problem with this Society today is that the home is being attacked and assaulted and no longer wields any influence. And, this is one more step, however well intentioned the Sponsors are, to attack the beauty, the sanctity, and the essentialness of having the home the center of life and society. And, lastly, just let me say, it isn't necessary. We have the 14th Amendment which provides for equal protection, the Supreme Court is recognizing. This means no invidious sexual discrimination. But, I just want to leave you with the words from a great play that Katherine Hepburn recently appeared in where she portrayed the life of a great clothes designer, Coco Chanel. And, when asked about women's equality, she said that, "Women don't need equality. They need Independence. For most women, equality is a step down."

Source: Hyde, Henry. "Remarks at Hearings before the Subcommittee on the Constitution of the Committee on the Judiciary, U.S. Senate, 95th Congress, 2nd Session, on Joint Resolution to Extend the Deadline for Ratification of the Equal Rights Amendment," August 2, 3, and 4, 1978. Washington, DC: Government Printing Office, 1979, pp. 319–321.

THE PREGNANCY DISCRIMINATION ACT, 1978

*Historically, one of the greatest impediments in career advancement for American women has been the discriminatory treatment received from employers when women become pregnant. For many years, women could be fired, passed over for promotions they had earned, subjected to criticism for prioritizing kids over work, and otherwise marginalized in the workplace by their employers. Pregnant women and their supporters hoped that when prohibitions against sex discrimination were added to the 1964 Civil Rights Act, these punitive practices would come to an end. In 1976, though, the U.S. Supreme Court ruled in Gen-*eral Electric Company v. Gilbert *that pregnancy discrimination was not a form of sex discrimination. In the aftermath of this decision, which baffled and enraged women's rights activists, calls for a bill that would formally protect pregnant women from discrimination in the workplace quickly escalated. The Pregnancy Discrimination Act (PDA), passed by Congress and signed by Democratic president Jimmy Carter in 1978, was Washington's answer to those demands.*

An Act

To amend Title VII of the Civil Rights Act of 1964 to prohibit sex discrimination on the basis of pregnancy.

Be it enacted by the Senate and House of Representatives of the United States of America in Congress assembled,

That section 701 of the Civil Rights Act of 1964 is amended by adding at the end thereof the following new subsection:

"(k) The terms 'because of sex' or 'on the basis of sex' include, but are not limited to, because of or on the basis of pregnancy, childbirth, or related medical conditions; and women affected by pregnancy, childbirth, or related medical conditions shall be treated the same for all employment-related purposes, including receipt of benefits under fringe benefit programs, as other persons not so affected but similar in their ability or inability to work, and nothing in section 703(h) of this title shall be interpreted to permit otherwise. This subsection shall not require an employer to pay for health insurance benefits for abortion, except where the life of the mother would be endangered if the fetus were carried to term, or except where medical complications have arisen from an abortion: Provided, That nothing herein shall preclude an employer from providing abortion benefits or otherwise affect bargaining agreements in regard to abortion."

Sec. 2. (a) Except as provided in subsection (b), the amendment made by this Act shall be effective on the date of enactment.

(b) The provisions of the amendment made by the first section of this Act shall not apply to any fringe benefit program or fund, or insurance program which is in effect on the date of enactment of this Act until 180 days after enactment of this Act.

Sec. 3. Until the expiration of a period of one year from the date of enactment of this Act or, if there is an applicable collective-bargaining agreement in effect on the date of enactment of this Act, until the termination of that agreement, no person who, on the date of enactment of this Act is providing either by direct payment or by making contributions to a fringe benefit fund or insurance program, benefits in violation with this Act shall, in order to come into compliance with this Act, reduce the benefits or the compensation provided any employee on the date of enactment of this Act, either directly or by failing to provide sufficient contributions to a fringe benefit fund or insurance program: Provided, That where the costs of such benefits on the date of enactment of this Act are apportioned between employers and employees, the payments or contributions required to comply with this Act may be made by employers and employees in the same proportion: And provided further, That nothing in this section shall prevent the readjustment of benefits or compensation for reasons unrelated to compliance with this Act.

Source: Pregnancy Discrimination Act of 1978. Public Law 95-555, 92 Stat. 2076, S. 995, enacted October 31, 1978.

TITLE IX "POLICY INTERPRETATION" LEVELS THE PLAYING FIELD FOR MALE AND FEMALE COLLEGIATE ATHLETES, 1979

Title IX of the Education Amendments of 1972 is a federal law prohibiting gender discrimination in any education programs and activities that receive financial aid from the federal government. Although Title IX had a broad impact on the American education system from its very inception, it is best known in the broad public consciousness for the tremendous changes it prompted in high school and intercollegiate athletics. In 1971, the year before Title IX was passed, fewer than 300,000 girls participated in high school athletics in America. More than 40 years later, the number of girl high school athletes was nearly 3.3 million. A similar revolution took place on university and college campuses across the country. In 1971 there were only about 30,000 women competing in intercollegiate sports. By the mid-2010s, there were more than five times that number (150,000), and the number was rising. The visibility of high school and intercollegiate sports for girls is also higher than ever before.

The Office for Civil Rights (OCR) of the U.S. Department of Education enforces Title IX. It does so in accordance with regulations—called an Intercollegiate Athletics Policy Interpretation—issued on December 11, 1979. This 1979 policy interpretation, key portions of which are excerpted below, remains current policy.

1. Legal Background

A. The Statute

Section 901(a) of Title IX of the Education Amendments of 1972 provides:

- No person in the United States shall, on the basis of sex, be excluded from participation in, be denied the benefits of, or be subjected to discrimination under any education program or activity receiving Federal financial assistance.

Section 844 of the Education Amendments of 1974 further provides:

- The Secretary of [HEW] shall prepare and publish ! ! ! proposed regulations implementing the provisions of Title IX of the Education Amendments of 1972 relating to the prohibition of sex discrimination in federally assisted education programs which shall include with respect to intercollegiate athletic activities reasonable provisions considering the nature of particular sports.

Congress passed Section 844 after the Conference Committee deleted a Senate floor amendment that would have exempted revenue-producing athletics from the jurisdiction of Title IX.

B. The Regulation

The regulation implementing Title IX is set forth, in pertinent part, in the Policy Interpretation below. It was signed by President Ford on May 27, 1975, and submitted to the Congress for review pursuant to Section 431(d)(1) of the General Education Provisions Act (GEPA).

During this review, the House Subcommittee on Postsecondary Education held hearings on a resolution disapproving the regulation. The Congress did not disapprove the regulation within the 45 days allowed under GEPA, and it therefore became effective on July 21, 1975.

Subsequent hearings were held in the Senate Subcommittee on Education on a bill to exclude revenues produced by sports to the extent they are used to pay the costs of those sports. The Committee, however, took no action on this bill.

The regulation established a three year transition period to give institutions time to comply with its equal athletic opportunity requirements. That transition period expired on July 21, 1978.

II. Purpose of Policy Interpretation

By the end of July 1978, the Department had received nearly 100 complaints alleging discrimination in athletics against more than 50 institutions of higher education. In attempting to investigate these complaints, and to answer questions from the university community, the Department determined that it should provide further guidance on what constitutes compliance with the law. Accordingly, this

Policy Interpretation explains the regulation so as to provide a framework within which the complaints can be resolved, and to provide institutions of higher education with additional guidance on the requirements for compliance with Title IX in intercollegiate athletic programs.

III. Scope of Application

This Policy Interpretation is designed specifically for intercollegiate athletics. However, its general principles will often apply to club, intramural, and interscholastic athletic programs, which are also covered by regulation. Accordingly, the Policy Interpretation may be used for guidance by the administrators of such programs when appropriate.

This policy interpretation applies to any public or private institution, person or other entity that operates an educational program or activity which receives or benefits from financial assistance authorized or extended under a law administered by the Department. This includes educational institutions whose students participate in HEW funded or guaranteed student loan or assistance programs. For further information see definition of "recipient" in Section 86.2 of the Title IX regulation.

IV. Summary of Final Policy Interpretation

The final Policy Interpretation clarifies the meaning of "equal opportunity" in intercollegiate athletics. It explains the factors and standards set out in the law and regulation which the Department will consider in determining whether an institution's intercollegiate athletics program complies with the law and regulations. It also provides guidance to assist institutions in determining whether any disparities which may exist between men's and women's programs are justifiable and nondiscriminatory. The Policy Interpretation is divided into three sections:

- Compliance in Financial Assistance (Scholarships) Based on Athletic Ability: Pursuant to the regulation, the governing principle in this area is that all such assistance should be available on a substantially proportional basis to the number of male and female participants in the institution's athletic program.
- Compliance in Other Program Areas (Equipment and supplies; games and practice times; travel and per diem, coaching and academic tutoring; assignment and compensation of coaches and tutors; locker rooms, and practice and competitive facilities; medical and training facilities; housing and dining facilities; publicity; recruitment; and support services): Pursuant to the regulation, the governing principle is that male and female athletes should receive equivalent treatment, benefits, and opportunities.
- Compliance in Meeting the Interests and Abilities of Male and Female Students: Pursuant to the regulation, the governing principle in this area is that the athletic interests and abilities of male and female students must be equally effectively accommodated. . . .

5. Application of the Policy—Levels of Competition

In effectively accommodating the interests and abilities of male and female athletes, institutions must provide both the opportunity for individuals of each sex to participate in intercollegiate competition, and for athletes of each sex to have competitive team schedules which equally reflect their abilities.

Compliance will be assessed in any one of the following ways:

1) Whether intercollegiate level participation opportunities for male and female students are provided in numbers substantially proportionate to their respective enrollment; or
2) Where the members of one sex have been and are underrepresented among intercollegiate athletes, whether the institution can show a history and continuing practice of program expansion which is demonstrably responsive to the developing interest and abilities of the members of that sex; or
3) Where the members of one sex are underrepresented among intercollegiate athletics, and the institution cannot show a continuing program of program expansion such as that cited above, whether it can be demonstrated that the interests and abilities of the members of that sex have been fully and effectively accommodated by the present program.

Compliance with this provision of the regulation will also be assessed by examining the following:

1) Whether the competitive schedules for men's and women's teams, on a program-wide basis, afford proportionally similar numbers of male and female athletes equivalently advanced competitive opportunities; or
2) Whether the institution can demonstrate a history and continuing practice of upgrading the competitive opportunities available to the historically disadvantaged sex as warranted by developing abilities among the athletes of that sex.

Institutions are not required to upgrade teams to intercollegiate status or otherwise develop intercollegiate sports absent a reasonable expectation that intercollegiate competition in that sport will be available within the institution's normal competitive regions. Institutions may be required by the Title IX regulation to actively encourage the development of such competition, however, when overall athletic opportunities within that region have been historically limited for the members of one sex.

6. Overall Determination of Compliance

The Department will base its compliance determination under . . . the regulation upon a determination of the following:

a. Whether the policies of an institution are discriminatory in language or effect; or

b. Whether disparities of a substantial and unjustified nature in the benefits, treatment, services, or opportunities afforded male and female athletes exist in the institution's program as a whole; or

c. Whether disparities in individual segments of the program with respect to benefits, treatment, services, or opportunities are substantial enough in and of themselves to deny equality of athletic opportunity.

Source: Policy Interpretation: Title IX and Intercollegiate Athletics, *Federal Register,* 44, no. 239, December 11, 1979.

PRESIDENT CARTER RESPONDS TO ILLINOIS'S REJECTION OF THE EQUAL RIGHTS AMENDMENT, 1980

After Congress voted in 1979 to extend the deadline for ratification of the Equal Rights Amendment (ERA) to 1982, ERA advocates strategized where best to focus their efforts on getting the last three state ratifications necessary to enshrine the ERA in the Constitution. One of their chief targets was Illinois, the lone northern industrial state that had yet to ratify the amendment. In a bid to put public pressure on Illinois lawmakers to support ratification, the National Organization for Women (NOW) engineered a pro-ratification parade in Chicago in May 1980 that drew as many as 85,000 marchers. But Illinois was the home state of Phyllis Schlafly, the single most prominent anti-ERA activist in the country, and she organized the state's cultural conservatives into a formidable lobbying force in opposition.

On June 18, 1980, a resolution in the Illinois House of Representatives resulted in a vote of 102–71 in favor of ratification. But since the state's laws required a three-fifths majority on constitutional amendments, the measure actually failed by five votes. Later that same night, Democratic president Jimmy Carter, an ERA supporter, tried to bolster the flagging spirits of ERA advocates at a fund-raising dinner.

In 1966 I gave up a seat in the Georgia Senate and ran for Governor. No one knew who I was when I began. I spent all the money I had. I borrowed more than I could afford. I lost 22 pounds. I missed making the runoff for Governor by 21,000 votes. It was a disappointment, I admit, but the morning after the 1966 election I met with a very small group of folks, and they asked me what I was going to do for the next 4 years. I said, "I'm going to run for Governor." And in 1970 I was elected. I did not intend to lose.

In 1947 we had our first child, a son, who was born in Virginia. We wanted very much for the next child to be a daughter. But in 1950, in Hawaii, Chip was born, and we wanted very much for the next child to be a daughter. [Laughter] In 1952 Jeffery was born. It was a disappointment, I admit. That was in 1952. And 1955 went by and 1960 went by and 1965 went by. And finally came 1967, and the entire family burst into tears when Rosalynn announced—the doctor let her do it—that we finally had a daughter: Amy. We had some disappointments on the way, but we did not intend to lose.

In 1974 I announced that I was going to run for President. I invited some major political reporters down to Plains and to Atlanta to talk to me, and I made what I considered to be a major address to the Nation at the National Press Club. A few days later they had the miniconvention in Kansas City, December 3, 1974. I waited eagerly for the Gallup poll to come out. They had 36 names in the Gallup poll: more than a dozen Senators, several Members of the House, several Governors, Julian Bond, Ralph Nader, Benjamin Spock. [Laughter] They didn't have Jimmy Carter on the list. But less than 2 years later I was elected President. It was a difficult struggle, but I did not intend to lose.

Not too many months after that, we faced the prospect of continued war in the Middle East—in 30 years, four wars, thousands of young people killed on both sides, atmosphere filled with hatred. International borders were an insurmountable obstacle to communication and to peace. We went to Camp David—myself, President Sadat, Prime Minister Begin. After the first 3 days they did not speak to each other. For 10 solid days neither Begin nor Sadat talked to one another at all about the peace agreement.

Sunday morning we thought we had failed. It was a major disappointment. But Sunday afternoon we signed the Camp David accords, and not many months after, the peace treaty between Israel and the major Arab country. It was a disappointment along the way, but we did not intend to lose.

This afternoon in Illinois there was a vote, 102 to 71, a major majority: ERA was not ratified by the Illinois legislature, a major disappointment. But we do not intend to lose.

The history of our Nation is filled with personal reminiscences. Every one of you here could list things in your own life where you had a major goal or a major aspiration or a major hope or a yearning deep in your heart for something you thought was important—with obstacles and disappointments all along the way, plenty of chance to be discouraged, plenty of chance to blame others for a failure, plenty of chance to separate yourself from others who were involved in the same noble endeavor. But you persisted, and you triumphed.

Ours is the greatest nation on Earth, the greatest democratic experiment in the history of humankind. But for decades, generations, our Constitution permitted slavery of human beings. Americans were not given the right to vote directly for their own United States Senator; women were not permitted to vote. Had there been timidity on the part of Americans, had there been discouragement that brought an end to struggle, our Nation would never have improved.

We've almost wiped clean the legal, permissive discrimination against a group of human beings in our Nation. Not quite. There is only one group, as you well know, against whom laws can still be passed patently depriving American citizens of their civil or human rights, and that is against women. It's a noble struggle. It's difficult. Massive forces are mounted against us. The most abominable distortions are promulgated as the truth. Political pressures are exerted on often well-meaning members of State legislatures. It's not an easy task, but there is no reason for us to fail.

Six Presidents who lived before me in the White House have endorsed and supported the equal rights amendment. Thirty-five States, as you know, have already ratified the equal rights amendment. The Democratic and Republican platforms have endorsed the equal rights amendment. The overwhelming majority of Americans in almost every poll, or every one, so far as I know, favor the equal rights amendment. But discrimination still exists of a legal kind.

Women have not been deprived of responsibility. More than a fourth of all the households in this Nation are headed by women. Women have not been deprived of the burden of labor. Forty-three percent of our workforce is comprised of women. What women have been cheated of is equal wages, equal opportunities in education, equal opportunities under the law, equal opportunities to hold property, equal opportunities for human dignity, equal opportunities to realize the hopes of a human life and to utilize the talent that God has given.

This is a smirch on America, not yet to have succeeded in ratifying the equal rights amendment. I'm concerned about every one of you here, because I know what you go through. I meet every month with the presidents of most women's organizations, to share ideas and to share plans and to assign responsibilities, for telephone calls, for luncheons at the White House with the Governors and the speakers of the house and the majority leader and the minority leader of the State legislatures which still have not yet ratified the equal rights amendment. We make numerous calls. My whole family, my whole administration is committed to this struggle: to say that equality of rights under the law shall not be denied or abridged by the United States or any State on account of sex. A simple statement, but one with profound significance.

My message is, don't be discouraged. We have had a setback this afternoon. It means we'll have to struggle harder, we'll have to unify ourselves more closely. We'll have to realize that this is not a time to cast stones at one another or to try to assign blame for a disappointing day. It's a time for the marshaling of forces and to realize that together we will not fail.

We did not get in this fight to lose, and we do not intend to lose. We will ratify the equal rights amendment for the United States of America.

Source: Carter, Jimmy. "Equal Rights Amendment: Remarks at a Fundraising Dinner, June 18, 1980." *Public Papers of the Presidents of the United States, Jimmy Carter, 1980–1981, Book 2.* Washington, DC: Government Printing Office, 1982, pp. 1133–1135.

MORAL MAJORITY LEADER JERRY FALWELL LAMENTS "ASSAULTS" ON THE TRADITIONAL FAMILY, 1980

During the 1970s and 1980s, fundamentalist Baptist televangelist Jerry Falwell (1933–2007) became one of the most influential power brokers in the Reagan-era Republican Party. In 1979 Falwell founded the Moral Majority, an organization of evangelical Christian conservatives that quickly became a major force in American politics. Falwell and his organization criticized women who pursued careers, condemned "immoral" forces in

American culture such as homosexuality and materialism and sex outside of marriage, and urged the nation to return to a more traditional, God-centered life that placed husbands and fathers as the spiritual leaders of families and women as their devoted followers. All of these themes are touched upon in the following excerpt from Falwell's 1980 book, Listen, America!

There are only three institutions God ordained in the Bible: government, the church, and the family. The family is the God-ordained institution of the marriage of one man and one woman together for a lifetime with their biological or adopted children. The family is the fundamental building block and the basic unit of our society, and its continued health is a prerequisite for a healthy and prosperous nation. No nation has ever been stronger than the families within her. America's families are her strength and they symbolize the miracle of America.

Families in search of freedom to educate their children according to religious principles originally settled this land. Families in search of religious freedom, determined to work and enjoy the fruits of their labor, tamed this wild continent and built the highest living standard in the world. Families educating their children in moral principles have carried on the traditions of this free republic. Historically the greatness of America can be measured in the greatness of her families. But in the past twenty years a tremendous change has taken place.

There is a vicious assault upon the American family. More television programs depict homes of divorced or of single parents than depict the traditional family. Nearly every major family-theme TV program openly justifies divorce, homosexuality, and adultery. Some sociologists believe that the family unit, as we know it, could disappear by the year 2000. Increased divorce and remarriage have broken family loyalty, unity, and communications. We find increased insecurity in children who are the victims of divorced parents. Many of these children harden themselves to the possibility of genuine love, for fear that they will be hurt again. Their insulated lives make them poor future candidates for marriage, and many young people have no desire to marry whatsoever. But I believe that most Americans remain deeply committed to the idea of the family as a sacred institution. A minority of people in this country is trying to destroy what is most important to the majority, and the sad fact is that the majority is allowing it to happen. Americans must arise and accept the challenge of preserving our cherished family heritage.

I quote again from the *Washington Post* poll of December 16, 1979, "Americans' Hopes and Fears About the Future": "To be alone—those are dreadful words to most Americans, expressed repeatedly in this era supposedly dedicated to self." I recently read that one of our leading political commentators said that loneliness will be a major political issue in the 1980s. God said in the Book of Genesis that it was not good that man should be alone. God made men and women with the need for fellowship and the desire for a family life.

The home was the first institution established by God. God's program cannot be improved. In the Book of Genesis in the Bible we find these words: "And the LORD God caused a deep sleep to fall upon Adam, and he slept: And he took one of his ribs, and closed up the flesh instead thereof; And the rib, which the LORD God had taken from man, made he a woman, and brought her unto the man. And Adam said, This is now bone of my bones, and flesh of my flesh: She shall be called Woman, because she was taken out of Man. Therefore shall a man leave his father and his mother, and shall cleave unto his wife: And they shall be one flesh. And they were both naked, the man and his wife, and were not ashamed." (Gn. 2:21–25) Nothing is more right than a man and a woman joined together in holy wedlock. As a family, they are in submission to the Lordship of Jesus Christ—the most heavenly thing on earth.

A commentator from one of the major networks once asked me, "What right do you Baptists have to promote your ideas about the family being the acceptable style for all of humanity?" I replied that it was not Baptists who started the family; it was God Almighty, and He is not a Baptist. God made a helpmeet for man. The family is that husband–wife relationship that God established in the Garden of Eden, later producing children. God gave Adam authority and dominion over the creation and told him to multiply and replenish the earth. The family is that basic unit that God established, not only to populate but also to control and contain the earth. The happiest people on the face of this earth are those who are part of great homes and families where they are loved, protected, and shielded. When I have been out having a long, hard day, often in a hostile environment, it is great to walk into my home, to close the front door, and to know that inside the home there are a wife and children who love me. Home is a haven to which I run from the troubles of this world, a place of security and warmth, where each member has the knowledge of belonging. Most of the people who are leading the antifamily efforts in America are failures in the family business because they have not committed their lives to Jesus Christ and so do not know His perfect plan for their lives.

The single most important influence on the life of a child is his family.

The strength and stability of families determine the vitality and moral life of society. Too many men and women, trying to protect their own sinfulness and selfishness, are for the desires of self-gratification destroying the very foundation of the family as we know it. In the war against the family today, we find an arsenal of weapons. The first weapon is the cult of the playboy, the attitude that has permeated our society in these last twenty years. This playboy philosophy tells men that they do not have to be committed to their wife and to their children, but that they should be some kind of a "cool, free swinger." Sexual promiscuity has become the life style of America. The cult of the playboy is more than just a revolution of dirty magazines. It represents a life style that ultimately corrupts the family. Men are satisfying their lustful desires at the expense of family.

The second weapon against the family is the feminist revolution. This is the counterreaction to the cult of the playboy. Many women are saying, "Why should I be taken advantage of by chauvinists? I will get out and do my own thing. I will stand up for my rights. I will have my own dirty magazines." Feminists are saying that self-satisfaction is more important than the family. Most of the women who are leaders in the feminist movement promote an immoral life style.

In a drastic departure from the home, more than half of the women in our country are currently employed. Our nation is in serious danger when motherhood is considered a task that is "unrewarding, unfulfilling, and boring." I believe that a woman's call to be a wife and mother is the highest calling in the world. My wife is proud to be called a housewife. She is dedicated to making a happy and rich life for us and our three children. She does not consider her life work of making my life happy and that of loving and shaping the lives of our precious children inconsequential or demeaning. Women who choose to remain in the home should never feel inferior to those working outside, but should know they are fulfilling God's command for the home.

We have been living in a distorted and decaying society where women are made to feel a loss of self-esteem and a loss of status when they choose to be full-time housewives. Women are finding today that they feel they must justify themselves if they choose to remain in the home. Edith Schaeffer, in her book *What Is a Family?* points out the glory and the seriousness and responsibility of being a full-time housewife. Answering the question, "What is a family?" she says: "A formation center for human relationships—worth fighting for, worth calling a career, worth the dignity of hard work." She says, "The family is the place where the deep understanding that people are significant, important, worthwhile, with a purpose in life, should be learned at an early age. The family is the place where children should learn that human beings have been made in the image of God and are therefore very special in the universe." (p. 69) She says: "The environment in a family should be conducive to the commencement of natural creativity, as natural as breathing, eating, and sleeping. A balanced, created person can come forth, developing and branching out in a wide number of areas, if some amounts of imagination and care are used. The first requirement is a dignity of attitude toward the family. This dignity involves accepting the seriousness and excitement of having your own home be a very specific creativity center. Given one, two, three, or more new little beings, one at a time, adopted or born to you, you have an opportunity to develop a growing, changing, constantly better environment for budding and blossoming creativity . . . someone has to have time to give to this." (p. 58)

It is sad that we find in our major magazines articles such as that in the July 9, 1979, *U.S. News & World Report* entitled, "Full-time Homemaking Is Now 'Obsolete,'" It says: "Shirley Johnson, the Vassar economist, figures that for each additional $1,000 a woman earns, the chance of divorce increases by 2 per cent." A January 15, 1979, *U.S. News & World Report* article entitled, "Working Women Joys and Sorrows" states, "Women are swelling the work force at a rate of almost 2 million every year—a phenomenon that is beginning to transform everyday life in the United States. From astronaut to zoologist, nearly every occupation has been invaded by women, who are pouring into the job market almost twice as fast as men. More than half of our country's 84 million women, including a majority of mothers with school-age children, now work or seek jobs. So dramatic is the shift from homemaking to careers that Eli Ginzberg, head of the National Commission for Manpower Policy, describes it as 'bigger than the atomic bomb or nuclear power.' Ginzberg predicts that the desire of women for jobs ultimately may alter the lives of every American: 'It changes the relationship of men to women; it changes the relationship of mothers to children.'" Edith Schaeffer knows the security and love a family can give to each of its members. She says, "Family bridges the centuries and is not meant to be represented by splintered, shattered, broken human counterparts. Togetherness in sickness and in health is to be 'till death do us part' . . . it is while we are in the land of the living that the family is meant to care for each other, and to be a real shelter—from birth to old age." (p. 118)

Many women today say that they must work for economic reasons. Although inflation has placed a financial burden on the family, we are overly concerned about materialistic wealth. Many Americans consider it more important to have several cars in the driveway, a beautiful house, and two color television sets than to have a stable home environment for their children.

Men and women are seeking easy divorces. The October 15, 1979, *U.S. News & World Report* said that demographers estimate that 45 per cent of infants born in 1980 will live in one parent families for at least part of their childhood. A person's character is determined by the pledges and promises he or she makes. A man or woman who does not keep his or her word can hardly be a good example to children, but thousands of men and women who have made a pledge of marriage, an eternal pledge of marriage, are breaking that promise in front of impressionable children.

Young people are living together today because they have observed parents who thought little of the eternal commitment they made to each other in their marriage vows. Couples living together cannot experience, however hard they try, the intimacy, security, and genuine love of a stable marriage in a relationship that is anything less than 100 per cent commitment. Parents are failing to teach their children a sense of commitment to relationships. Only marriage fulfills basic human needs for security and love.

An article by Judy Mann entitled, "We're a Lot Freer, But Is It So Good?" in the January 4, 1980, *Washington Post* states, "So what's ahead? What's ahead for the eighties for the baby-boom generation, the generation that gave us the free-speech movement, free sex, free dope, free Vietnam, the generation that liberated homosexuals, women and finally men? . . . As the seventies came around, we rejected homemaking and plunged into careers. Women who went to work knew they were spending a lot less time with their children than mothers who did not. Parents came up with the theory that it wasn't the quantity of time we spent with our children that counted but the quality. People who challenged this were attacked as antifeminists.

"We focused on day care for children as the single greatest worry of working mothers, and everyone assumed we meant day care for little kids. For a few years we did. But what of the teenagers who come home now from junior high school and high school to empty houses all around the neighborhood? Listen to the working mother of two teen-age daughters: 'I'm a single parent. I have to work. I can't be here every afternoon. There's no way I can know everything that goes on.'

"We're in something of a fix. How should we teach our children about the sanctity of marriage when we're in the process of divorcing a second or third spouse? How do we tell them drugs are dangerous and they should stay away from them when they can get pot in our dresser drawers? How do we expect them to excel in the public schools when we come home from work too tired to help them study?

"The baby-boom generation seems to have survived its social experiments and we've had a lot of fun but something is happening to our children and attention must be paid. The warning signals—illiteracy, teen-age suicides, burnouts, people who are unemployable—are all around us, sending us signals that while we may have created a better world for ourselves, it is not a safer one for our children.

"This is not the stuff of marches, of protests. We are adults now. This time we are the parents. We can't take over the high-school administration building in an effort to get dope out of the restrooms and learning back into the classrooms. We have to be cautious, mature, thoughtful, resourceful, and persuasive. We who challenged and discarded the standards and life styles of our parents now have the far trickier task of fashioning new standards for our children, searching for mutually acceptable guidelines between the freedoms we enjoy as adults and the freedoms they want for themselves as children. And somehow, both the fathers and mothers are going to have to realize that it takes more than a little quality time to raise children: It takes large quantities of high-quality time.

"Whether we do it through more part-time work for fathers and mothers, through more flexitime, through parental leave of absence, through the thirty-hour work week, parental co-operatives, and other forms of sharing child-raising responsibilities, we now need to free more of our time to raise our children.

"In the eighties, the baby-boom generation is finally going to have to grow up."

The answer to stable families with children who grow up to be great leaders in our society and who themselves have stable homes will not come from, as Judy Mann states, more part-time work for fathers and mothers, or parental leaves of absence, or thirty-hour weeks, or parental co-operatives and other forms of sharing childraising responsibilities. It will come only as men and women in America get in a right relationship to God and His principles for the home. Statistics show that couples who profess a born-again relationship have much happier, healthier marriages. In a January 22, 1979, *U.S. News & World Report* interview with Dr. Robert B. Taylor, specialist in family medicine, entitled, "Behind the Surge in Broken Marriages," Dr. Taylor says: "We find that couples who are actively religious tend to have more stable marriages. Worshiping together and attending church activities help develop strong couple bonds that are very hard to break." The Bible gives men and women God's plan.

Scripture declares that God has called the father to be the spiritual leader in his family. The husband is not to be the dictator of the family, but the spiritual leader. There is a great difference between a dictator and a leader. People follow dictators because they are forced to do so. They follow leaders because they want to. Good husbands who are godly men are good leaders. Their wives and children want to follow them and be under their protection. The husband is to be the decision-maker and the one who motivates his family with love. The Bible says that husbands are to love their wives even as Christ also loved the church and gave Himself for it. A man is to be a servant to his family while at the same time being a leader. A husband and father is first of all to be a provider for his family. He is to take care of their physical needs and do this honestly by working and earning an income to meet those needs. Then he is to be a protector. He is to protect them not only from physical harm but from spiritual harm as well. He is to protect them from television programs and from magazines that would hurt them. Child abuse involves much more than physical abuse. We have little children today who are growing up in homes where mothers and fathers literally hate each other. Those children are living in a constant perpetual hate war that is destroying them. A father has a God-given responsibility to lead his family in their worship of God. A father is to be a godly example to his wife and children; he must be consistently living a good life style before his family. He is to pray with his family and read to them from the Word of God. A man cannot do these things if he does not know Jesus Christ as his Lord and Savior. The Bible says, "But as many as received him, to them gave the power to become the sons of God, even to them that believe on his name." (Jn. 1: 12) The love of God is available to every man, and God has made an offer to us and asked us to receive the gift of salvation. Until men are in right relationship with God, there is no hope for righting our families of our nation. Because we have weak men we have weak homes, and children from these homes will probably grow up to become weak parents leading even weaker homes.

Dr. Harold M. Voth, M.D., senior psychiatrist and psychoanalyst at the Menninger Foundation, Topeka, Kansas, has said, "The correct development of a child requires the commitment of mature parents who understand either consciously or intuitively that children do not grow up like Topsy. Good mothering from birth on provides the psychological core upon which all subsequent development takes place. Mothering is probably the most important function on earth. This is a full-time, demanding task. It requires a high order of gentleness, commitment, steadiness, capacity to give, and many other qualities. A woman needs a good man by her side so she will not be distracted and depleted, thus making it possible for her to provide rich humanness to her babies and children. Her needs must be met by the man, and above all she must be made secure. A good man brings out the best in a woman, who can then do her best for the children. Similarly, a good woman brings out the best in a man, who can then do his best for his wife and children. Children bring out the best in their parents. All together they make a family, a place where people of great strength are shaped, who in turn make strong societies. Our nation was built by such people."

Source: Falwell, Jerry. *Listen, America!* New York: Doubleday, 1980, pp. 121–130. Copyright © 1980 by Jerry Falwell. Used by permission of Doubleday, an imprint of the Knopf Doubleday Publishing Group, a division of Penguin Random House LLC. All rights reserved.

PRESIDENT CARTER ASKS FOR SUPPORT FROM A WOMEN'S LABOR UNION, 1980

On September 29, 1980, deep in the stretch run of a presidential reelection campaign against Republican nominee Ronald Reagan, Democratic president Jimmy Carter attended the 37th Tri-Annual Convention of the International Ladies' Garment Workers' Union. In his remarks, excerpted below, he asserted that his Democratic Party was the only viable choice for working women determined to secure equal treatment in American society— including the workplace.

I am proud to be President of a great nation that stands up for human rights, not only in our own country but around the world, just as this union was standing up for human rights long before most of us were born. . . .

And I'm also proud to stand before you as the standard-bearer of the one political party that represents the historic concerns of America's working people, and that is your and my Democratic Party of the United States.

I lead this party as its nominee in the crucial election of 1980 because of your help. And I am proud to share that leadership with a great friend of labor and the best Vice President that any President ever had, Fritz Mondale.

There are a lot of things that bind us closely together. I'm very proud to run with the support of a union that believes that our society has a moral obligation to do the most for those who have the least. That's what compassionate, democratic government is all about. That is what this campaign is all about. That is why you and I are fighting side by side, and that is why you and I are going to win November the 4th.

I feel confident about that prediction because this union has been fighting and winning for 80 years. You have fought for better wages, better working conditions for your own members, but you've done something more than that. For 80 years, you've fought to make our country live up to its own ideals. You've never cared what color someone might be or what nationality or what language they might speak or what sex they are or what religion they practice, because this union is serious about equality and social justice and democracy.

Five weeks from tomorrow the American people will make a choice that will affect every gain that you have fought so hard to achieve for the last 80 years. All of those gains, all of that progress is at stake, from the minimum wage to human rights. Never in my lifetime has our country faced such a stark choice—between two parties, yes, between two candidates, yes, between two totally different philosophies, yes; also, between two futures, for you, for your families, for those you love, and for our country.

I came here to talk to you briefly about that choice and what it means to working people and, especially today, about working women. It should be an easy choice, because all you have to do is follow the same good advice the ILG has been giving for years. When you pick a candidate and when you pick a party, just look for the union label.

Before a candidate tells you what he's going to do, first find out what he's already done. I think that's a pretty good standard. Before someone says he's a friend of the working people, take a look at his record. Look at which candidate stands up for the needs of America's working people, which party looks out for the people who have to work day in and day out, which candidate has fought with you, alongside of you, when the working people's interests were at stake.

Let me tell you briefly where I stand, what I've been fighting for with your help since the first day I was inaugurated President.

I believe, as you do, that people have a right to a decent living, and that's why we fought together for the largest and most certain continual increase ever in history in the minimum wage. We won that fight over tremendous opposition, and now 4 million Americans are living better lives today and all Americans, because of that, really live better lives.

I believe, as you do, that in the nation with the richest agriculture in the history of the entire world there can be no excuse for allowing anyone to go hungry. And that's why you and I fought to eliminate the cash requirement for purchasing food stamps. And we won that fight, and a lot of people today are not hungry because we fought together.

And I believe, as you do, that every worker has a right to be employed in a place that's safe and healthy. And that's why we've worked to improve OSHA and successfully defended it against attempts to destroy it. These attempts might still be launched in the future, but with you and I working together they will not succeed, and Americans will be protected where they work.

And I believe, as you do, that the best way to put young people to work is not to guarantee them lower wages, but to give them the training and the work experience they need to fit into the job market. I want to make sure there's a job for every young person to fill. As a matter of fact, I want to be sure that in America, there is a job for every person who's able to work to fill.

Full employment is my goal, and full employment is your goal. And that's why I'm working with the ILG to protect jobs from unfair import competition. And that's why you and I've worked together to increase American textile exports. In the last 2 years, we've had some success. Textile imports in the last 2 years are down, and in the last 2 years, American exports of textiles are up $2 billion. That trend is in the right direction, and we're going to keep it moving that way. This is your characteristic, because for 80 years you have fought to eliminate the sweatshop. And we must not let the sweatshop win, from abroad, the battle that you won against the sweatshop here at home. . . .

And I also do not believe that the answer to our Nation's complex economic problems is a monstrous, ill-conceived tax giveaway to the very rich—Reagan-Kemp-Roth, a plan that would give the most to those who already have the most, a plan that may be the most ill-advised and inflationary proposal ever put before the Congress. I believe that the real answer is for you and me to work together not only to defeat Reagan-Kemp-Roth but also to defeat those who support it.

And more general in nature but equally important, I believe that the real answer is a good partnership between labor, business, and the public, to revitalize and to modernize American industry, to help American workers become even more productive and where necessary, better trained. With your help we will build that partnership and achieve those goals. Every one of these positions and many more that I could name carries the ILG union label, and so does this one: All Americans, women and men alike, should have the same fundamental rights. And those rights should be enshrined where the rights of Americans are supposed to be enshrined, in the Constitution of the United States of America.

We simply cannot afford top public officials who ignore the real problems of American working women, who would deny women the constitutional protection of their equal rights, who seem to believe that women, like children, should be seen and not heard. I totally reject that view. I support ERA. Not only do I support ERA, but my six predecessors in the White House also supported it, Democratic and Republican Presidents. Even the Republican Party supported ERA for 40 years, until this year. The new Republican leaders have turned their backs on American women. Some of them say they are not opposed to women's rights; they just want to let the States do it. That's what the enemies of women's suffrage said 70 years ago, "Leave it to the States." That's what the enemies of civil rights said 20 years ago, "Leave it to the State."

Throughout the United States there are hundreds and hundreds of laws that discriminate against women. Fragment this series of laws among 50 different States, and you get some idea of what leaving it to the States really means. Make no mistake, this is not just a theoretical question. Equal rights for women is a bread and butter issue. For every dollar that men are paid, women are only paid 59 cents for the same amount of work. That is wrong. In many parts of our country women cannot work or borrow or dispose of their property on equal terms. That, too, is wrong. Equal pay for equal work!

Equal pay for equal work is a standard that ILG set a long time ago. It's the time now that the rest of the country caught up with you. Women make up 43 percent of the work force; a fourth of American households are headed by women—more and more American families depend on the wages that women bring home. When we help women to achieve greater economic rights, we are helping the American family. That's why we must put muscle behind our antidiscrimination laws, why we've toughened the Equal Employment Opportunity Commission, why I personally have appointed more women to top Federal positions and more women judges to the Federal bench than all previous Presidents in the 200-year history of our Nation combined. And that's why we have boosted women employees in the Federal Government by 66,000, at a time when overall Federal employment was going down because of increased efficiency. And that's why we've strengthened the support of day care, why we've pioneered pacesetting innovations like flexitime and compressed time to help women meet both job and family responsibilities.

I'm the father of a little girl, and I'm also the grandfather of a little girl, and I want them to have the same kind of opportunities that my sons and my grandsons have.

I'd like to remind you again that ERA is not just a question of laws; it's a clarion call to end an historic injustice. It's a signal that we are really one Nation, with liberty and justice for all—all men and, at long last, all women. You understand the special problems of working women, because more ILG'ers are working women, women who work to support themselves and their families, women whose paychecks are not a luxury but a necessity.

You've not had an easy historic road. The men and women of the ILG have worked to send your sons and daughters to college, to law school, to medical school, sometimes based on the lowest possible wage. One of my own assistants in the White House, in fact the one who helped me write this speech, is the grandson of two members of the old local 38. His grandmother was a sweatshop seamstress at a time when the great shirtwaist strike of 1909, when 20,000 people, most of them women, rose up to demand the right to be treated with simple human decency. That strike holds a lesson for today's battle for ERA. On the ILG picket lines, immigrant girls of 14 and 15 years of age were joined by wealthy women from the suffragist movement; the women of 5th Avenue and the women of the Lower East Side joined together in solidarity because both believed in the dignity of women as human beings and also because both groups of women believed in the promise of America.

All of us who are fighting for ERA today are part of that same battle which began so many years ago. We must persevere until the battle is won and the equal rights amendment is inscribed in the Constitution of the United States.

But let me say, in closing, that the rights of women, the rights of minorities, the rights of those who are afflicted and oppressed, the rights of free speech and free expression, the rights of working people to organize and bargain collectively—these are fundamental human rights. They are the rights that our Nation represents. These are the rights that are worth fighting for, and these are the rights of our Nation which I will defend as long as I am President.

Let me dip just once more into ILG history before I close. Many of you will remember the old Italian Dressmakers Local 89 radio program on WEVD. The program always began with a song. The title of the song was "Bread and Roses." That same phrase—"Bread and Roses"—was one of the most famous rallying cries of the early American labor movement. It meant, of course, that labor was not struggling only for material benefits, but for the value and the ideals that give life its meaning and its beauty.

That old rallying cry is as good a description as any of what our country means to our own people and also to people all over the world. I want to continue that struggle side by side with you over the next 4 years. So let us go forward together to win an election and to build a future that gives us bread—and roses, too.

Thank you very much, and God bless you.

Source: Carter, Jimmy. "Remarks at International Ladies Garment Workers Convention (September 29, 1980)." *Public Papers of the Presidents of the United States, Jimmy Carter, 1980–1981, Book 3.* Washington, DC: Government Printing Office, 1982, pp. 1949–1953.

PRESIDENT OF HUNTER COLLEGE TOUTS THE ERA'S BENEFITS FOR WOMEN'S EDUCATION, 1984

The failure of the Equal Rights Amendment (ERA) to secure the requisite approval from 38 states by 1982 was a crushing blow to its proponents. But rather than give up, ERA supporters in Washington begin reintroducing new ERA bills in Congress on an annual basis. The following statement in support of the ERA by Hunter College president Donna Shalala (who went on to serve as secretary of the Department of Health and Human Services for both terms of the Clinton administration) was delivered at 1984 congressional hearings on the ERA. The document then provides excerpts from a tense exchange between Shalala and conservative Republican senator Strom Thurmond of South Carolina, who had a long record of condemning the ERA as anti-family.

Good morning. I am Donna Shalala, President of Hunter College of the City University of New York. I am here today to speak in favor of the Equal Rights Amendment. That Amendment would finally make it unconstitutional to deny any individual's equal rights on account of sex in any area of government action. No longer would women be required to rely on the patchwork of anti-discrimination laws to enforce their rights to equal opportunity and equal treatment, nor would they bear the substantial risk that the claim for equality is unenforceable, because the government does not stand behind it, or insupportable because of some exception in the laws.

In no area of public life is the ERA more important than in education. In virtually every aspect of education, both public and private, sex domination continues to exist. Today, I'm here to discuss the extent of that discrimination and its impact on women.

I need not elaborate on the importance of education in determining one's life opportunities. By denying equal access to education to a woman, we narrow her choices and options in employment, income and mobility.

The ERA is central to ensuring women's equal right to education. It will provide women with a permanent constitutional basis to assert that right. It will provide an important constitutional backdrop to the statutes designed to ensure equality and, thus, eliminate any necessity for such statutes to be liberally construed to achieve equality. It will insulate women's rights from political pressure. It will end efforts to repeal existing antidiscrimination statutes, to create special exceptions to the equality principle in antidiscrimination statutes, and to limit the remedies or means to enforce equality. Finally, it would free this Congress to implement women's equality in an efficacious and cost effective manner.

I. Sex Discrimination In Education

Discrimination based on sex in institutions creates a host of problems for female students and employees on every level. While women now have better access to education (helped substantially by Title IX) they still face the heavy burden of

proving themselves in many areas. The resulting patterns are evident in employment of women in education, admissions, courses of study and athletics. Without
a constitutional amendment, the gains women have won are vulnerable to political
whim.

Admission and Course of Study for Women

In its 1981 report *Title IX: The Half Full, Half Empty Glass*, the National Advisory
Council on Women's Educational Programs described some of the discrimination
that limits women's educational opportunities. The following examples illustrate
widespread sex discriminatory policies:

- Because it had few dormitories for women and would not permit them to
  live off campus, the University of North Carolina accepted only one-quarter
  of the women who applied for admission while admitting half of the male
  applicants.
- At the New York State College of Agriculture at Cornell, women were requested
  to have SAT scores 30 to 40 points higher than those of entering men.
- A male applicant at Penn State was five times more likely to be admitted than
  a female.

Although Title IX outlawed these particular discriminatory practices especially in
professional and graduate programs, the percentages of women enrolled in certain
courses of study still fall short of full access to these programs. In 1980, the proportion of women in medical school was 26 percent; in law school 34 percent; in
dental school 17 percent; and in veterinary school 39 percent. Women earned only
30 percent of doctorates awarded in 1980.

The problems in secondary and postsecondary education are even more severe;
almost half of all programs are still overwhelmingly segregated by sex. Seventy-two
percent of all women in vocational education in 1978 were still enrolled in predominantly female clerical programs or in home economics classes. The percentage of women enrolled in training that leads to higher-paid typically male skills
is still quite low. Seventeen percent in agricultural programs, 18% in trade and
industrial programs, and 20% in technical programs. These figures overstate the
progress because these broad job categories include predominately female trades
such as cosmetology.

The importance of skill training for women for high-paid jobs, usually reserved
for men, cannot be underestimated. One-half of all women in this country work,
and two-thirds of them work out of economic necessity. With rising divorce rates,
the economic cushion of a spouse's income can no longer be assumed. As noted by
the National Advisory Council on Economic Opportunity, "Poverty among women
is becoming one of the most compelling social facts of this decade. If the proportion of the poor who are in female-headed families were to increase at the same
rate as it did from 1956–1977, the poverty population would be composed solely
of women and their children in the year 2000."

Occupations historically reserved for women are undergoing enormous change. An estimated 80 percent of women currently working are now concentrated in occupations which are rapidly declining or becoming obsolete as a result of technological advances. Jobs such as bank teller, telephone operator and clerical worker are undergoing major changes. These changes will result in dramatically fewer available jobs in fields in which women have been concentrated and greater technological skill requirements in the remaining jobs. An unskilled woman will be displaced and may become permanently unemployed.

Moreover, a variety of forces have kept women out of predominantly "male" jobs. First and foremost is the fact that many jobs—e.g. plumber, electrician, auto mechanic—are still performed almost exclusively by men in our society. This fact alone deters many teenage girls from even considering such fields, or from employment even if they have been trained. Just as teenage girls do not try out for the high school football team or seek to join a "boys only" school club or extracurricular activity, many do not even enroll for the auto mechanics course that only boys take.

Not only are there subtle societal norms that give young women implicit messages, girls are expressly discouraged from pursuing certain educational opportunities. Discriminatory counselors believe and tell girls that "dirty" work is not appropriate for them. Many counselors warn girls to avoid jobs in which they could face harassment (verbal and physical) rather than counseling them how to avoid the harassment. The result is that those girls who achieve academically despite this discouragement are likewise excluded from and discouraged in the job market. Women are harassed in many job environments, and many employers refuse to consider hiring females for "male" jobs, such as plumbers, electricians, etc.

The failure actively to recruit female students into traditionally male courses is sex-based discrimination in recruiting and training. It effectively endorses and perpetuates the pattern of discrimination that has kept women out of high-paying blue-collar skilled craft jobs. The notion that a girl should be discouraged or not encouraged in acquiring the special skills demanded by these changes, unless she herself exhibits an intense desire to do so, is economically catastrophic to women and fails to recognize the depth of the forces deterring her.

Women are also discouraged from courses of study in math and science with virtually the same force as they are discouraged from skilled jobs and vocational training. The stereotype that women are not good at math and science is still widely indulged even though these are extremely important areas of future employment. The result of this historic unfair exclusion of women from math and the sciences has proven difficult to overcome. It is reflected in the counsel that girls receive as they choose a course of study.

There are severe consequences to the cultural bias that math and science are properly in the male domain. In 1981, only half of college-bound girls, compared to two-thirds of college-bound boys, had completed four years of high school math. The gap in enrollments, especially in advanced courses, persists despite the assistance of Title IX.

A study of math enrollments by the Project on Equal Educational Rights of the NOW Legal Defense in Education Fund in 113 school districts in Michigan in the fall of 1981 confirmed this pattern. Boys outnumbered girls two to one in computer math courses. In one school district the percentage of girls in computer math was as low as 22 percent. Girls were 40 percent of the students in calculus and 43 percent of the students in trigonometry. Advanced science courses had enrollments as low as 19 percent female.

This difference in course-taking is chiefly responsible for the lower achievement rates of girls that many studies have reported. While boys and girls tend to do equally well in math at elementary school levels, girls' math scores drop behind in junior high and fall further behind at the high school and college level. The disparity between boys' and girls' scores disappears, however, when the data are controlled for years of math taken in school. These findings confirm that it is primarily lack of exposure and practice that keeps girls behind boys' achievements in math and other technical studies.

The problem of women's exclusion from math training and their resultant loss of opportunity is exacerbated by the fact that sex-segregated schools at the elementary and secondary level are tolerated under both Title IX and the equal protection clause of the Fourteenth Amendment. In 1977, the U.S. Supreme Court upheld on an equal protection challenge the exclusion of a Philadelphia girl from the all-male Central High, one of the city's two academic high schools, and the one with the best reputation and the most prestigious graduates. The other academic school, the all-female Girls High, was good but not quite on a par with "Central." The appellate court ruled in favor of "separate but equal," emphasized that Central and Girls High were comparable in quality, academic standing and prestige—and ignored the superior science facilities and reputation of Central. Last month, a Pennsylvania state court ordered Central High to admit girls. However, that decision was based in part on the state Equal Rights Amendment.

Schools for boys typically offer superior math and science opportunities. Girls, therefore, are often barred from entering programs in which math and science learning is required. The evidence confirms that girls, like most people, gain confidence in their ability to perform a difficult task only after they have tried it. The exclusion from a superior program of education can be fatal to any woman's development of interest and abilities in math and science.

Judging from the educational programs that prepare future professionals in these fields, women are likely to stay substantially underrepresented in scientific and technical fields. While the trend has been slightly upward over the last decade, young women are still enrolling in education for these fields in significantly smaller numbers than are men. For example, in 1980, only 30 percent of all college graduates specializing in computer and information sciences were women. There have been modest recent gains, but women are still a small minority in educational programs in these fields. In 1976, while women were 40 percent of the labor force, they held only 13 percent of the jobs in math, computer and life science. Women have historically been missing from other expanding career fields as well. In 1976, women held only 7.5 percent of the jobs in the physical sciences and one percent of the jobs in engineering.

The implications of these statistics for the nation's future are staggering. At a time when our society is moving into an advanced technological era, we need to develop every citizen's ability to contribute. Instead, half the population is effectively excluded from these fields.

Sports and physical activity are another important area of student life that would be affected by the equal rights amendment. The strongly held stereotypes about women's athletic abilities have begun to be challenged. Today girls and women have more opportunity to participate in athletics—either for recreation or in competition—than they did before the passage of Title IX. But we have a long way to go.

Title IX has to date been interpreted to require institutions to provide a selection of sports and a level of competition that effectively accommodate the interests and abilities of both sexes. Women and men, boys and girls, must be provided comparable equipment and supplies, travel and per diem allowances, opportunity to receive coaching and academic tutoring, publicity, scheduling of game and practice times, scholarship aid, medical, housing, and dining facilities. Since the passage of Title IX the increase in women's and girls' enrollment in athletic programs reflects the active desire that girls and women had for sports participation that was denied to them. However, the current data on girls' participation in athletics shows how far we have to go before programs reflect full and fair participation for women.

- Last year only 35% of the high school varsity athletes were girls.
- In 1980, the average budget for a women's athletics program was 16.4% of the total athletics budget.
- During the 1977–78 school year, the average Big 10 school athletic budget for women was between $250,000 at smaller schools and $750,000 at larger schools. In the same year, however, the average men's Big 10 athletic was 3 million dollars.

While women still have a long way to go to achieve equality of opportunity in athletic participation, the gains in athletics for women are at risk today. The current Administration wants to severely limit Title IX in a way that would virtually eliminate athletics from coverage by that Act. For women to lose these gains would not only deny talented women careers in athletics. It would deny all young women the health, well-being and emotional and physical development that comes with sports and a full range of physical education participation. It would also guarantee that all women must continue to labor under the stereotype that women are innately weak, because as women continue to be denied opportunities for physical development and the incentives for that development, the stereotypes remain unchallenged and the talented athletic woman remains an aberration. For girls, as much as for boys, physical development through athletics is a crucial part of their education. Today, we continue to deny our girls and women this access to a full education. . . .

Responses to Questions of Senator Thurmond.

Question 1:

Dr. Shalala, over the years segregation has been a policy and practice of exclusion. I doubt that anyone would contest this statement insofar as it applies to separation of the races. However, it appears that most all-women's colleges were established for the specific purpose of promoting equality between the sexes in the area of education. These all-female institutions do a great deal to bring about equality for women by producing graduates who become scientists, educators, and political leaders. In this way, women's colleges enhance opportunities for women. If the Equal Rights Amendment were to become a part of our body of law, wouldn't those who have traditionally promoted equal opportunity for women through support of single-sex colleges be put in an untenable philosophical position?

The simple answer to your question is no, absolutely not; but let me elaborate. Private women's colleges, as I pointed out in my earlier reply respecting all private institutions, very well may not come within the sweep of the ERA because the ERA applies only to state action. So it may be that the affirmative action exception for private women's colleges will have no practical impact.

In the unlikely event that particular private colleges do come under ERA, it is important to look at the status of women's colleges in light of the history of women's education. Most private all-women's colleges were established in a time when women were excluded from education in male institutions. The policy and practice of exclusion of girls and women from education, like the policy and practice of racial exclusion, is long-standing and well documented.

Private all-women's colleges were established with the specific purpose of providing women the education that they would otherwise be denied on account of their sex. Lack of resources for women's education made any "purpose of promoting equality between the sexes" a lofty ideal rather than a specific purpose.

Notwithstanding this lack of resources, women's institutions have made a great contribution to this country and to improving the status of women. Among other accomplishments, they have produced graduates who have become scientists, educators, and political leaders of great stature in proportions that far exceed what might be expected from their enrollments. This may be true in part because such women are educated in an environment free from the well-documented detriments to female leadership in the classroom climate of coeducational institutions that is often hostile to female students.

The touchstones of affirmative action is that the action be specially designed and serves to overcome the effects of historic discrimination and to provide opportunities and environments for learning not readily available elsewhere, and thus promote equality. This concept is inherent to the Equal Rights Amendment, not contrary to it. An all-women's institution that actually serves the purpose of providing education and training that truly advances women's role in society and that does not perpetuate traditional stereotypes, is not in an untenable philosophical position in the context of the Equal Rights Amendment at all.

Until coeducational institutions offer women and girls the same educational opportunities and the same supportive environment for learning as are offered to men, the need will continue for institutions that are devoted to the education and advancement of women. Using objective measures, it can be determined when the goal of equal opportunity has been reached and affirmative action is no longer necessary.

Question 2:
There are two ways that Congress can bring about greater equality in education for women in the field of education. One is through the enactment of specific statutes and the other is, supposedly, through the passage of the Equal Rights Amendment. Do you think that inequalities in education for women can be adequately addressed through the enactment of specific pieces of legislation? If not, why not?

This question assumes that a constitutional amendment and specific pieces of legislation can be equally effective alternatives for creating law. This assumption is inaccurate because it ignores the primacy of the Constitution in defining the priorities of rights and protections concerning the relationship of the government to individuals. The Equal Rights Amendment and statutes are not equal alternatives to the same end.

The ERA is needed to establish once and for all that discrimination on account of sex by any level or branch of government in any aspect of its dealings is no longer an option. No statute or collection of statutes can achieve that result.

As I noted in my written and oral testimony, this Administration's efforts to narrow the reach of Title IX only to those specific programs receiving federal funds, but not for programs benefitting from federal tuition aid, demonstrate dramatically how women's right to equality may be undermined by executive action.

Despite the Supreme Court's holding that Title IX is modelled after Title VI, . . . several courts have cited the fact that racial discrimination is clearly proscribed by the Constitution while sex discrimination is not, including that Title IX should not receive the broad enforcement as Title VI . . .

Women need the important statement of principle that "equal rights shall not be denied on account of sex," unburdened by exceptions that typically appear in statutes. Girls for far too long have had to stand by while boys and men continue to receive valuable training and experience in sex-segregated schools and programs for the sake of tradition and the preservation of cherished stereotypes. A prime example is women's long exclusion, even under Title IX, from Philadelphia's prestigious all-male Central High. This exclusion was only finally overcome last year under the Pennsylvania State Constitution's ERA and Equal Protection Clause and the Fourteenth Amendment of the U.S. Constitution when, in *Newberg v. Board of Public Education,* ... the plaintiff proved that boys in Central receive three times the science, math, and gifted student training opportunities as the girls receive in the supposedly comparable Girls High. That case could not be brought under Title IX because of exceptions to this useful, but flawed, statute.

Even with the ERA, statutes will be needed. Statutes are the means of implementing the equality mandate of the Constitution in an orderly and thoughtful fashion and in a manner that is both efficient and cost-effective. Indeed, the two-year waiting period following ratification provides Congress and the States the time within which to consider and enact implementing changes in their statutes. It is in this supportive implementing role that statutes are the most useful.

Question 3:
Dr. Shalala, it has been concluded by some commentators that no law will ever make women equal—not even a "constitutional law." This conclusion is based upon the premise that making oneself equal is the responsibility of each individual. Supposedly, an individual can start the move toward full equality by developing a very real sense of self-worth as a person by acting in such a manner that he or she will be accepted as an equal by those around that individual as a matter of course. This theory ties in with your citation of the fact that of the women enrolled in vocational training, only a very small percentage take courses that prepare them for the higher paid, typically male skilled jobs. Doesn't this situation stem more from the way women perceive themselves in society than from sex discrimination in vocational education?

The target of equal rights under law is not sameness. The opportunities for women to develop a sense of self-worth and to benefit themselves by means of drive and determination are still heavily burdened in all aspects of education and employment in ways that men never face. Women, because they are women, are frequently and consistently denied jobs or promotions or made the objects of unwanted sexual demands. Such treatment is always demeaning and demoralizing. But it is even more so where, as is often true with women because of discrimination past and present, one's options are extremely limited. Under these circumstances, to explain away the current status of women as due to the individual's failure to develop a sense of self-worth ignores the persistent influence of the opinions of teachers, counsellors, neighbors, and friends about the proper role of women in society. However confident and self-assured an individual may be, she can't make it on her own, and everyone requires the support of others. . . . In non-traditional work situations, women not only face discrimination and harassment, they are also virtually excluded from social groupings in the workplace and from informal communication networks important to learning skills and finding better jobs, among other things. . . . Some researchers have concluded that men want and affirmatively act to keep women out of such traditionally male jobs to protect their own status.

Every day women of great courage, individual self-possession, drive, and determination endure low-paying dead-end jobs to keep their families together and face demeaning sexual harassment and discrimination in the bargain. Those knowledgeable about the extent of discrimination against and harassment of women know that the problem is not essentially a lack of sense of self-worth on the part of women. Rather it is a denial of opportunity for women and the resulting perception on the woman's part that "If I rock the boat here, I may have no job at all."

The ERA will send an authoritative message to the entire country that women are entitled to the same aspirations, support, and training that men can take for granted.

Source: Shalala, Donna E. "Prepared Statement and Responses to Questions from Senator Thurmond, Hearings on 'The Impact of the Equal Rights Amendment.'" Subcommittee on the Constitution of the Committee on the Judiciary, United States Senate, 98th Congress, Part 1. Serial J-98-42. Washington, DC: Government Printing Office, 1985, pp. 117–123.

AN ECONOMICS PROFESSOR EXPLORES COMPARABLE WORTH IN THE AMERICAN WORKPLACE, 1985

One of the most persistent problems facing American women has been the disparity in the wages paid to male and female workers in a wide range of professions and industries. During the 1970s and 1980s, reformers determined to address this issue examined a variety of proposals. Many of these proposals were grounded on the concept of "comparable worth." In the following essay, which was first presented at a meeting of the American Statistical Association before being published in the Department of Labor's Monthly Labor Review, *Wellesley College professor of economics Carolyn Shaw Bell (1920–2006) explained how "comparable worth" might act to reduce or even eliminate longstanding wage disparities between genders (and different races/ethnic groups). In addition to her influential work as an economist, Bell was known throughout her career as a dedicated advocate for women in the economics profession.*

Comparable Worth: How Do We Know It Will Work?

The title of this article poses a question to which there is a very short answer. We don't. We are completely unable to predict the outcomes of an effective comparable worth policy, whether mandated by law or adopted by private decisionmakers. Our ignorance stems from the lack of data with which to build a viable economic model. The issue is, of course, too new for historical evidence or even case studies to provide much help.

The dearth of useful data is due primarily to the fact that comparable worth itself comprises several different issues. Most of these issues have, in fact, emerged from analyzing statistics gathered for other purposes. But comparable worth has frequently been proposed as a solution without clearly defining the problem, partly because of insufficient data, and partly because of insufficient analysis of existing data.

The following discussion will elaborate on these statements. It concludes that efforts to design data collecting systems or even to tabulate and amass those data that already exist lag behind efforts to litigate and legislate comparable worth. It is highly likely, therefore, that comparable worth as a policy will be adopted or rejected on the basis of factors other than reasoned analysis.

Defining comparable worth

The term "comparable worth" is difficult to define. Whatever it is, the concept emerged after the passage of the Civil Rights Act of 1964. Title VII of the act makes it an unlawful employment practice for any employer to discriminate on the basis of race, color, religion, sex, or national origin. Title VII specifically mentions hiring and discharge, compensation and conditions of employment, and the limiting of opportunities for employment.

Nowhere in the 1964 act, or in the legislative history preceding its passage, or in its predecessor, the Equal Pay Act of 1963, was the term comparable worth mentioned or its essence discussed in other ways. So the concept did not originate with Title VII, whether or not it can be justified by that legislation. Rather, the notion of comparable worth emerges from a specific interpretation of statistical estimates. These estimates show a significant and continuing disparity between men's wages and women's wages, and between the wages of blacks and whites. The data describe an existing condition, which the use of comparable worth seeks to remedy. It must be noted at once that most discussions move from simple descriptive statistics to comparable worth as the remedy with little attempt at analyzing the data, assessing their applicability, or rigorously defining the problem.

Examples of the difficulties in defining comparable worth and its aims abound in the press. When the issue arose during the 1984 Presidential campaign, one political writer identified the concept as "a means of raising the income of working women." More recently, however, another commentator defined comparable worth as a "practice . . . designed to increase the pay of workers in female-dominated fields such as nursing to a level of men in a field requiring comparable labor."

These two quotations share one characteristic: they both report comparable worth as a solution to a problem. But they identify different problems. One view, widely held, sees comparable worth as a remedy for low incomes and growing poverty among women. Another suggests that comparable worth is the remedy for the earnings differential between male jobs and female jobs. Proponents of both rely on statistics to describe the problem.

The case for comparable worth as a remedy for poverty among women is a very general or macroeconomic statement referring to women in aggregate. Thus, those who seek to remedy such a poverty quote data on earnings of women compared to men and, most frequently, the familiar figure that full-time year-round workers who are female earn about 60 percent as much as their male counterparts. They then explicitly or implicitly translate these earnings figures into income.

The preponderance of low incomes among women can be found in many different sets of statistics. To advocate comparable worth as a means of raising these incomes, however, often rests on the premise that discrimination against women exists in the workplace. The same assertion is required in the other line of advocacy, which sees comparable worth as a remedy not so much for poverty as for differences in wages.

This second notion of comparable worth has frequently been called "pay equity" and proposes to do away with obvious and sometime noteworthy differentials in wages between occupations. Again, statistical evidence can be quoted at length. However, unlike the estimates cited in support of comparable worth as a general remedy for poverty among women, these data refer to one market and, hence, constitute the microeconomic approach.

The use of data on interoccupational wage disparity can be illustrated by testimony before a 1984 congressional hearing that contrasted monthly salaries for city or State government workers in various job classifications—for example, a senior carpenter at $1,080 and a senior legal secretary at $665, or a senior accounting clerk at $836 in pay and a streetsweeper at $758. Jobs paying higher wages were found to be held almost exclusively by men, with women dominating the lower-wage jobs. Again, the proposed remedy (without any very careful delineation of the problem) was to implement comparable worth in determining wages.

Is discrimination the culprit?

The discrimination charge also rests on statistical evidence. First, occupational data from the Bureau of the Census, the Bureau of Labor Statistics, and other public and private sources have been tabulated to show the percentages of males and females in various jobs, which can then be classified as male-dominated (or male-intensive), female-dominated, or neutral.

Exactly what percentage of jobholders in an occupation must be of the same sex for it to be sex-typed is not often discussed, and yet this is a good example of the kind of analysis that needs to be undertaken. Because women make up about half the labor force, one could argue that the only "neutral" occupations are those with between 45 percent and 55 percent female jobholders. But because women make up less than half the full-time labor force, this definition can be disputed. Other rules for sex-typing of jobs can easily be devised; the point is that insufficient research has been done to establish general agreement on this rather simple point. It is also true that substantial movement of women between men's and women's jobs occurs.

Notwithstanding, comparable worth advocates and opponents alike refer to "men's jobs" and "women's jobs." Of course, these terms have also been used for years by anthropologists, historians, and other observers of various cultures and of the division of labor between the sexes. What is at issue is an attempt to use statistics to turn this condition into a problem and to advocate comparable worth measures as a solution.

Following the sex-typing of jobs, the pay disparity argument turns to the data on wages and earnings in each occupation. Most arrays find women's jobs at the low end of the pay scale with men's jobs at the upper end, and some remarkably persuasive inverse correlations between the proportion of jobholders who are female and the level of earnings have been calculated.

There are then two ways by which to conclude that discrimination exists. One is to assume that women are being confined to the lower-wage jobs. The other is to hold that women tend to enter certain occupations, and that those jobs pay less because they are "female jobs." Both arguments can be found in the literature, although they have different implications with respect to the remedy of comparable worth, defined in this case as pay equity.

If discrimination exists because women are crowded into low-paying jobs, then the immediate remedy would appear to be removal of the barriers to their employment in high-paying occupations; presumably, this remedy was made available by Title VII. The argument for the new remedy of comparable worth rests on the charge that Title VII has not worked, and that not enough progress in job integration has occurred since the 1964 Civil Rights Act was passed. Thus, something stronger than merely making discrimination illegal is needed, something like an adjustment of wages.

If, on the other hand, the discrimination exists because all jobs held predominately by women (for whatever reason) are paid less than all jobs held predominately by men because women's work is valued less, then removing obstacles to employment would not have any effect. Indeed, evidence exists that, as formerly male jobs (stenographers at the turn of the century and bank tellers during the postwar years) have become almost exclusively female, relative pay levels for those occupations have fallen. It follows, according to this line of reasoning, that it will do no good to admit women to men's jobs, that what is needed is to raise the prevailing low levels of pay for female jobs. Hence, the need for comparable worth.

Source: Bell, Carolyn Shaw. "Comparable Worth: How Do We Know It Will Work?" *Monthly Labor Review,* December 1985, pp. 5–7.

Chapter 7: 1990–2008: Gains for Women's Rights amid Calls for a Return to Traditional Gender Roles

The 1990s began with a groundbreaking case about sexual harassment in the workplace involving Clarence Thomas, judge of the U.S. Court of Appeals for the District of Columbia Circuit (and previously chair of the Equal Employment Opportunity Commission, 1982–1990), and Anita Hill, a professor of law at the University of Oklahoma. Hill had worked with Thomas at the EEOC (and at the U.S. Department of Education's Office of Civil Rights). In his confirmation hearings to become a justice of the Supreme Court (1991), the Senate Judiciary Committee approached Anita Hill during its routine background investigation of Thomas, because of their work history. When she informed investigators that Thomas had sexually harassed her while they both worked at the EEOC, she was asked to testify at the Senate hearings. Hill testified that Thomas had repeatedly asked her to go out with him and when she refused, he retaliated. He talked about his sexual prowess and frequently included descriptions of sexual acts and his sexual anatomy in his conversations with her. In the hearing, Hill was questioned by 14 white men, all members of the Senate Judiciary Committee. Hill and Thomas were both African Americans who came from modest rural backgrounds and had worked their way to the highest echelons of law. During her testimony, Professor Hill soberly and calmly recounted the acts she had witnessed when working with Thomas. Thomas, on the other hand, denied all of the claims she made and referred to the hearing as a "high-tech lynching for uppity blacks." In the end, the Senate Judiciary Committee confirmed Clarence Thomas's nomination to the U.S. Supreme Court, where he continued to sit as of mid-2017.

At the time of the hearing, which was nationally televised, public opinion polls showed that Americans were more likely to believe Thomas than Hill, most likely because of the negative characterizations of Hill that were offered by many of Thomas's supporters. Another confounding factor was that Hill "followed" Thomas from the Civil Rights Office to the EEOC in spite of the fact that he had allegedly abused her. Hill's supporters believed that the lengthy and debasing hearing she faced at the hands of the 14 white men on the Judiciary Committee would increase the public's awareness of sexual harassment in the workplace and encourage more women who had experienced it to report it. But some activists feared that the demeaning treatment Professor Hill received from the members of the Senate committee would discourage other women from coming forward. The media attention given to Thomas's confirmation hearing did increase public awareness, and more women did come forward with complaints about sexual harassment in the workplace. The public was educated about the types of sexual harassment to which women can be subjected, learning that acts that created a hostile work environment, as well as *quid pro quo* harassment (e.g., promising raises or promotions in return for sexual "favors"), were harmful and illegal. The prevalence of sexual harassment of women and girls in American society also became a growing topic of debate.

In an interview conducted in 2014 with Irin Carmin of MSNBC, Hill discussed her motives for working at the Equal Employment Opportunity Commission when Thomas was there. She said she wanted to address discrimination in the workplace. Sexual harassment was not regarded as a serious issue by many judges, and she wanted to address it.

Sex Discrimination in the Workplace

In 1991, the U.S. Supreme Court heard the case of *United Auto Workers v. Johnson Controls*. Johnson Controls was a company that manufactured batteries. The production process involved exposure to high levels of lead. When the company discovered that eight pregnant employees had higher levels of lead in their blood than the Occupational Safety and Health Administration considered safe, Johnson Controls instituted a policy that no women employees—except those who could medically document infertility—could work in any jobs that exposed them to high lead levels. The United Automobile Workers charged the company with sex discrimination in violation of Title VII of the Civil Rights Act (1964). Title VII states that it is "an unlawful employment practice for an employer . . . to discriminate against any individual with respect to his [sic] compensation, terms, conditions, or privileges of employment, because of such individual's race, color, religion, sex, or national origin." The Supreme Court ruled that the company's gender-specific rule was biased and inequitable because it permitted fertile men, but not fertile women, to decide whether to work in jobs where they were subjected to lead exposure while manufacturing batteries.

In 1993, another sexual harassment case (*Harris v. Forklift Systems*) went before the Supreme Court. The case involved a woman, Teresa Harris, who had worked at the company from 1985 to 1987. Harris claimed that the president of the company had repeatedly made sexually explicit comments and sexual advances to her at work in front of other employees. Harris had directly confronted the company president about his behavior; he claimed he was just joking around and promised not to repeat the behavior. Harris decided to stay in the job. But when the employer resumed the behavior, she quit the job and sued, claiming that his actions had created a hostile work environment for her. The Tennessee district court ruled that while the employer's behavior would most likely have made any reasonable woman uncomfortable, Harris had not provided sufficient evidence to prove that it had constituted sexual harassment. The Supreme Court reversed the decision of the court of appeals, but the case was settled privately.

The Americans with Disabilities Act (1990)

A key development during this period of U.S. history was the passage of the Americans with Disabilities Act (ADA), the country's first civil rights law addressing the needs of people with disabilities. The law prohibits discrimination in employment, public services, public accommodations, and telecommunication.

President Clinton and Workplace Issues

Bill Clinton was elected in 1992 and assumed office in 1993. Early in his first term in office (1993), he signed into law the Family and Medical Leave Act (FMLA). The law was deemed necessary to provide the increasing number of women in the labor force with time off from work to care for dependent family members. The FMLA grants all eligible employees—men as well as women—up to 12 weeks of *unpaid* leave and job security for approved medical and family reasons, including personal or family illness, family military leave, pregnancy, adoption, or the foster care placement of a child; however, not all U.S. employees are eligible for the FMLA. Eligibility requirements include having worked at the same company for 12 months, for a minimum of 1,250 hours over that period, in a public or private company that employed at least 50 workers. While the FMLA has provided needed time away from work for many employees, it has been criticized for not requiring employers to pay the worker during the leave. Another drawback is that many workers are employed by companies that do not have 50 or more employees, so they are not eligible for the FMLA benefits.

Welfare Reform

In 1996, President Clinton signed the Personal Responsibility and Work Opportunity Reconciliation Act (PRWORA) into law. The number of people receiving welfare benefits increased between 1989 and 1994, reinforcing the negative stereotypes of welfare recipients. The existing program, Aid to Families with Dependent Children, was replaced with the Temporary Assistance for Needy Families (TANF).

The primary requirements and intended effects of PRWORA were (1) ending welfare as an entitlement program, (2) requiring recipients to begin working after two years of receiving benefits, (3) placing a lifetime limit of five years on benefits paid by federal funds, (4) aiming to encourage two-parent families and discouraging out-of-wedlock births, and (5) enhancing enforcement of child support. The act was strongly criticized because of the racist and sexist assumptions that motivated it. Studies of the short-term impact of the act showed that it succeeded in getting people to work. Between 1996 and 2000, the employment rate among never-married mothers increased from 63 percent to 76 percent. Poverty among single-parent families headed by women, as well as the general poverty rate, dropped. But the people at the very bottom of the economic ladder were left behind. Extreme poverty increased. The act reinforced traditional ideas about women's and men's roles by promoting work and marriage, and by aiming to reduce out-of-wedlock births and to increase two-parent families.

The Defense of Marriage Act

In 1996, the U.S. Congress enacted the Defense of Marriage Act (DOMA), which limited the legal definition of marriage to one man and one woman. DOMA was prompted by an increasing acceptability of same-sex marriage. It allowed states to refuse same-sex marriages that were legal in states that recognized them. It was struck down by the U.S. Supreme Court in 2013 in *United States v. Windsor*.

Women in the Military

Women have assisted the U.S. military in many roles since the nation was formed. But they were prohibited from serving in combat until 2013. Changes in policy regarding women's participation in the military have occurred slowly. Women were only allowed to serve in military positions in times of war until 1948, when Congress passed the Women's Armed Services Integration Act. This allowed women to hold permanent positions in the military, including during peacetime. During the Vietnam conflict,[1] 11,000 women served in the military, nearly all of whom were nurses. It wasn't until after the Vietnam War (in 1976) that women students were permitted to enroll in four of the military academies. In 1978, women sailors and marines were allowed to serve on non-combat ships (Task and Purpose 2017).

In the early 1990s, under the first Bush administration, the United States was involved in the Gulf War (August 2, 1990–February 28, 1991). Congress had just authorized women to fly in combat planes and to serve on combat ships. During the combat phase (referred to as "Desert Storm"), 41,000 military women served. Two were taken prisoner by the Iraqi military. However, in 1994 the Department of Defense announced that women could not serve in units whose primary purpose was on-the-ground combat. No additional changes in policy regarding women's roles in the military occurred until the 21st century (Task and Purpose 2017).

Women in Space

In 1989, Eileen Collins (born 1956) was accepted at the competitive Air Force Test Pilot School at Edwards Air Force Base. In 1990, she became only the second woman to graduate as a test pilot and was selected to be an astronaut by NASA. In February 1995, Collins became the first female astronaut to pilot a space shuttle

---

1. The United States had been involved in the Vietnam conflict since the 1950s, but its involvement escalated in the 1960s. The peak year of U.S. involvement was 1969. A peace agreement was signed in 1973, but fighting continued until approximately 1975.

mission when she served as second-in-command of the shuttle *Discovery*. In 1997, Collins piloted her second mission, on the shuttle *Atlantis*, during its delivery of 7,000 pounds of equipment to the Russian space station *Mir*. When she was chosen by NASA to become its first female shuttle commander, she had already flown over 400 miles in space. Under Collins's command, the space shuttle *Columbia*[2] made history in July 1999, when it blasted off from Cape Canaveral to deliver a $1.5 billion telescope, the Chandra X-ray Observatory, into orbit. Chandra is in a 64-hour orbit around Earth and as of 2017 is still in orbit.

Traditional Gender Roles and Sexual Abstinence in the Bush Era

Republican George W. Bush served as president of the United States from 2001 to 2009, and during his two terms in office, federal policies and priorities took a more socially conservative direction than had been seen during the Clinton administration. Bush described himself as a born-again Christian whose religious beliefs strongly influenced his presidential actions. Bush took an anti-abortion stance, which was accompanied by numerous restrictions on the use of contraception. He continued (or resumed) abstinence-only sex education programs in public schools, which provided little or no information about effective use of contraception. He also instituted or supported existing federal programs that emphasized the importance of heterosexual marriage as a solution to social problems such as poverty and crime. He endorsed marriage among single mothers who were receiving federal assistance, as a way to reduce dependence on welfare. Thus, even though the most dramatic event during his presidency was the attack on the United States on September 11, 2001 (and the resulting prolonged involvement of the U.S. military in the Middle East), the Bush administration also enacted significant policies designed to restore the traditional idea of gender roles, including men's role as fathers, and sexuality only within the confines of heterosexual marriage. Cultural conservatives praised these efforts, but many women's rights activists and other progressive observers expressed concern that some of these changes amounted to a "war on women."

Strengthening Traditional Marriage and Responsible Fatherhood

In his decision regarding the reauthorization of the 1996 welfare reform act, which set forth clear goals designed to increase the number of two-parent families and to reduce out-of-wedlock childbearing, Bush endorsed specific programs that would attempt to further formalize the goals. The original welfare reform that was set in place in the Clinton administration took notice of demographic changes in marriage, divorce, and birth rates. Marriage rates were declining (especially among

---

2. *Columbia*'s last journey was in 2003 when it disintegrated upon reentry, killing all seven astronauts aboard, including Dr. Laurel Salton Clark (1961–2003), a medical doctor who was serving as a mission specialist.

African Americans), divorce rates had stabilized at a high level, and an increasing proportion of babies were born to unmarried mothers. The latter trend was more prominent among African Americans.

Bush embraced the marriage movement's[3] goals and tactics, which included educating young people about the necessity of traditional heterosexual marriage that included a wage-earning husband and father. He created the Healthy Marriage Initiative within the U.S. Department of Health and Human Services' Administration for Children and Families.

Bush attributed many of the problems of low-income neighborhoods to families headed by single mothers whose children's fathers were uninvolved with the children. Irresponsible fathers, from his perspective, were those who did not provide sufficiently for their families and did not serve as appropriate role models or disciplinarians for their children. Also missing were healthy relationships between parents. The Administration for Children and Families funded dozens of organizations across the United States to provide "Responsible Fatherhood" activities to strengthen engagement between fathers and their children, to improve employment and opportunities for economic mobility, and to strengthen relationships between couples who were meant to be co-parenting their children. The Bush administration created the Healthy Marriage and Responsible Fatherhood (HMRF) initiative, allocating $150 million to a discretionary grant program originally authorized under the Deficit Reduction Act of 2005 and reauthorized under the Claims Resolution Act of 2010.

During his first campaign, supporters carried signs and banners that read "W is for Women!" But as his administration unfolded, many of his priorities and policies were designed to undo much of the progress in women's rights that had taken place since the 1970s. In fact, George W. Bush adopted many of the policies that Ronald Reagan had instituted during his presidency in the 1980s. Bush had the support and encouragement of ultraconservative members of the U.S. Congress, who were emerging as a powerful political bloc. The term "war on women," which became a major part of the national conversation about the Republican Party's attempt to curtail women's access to reproductive rights, was coined by Tanya Melich, a conservative Republican, who in 1996 wrote about her party's growing hostility toward modern women.

The Bush administration supported a "Family Time Flexibility Act," declaring that it would give working mothers more flexibility when it came to balancing employment with family responsibilities. In reality, it was directed toward meeting employers' needs rather than employees'. Employers had the legal authority to adjust to their changing needs for labor by extending employees' time off when the need for labor was lower or by paying overtime when the need was greater. This could produce unpredictable work schedules, which are problematic for parents who need to find child care.

---

3. The marriage movement was a coalition of religious groups and intellectuals that sought to restore traditional, heterosexual marriage.

George W. Bush's priorities were also reflected in his restructuring of various departments in the federal government and in the appointments he made to fill positions in those departments. He also authorized deletion of information from government publications (or Web sites) that provided employees with knowledge about their rights. This was particularly noteworthy in the Women's Bureau, a division of the U.S. Department of Labor.

In appointing members to the National Advisory Committee on Violence Against Women, Bush's attorney general, John Ashcroft, named two women from the Independent Women's Forum (IWF), an organization that opposed the Violence Against Women Act (created by Joe Biden in 1993).[4] The Independent Women's Forum also opposed affirmative action; Title IX, which provided for equal educational opportunity; Take Our Daughters to Work Day; and women in combat. Bush appointed a former president and CEO of IWF to be a delegate to the United Nations Commission on the Status of Women. IWF also discounted reports of rape, wage discrimination, domestic violence, and gender bias in schools as false or exaggerated (Ivins 2004).

The (Anti-) Birth Control Revolution of 2000–2009

In the first budget George W. Bush sent to Congress (April 9, 2001), he deleted a clause requiring insurance companies to cover contraceptives for federal employees. House Democrats later reinstated the requirement. But the person Bush appointed as deputy assistant secretary for the Office of Population Affairs (which advised the administration about a wide range of topics related to reproduction) was a member of the Family Research Council, a conservative think tank; she told the *Washington Post* that she and the organization were happy with Bush's attempt to remove the requirement for insurance policies to provide federal employees with birth control coverage because "contraception is not a medical necessity" (Finlay 2006).

Close examination of the material about contraception promulgated by the Bush administration reveals that erroneous information was included. For instance, until the summer of 2002, the National Institutes of Health (NIH) maintained that women who had an abortion were at no greater risk of breast cancer than those who had not undergone the procedure. But under Bush, the NIH released a fact sheet that said the evidence was "unclear." In a similar incident, a Centers for Disease Control and Prevention fact sheet was altered to downplay the effectiveness of condoms in reducing the spread of sexually transmitted diseases. Rep. Henry Waxman and other Democratic lawmakers stated that "information that used to be based on science is being systematically removed from the public when it conflicts with the administration's political agenda" (Finlay 2006).

---

4. The Violence Against Women Act was reauthorized by bipartisan majorities in Congress in 2000, and again in December 2005. It was signed by President Bush.

Bush's Anti-Abortion Stance

Bush's personal stance against abortion influenced many of the United States' international policies. For instance, on his first day in office, he implemented a policy that required nongovernmental organizations (NGOs) receiving federal funds to agree not to perform abortions or to actively promote abortion as a method of family planning in other nations. In 2002, Bush withdrew funding from the United Nations Population Fund because it facilitated China's one-child policy, which frequently involved termination of pregnancies.

President Bush also signed a law that holds that a person who commits certain federal violent crimes and thereby causes the death of, or bodily injury to, a fetus shall be guilty of a separate offense, whether or not the person knew the mother was pregnant or intended to harm the fetus.

Abstinence-Only Sex Ed Policies

The federal government has consistently funded abstinence-only-until-marriage programs since early in the Reagan administration.[5] Funding for these unproven programs grew exponentially from 1996 until 2006, particularly during the years of the George W. Bush administration. As part of the 1996 welfare reform bill, Congress enacted a $50 million per year program to fund abstinence education.

In 2006, the Administration for Children and Families announced a new funding plan and vision for abstinence-only programs. The new promotion program presented sexual abstinence prior to marriage as an approach that would lead to a happier life, including having a healthier marriage and healthier children; earning more money; being honorable and more "responsible" parents; having integrity; attaining a better education; having fewer psychological disorders; avoiding drug, alcohol, and tobacco use; committing fewer crimes and staying out of prison; and having a longer lifespan (SIECUS 2010).

Between 2006 and 2009, funding levels stabilized; in 2010 they declined significantly . Abstinence-only education programs prohibit discussion of contraception, thus failing to provide sexually active teens with information on how to protect themselves from pregnancy and sexually transmitted infections. In some cases, the programs provide misinformation to students.

In 2007, findings from a congressionally mandated study found that federally funded abstinence-only-until-marriage programs (funded under the newer Community-Based Abstinence Education program) had no beneficial impact on young people's sexual behavior. The study, conducted by Mathematica Policy Research over nine years, at a cost of almost $8 million and on behalf of the Department of Health and Human Services, closely examined four of the "most

---

5. The Adolescent Family Life Act (AFLA) was signed into law in 1981 as Title XX of the Public Health Service Act. In addition to providing comprehensive support services to pregnant and parenting teens and their families, AFLA was established to promote "chastity" and "self-discipline."

promising" Community-Based Abstinence Education programs for intensive study. After following more than 2,000 teens for as long as six years, the evaluation found that none of the programs was able to demonstrate a statistically significant beneficial impact on young people's sexual behavior. The Community-Based Abstinence Education program was ended in 2010.

Gender Stereotypes in Abstinence-Only Programs

In addition to their ineffectiveness, abstinence-only programs promote gender stereotypes. Women are portrayed as passive, relational, and relatively unsexual, while men are aggressive, detached, and hypersexual. There is little to no discussion of the ways in which women and men are similar in terms of sexual desires. The contents of abstinence-only curricula are also usually heteronormative (Beechey and Moore 2015).

References

"Anita Hill Talks Feminism, Sexual Harassment, and Clarence Thomas." MSNBC, March 27, 2014. http://www.msnbc.com/msnbc/anita-hill-her-regrets (accessed September 27, 2017).

Beechey, Susanne, and Leah Curran Moore. "Gender in the Adoption and Implementation of Sex Education Policy." *Open Journal of Social Sciences* 3, no. 7 (2015).

Burke, Michael. "Welfare Reform 20 Years Later: What Worked, What Didn't?" *USA Today*, August 21, 2016.

Finlay, Barbara. *George W. Bush and the War on Women: Turning Back the Clock on Progress*. Zed Books, 2006.

Ivins, Molly. "He Loves Us Not: For the Last Four Years, George Bush Has Been Waging a Stealth Campaign against Women." *Mother Jones*, September/October 2004. http://www.motherjones.com/politics/2004/09/he-loves-us-not (accessed September 27, 2017).

Kamarck, Kristy. *Women in Combat: Issues for Congress*. Congressional Research Service, 2016. https://fas.org/sgp/crs/natsec/R42075.pdf (accessed September 27, 2017)

National Aeronautics and Space Administration (NASA). "First American Woman in Space." 2013. https://www.nasa.gov/multimedia/imagegallery/image_feature_2533.html.

Ryan, Michael. "A Ride in Space." *People*, June 23, 1983.

Sexuality and Information Council of the United States (SIECUS). "A History of Federal Abstinence-Only-Until-Marriage Funding FY10." 2010. http://www.siecus.org/index.cfm?fuseaction=page.viewpage&pageid=1340&nodeid=1.

Task and Purpose. "History: A Timeline of Women in the Military." 2017. http://taskandpurpose.com/timeline-history-women-us-military.

A MOMENTOUS SEX DISCRIMINATION RULING IN *UAW V. JOHNSON CONTROLS*, 1991

In 1977 Johnson Controls decided to bar all female employees (except those with medically documented infertility) from working in its battery manufacturing facilities in any position where they might be at risk of exposure to blood lead levels higher than recommended by the Occupational Safety and Health Administration (OSHA). The rationale for this policy was that the company wanted to keep potentially pregnant women employees from excess lead exposure. After Johnson Controls announced this decision, however, women's rights groups and labor organizations warned that if such policies became widespread, millions of women employed in jobs involving exposure to hazardous chemicals and toxins might be at risk of losing their jobs or advancing in their careers.

The United Auto Workers (UAW) subsequently filed a lawsuit against Johnson Controls' policy, charging that the new rule violated gender discrimination protections enshrined in Title VII of the Civil Rights Act of 1964. Both a district court and an appeals court sided with Johnson, but on March 20, 1991, the Supreme Court ruled unanimously that the company's "fetal-protection policy is sex discrimination forbidden under Title VII." The decision was a momentous one, wrote Gillian Thomas, an attorney with the American Civil Liberties Union (ACLU) Women's Rights Project, for it "marked the end of Muller v. Oregon's 'mothers first, workers second' framing of American womanhood. . . . With Johnson Controls, no longer was a woman's biology to be society's destiny; thanks to Title VII, it was returned to her, at least when it came to decisions about how and where she earned a paycheck." Following are excerpts from the Court's decision, which was written by Justice Harry Blackmun.

In this case, we are concerned with an employer's gender-based fetal-protection policy. May an employer exclude a fertile female employee from certain jobs because of its concern for the health of the fetus the woman might conceive?

I

Respondent Johnson Controls, Inc., manufactures batteries. In the manufacturing process, the element lead is a primary ingredient. Occupational exposure to lead entails health risks, including the risk of harm to any fetus carried by a female employee.

Before the Civil Rights Act of 1964, 78 Stat. 241, became law, Johnson Controls did not employ any woman in a battery-manufacturing job. In June, 1977, however, it announced its first official policy concerning its employment of women in lead-exposure work:

"[P]rotection of the health of the unborn child is the immediate and direct responsibility of the prospective parents. While the medical profession and the company can support them in the exercise of this responsibility, it cannot assume it for them without simultaneously infringing their rights as persons."

". . . Since not all women who can become mothers, wish to become mothers, (or will become mothers), it would appear to be illegal discrimination to treat all who are capable of pregnancy as though they will become pregnant."

Consistent with that view, Johnson Controls "stopped short of excluding women capable of bearing children from lead exposure," but emphasized that a woman who expected to have a child should not choose a job in which she would have such exposure. The company also required a woman who wished to be considered for employment to sign a statement that she had been advised of the risk of having a child while she was exposed to lead. The statement informed the woman that, although there was evidence "that women exposed to lead have a higher rate of abortion," this evidence was "not as clear . . . as the relationship between cigarette smoking and cancer," but that it was, "medically speaking, just good sense not to run that risk if you want children and do not want to expose the unborn child to risk, however small. . . ."

Five years later, in 1982, Johnson Controls shifted from a policy of warning to a policy of exclusion. Between 1979 and 1983, eight employees became pregnant while maintaining blood lead levels in excess of 30 micrograms per deciliter. This appeared to be the critical level noted by the Occupational Health and Safety Administration (OSHA) for a worker who was planning to have a family. The company responded by announcing a broad exclusion of women from jobs that exposed them to lead:

". . . [I]t is [Johnson Controls'] policy that women who are pregnant or who are capable of bearing children will not be placed into jobs involving lead exposure or which could expose them to lead through the exercise of job bidding, bumping, transfer or promotion rights."

The policy defined "women . . . capable of bearing children" as "[a]ll women except those whose inability to bear children is medically documented." It further stated that an unacceptable work station was one where, "over the past year," an employee had recorded a blood lead level of more than 30 micrograms per deciliter or the work site had yielded an air sample containing a lead level in excess of 30 micrograms per cubic meter.

II

In April, 1984, petitioners filed in the United States District Court for the Eastern District of Wisconsin a class action challenging Johnson Controls' fetal-protection policy as sex discrimination that violated Title VII of the Civil Rights Act of 1964, as amended, 42 U.S.C. § 2000e *et seq.* Among the individual plaintiffs were petitioners Mary Craig, who had chosen to be sterilized in order to avoid losing her job, Elsie Nason, a 50-year-old divorcee, who had suffered a loss in compensation when she was transferred out of a job where she was exposed to lead, and Donald Penney, who had been denied a request for a leave of absence for the purpose of lowering his lead level because he intended to become a father. Upon stipulation of the parties, the District Court certified a class consisting of "all past, present and future production and maintenance employees" in United Auto Workers bargaining units at nine of Johnson Controls' plants "who have been and continue to be affected by [the employer's] Fetal Protection Policy implemented in 1982."

The District Court granted summary judgment for defendant-respondent Johnson Controls. Applying a three-part business necessity defense derived from fetal-protection cases in the Courts of Appeals for the Fourth and Eleventh Circuits, the District Court concluded that, while "there is a disagreement among the experts regarding the effect of lead on the fetus," the hazard to the fetus through exposure to lead was established by "a considerable body of opinion"; that, although

"[e]xpert opinion has been provided which holds that lead also affects the reproductive abilities of men and women . . . [and] that these effects are as great as the effects of exposure of the fetus . . . a great body of experts are of the opinion that the fetus is more vulnerable to levels of lead that would not affect adults;"

and that petitioners had "failed to establish that there is an acceptable alternative policy which would protect the fetus." The court stated that, in view of this disposition of the business necessity defense, it did not "have to undertake a bona fide occupational qualifications (BFOQ) analysis."

The Court of Appeals for the Seventh Circuit, sitting en banc, affirmed the summary judgment by a 7-to-4 vote. The majority held that the proper standard for evaluating the fetal-protection policy was the defense of business necessity; that Johnson Controls was entitled to summary judgment under that defense; and that, even if the proper standard was a BFOQ, Johnson Controls still was entitled to summary judgment. . . .

With its ruling, the Seventh Circuit became the first Court of Appeals to hold that a fetal-protection policy directed exclusively at women could qualify as a BFOQ. We granted certiorari, to resolve the obvious conflict between the Fourth, Seventh, and Eleventh Circuits on this issue, and to address the important and difficult question whether an employer, seeking to protect potential fetuses, may discriminate against women just because of their ability to become pregnant.

III

The bias in Johnson Controls' policy is obvious. Fertile men, but not fertile women, are given a choice as to whether they wish to risk their reproductive health for a particular job. Section 703(a) of the Civil Rights Act of 1964 prohibits sex-based classifications in terms and conditions of employment, in hiring and discharging decisions, and in other employment decisions that adversely affect an employee's status. Respondent's fetal-protection policy explicitly discriminates against women on the basis of their sex. The policy excludes women with childbearing capacity from lead-exposed jobs, and so creates a facial classification based on gender. Respondent assumes as much in its brief before this Court.

Nevertheless, the Court of Appeals assumed, as did the two appellate courts who already had confronted the issue, that sex-specific fetal-protection policies do not involve facial discrimination. These courts analyzed the policies as though they were facially neutral, and had only a discriminatory effect upon the employment opportunities of women. Consequently, the courts looked to see if each employer in question had established that its policy was justified as a business necessity. The business necessity standard is more lenient for the employer than the statutory BFOQ defense. The Court of Appeals here went one step further and invoked the burden-shifting framework set forth in *Wards Cove Packing Co. v. Atonio* (1989), thus requiring petitioners to bear the burden of persuasion on all questions. The court assumed that, because the asserted reason for the sex-based exclusion (protecting women's unconceived offspring) was ostensibly benign, the policy was not sex-based discrimination. That assumption, however, was incorrect.

First, Johnson Controls' policy classifies on the basis of gender and childbearing capacity, rather than fertility alone. Respondent does not seek to protect the unconceived children of all its employees. Despite evidence in the record about the debilitating effect of lead exposure on the male reproductive system, Johnson Controls is concerned only with the harms that may befall the unborn offspring of its female employees. Accordingly, it appears that Johnson Controls would have lost in the Eleventh Circuit under *Hayes* because its policy does not "effectively and equally protec[t] the offspring of all employees." This Court faced a conceptually similar situation in *Phillips v. Martin Marietta Corp.* (1971), and found sex discrimination because the policy established "one hiring policy for women and another for men—each having pre-school-age children." Johnson Controls' policy is facially discriminatory, because it requires only a female employee to produce proof that she is not capable of reproducing.

Our conclusion is bolstered by the Pregnancy Discrimination Act of 1978 (PDA), in which Congress explicitly provided that, for purposes of Title VII, discrimination "on the basis of sex" includes discrimination "because of or on the basis of pregnancy, childbirth, or related medical conditions."

"The Pregnancy Discrimination Act has now made clear that, for all Title VII purposes, discrimination based on a woman's pregnancy is, on its face, discrimination because of her sex."

In its use of the words "capable of bearing children" in the 1982 policy statement as the criterion for exclusion, Johnson Controls explicitly classifies on the basis of potential for pregnancy. Under the PDA, such a classification must be regarded, for Title VII purposes, in the same light as explicit sex discrimination. Respondent has chosen to treat all its female employees as potentially pregnant; that choice evinces discrimination on the basis of sex.

We concluded above that Johnson Controls' policy is not neutral, because it does not apply to the reproductive capacity of the company's male employees in the same way as it applies to that of the females. Moreover, the absence of a malevolent motive does not convert a facially discriminatory policy into a neutral policy with a discriminatory effect. Whether an employment practice involves disparate treatment through explicit facial discrimination does not depend on why the employer discriminates, but rather on the explicit terms of the discrimination. In

Martin Marietta, supra, the motives underlying the employers' express exclusion of women did not alter the intentionally discriminatory character of the policy. Nor did the arguably benign motives lead to consideration of a business necessity defense. The question in that case was whether the discrimination in question could be justified under § 703(e) as a BFOQ. The beneficence of an employer's purpose does not undermine the conclusion that an explicit gender-based policy is sex discrimination under § 703(a) and thus may be defended only as a BFOQ.
. . .

In sum, Johnson Controls' policy

"does not pass the simple test of whether the evidence shows 'treatment of a person in a manner which, but for that person's sex, would be different.'"

We hold that Johnson Controls' fetal-protection policy is sex discrimination forbidden under Title VII unless respondent can establish that sex is a "bona fide occupational qualification."

IV

Under § 703(e)(1) of Title VII, an employer may discriminate on the basis of "religion, sex, or national origin in those certain instances where religion, sex, or national origin is a bona fide occupational qualification reasonably necessary to the normal operation of that particular business or enterprise."

We therefore turn to the question whether Johnson Controls' fetal-protection policy is one of those "certain instances" that come within the BFOQ exception.

The BFOQ defense is written narrowly, and this Court has read it narrowly. We have read the BFOQ language of § 4(f) of the Age Discrimination in Employment Act of 1967 (ADEA), which tracks the BFOQ provision in Title VII, just as narrowly. Our emphasis on the restrictive scope of the BFOQ defense is grounded on both the language and the legislative history of § 703.

The wording of the BFOQ defense contains several terms of restriction that indicate that the exception reaches only special situations. The statute thus limits the situations in which discrimination is permissible to "certain instances" where sex discrimination is "reasonably necessary" to the "normal operation" of the "particular" business. Each one of these terms—certain, normal, particular—prevents the use of general subjective standards and favors an objective, verifiable requirement. But the most telling term is "occupational"; this indicates that these objective, verifiable requirements must concern job-related skills and aptitudes. . . .

Johnson Controls argues that its fetal-protection policy falls within the so-called safety exception to the BFOQ. Our cases have stressed that discrimination on the basis of sex because of safety concerns is allowed only in narrow circumstances. In *Dothard v. Rawlinson,* this Court indicated that danger to a woman herself does not justify discrimination. We there allowed the employer to hire only male guards in contact areas of maximum-security male penitentiaries only because more was at stake than the "individual woman's decision to weigh and accept the risks of employment." We found sex to be a BFOQ inasmuch as the employment of a female guard would create real risks of safety to others if violence broke out because the guard was a woman. Sex discrimination was tolerated because sex was related to the guard's ability to do the job—maintaining prison security. We also required in *Dothard* a high correlation between sex and ability to perform job functions, and refused to allow employers to use sex as a proxy for strength although it might be a fairly accurate one.

Similarly, some courts have approved airlines' layoffs of pregnant flight attendants at different points during the first five months of pregnancy on the ground that the employer's policy was necessary to ensure the safety of passengers. In two of these cases, the courts pointedly indicated that fetal, as opposed to passenger, safety was best left to the mother. We considered safety to third parties in *Western Airlines, Inc. v. Criswell, supra*, in the context of the ADEA. We focused upon "the nature of the flight engineer's tasks," and the "actual capabilities of persons over age 60" in relation to those tasks. Our safety concerns were not independent of the individual's ability to perform the assigned tasks, but rather involved the possibility that, because of age-connected debility, a flight engineer might not properly assist the pilot, and might thereby cause a safety emergency. Furthermore, although we considered the safety of third parties in *Dothard* and *Criswell*, those third parties were indispensable to the particular business at issue. In *Dothard*, the third parties were the inmates; in *Criswell*, the third parties were the passengers on the plane. We stressed that, in order to qualify as a BFOQ, a job qualification must relate to the "essence," or to the "central mission of the employer's business." . . .

The unconceived fetuses of Johnson Controls' female employees, however, are neither customers nor third parties whose safety is essential to the business of battery manufacturing. No one can disregard the possibility of injury to future children; the BFOQ, however, is not so broad that it transforms this deep social concern into an essential aspect of battery-making.

Our case law, therefore, makes clear that the safety exception is limited to instances in which sex or pregnancy actually interferes with the employee's ability to perform the job. This approach is consistent with the language of the BFOQ provision itself, for it suggests that permissible distinctions based on sex must relate to ability to perform the duties of the job. Johnson Controls suggests, however, that we expand the exception to allow fetal-protection policies that mandate particular standards for pregnant or fertile women. We decline to do so. Such an expansion contradicts not only the language of the BFOQ and the narrowness of its exception, but the plain language and history of the Pregnancy Discrimination Act.

The PDA's amendment to Title VII contains a BFOQ standard of its own: unless pregnant employees differ from others "in their ability or inability to work," they must be "treated the same" as other employees "for all employment-related purposes." This language clearly sets forth Congress' remedy for discrimination on the basis of pregnancy and potential pregnancy. Women who are either pregnant or potentially pregnant must be treated like others "similar in their ability . . . to work." In other words, women as capable of doing their jobs as their male counterparts may not be forced to choose between having a child and having a job. . . .

Employment late in pregnancy often imposes risks on the unborn child, but Congress indicated that the employer may take into account only the woman's ability to get her job done. With the PDA, Congress made clear that the decision to become pregnant or to work while being either pregnant or capable of becoming pregnant was reserved for each individual woman to make for herself.

We conclude that the language of both the BFOQ provision and the PDA which amended it, as well as the legislative history and the case law, prohibit an employer from discriminating against a woman because of her capacity to become pregnant unless her reproductive potential prevents her from performing the duties of her job. We reiterate our holdings in *Criswell* and *Dothard* that an employer must direct its concerns about a woman's ability to perform her job safely and efficiently to those aspects of the woman's job-related activities that fall within the "essence" of the particular business.

V

We have no difficulty concluding that Johnson Controls cannot establish a BFOQ. Fertile women, as far as appears in the record, participate in the manufacture of batteries as efficiently as anyone else. Johnson Controls' professed moral and ethical concerns about the welfare of the next generation do not suffice to establish a BFOQ of female sterility. Decisions about the welfare of future children must be left to the parents who conceive, bear, support, and raise them, rather than to the employers who hire those parents. Congress has mandated this choice through Title VII, as amended by the PDA. Johnson Controls has attempted to exclude women because of their reproductive capacity. Title VII and the PDA simply do not allow a woman's dismissal because of her failure to submit to sterilization.

Nor can concerns about the welfare of the next generation be considered a part of the "essence" of Johnson Controls' business. Judge Easterbrook in this case pertinently observed:

"It is word play to say that 'the job' at Johnson [Controls] is to make batteries without risk to fetuses in the same way 'the job' at Western Air Lines is to fly planes without crashing."

Johnson Controls argues that it must exclude all fertile women because it is impossible to tell which women will become pregnant while working with lead. This argument is somewhat academic in light of our conclusion that the company may not exclude fertile women at all; it perhaps is worth noting, however, that Johnson Controls has shown no "factual basis for believing that all or substantially all women would be unable to perform safely and efficiently the duties of the job involved."

Even on this sparse record, it is apparent that Johnson Controls is concerned about only a small minority of women. Of the eight pregnancies reported among the female employees, it has not been shown that any of the babies have birth defects or other abnormalities. The record does not reveal the birth rate for Johnson Controls' female workers, but national statistics show that approximately nine percent of all fertile women become pregnant each year. The birth rate drops to two percent for blue collar workers over age 30. Johnson Controls' fear of prenatal injury, no matter how sincere, does not begin to show that substantially all of its fertile women employees are incapable of doing their jobs.

VI

A word about tort liability and the increased cost of fertile women in the workplace is perhaps necessary. One of the dissenting judges in this case expressed concern about an employer's tort liability, and concluded that liability for a potential injury to a fetus is a social cost that Title VII does not require a company to ignore. It is correct to say that Title VII does not prevent the employer from having a conscience. The statute, however, does prevent sex-specific fetal-protection policies. These two aspects of Title VII do not conflict.

More than 40 States currently recognize a right to recover for a prenatal injury based either on negligence or on wrongful death. According to Johnson Controls, however, the company complies with the lead standard developed by OSHA and warns its female employees about the damaging effects of lead. It is worth noting that OSHA gave the problem of lead lengthy consideration, and concluded that

"there is no basis whatsoever for the claim that women of childbearing age should be excluded from the workplace in order to protect the fetus or the course of pregnancy."

Instead, OSHA established a series of mandatory protections which, taken together, "should effectively minimize any risk to the fetus and newborn child." Without negligence, it would be difficult for a court to find liability on the part of the employer. If, under general tort principles, Title VII bans sex-specific fetal-protection policies, the employer fully informs the woman of the risk, and the employer has not acted negligently, the basis for holding an employer liable seems remote, at best. . . .

The tort liability argument reduces to two equally unpersuasive propositions. First, Johnson Controls attempts to solve the problem of reproductive health hazards by resorting to an exclusionary policy. Title VII plainly forbids illegal sex discrimination as a method of diverting attention from an employer's obligation to police the workplace. Second, the spectre of an award of damages reflects a fear that hiring fertile women will cost more. The extra cost of employing members of one sex, however, does not provide an affirmative Title VII defense for a discriminatory refusal to hire members of that gender. Indeed, in passing the PDA, Congress considered at length the considerable cost of providing equal treatment of pregnancy and related conditions, but made the "decision to forbid special treatment of pregnancy despite the social costs associated therewith."

We, of course, are not presented with, nor do we decide, a case in which costs would be so prohibitive as to threaten the survival of the employer's business. We merely reiterate our prior holdings that the incremental cost of hiring women cannot justify discriminating against them.

VII

Our holding today that Title VII, as so amended, forbids sex-specific fetal-protection policies is neither remarkable nor unprecedented. Concern for a woman's existing or potential offspring historically has been the excuse for denying women equal employment opportunities. Congress in the PDA prohibited discrimination on the basis of a woman's ability to become pregnant. We do no more than hold that the Pregnancy Discrimination Act means what it says.

It is no more appropriate for the courts than it is for individual employers to decide whether a woman's reproductive role is more important to herself and her family than her economic role. Congress has left this choice to the woman as hers to make.

The judgment of the Court of Appeals is reversed, and the case is remanded for further proceedings consistent with this opinion.

It is so ordered.

Source: *United Automobile Workers v. Johnson Controls*, 499 U.S. 187 (1991).

"WE'RE NOT A FAD": WOMEN MAKE INROADS IN CONGRESS, 1992–2002

During the 1990s, the U.S. Congress and many statehouses across the nation saw a surge in women members. This rapid growth in political representation changed political priorities, campaign messaging, and policy prescriptions at both the state and federal levels. The following overview of this momentous decade for women's political empowerment is excerpted from an exhibit of the U.S. House of Representatives history and archives department called "Women in Congress, 1992–2002."

On election Tuesday 1992, American voters sent as many new women to Congress as were elected in any previous decade, beginning a decade of unparalleled gains for women in Congress. In November 2002, women attained another historic milestone when the House Democratic Caucus elected 15-year veteran Nancy Pelosi of California as Democratic Leader—making her the highest ranking woman in congressional history.

Expectations for a "breakthrough" year for women had been high since the late 1970s; in fact, 1984 had been hopefully, but prematurely, advertised as the "Year of the Woman." Political observers discussed the rise of a "gender gap," predicting that 6 million more women than men would vote in the 1984 elections. When Congresswoman Geraldine Ferraro of New York was chosen as the Democratic candidate for Vice President that year—the first woman to appear on a major party ticket—expectations soared for a strong turnout by women at the polls. Jan Meyers of Kansas, one of a group of women running for national office in 1984, credited Ferraro's high profile with having "a very positive impact" on her campaign in suburban Kansas City for a House seat. Ferraro put women in the headlines, increased their credibility, and forced the Republican Party to focus on women voters, Meyers said shortly after winning a seat in Congress. Some expected women to vote as a bloc on the hot-button issues that were important to them—reproductive rights, economic equality, and health care; the emergence of a women's voting bloc had been predicted since the passage of the 19th Amendment. But this bloc failed to materialize in 1984, and Ferraro and Democratic presidential candidate Walter Mondale of Minnesota lost in a landslide to the incumbent President Reagan.

In 1992, women went to the polls, energized by a record-breaking number of women on the federal ticket. The results were unprecedented; the 24 women who won election to the U.S. House of Representatives for the first time that November comprised the largest number elected to the House in any single election, and the women elected to the Senate tripled the number of women in that chamber. Dubbed the "Year of the Woman," 1992 also marked the beginning of a decade of remarkable gains for minority women. Twenty-three of the 34 African-American, Hispanic-American, and Asian-Pacific-American women who have served in Congress were elected between 1992 and 2005.

California's 1992 congressional races were a microcosm of the changes beginning to take place nationally. During the 102nd Congress, from 1991 to 1993, women held three seats on the California congressional delegation—roughly 6 percent. In 1992, a record 71 California women were nominated to run in the fall elections for federal and state offices; nationally 11 women won major party nominations for Senate races, while 106 women contended for House seats in the general election. "The days of cold lonely fights of the '60s and '70s, when women were often laughed at as we tried to push for new opportunities, are over," said Lynn Schenk, a congressional candidate from San Diego. "No one's laughing now. If people truly want someone to be an agent of change, I'm that person. And being a woman is part of that." Five new women Members from California, including Schenk, were elected to the House in the fall of 1992 alone. Two others, Representative Barbara Boxer and former San Francisco Mayor Dianne Feinstein, won election as U.S. Senators, making California the first state with two women in the Senate. By the 109th Congress in 2005, 21 members of the California congressional delegation were women—38 percent of the state's total representation in Congress.

Women's impressive gains in 1992 were not the product of any one galvanizing event, but rather the confluence of several long-term trends and short-term election year issues. Demographics, global politics, scandal, and the ripple effect of the women's liberation movement all played a part in the results of that historic election.

In 1992, the incumbent candidates faced a tougher-than-usual contest for re-election. An economic downturn that had begun in 1991 was predicted to be the leading edge of a long-term recession. American business mired as the country transitioned to a peace-time economy after the fall of the Soviet Union and the end of the Cold War. The national focus shifted from the Soviet–American conflict and national security to areas where women's influence was more established—education, health care, welfare reform, and the economy. While Americans worried about their jobs, they watched apprehensively the resurgent Japanese economy and the reunification of Germany. The check-writing scandal in the House "bank" (operated by the Sergeant at Arms), where a large number of Representatives had overdrawn their accounts—in some cases on hundreds of occasions—also contributed to the anti-incumbent sentiment within the electorate that disdained business-as-usual politics in Washington. Moreover, the debate over the abortion issue had reached a divisive point, with a pro-life President in the White House and the Supreme Court considering a ruling that could have reversed *Roe v. Wade*.

The issue of whom President George H. W. Bush's administration would appoint to replace retiring Supreme Court Justice Thurgood Marshall became a galvanizing one for women candidates. Bush nominated Clarence Thomas, a conservative he had earlier appointed to the U.S. Court of Appeals. Thomas's antiabortion stance, as well as his opposition to affirmative action, made him a lightning rod for liberal groups and Democratic Senators. But his confirmation hearings became a public forum on sexual harassment in the workplace when Thomas's former aide Anita Hill accused him in televised hearings before the Senate Judiciary Committee of making unwanted advances. Beamed into millions of homes, the spectacle of the all-male Judiciary Committee offering Hill little sympathy and at moments treating her with outright hostility reinforced the perception that women's perspectives received short shrift on Capitol Hill. Seven Democratic women from the House marched in protest to address the caucus of their Democratic Senate colleagues, but they were rebuffed.

While controversy stirred by the Thomas–Hill episode provided good campaign rhetoric and a convenient media explanation for the "Year of the Woman," other contributing factors included the availability of funding, the growing pool of women candidates with elective experience, and the presence of a Democratic presidential candidate, who shared their beliefs on many of the issues (24 of the 27 women elected that fall were Democrats). Also significant were the effects of redistricting after the 1990 Census, the large number of retiring Members, and the casualties of the House banking scandal; the combination of these effects created 93 open seats in the U.S. House during the 1992 elections. Candidates of both genders embraced the popular theme of change in government by stressing their credentials as Washington outsiders, but women benefited more from this perception, because they had long been marginalized in the Washington political process. As Elizabeth Furse, a successful candidate for an Oregon House seat, pointed out during her campaign: "People see women as agents of change. Women are seen as outsiders, outside the good old boy network which people are perceiving has caused so many of the economic problems we see today."

For all the media attention paid to the "Year of the Woman," it was but a part of the larger trend of women's movement into elective office. A number of women expressed exasperation with the media focus that hyped the sensational news story but largely ignored more enduring trends and influences. "The year of the woman in retrospect was a small gain, but it was the start of what was a big gain," Senator Barbara Boxer observed a decade later. "I don't even think it was the year of the woman then, but it started the trend of electing more women." Others felt the label diminished women's achievement and reinforced perceptions that their impact on Congress was temporary. As Senator Barbara Mikulski of Maryland said: "Calling 1992 the Year of the Woman makes it sound like the Year of the Caribou or the Year of the Asparagus. We're not a fad, a fancy, or a year."

The trend that culminated in the 1990s had begun decades earlier in the state legislatures, where women began to accumulate political experience that prepared them to be legislators. The first Congresswoman with elective experience in a state legislature was Kathryn O'Loughlin McCarthy of Kansas. For decades McCarthy proved the exception to the rule; between her election to Congress in 1932 and 1970, when greater numbers of women began to serve in state capitols, hardly more than a dozen Congresswomen had held a seat in the state legislature or a statewide elective office. It was only in the last 30 years of the 20th century that women made significant gains in state legislatures and, subsequently, the U.S. Congress. For example, in 1970 women held about four percent (301 seats) of all the seats in state legislatures nationwide. In 1997 that figure plateaued at around 1,600, and for the next five years women made up about 22 percent of state legislators nationally. In 2003, 1,648 (22.3 percent) of the 7,382 state legislators in the United States were women.

Ultimately, however, the "Year of the Woman" spawned expectations that women candidates in subsequent elections could not realistically meet. Contrary to widely held beliefs, women were not about to change the political culture overnight—especially not on seniority-based Capitol Hill. Later political battles over issues such as reproductive rights, welfare reform, and the federal deficit dashed hopes that women would unite across party lines, subordinate ideology to pragmatism, and increase their power.

Moreover, the belief that sexism would be eradicated proved overly optimistic, as old stereotypes persisted. Along with Representatives Barbara Boxer and Marcy Kaptur of Ohio, Mary Rose Oakar of Ohio led a 1985 protest of House women demanding equal access to the House gym and fitness facilities. Unhappy that the women's gym lacked the modern exercise equipment, swimming pool, and basketball court accessible to the male Members, the three lawmakers made their pitch in a song belted out to the tune of "Has Anyone Seen My Gal?" before a meeting of the House Democratic Whips. However, women still contended with unequal access to gym facilities and other indications of sexism. Once when fellow freshman Leslie Byrne of Virginia entered an elevator full of Members, a Congressman remarked, "It sure is nice to have you ladies here. It spiffs up the place." Exasperated, Byrne quipped, "Yup, chicks in Congress." Another Member of the class of '92 observed that Congress had failed to keep pace with changes in American society. "Out in the real world, we took care of a lot of these basic issues between men and women years ago," said Lynn Schenk. "But this place has been so insulated, the shock waves of the '70s and '80s haven't quite made it through the walls."

After the 1992 elections, women Members were still in a distinct minority, although for the first time in congressional history they accounted for more than 10 percent of the total membership. Subsequent growth was slower, though steady.

On average since 1992, 10 new women have been elected to Congress each election cycle, while incumbency rates have remained well above 90 percent. In August 2005, women made up 15.5 percent of Congress—an all-time high. Some women noted that although they had failed to achieve numerical parity in Congress, they had dramatically altered the political culture within the electorate. "In previous years, when I have run for office, I always had to overcome being a woman," said Texas Senator Kay Bailey Hutchison. "All I've ever wanted was an equal chance to make my case, and I think we're getting to that point—and that's the victory."

Committee and Party Leadership

The women who entered office in record numbers in the 1990s soon accrued seniority in committees and catapulted into top leadership posts. This trend ran counter to historical precedent, although arguably the most powerful and influential woman to head a committee was one of the first: Mary T. Norton chaired four House committees during the 1930s and 1940s—Labor, House Administration, District of Columbia, and Memorials. However, Norton's experience was unusual and, tellingly, she never held a top leadership job in the Democratic Party during her 25 years in the House. As late as the spring of 1992, the iconic feminist Congresswoman Pat Schroeder observed that the wheels of sexual equality on Capitol Hill turned slowly. "It's not revolutionary, it's evolutionary," Schroeder said. "We get some appointments, we get some this, we get some that. But to think that women get any power positions, that we've become the bull elephants, that we're the kahunas or whatever, well, we're not."

Unlike the third generation of women in Congress, the fourth generation often chose to confront the institution less directly. Whereas Bella Abzug's generation worked against the congressional establishment to breach gender barriers, many women in the fourth generation worked for change from within the power structure. Women in the 1980s and early 1990s who moved into leadership posts did so largely by working within traditional boundaries—a time-honored approach that extended back to Mary Norton and Edith Nourse Rogers in the first generation of Congresswomen. The careers of Lynn Martin and Barbara Kennelly of Connecticut illustrate this tendency: Martin served as Vice Chair of the GOP Conference; Kennelly served as the Democratic Party's Chief Deputy Whip (a position created for her) and eventually became Vice Chair of the Democratic Caucus. Congresswoman Geraldine Ferraro also possessed an ability to work with the House leadership, particularly Speaker Tip O'Neill of Massachusetts, in a way her male colleagues perceived as "nonthreatening." As Ferraro's colleague Marge Roukema observed, Ferraro "takes a feminist stand but works only within the art of the possible." The Congresswoman's pragmatism struck a balance that was pleasing to both Capitol Hill insiders and feminists. Betty Friedan, founder of NOW, judged that Ferraro was "no cream puff; she's a tough dame." Other women who were influential in their parties followed a similarly pragmatic approach. "I worry about marginalizing women in the institution," said freshman Rosa DeLauro of

Connecticut in 1992. "It's a very competitive place, and what you need to do is build coalitions, and since there are 29 women who don't think alike, you build coalitions among women, and you build coalitions among men. If you sit there and say, 'I'm a woman, we're in the minority here,' then you're never going to get anywhere in this body."

Nevertheless, until 1992, women had been on the margins of institutional leadership. Fewer than 10 women had chaired full congressional committees, and just eight House and Senate women had held positions in the party leadership. The two highest-ranking women in the House were still at a considerable remove from the levers of power: Mary Rose Oakar was Vice Chair of the Democratic Caucus and Lynn Martin was Vice Chair of the Republican Conference in the 99th and the 100th Congresses (1985–1989). The highest-ranking woman in Senate history was Margaret Chase Smith of Maine, whom GOP peers elected Chair of the Republican Conference in the 90th through the 92nd Congresses (1967–1973).

Three women led committees in the 104th Congress (1995–1997): Jan Meyers chaired the House Small Business Committee, Nancy Johnson chaired the House Committee on Standards of Official Conduct, and Nancy Landon Kassebaum chaired the Senate Labor and Human Resources Committee. Kassebaum's post was particularly noteworthy, as she was the first woman in Senate history to head a major standing committee. However, by the end of the 104th Congress, Meyers, Johnson, and Kassebaum had either left their posts or retired from Congress. The only other women to chair congressional committees during this period were Senators Olympia Snowe (Small Business) and Susan Collins (Governmental Affairs) in the 108th and 109th Congresses (2003–2007).

But gradual changes in the 1990s had begun to alter the leadership makeup in ways that portended greater involvement for women. From the 103rd through the 108th Congresses (1993–2005), 12 more women moved into the leadership ranks. Representatives Susan Molinari, Jennifer Dunn of Washington, Tillie Fowler of Florida, and Deborah Pryce of Ohio served as the Vice Chair of the House Republican Conference from the 104th through the 107th Congresses, respectively. In the 108th Congress, Pryce, who first won election to Congress in the "Year of the Woman," became the highest-ranking woman in House GOP history when she was elected Chair of the Republican Conference. Her accomplishment was exceeded only by that of Congresswoman Nancy Pelosi of California, who had succeeded Representative Sala Burton of California in the House after her death in 1987. In 2001, Pelosi won the Democratic Caucus contest for Whip. Little more than a year later, when Representative Dick Gephardt of Missouri left the Democratic Party's top post, Pelosi overwhelmingly won her colleagues' support in her bid to become House Democratic Leader. This event garnered national and international attention.

Meanwhile, many of the women elected in the 1990s accrued seniority and, as a result, more important committee assignments. Though not yet apparent in the chairmanships of full committees, this power shift was evident in the chairmanships of subcommittees—a key prerequisite for chairing a full committee. Since the 80th Congress (1947–1949)—the first Congress for which such records are readily accessible—54 women have chaired House or Senate subcommittees. Three women—Margaret Chase Smith, Barbara Mikulski and Barbara Boxer—chaired subcommittees in both the House and the Senate. While just two women—Representatives Smith and Bolton—chaired House subcommittees in the 80th Congress (there were no women chairing Senate subcommittees at the time), by the 109th Congress in 2005, 10 women chaired subcommittees in the House and the Senate. More telling, roughly half the women in congressional history who chaired subcommittees attained these posts after 1992.

Representatives Pelosi and Pryce were on the leading edge of the spike in women elected to Congress. Pryce was elected to Congress at age 41 and attained her leadership post at 51. Pelosi arrived in the House at age 47 and was elected House Democratic Leader at 62. Behind these two leaders are a host of women who were elected in the latter 1990s. When elected, some of these women were 10 years younger than Pelosi and Pryce upon their arrival in Congress, giving them additional tenure to accrue seniority and power. If present trends continue and more and younger women are elected to Congress, women will likely become better represented in high committee posts and the leadership.

Source: Office of the Historian, U.S. House of Representatives, "The Decade of Women, 1992–2002" and "Committee and Party Leadership." Available online at http://history.house.gov/Exhibitions-and-Publications/WIC/Historical-Essays/Assembling-Amplifying-Ascending/Women-Decade and http://history.house.gov/Exhibitions-and-Publications/WIC/Historical-Essays/Assembling-Amplifying-Ascending/Leadership.

PRESIDENT CLINTON PRAISES WOMEN SERVING IN THE U.S. MILITARY, 1995

For roughly the first century and a half of America's history, women did not officially serve in the military, although several hundred fought in unofficial capacities—such as disguised as men—in the Civil War, and others supported various war efforts with cooking, laundry, and nursing. During World War I, however, both the U.S. Navy and Marine Corps allowed women to enlist. More than 25,000 women served their country in Europe or at home as nurses or in other support capacities. The presence of women in the U.S. military expanded again during World War II, when about 350,000 women served in the armed forces, most visibly as nurses but also in a range of clerical, driving, and other support roles.

The feminist movement of the 1960s and 1970s helped women make further inroads into areas of the U.S. military that had historically been closed to them. In the late 1970s the U.S. Coast Guard allowed women to serve in any position, and during the 1991 Gulf War, several historic firsts were recorded. During that conflict, Congress removed the ban on female pilots in combat, and women served in integrated units with men within a designated war zone. All told, more than 40,000 American women served in the Gulf War. In 1993, Congress passed a law allowing women to serve on U.S. Navy combat vessels.

In all of those conflicts of the 20th Century, American women gave their lives in service to their country. In belated recognition of that fact—as well as the service rendered by all women veterans—the United States in the mid-1980s approved plans for a memorial to honor all American servicewomen. The groundbreaking ceremony for this memorial was held at Arlington National Cemetery in Virginia on June 22, 1995. Following are excerpts from the remarks of President Bill Clinton (1946–) at the ceremony.

To all the remarkable servicewomen who surround me here, out in the audience and on the podium, let me say to all of you: Thank you for your service to America. We are all proud to be here to break ground on a memorial that will recognize a contribution that you have made far beyond the call of duty.

Women have been in our service, as has been said, since George Washington's troops fought for independence, clothing and feeding our troops and binding their wounds. They were in the struggle to preserve the Union as cooks and tailors, couriers and scouts, even as spies and saboteurs. Some were so determined to fight for what they believed that they masqueraded as men and took up arms.

Women were there during the two World Wars, and slowly, our military establishment that for decades had sought to limit women's roles brought them in to serve as WACS and WAVES, SPARS and WASPS and Women Marines. In our Nation's shipyards and factories, women helped to build democracy's arsenal. From the beaches of Normandy to the Pacific Islands, they endured bombs, torpedoes, disease, deprivation to support our fighting forces.

Despite this history of bravery and accomplishment, for very much too long women were treated as second class soldiers. They could give their lives for liberty, but they couldn't give orders to men. They could heal the wounded and hold the dying, but they could not dream of holding the highest ranks. They could take on the toughest assignments, but they could not take up arms. Still, they volunteered, fighting for freedom all around the world but also fighting for the right to serve to the fullest of their potential. And from conflict to conflict, from Korea to Vietnam to the Persian Gulf, slowly, women have overcome the barriers to their full service to America.

The past few decades have witnessed a remarkable series of firsts: the first woman company commander, the first female service academy graduate, the first woman skipper, the first female fighter pilot, the firsts that are here with us today. Twenty-five years ago this month, Anna Mae McCabe Hays became the first woman promoted to general. Hazel Johnson-Brown was the first minority woman to reach that rank. And 2 years ago, it was my honor to nominate the Secretary of the Air Force, Sheila Widnall, to become the first woman to head one of our service branches. I am honored to be with all of them today.

But just as important as these firsts are those who have followed them, proving that they were not an accident or an aberration, for women today are test pilots and drill sergeants, squadron commanders and admirals, academy instructors and service recruiters. I am very proud of the fact that during our administration almost 260,000 new positions in the military have been opened to women who wish to serve.

And I might say that this is a tribute not only to the women in the service but to the men in leadership positions who had the wisdom and the understanding and the ability to proceed with this remarkable transformation and strengthening of our military in a climate of tolerance and teamwork and respect. I know of no other institution in our society which could have accomplished so much in such an incredibly efficient and humane and professional way. And so we should be proud of all who played a role in that.

And let me say, before I go further, our Nation, as you know, is involved now in a great debate over the subject of affirmative action. Before people rush to judgment, I would like to remind all Americans that the United States military is the strongest in the world because it has found a way to make the most of the talents of every American without regard to gender or race. And as a nation, we must continue to search for ways to make the most of the talents of every American without regard to gender or race.

There are so many individual stories, the stories that this memorial will tell. But in their detail and drama, they help us understand more of what has occurred than the speeches we can give. Some of these women are here today, and I would like to ask them to stand:

Women like June Wandrey Mann, who volunteered for the Army Nurse Corps in the Second World War, who served 2 1/2 years overseas, from primitive field hospitals in Tunisia and Italy to a center for concentration camp survivors outside of Munich. In her courage and caring, Lieutenant Wandrey represents the best of America. Would you please stand. [*Applause*] Thank you. And I might add, you still look terrific in your uniform.

Women like Charity Adams Earley, who was mentioned earlier, the Women's Army Corps' first African-American officer. Along with thousands of other African-American veterans, both men and women, she helped our Nation act on a truth too long denied, that if people of different races could serve as brothers and sisters abroad, surely they could learn to live together as neighbors at home. Colonel, would you please stand. [*Applause.*] And I might add, she gives a resounding speech.

Women like U.S. Air Force Captain Teresa Allen Steith of the 60th Air Mobility Wing from Travis Air Force Base in California, who was among our first soldiers to set down in Haiti last year and who for 3 months helped planes and troops and cargo move in and out of the Port-au-Prince airport. Because she and the rest of our troops did their job so well, the people of Haiti now, remarkably, have a second chance at democracy. And this Sunday, this Sunday, they will be going to the polls to exercise their newfound rights for the first time in 5 years. And this time, they won't be stolen from them, thanks to people like you, Captain. Thank you very much, and God bless you.

Women like Barbara Allen Rainey, the mother of two daughters, the Navy's first female aviator, tragically the victim of a training crash. Her story reminds us that even in peacetime, those who wear the uniform face danger every day. Now she rests just behind me in the quiet of these sacred grounds.

This memorial will tell the stories of these women and hundreds of thousands more. It makes a long overdue downpayment on a debt that we will never fully repay, a debt we owe to generations of American women in uniform who gave and continue to give so much to our country, and a debt we owe yet to future generations of women who will in the future dedicate their own lives to the defense of our freedom.

May this memorial say to each and every one of them: We cherish your devotion; we admire your courage; we thank you for your service.

God bless you, and God bless America.

Source: Clinton, William. "Remarks at the Groundbreaking Ceremony for the Women in the Military Service Memorial in Arlington, Virginia, June 22, 1995." *Public Papers of the Presidents of the United States: William J. Clinton (1995, Book I).* Washington, DC: Government Printing Office, 1995, pp. 917–919.

DEBATING TITLE IX'S IMPACT ON COLLEGIATE ATHLETES, 1995

More than two decades after Title IX swept across American college campuses in the early 1970s, its impact was still being hotly debated. In many cases, opponents claimed that the gains being registered by women athletes were unfairly coming at the expense of their male counterparts, while advocates asserted that although Title IX had closed the gender inequality gap in university athletics, men's programs continued to enjoy favored status. These and other common talking points of the two sides can be seen in the following dueling testimonies at a congressional hearing specifically called in 1995 to examine whether Title IX was living up to expectations and whether it was having a deleterious impact on men's athletics—and especially popular and financially lucrative men's sports such as football and basketball. Speaking in support of the legislation are Christine H. B. Grant (1936–), representative for the National Association of Collegiate Women Athletics Administrators, and Wendy Hilliard, president of the Women's Sports Foundation. Speaking out against Title IX is T. J. Kerr (1949–2013), president of the National Wrestling Coaches Association.

Statement of Christine H. B. Grant

. . . From the late 1800s until 1972, men at the intercollegiate level enjoyed all of the varsity participation slots in the nation, opportunities often financially supported by both institutional funds as well as student fees from both male and female students. Thus, at many institutions, women were not only denied the opportunity to participate in varsity sports, they were also required to financially support the athletic opportunities for men! Any woman who desired to participate in club sports (the highest level of sport available to women) then had to pay for these opportunities out of their pockets again. Of course, men in varsity sports had all expenditures paid for them and, in addition, most received a totally free education, which today costs anywhere up to $100,000 each.

Although Title IX passed 23 years ago, men still command the lion's share of all sporting opportunities. The 1992 NCAA Gender Equity Study shows that women received only 29% of the participation opportunities and 28% of all athletic scholarships. In most instances student fees from women undergraduates are still used to support more than twice as many participation slots for men as women. Would such biased practices be accepted in any other area of our universities? I think not. What an injustice! What a farce it makes of both the letter and the spirit of federal law!

Rather than having hearings to determine how to protect football, our Congress should be having hearings on what must be done immediately to end these discriminatory practices at all levels of our educational institutions that are, supposedly, equally committed to both young women and young men. We are not talking about professional sport here; we are talking about giving youngsters an equal opportunity to experience the joys, the challenges, and the educational lessons of sport that directly contribute to their growth and development as people.

I primarily fault the Chief Executive Officers at our educational institutions for the current situation. For more than two decades, they have known the requirements of the Federal law and could have moved gradually into compliance. Far too many chose to take as long as they could to do as little as possible. In recent years, there has been a resurgence of a demand by female student-athletes for equal opportunities, coinciding with a time in which most universities found themselves in financial difficulties. Many hoped that the CEOS, through the NCAA Presidents Commission, would mandate cost-containment measures in intercollegiate athletics, especially in Division I. They could have eliminated the excesses in football and men's basketball and demanded reform of our costly recruiting system. On a national level, we could, for example, prohibit these teams from staying in hotels the night before home games; we could also drastically reduce their flashy 200-page media guides. These are but two examples of practices which cause 73% of the entire men's budget to go to these two sports. Through a proactive stance, the CEOs could have averted the current situation which now pits men's minor sports against women's sports (the have-nots against the have-nots), leaving intact enormous football and basketball expenditures and deficits. Blaming gender equity for the demise of men's minor sports is a red herring; they are being dropped because CEOs will not address the problem of habitual excessive spending, either on the institutional or the national level.

Although few schools have achieved compliance with Federal law, it can be done. I am happy to share with you an impressive list of institutions that have made the commitment to equal opportunity and are progressing toward that goal without dropping men's sports. The list reveals that lack of opportunity, not lack of interest, has kept women from participating in intercollegiate athletics. . . .

Given the facts I have presented today coupled with the additional data in my written testimony, it is preposterous for us to be considering anything other than expanding the opportunities for women to participate in sport. Equitable sporting opportunities for women can and must be realized, or none of us will be able to look our daughters or granddaughters in the eye to explain "why not."

Statement of T. J. Kerr

The NWCA (National Wrestling Coaches Association) is the voice of all wrestling coaches in the country. I shall also attempt to speak on behalf of all the young male athletes in this nation and their parents.

While we firmly agree with the letter and spirit of Title IX, we are firmly committed to the proposition that it is unconscionable to eliminate male programs or male athletes to satisfy a gender quota. Both the OCR [Office for Civil Rights of the Education Department] and the courts have expressed the opinion that a school is justified in dropping male athletes in order to comply with Title IX. We believe that this opinion misconstrues Congressional intent. . . .

As a threshold issue, you might ask—is there a crisis? Yes there is. Male gymnastics is almost extinct at the college level. Wrestling has relatively recently lost over 100 programs and may lose as many as 20 programs this year.

Programs in every sport have been dropped or reduced in number—soccer, baseball, tennis, swimming, etc.—even football and basketball. . . .

All male sports programs are at risk because of the proportionality rule/gender quota which the OCR has drafted. There are about 190,000 male college athletes in divisions I, II, and III. There are about 105,000 female athletes. How can proportionality be achieved when the present male to female ratio is 47–53? If the trend continues, administrators will have to eliminate about 100,000 male athletes to reach proportionality.

In 1972 when Congress enacted Title IX the college enrollment ratio nationally was 55%+ male. By the 21st Century 55% of the college population may well be female. The 55–45 female-to-male ratio sets up a gender quota which is impossible to achieve in no small part because females do not tend to compete in sports— particularly those like football and wrestling. Nor do they participate in a non-scholarship/walk-on capacity in anywhere near the number which males do. . . .

School administrators believe that they must achieve proportionality. Many are unable, because of budget constraints, to add female sports programs, so these administrators drop male programs or "cap" sports by dropping the non-scholarship or walk-on athlete. . . .

Programs should not be eliminated because athletes matriculate at a school in the good faith belief that the administration will honor its commitment to provide a program for their four years of college. It is a devastating betrayal for these young men when they learn that their faith has been misplaced. It is worse when they are informed that the reason for the elimination of their program is Title IX or gender equity. . . .

I have sought in my program [at California Bakersfield] to work with the many young men who otherwise would not be able to attend college, and I know I speak for the coaches of all male programs when I say that the elimination of male opportunities will greatly affect the future generation of young men.

All statistics reflect that the opportunities existing for females is much greater than for males. For example, wrestling is the sixth most popular high school sport in the nation. There is, however, only one college program for every 33 high school wrestling programs. Of the top ten female sports, the worst ratio is about 22–1 and the best ratio is about 11–1. High school females have greater opportunities to compete at the collegiate level in every counterpart sport except golf and gymnastics.

As these disparities continue to grow as male programs are eliminated, high school and junior high school male programs will atrophy and die. Many kids, without the option of participating in athletics, will choose antisocial activities.

Unfortunately, at present, there is hardly a male high school athlete who is unaware of Title IX and the OCR's approach to gender equity. Expectedly, these males are angry and their morale is sinking. . . .

Gender equity . . . should not be synonymous with gender quotas. The OCR's gender quota, which masquerades as the proportionality rule, is now an anachronism which should be abolished.

Statement of Wendy Hilliard

I went to college in the 1980s when Title IX was supposedly in force. My sport [of rhythmic gymnastics] wasn't offered at the varsity level. I did not receive an athletic scholarship. I had to work my way through college, and pay for my athletic training, yet graduated from New York University with honors. The month before graduation, I missed the1988 Olympic trials by .05 of a point. Why didn't I, as one of the best in the entire country in my sport, and at the top of my class as a student, have the opportunity for an athletic scholarship? There are still many women who are asking that question today. Twenty-three years after the passage of Title IX, women are still receiving only 35% of all college athletic opportunities. . . .

The Women's Sports Foundation's primary mission is education. We believe it is important for the general public and Congress to know the facts rather than be guided by popular mythology and misconceptions promoted by those who oppose Title IX. Thus, I would like to address issues often raised in discussion about the law.

Do men's non-revenue sports have to be eliminated in order for schools to comply with Title IX?

The purpose of laws prohibiting discrimination is to bring the disadvantaged population up to the level of the advantaged population, not to treat men's minor sports like women's sports who weren't given a chance to play. If we are going to expand opportunities for women to participate in athletics without cutting men's non-revenue sports such as wrestling, swimming, and gymnastics, there has to be a reduction of current expenditures on existing men's teams and a transfer of those resources to women's programs. . . .

[Hilliard goes on to list a variety of potential cost-saving measures, including savings in housing, travel, facility construction, and media expenditures for men's teams.]

Are women less interested in playing sports than men?

There are those who would persuade the committee to conclude that women aren't as interested in athletic opportunities as men, citing lower participation numbers in NCAA member institutions, the lack of "walk-ons" on women's teams and lower participation numbers in high school sports.

The issue of interest of female athletes is a critical one. **Opportunity drives interest and ability.** Title IX's purpose includes redressing historic discrimination. **There is no lack of interest and ability on the part of males or females** to participate in the finite number of opportunities available at the collegiate level. . . . [T]he real question is how do you demonstrate that the schools' limited opportunities to participate are apportioned in a fair manner . . .

A simple analogy may be helpful. You are a parent who has a son and a daughter. For many years, you have given your son, on the occasions of his birthday and holidays, baseballs, gloves, footballs, hockey sticks, and other sports equipment. His room is full of sports implements—a veritable palace of athletic privilege. One day, your daughter comes to you complaining that her brother won't let her borrow his glove so she can have a catch with her girlfriends. Would you tell her to go out and work so she can buy her own glove or would you explain to your son how important it is to share? Would you change your commitment to the importance of sharing and treating your children equally if your son advanced the argument that his sister would destroy, lose, or in some other way damage his glove—or his football?

Source: Statements of Christine H. B. Grant, T. J. Kerr, and Wendy Hilliard. *Hearing on Title IX of the Education Amendments Act of 1972: Hearing before the Subcommittee on Postsecondary Education, Training, and Life-Long Learning of the Committee on Economic and Educational Opportunities.* U.S. House of Representatives, 104th Congress, 1st session, May 9, 1995.

PRESIDENT CLINTON ANNOUNCES AMERICA'S FIRST WOMAN SPACE MISSION COMMANDER, 1998

In 1998 the American public learned that yet another historic "first" in women's history was at hand—the nation was about to have its first female space mission commander, an Air Force colonel and NASA astronaut named Eileen Collins (1956–). This announcement, made by President Bill Clinton (1946–) on March 5, was widely recognized as clear and dramatic evidence that the career and life opportunities available to American girls and women were continuing to steadily expand.

The mission commanded by Collins, who had first gone into space in 1995 as pilot of the Discovery *space shuttle (STS-63), was a success. In a 1999 mission (STS-93) Collins guided the* Columbia *space shuttle into space, where it successfully deployed the Chandra X-ray Observatory, a powerful telescope for scientists to study distant stars, black holes, and other astrological phenomena, during its six-day mission (July 22–27). In 2005 Collins commanded a second space shuttle flight, the* Discovery *(STS-114), which docked with the International Space Station during its two-week sojourn (July 26–August 9).*

Forty years ago, *Life* magazine introduced America's first astronauts to the world, noting that the seven *Mercury* astronauts were picked from, quote, "the same general mold." They were all military pilots. They were all in their thirties. They all had crewcuts. They were all men. And they really were all true American heroes. But heroes come in every size and shape and gender. Today we celebrate the falling away of another barrier in America's quest to conquer the frontiers of space and also to advance the cause of equality.

I'm proud to be here to congratulate Colonel Eileen Collins on becoming the first woman to command a space shuttle mission. She may not fit the exact mold of 40 years ago, but she clearly embodies the essential qualities of all our astronauts, then and now, the bold, restless, pioneering spirit that had made our Nation great. And as we've already heard, the story of her life is a story of challenges set and challenges met. That is also the story of our space program.

When it comes to exploring space and the unknown, the word "impossible" is not in our vocabulary. We have always recognized the limitless possibilities of seemingly impossible challenges.

A generation ago, President Kennedy said within a decade we would send an American to the Moon and bring him safely back to Earth. By 1969, Neil Armstrong and Buzz Aldrin had left their footprints on the Moon. We said, in our time, that we would visit the planets of the solar system. And last Fourth of July all Americans, with the help of a robot called *Sojourner,* got a chance to rove the surface of Mars and meet red rocks named Scooby Doo and Barnacle Bill.

Thirty-six years after John Glenn made his history-making space flight in a capsule the size of a compact car, he's not only going back into space, but we are poised to build an international space station the size of a football field. America has indeed become, as President Kennedy hoped, the world's leading spacefaring nation, a distinction we must keep in the 21st century.

Colonel Collins will lead us in this effort, commanding a mission to launch a telescope that will allow us to peer into the deepest reaches of outer space. Our balanced budget for 1999 will support, in fact, 28 new space missions, missions that will help us decipher more of the mysteries of black holes, of ancient stars, and of our Earth itself. Indeed, later today NASA will be making some exciting new announcements on the results of the *Lunar Prospector* mission, currently orbiting the Moon.

The knowledge we gain from our space missions could help us treat diseases here on Earth, from osteoporosis to ovarian cancer. It could make our farms more productive. It could help us meet the challenge of global climate change. And perhaps help us to uncover the very origins of life itself.

All Americans, especially our young people, have important roles to play in making these plans a reality. They have to begin by taking their studies, especially their studies in math and science, seriously.

Last week we learned that our leading spacefaring Nation is not faring very well when it comes to achievement of high school seniors in math and science. This is unacceptable. As we prepare for an information age that will require every student to master not just the basics of reading and math but algebra, geometry, physics, and computer science, I call on every parent, every school, every teacher to set higher expectations for our children. And I call upon all of our students—and I know that Hillary and Eileen will today—to take these challenging courses, so that we can all be prepared for the known and still unknown challenges of the future.

And I call on all young girls across America and their parents to take inspiration from Colonel Collins' achievement.

Let me remind you of something she was too modest to say. She has a distinguished degree from Syracuse University. She came up through the ROTC program. She began her high school education in community college. I want every child in this country to know that we have opened the doors of college to all Americans, that community college is virtually free for all children now, that everybody can make this start and nobody needs to put blinders on their aspirations for the future. She is proof.

I want to say, especially to the little girls who will hear Eileen Collins and these who will see her and to their parents, let's remember that at a time when very few girls were taking the hardest math and science courses, Colonel Collins was taking them and mastering them. She did in part because of the unfailing support of her parents who set high expectations and told her she could do anything she set her mind to. She never gave up, and one by one her dreams came true.

I think our country owes a great debt of gratitude to her parents, and I hope that more will follow her direction. And perhaps with her well-justified new fame, notoriety, the greatest mark Colonel Collins will make will not just be written in the stars but here on Earth, in the mind of every young girl with a knack for numbers, the gift for science, and a fearless spirit. Let us work to make sure that for every girl and every boy, dreams and ambitions can be realized, and even the sky is no longer the limit.

Thank you very much.

Source: Clinton, William. "Remarks Announcing the Selection of Lieutenant Colonel Eileen M. Collins, USAF, as the First Woman Space Mission Commander, March 5, 1998." *Public Papers of the Presidents of the United States: William J. Clinton (1998, Book I).* Washington, DC: Government Printing Office, 1995, pp. 331–332.

FIRST LADY HILLARY CLINTON AND PRESIDENT BILL CLINTON ON EQUAL PAY FOR WOMEN, 1999

On April 7, 1999, First Lady Hillary Rodham Clinton (1947–) and President Bill Clinton (1946–) co-hosted a special White House roundtable discussion on wage discrimination against women and steps that could be taken to achieve equal pay in American workplaces. Following are excerpts from the remarks of both the First Lady (who 17 years later would become the first woman ever to earn the presidential nomination of a major party) and the president.

First Lady: Thank you and welcome to the White House. Please be seated. We are delighted to have you here this afternoon to help commemorate Equal Pay Day, which is tomorrow. I'm glad to see so many both new and old faces in the fight for equal pay. And we know that this is a struggle that has taken some time. We've made a lot of progress, but I hope that we'll eventually see the end of Equal Pay Day, because the goal will have been achieved and we won't have to have any sessions like this, where we continue to talk about it.

We know that women who walk into the grocery store are not asked to pay 25 percent less for milk. They're not asked by their landlords to pay 25 percent less for rent. And they should no longer be asked to try to make their ends meet and their family incomes what they should be by having 25 percent less in their paychecks. . . .

In a few minutes, we're going to hear from our four panelists. They will be able to tell you in their own words why they are here. But when you have heard from Professor Nancy Hopkins, Sanya Tyler, Carolyn Gantt and Patricia Higgins, you will appreciate—as I think all of us who've ever been in the world of work do—the struggles and the challenges and the victories that they have faced, and the way they represent so many other women.

One of my staff members was home for the holidays last week, and there was a cartoon stuck up on the refrigerator in her house. I mean, that's where everybody keeps all of their reminders, their namesakes, their children's drawings, and all the important documents, at least in my experience. And her mother, without knowing anything about this day and this particular commemoration, had cut out a cartoon which showed six people sitting around a conference room table, all in suits, all wearing glasses, all men. And one of them announces, gentlemen, we must cut our expenses in half, so I'm replacing each of you with a woman.

Now, clearly, things are not as bad as the cartoon. You know, they have to exaggerate to get our attention. And things clearly have improved. As a recent Council of Economic Advisers report makes clear, the gap between women's and men's wages has narrowed since 1963. But women still bring home only about 75 cents for every man's dollar.

And I think it's important that, despite this long-time inequity, there are still those who claim that this is a made-up problem, that any wage gap between men and women can be explained away by the choices that women make. And we all know that individual women, thank goodness, make different choices—that women, for personal reasons, or other professional reasons, may choose a particular career or work pattern that results in lower wages. But this is not an accurate finding, and those who promote it should look at the entire picture and the studies that have been repeatedly which demonstrate the contrary.

Women at all ages, when you adjust for differences in education, experience and occupation—as a recent CEA study report reminds us—there is still a sizeable gap between men's and women's salaries that can best be explained by one phenomenon, the continuing presence and the persistent effect of discrimination—sometimes in very subtle ways. And we'll hear about some of that from one of our panelists.

In fact, recently, an important report issued by the Massachusetts Institute of Technology—which one of our panelists will discuss—looked at pay equity among tenured faculty and found that women at the School of Science were discriminated against in diverse areas, including hiring, awards, promotions, committee assignments and the allocation of resources such as lab space and research dollars. This report showed that even women who supposedly break through the glass ceiling and reach the highest echelons of their professions still find themselves bumping up against some gender discrimination.

So I think it's fair to say that when you have some of the best scientists in the world taking a look at this issue in one institution and coming to these conclusions, and then that, in turn, supports the broader findings that have been derived from looking at society at large, we know that we do have a wage gap that we have to address. And it's not just a gap in wages, it's a gap in our nation's principles and promises. . . .

[*First Lady Hillary Rodham Clinton then introduced her husband, President Bill Clinton.*]

The President: I'd like to make just a few brief points. Hillary has made most of the points that need to be made, and we all know here we're preaching to the saved in trying to get a message out to the country. But I'd like to point out as I tried to do in the State of the Union that the time in which we are living now in terms of our economic prosperity is virtually unprecedented. We had 4.2 percent unemployment last month.

I remember a meeting I had and a huge argument I had in December of 1992 when I had been elected but not inaugurated President, about how low we could get unemployment before inflation would go up. And all the traditional economists said, man, when you get below six percent, you know, you will just see what will happen. And the American people turned out to be a lot more productive, a lot more efficient; technology turned out to be a lot more helpful; we were in a much more competitive environment. So now, we have 4.2 percent unemployment, lowest rate since 1970, lowest peacetime unemployment since 1957, 18 million new jobs.

But we still have some significant long-term challenges in this country. We have pockets of America—in rural America, in urban America; our medium-size industrial cities; our Native American reservations—which have not felt any of the impact of the economic recovery. We still have substantial long-term challenges to Social Security, to Medicare. And we still have a significant fact of inequality in the pay of women and men.

And the central point I would like to make is that we should not allow the political climate or anything else to deter us from concentrating our minds on the fact that this is a precious gift that the American people have received, even though they have earned it. Countries rarely have conditions like this. If we can't use this moment to deal with these long-term challenges, including the equal-pay challenge, when will we ever get around to it? . . .

And those of us who are old enough to remember what the economy was like in the 1970's with the long gas lines, what it was like in the 1980's when we had the so-called bicoastal economy and my State and Senator Harkin's State had double-digit unemployment in county after county—I'm telling you, when times get tough and then you go around and try to talk to people about problems like this, their eyes glaze over because even the people who would benefit, they're just trying to keep body and soul together. They're worried about holding on to what they have. We have an opportunity now to make a better America for our children, for all of our children.

The second point I want to make is the one I made jokingly in the story about Tom and me having the privilege of living with women who make more money than we do. And that is that this is not just a women's issue. The women who are discriminated against often are in families, raising children with husbands who are also hurt if their wives work hard and don't have the benefits of equal pay. A lot of the women who are single mothers are out there working, and they have boy children as well as girl children. This is not just a gender issue, and men should be very interested in this.

I can say furthermore that I believe that it would be good for our overall economy. You know, you hear all these problems that they say it will cause the economy if you do this. All this stuff is largely not true. I mean, every time we try to make a change to have a stronger society, whether it's a raise in the minimum wage or cleaning up the environment or passing the family leave law, the people that are against it say the same thing. And we now have decades of experience in trying to improve our social fabric. And America has had a particular genius in figuring out how to do these things in a way that would permit us to generate more economic opportunity and more jobs and more advances.

I'd like to make a third point not in my notes, but Hillary made me think of it. There are these people now who are out there saying, "Well, there really isn't much of an equal pay problem because it's almost exclusively confined to women who have children. And women who have children have to have more intermittent periods in the workplace"—you've heard all the arguments—"and once you factor that out, well, there's no problem."

Well, I have two reactions to that. First of all, if you take that argument to its logical conclusion, we would be depopulating America before you know it. No one else has really figured out any way to bring children around, as far as I know.

Secondly, if that is true, it still doesn't make it right. If you give the people the entire argument—which I don't think the analysis supports—but if you did, what does that mean? It means that an important part of the equal pay battle should be strengthening the family and medical leave law, for example, something I've been trying to do without success ever since we signed the first bill. It ought to apply to more companies. It ought to be more extensive. It ought to cover more situations. We've proved that we can do this without hurting the economy.

And if you believe that having children is a significant factor here and if you believe as I do that's the most important work of any society, then why shouldn't we continue with something that's done so much good, this family leave law, to find other ways to do it, to find other incentives for flex-time, all kinds of things we could be doing if this is a problem.

Now, finally, let's talk a little bit about what I think we can do about this right now. Earlier this year, I asked Congress to pass two measures to strengthen our wage discrimination laws and to boost enforcement of existing ones. I ask Congress again to pass the $14 million equal pay initiative that's in our balanced budget to help the EEOC identify and respond to wage discrimination, to educate employers and workers about their rights and responsibilities—you'll hear some pretty impressive people talk about that on our panel in a moment—and to help bring more women into better-paying jobs.

Again, I ask the Congress to pass the "Paycheck Fairness Act" sponsored by Senator Daschle and Congresswoman DeLauro, which would put employers on notice that wage discrimination against women is just as unacceptable as discrimination based on race or ethnicity. Under current law, those who are denied equal pay because of race can receive compensatory and punitive damages. This new legislation would give women the same right. It will make a difference. It would protect employees who share salary information from retaliation. It would expand training for EEOC workers, strengthen research, establish an award for exemplary workers.

We can do more. Today I'm pleased to announce that we want to strengthen our legislation by requiring the EEOC to determine what new information on workers' salaries they need to improve enforcement of wage discrimination laws and to find a way to collect that information. The new provision would call on the EEOC to issue a new rule within 18 months to gather, in the most effective and efficient way possible, pay data from companies based on race, sex, and national origin of employees.

Addressing wage discrimination takes courage, as our panelists can tell you. It takes courage as an employee to speak out, to gather evidence, to make the case. It takes courage as an employer to recognize problems in pay equity and take steps to remedy them.

Just recently—let me just mention the experience of one of our panelists—we saw this courage among the administrators and women scientists at MIT, one of our country's most outstanding institutions of higher education. Together, they looked at the cold, hard facts about disparities in everything from lab space to annual salary. They sought to make things right, and they told the whole public the truth about it, which is a rare thing. And I appreciate what they did. I commend them. I hope their success and their example can be replicated throughout our country.

Now again I say, this should not be a partisan issue. It should be an American issue. And as you argue through these matters this year, I ask you, every time you are in contact with any person in a position to vote on this in Congress or influence a vote in Congress, ask them this simple question: If we don't deal with this now, when will we ever get around to it?

Thank you very much.

[*Secretary of Labor Alexis Herman thanked the president and First Lady and made brief remarks. She then introduced the roundtable participants, and each made brief remarks on their perspective on equal pay issues.*]

The President. I would like to just start. We're going to do a little roundtable and just give the participants a chance to answer a few questions and amplify on their remarks. And taking account of Sanya Tyler's voice problems, I still want to ask her one question, because obviously the situation at Howard and the situation at MIT were resolved in different ways.

After you won the lawsuit, did you feel that the administration treated you and other people who were in the same situation fairly? Did you feel like that the work environment was worse, and did you believe that the program also began to get more support, as well as on the wages? Was Title IX and the other efforts you made, did you get more support for the program, as well as for your income?

[Ms. Tyler, head coach of women's basketball at Howard University, said she was proud of the university's response after she won her Title IX discrimination suit, indicating that the current president made it clear that women had a significant role not only in the sports program but also in the development and leadership of the university. The First Lady then called on Professor Nancy Hopkins, Massachusetts Institute of Technology (MIT), who stated that 5 years ago there were only 15 tenured women in MIT's School of Science and that discrimination against women at MIT was subtle and difficult to identify. She said that when an incident inspired her to prepare a strong letter of complaint to MIT's president, the other female faculty members all signed the letter and gathered data on the problem. After reviewing the data, MIT administrators took immediate action to institute changes. The First Lady agreed that often such problems were not readily apparent, and she commended MIT for its action.]

The President. You know, the question that I wanted to ask, because this MIT thing is so unusual, is, do you believe that they knew it was going on before? And if they didn't know it was going on before—but all the women you went to had immediately related in the same way you did and signed up—how did it happen? Because I think this is something that data may not tell you. But I think this is what is really important, because there may be a lot of organizations out there where this sort of just creeps in, but the people now running these organizations don't know it.

And what I'm hoping is that—it's not like— it may not be as overt as it was when Carolyn was in the workforce, so how do you think this happened? It's very impressive that the president said, "Okay, let's go do the right thing." But that raises the question of how did it happen in the first place?

[Professor Hopkins stated that the top levels where power resided were the last frontier of the civil rights/affirmative action process. She said that the discrimination there wasn't conscious, and thus the women themselves weren't aware of it; however, gender bias that was small in each instance added up to 20 percent pay.]

The President. Let me ask a specific question. Do you think—if there was no deliberate policy to hire all these people at a lower salary, and then not to raise them at some point to a comparable salary, and there was never a systematic policy, do you believe that—here's what I'm trying to get at—is there a still, sort of in the minds of at least the men who are making these hiring or pay decisions, this notion that there's a marketplace out there, and it's a big deal for a woman to be a tenured professor at MIT? And therefore, this was a market-based decision; this is what I can get this talent for; and this is what I'm going to pay? Is that what you think happened? And if not, what is it that you think happened?

[*Professor Hopkins said that men approached these decisions differently than women, and that women had to share in the decision-making power. The First Lady then introduced Carolyn Gantt, an employee at a Washington, DC, senior center, who during her career had witnessed men with the same or lesser qualifications, in the same or lesser jobs, receiving more benefits and higher pay. When Mrs. Clinton asked how she became aware of the situation, Ms. Gantt replied that contacts in the community gave her access to lists of how much individuals in her organization were paid, and her knowledge of individuals' duties and qualifications led her to recognize the disparity in compensation. After going to the organization's board, she got a promotion but became a pariah. When she moved into a new position in the District of Columbia government, she encountered the same situation.*]

The President. Let me just use this remarkable woman's case as an illustration of a point I made in my remarks, that this is something that imposes great economic costs on the society as a whole.

You have seven children, right?

Ms. Gantt.   I still have seven, but they're grown. [*Laughter*]
The President. And you're still working part-time? And how old are you?
Ms. Gantt.   Do you really want me—[*Laughter*]
The President. Let me ask you this. Let me ask you another question. You are—
Ms. Gantt.   —[*inaudible*]—category. [*Laughter*]

The President. I know I shouldn't have asked. [*Laughter*] The reason I ask you is because you look so much younger than you are. [*Laughter*]

But let me ask—the point I wanted to make is, she has been for some time eligible for Social Security. Here's the point I want to make about the issue. You know we're having this big Social Security debate here now, and we're in an argument in the Congress about how to save Social Security. Why? Because the number of people over 65 are going to double between now and the year 2030. And the Trust Fund runs out of money in 35 years. And for it to be stable, it needs to last for 75 years. But in addition to that, we need to lift the earnings limit for people who work when they're over 65, I think, so they can still draw their Social Security, number one. And number two, we need to have a remedial program to deal with the fact that the poverty rate among single elderly women is twice, almost twice the general poverty rate among seniors in this country.

Why? A lot of it is because of stories like this. So you've either got people like this remarkable lady who is healthy enough and, as you can see, more than quite alert and on top of things and energetic, who continue to work on and on, or you have people who can't do that, and they are twice as likely to be living in poverty even when they draw Social Security.

This is another of the consequences of this. And so the rest of you are going to have to pay to fix this, unless you just want to let it go on. And I don't think, since we have some money to fix it now, I presume none of us want to let it go on, and we'd like to fix it.

But we should understand that none of this—this kind of discrimination is not free to the rest of us, as well. Just because you haven't felt it directly doesn't mean that you're not weakened and lessened because of the quality of life, the strength of your society, the fabric of it is not eroded by this. And that's the point I wanted—I didn't want to embarrass her about her age, but I think it's important that you understand that this is a cost imposed on the whole society. And one of the big efforts we're going to make this year in this saving Social Security is to do something about this dramatic difference in the poverty rate. And it would be much, much lower if no one had ever had the experiences you just heard described.

[*Secretary Herman commented that the pension gap was even greater than the 75-cents-to-every-dollar gap for regular wages and that only 40 percent of women had pension coverage. The First Lady then introduced Patricia Higgins, a nurse who had encountered subtle wage discrimination in her field. She said that while the profession required idealism and dedication, medical advances meant that levels of training, skill, and responsibility had increased, and compensation should also increase. Secretary Herman commented that many institutions had good policies and procedures that were often not supported in practice. She said the administration was supporting legislation to share salary information without fear of reprisal and asked Ms. Tyler if she thought that would be helpful. Ms. Tyler stated that pursuing her case in court had been very successful and had generated real dollars for the many coaches affected.*]

The President. Thank you very much. Let me say on behalf of all of us, we're delighted that you're here. We especially thank Senator Harkin and Congresswoman Eleanor Holmes Norton for their leadership, and we thank our panelists. They were all terrific.

Thank you very much.

Source: Clinton, William. "Remarks in a Roundtable Discussion on Equal Pay, April 7, 1999." *Public Papers of the Presidents of the United States: William J. Clinton (1999, Book I).* Washington, DC: Government Printing Office, 1999, pp. 512–516.

PERSPECTIVES ON MANHOOD AND CHANGING GENDER ROLES FROM THREE MEN, 2000–2009

Since the magazine published its first issue in 1983, Voice Male has explored issues of manhood and gender justice from a progressive, pro-feminist viewpoint. Although women and their perspectives are represented in its pages, most of Voice Male's articles and essays are written by men examining the societal forces and personal challenges that pose obstacles to more positive and egalitarian gender relations. Following are three articles from Voice Male from 2000 to 2009 in which contributors explore issues such as gender-based divisions of parenthood responsibilities, boys' stunted understandings of manhood, and the importance of women coaches in youth sports.

"When Fathers Mother"

By Donald N. S. Unger
Summer 2000

It's not easy being a mother, is it? the librarian says, smiling, as I change my then six-month-old daughter's diaper on a desk in the back room.

I close my eyes briefly, try not to grit my teeth, remember to breathe.

"I'm not *being* a mother," I tell her, as softly as I can manage. "I'm *being* a *parent*."

"You're doing what mothers usually *do*," she tells me. And I think it best to let the conversation die there. I don't have the time, the energy or the tact. In situations like that, almost a daily occurrence when I'm out with my daughter, it's as though I lose my voice.

I had been "invited" to work, to score entrance exams for the freshman writing course I was teaching; I was taking care of my daughter, Rebecca, four days a week that term, but, in a fit of the kind of flexibility that I realize is rarely extended to working mothers, my department chair had suggested that I bring the baby with me for the morning, rather than miss all the fun.

So I came in early, folding playpen in tow, took my daughter into the back offices in the library, where we would be working, stripped her, fed her, cleaned her up, changed her, and got her dressed again, while the librarians buzzed in and out doing their work—and giving their commentary.

Does it sound lighthearted, a harmless observation about statistical reality? Does complaining about this make me seem thin-skinned? Try this if you're a working woman, particularly in one of the professions, a doctor, a lawyer: Someone observes you at work and says, "It's not easy being a man, is it?"

All in good fun? In today's atmosphere, a statement like that is close to actionable.

I don't want to get into issues of "oppression envy" here. For the record: it would be silly to argue that men have suffered, or suffer now, discrimination on anything like the scale that women have had to deal with throughout history. Still, as is becoming increasingly obvious, we've had *half* a revolution in the last 30 years, made great strides toward opening up a broad range of jobs to women, certainly made a good start toward leveling the playing field in outside-the-home employment; on the domestic side, increasingly, no one's home.

A good piece of this is due to economics. The same 30 years that have marked professional progress for women have seen a stagnation in middle-class wages that all but requires both partners in the household to work. But, as first-wave feminists were quick to point out, the language we use also has a profound impact on how we see ourselves and each other, how we interpret the world and our roles in it, what we see as possible and what we even lack words to effectively describe.

We've had an incomplete, somewhat one-sided, linguistic revolution: we've done a great deal to truly neuter the neuter pronouns and other terms that, in English, have traditionally been male. If these changes have not yet completely suffused our society, the battle is still essentially over: college writing programs routinely require nonsexist usage, as do the style books of all the major publishing houses; when you call a department head a "chair" rather than "chairman," people don't scold you anymore that you've referred to the person as a piece of furniture.

And on the other side, the language of domestic work, the words we use to describe the roles usually ascribed to women? That hasn't changed, nor does there seem to be any movement afoot to work toward or facilitate that change: "to mother" is to care for and to nurture; "to father" essentially means to inseminate. The somewhat antiseptic phrase "to parent" has some currency, but reflexively, as with the librarian, what people fall back on is female-centered language. This leaves men out, makes us invisible, takes away our voice, in a care-giving role that, cultural critics on both the left and the right agree, is being dangerously neglected.

I don't say this because I want "points." I haven't been active in caring for my daughter because I'm looking to earn a merit badge. I would like my gender to be as invisible and unworthy of commentary as is increasingly the case for women who do a broad variety of jobs, from physicians to carpenters. But I do want my existence as a parent to be acknowledged, and not just as an oddity. I want linguistic parity.

More than two decades ago, in *Language and Woman's Place*, Robin Lakoff observed that to call a man a "professional" identifies him as a doctor or a lawyer or someone else in a respected occupation; to call a woman the same thing implies that she is a prostitute. Similarly, to be a "master" is to have power over something; to be a "mistress" is to have an illicit sexual relationship. She identified this "lack of linguistic equivalence" as one of the keystones of inequality. She was right. And it cuts both ways.

Some people understand this intuitively, and it is in them that I find hope.

Several summers ago, my mother and I took Rebecca, then two years old, on her first subway ride, to the Museum of the American Indian. The train was standing room only when we got on in Brooklyn. I held her against my chest with one arm, her legs wrapped around my waist, my other hand light on one of the support poles—but this didn't last long. A middle-aged Jamaican woman, sitting across the aisle from where I was standing, got up and gestured me into her seat.

"It takes two to tango," she said to my mother over the din of the train, nodding approvingly in my direction. "It takes a mother *and* a father." A simple statement, and a small sacrifice on her part, but one that touched me deeply because it's so rare. My wife and I have been impressed to discover, in the last couple of years, that, in our generally unfortunate cultural context, parenthood is one of the few things that trumps race—by which I mean, parenthood is one of the few bridges over the chasm of race, and creates more, and easier, interracial interaction, more real and perceived common ground, than almost anything else; but what this woman was doing, in addition to reaching across that divide, was ignoring gender as well: she read me as a parent with a child and, in spite of the fact that it is traditionally men who give up seats to women, younger people who give up seats to older, her respect for parenthood propelled her toward a different kind of etiquette.

The *language* she used, moreover, was perfect; two simple sentences, the second of which contained a quiet but clear, straight equivalence between "mother" and "father," no sarcasm, no lifted eyebrow. For a brief moment, I existed; she gave me space and, in *her* choice of words, because we exist not just in other people's eyes but reflected in the words with which they choose to describe us, she gave me voice.

"Getting Out of the Man Box"

By Doug Ginn
Winter 2001

Last year, a female cofacilitator and I were leading a discussion on gender roles with a group of white, lower- to middle-class, high-school-age boys. Our first activity was to brainstorm what it meant to "act like a man." On a sheet of newsprint we wrote their suggestions inside a square box, which we said represented the traditional view of masculinity. Around the box, we wrote the consequences a man might face if he tried to step out of the "box of conformity." The result? Name calling, threats, violence: these kids knew what was up. They were becoming men in the same culture that produced me. Misogyny, homophobia, and even violence were a part of life. This state of affairs seemed natural to them.

For the rest of the session, we discussed the ways gender roles are reinforced. I kept emphasizing the box as a visual metaphor to show how dominant, white masculinity is confining and rigid—besides being dangerous and destructive. Through the exercise, I hoped these teenage boys might glimpse what it was like to transgress their gender, to see the possibilities doing so opens. After a while, one of the older boys said something that shook the ground beneath my soapbox and made the square, visual metaphor on the newsprint behind me seem irrelevant. "I don't know," he said, "I kind of like being inside the box."

Yes, he admitted, "acting like a man" meant you often had to seek out danger to prove yourself, but the danger could be fun. Yeah, you had to disrespect girls and gays with your friends, but that's how you got to be a part of their clique. Most important, acting like a man gave you power and privileges in this society that were withheld from most other groups of people. Despite the fact that "being a man" meant dominating others and never showing vulnerability, the payoff, for this teenage male anyway, was still worth it. And, as it turned out for the group, he was not alone in feeling that way.

Only four years earlier, I had been in the same place as he was—uncertain about the world but grasping for some way of explaining it. In those four years, I have gone through many transformations; I still am, as it's an ongoing process. Yet somewhere along the line, I forgot what it was like to be numb to the pain of others. This boy's comment triggered memories of being a desensitized teenager, struggling to feel in a desensitizing culture.

My parents did as much as they could to teach me about the world and the importance of caring for other people. They tried to explain why violence was never the answer; that there was never an excuse for violence against women; that you should always respect those with different lifestyles and opinions. I am the man I am today because of them—but the hardest part of the journey had to be walked alone. There wasn't much my parents could do during the years between beginning junior high and graduating from high school. I didn't want to be shielded anymore. I wanted to stand on my own two feet, and that meant walking face first into the oncoming wave of adolescence.

The media landscape through which I wandered was relatively the same as the one this group of teenage boys was experiencing. It's a world where society is corrupt and everyone screws everyone, so you might as well get yours while you can. The only thing that really matters is being hyper-cool. Any sort of brutality can be made acceptable if it's sexy enough. This world isn't much different from the one that most adults consume every day, but adults have other things to occupy their minds—paying the bills, raising kids, trying to be good role models. For young people, this corrupt world is our whole world.

We don't immediately accept it, of course. We want to believe that there is goodness in the world, but the positive role models get fewer and fewer the farther we get from the world of our parents. At first, "polite society" filled me with rage because it stank of falseness, but the only outlet for this rage was mediated (and medicated)—through TV, music, and movies. The violence had to be extreme, the sex ultra-raunchy, and the music aggressive and loud. The more cracks that appeared in society's civilized facade, the more jaded I made myself. Eventually, it became a source of pride. Anyone who still cared about "saving the world" was naive and open to ridicule. Now, I can see this whole process happening at an even earlier age as I watch young people growing up.

The flipside to this depressing tale is that I eventually grew tired of being unable to feel any real emotions. The power and privilege that came from staying "inside the box" felt hollow. I wanted to try being something other than ultra-jaded and hyper-cool. When I got to college, studying history, theory, and politics stirred up the embers in my stomach, and as passion returned to my heart, I found a healthy outlet working with organizations dedicated to social change—not on a fly-by-night basis, but as a long-term project spanning, I hope, the rest of my life.

Too few young adults get the chance to explore the opportunities college offers, and many young men who do get to college have already grown too accustomed to the "box" of masculinity to be able to give it up. To seriously challenge sexism, instead of just preaching, we need to acknowledge how difficult it is for young boys to adopt any other persona but the traditional, dominant, masculine one. There have to be outlets for young boys to channel their anger into healthier forms of expression, and we need to mitigate that anger by honestly engaging with them from a very early age. Most important, men, and especially young men, need to set the example of a masculinity that is lived "outside the box."

"Coaching Our Kids"

By Michael Messner
Spring 2009

Campbell Weber is a single divorced father who coaches his son Robbie's Little League Baseball team. Campbell is college-educated, but his economic resources are thin. When I asked him if he would coach again the next year, for what would be Robbie's final year in Little League baseball, he thoughtfully considered the meaning and importance of his doing so:

"I'll only coach if Robbie wants me to—if he's embarrassed, I won't do it. But I'd really like to. This year would be my last year, because next year he'll be into high school, so I'm treasuring this time that I can spend with him. I'm not a well-off man, so the only thing that I'm leaving Robbie is the time that I spend with him, and that's really important to me. My dad died when I was sixteen, and I was at boarding school and I didn't get to do things with him; he wasn't a go-out-and-do-things kind of guy. We never went out and threw the baseball around, that sort of thing. I've made sure that Robbie and I do a lot of stuff together, because those are the memories he's gonna have. And that's what he gets."

When Campbell Weber punctuated his statement with the words, "And that's what he gets," it gave me a sad stab of recognition and memory. My own father had a very successful public life as a high school teacher, a coach, and a naval officer. He was very busy, so I spent far more time with my mom and sisters than I did with him. His relative absence from my life added tremendous emotional salience to the rare moments I did get to spend with him, and many of those moments were organized around sports.

I am a father now too. Both of my sons are in their teens, but when they were younger they both played community-based youth sports. Stepping onto a soccer field, a basketball court, or (especially) a Little League Baseball field with my sons immediately brought up visceral feelings and what felt like ancient memories. I felt a sense of continuity that stretched from my father, who died many years ago, through me and to my sons. I wanted the playing field to be a place where I could connect with my sons, though I did not want it to be *the only place*, or even necessarily the most important place.

These continuities from my childhood were experienced against a shifting backdrop; something fundamental had changed since I was a boy. Now, there were girls—scores of them, hundreds of them—out there on our community's playing fields. Unlike my childhood in the 1950s and 1960s, when there were almost no opportunities for girls to play sports, today millions of girls participate in organized soccer, baseball, softball, basketball and other sports. This, to me, is one of the many positive achievements of the feminist movement, during my lifetime. Another apparent change struck me when we arrived at our six-year-old son Miles's first soccer practice: I was delighted to learn that his coach was a woman. Coach Karen, a mother in her mid-thirties, had grown up playing lots of sports. She was tall, confident and athletic, and the kids responded well to her leadership. "Great, a woman coach!" I observed cheerily. "It's a new and different world than the one that I grew up in." But over the next twelve years, as I traversed with Miles and eventually with his younger brother Sasha many seasons of youth sports, we never had another woman head coach. It's not that women weren't contributing to the kids' teams. All of the "team parents" (often called "team moms")—parent volunteers who did the behind-the-scenes work of phone-calling, organizing weekly snack schedules and team parties, collecting money for a gift for the coaches—were women.

Women head coaches were very few and far between. This stimulated the feminist researcher in me. How is it possible in this day and age, I wondered, that only 13 percent of the soccer coaches, and 6 percent of the baseball and softball coaches, are women? Why was it that the women coaches were clustered around girls' teams, and around the very youngest kids' teams? And why did most women coach for just one year, before quitting? This began for me a seven-year-long research project that explored the gender and family dynamics of youth sports coaches in my community.

Watching, and especially listening to the voices of women coaches, I learned a great deal about how an "old boys' network" makes it very difficult for women to break into coaching, and how informal (and I am convinced, mostly unconscious) words and actions by men coaches make youth sports coaching a chilly, unwelcome climate for the few women who do coach. As you move up past coaching five-, six- and seven-year-olds and begin to enter the intermediate and older age groups, the coaches told me, everything gets more "serious." As coaches increasingly emphasize winning, they yell at the kids more, adopt more extreme "drill sergeant" styles on the playing fields, use their bodies and voices in more intimidating ways, and most of the women coaches bail out.

More than one woman coach who quit, or cycled back to remain working with the youngest kids, told me, "I just couldn't take that." But here is the surprise I learned through my research: a lot of the men coaches could not take it either. The women coaches think that all of the men are uniformly "confident" in coaching. To be sure, women coaches are subjected to a great deal of gendered scrutiny—"Is she really qualified to coach my son?"—and men coaches are usually just assumed to know what they are doing, until they prove otherwise. However, many men reported to me that they felt insecure about taking on such a public position in their kids' lives. And several told me that they opted out of coaching the higher-aged kids' teams for precisely the same reasons that the women had dropped out. When it got "too serious," when the values of the league shifted toward narrow conceptions of toughness, competition and winning, many of the men bailed out, just as had most of the women.

Will Solomon, a baseball coach with lots of sports experience, told me "there's no way" he would go on to coach his son's baseball team at the twelve-year-old age level.

"It gets so *serious* at that level," he said. I had observed Will to be a fun and supportive coach, very low-key and good with all the kids. I especially appreciated his style, because my son Sasha had had a less than successful season before playing on Will's team. Suddenly, Sasha was swinging the bat better, and making good consistent contact, sometimes ripping solid line drive hits. It seemed to me that Sasha was just more relaxed, looser, and I attributed that to the lower pressure, the fun context that Will had created on the team. I asked Will if he intended to volunteer to coach the next season, and his response was unequiv-ocal: "Ha! There's no way I'll coach in the Majors next spring. Anyway, I doubt they'd have me." When I asked him why, he said, "I figure I'd be considered not serious enough." "I don't get it," I said, "you are a great coach, and I'm not sure too many people in town have more sports experience than you." "I guess it's a couple of things," he explained. "One, I don't think they'd want me to because I'm not as focused on the baseball side of it as I am on the sort of kids' side of it, and I think [in the Majors] they start to get real serious about the baseball side. And the other thing is that there does form sort of a club among these coaches at the Major League level which I didn't see at the [younger kids'] level. So I think probably they wouldn't want me, you know. I mean the kids would. But the coaches, the powers-that-be wouldn't."

Will Solomon's words illustrated a clear pattern that emerged in my years of research. At the younger levels, there is more elbow room for coaches—men and some women—to deploy what I call "kids knowledge" as the underlying philosophy of their coaching strategies. As the kids get older, coaches move very noticeably to what I call "sports knowledge." This transformation radically shifts the kids' playing experiences away from a "kids knowledge" emphasis on universal participation, trying out different positions, having fun, engaging in healthy exercise, and learning to cooperate with teammates. The shift to a "sports knowledge" value system shifts the kids' experience toward a focus on perfecting skills, strategic attempts to win games and championships, aggressive competition, a decline in empathy when a kid gets hurt, specialization of kids' roles on teams, and the emergence of a star system that marginalizes the less skilled kids. This values shift—and the way it's embodied and enforced by the "inner circle" of men coaches—is what causes most women, and many men, to say "not for me."

It strikes me that this is a wonderful example of how the interests of women are congruent with the interests of many men—a majority of men, really—who are made to feel uncomfortable and are marginalized by narrow expressions of masculinity. Creating more space for women in youth sports coaching will also expand the space for more kinds of men to participate—and vice-versa. I've observed this already happening on a small scale in youth soccer (albeit not that I can see in baseball). Women are actively trying to recruit more women coaches, are supporting each other to hang in there and to thrive, and are working with male allies to instill their teams and leagues with positive coaching values and practices.

I am convinced that it is very important to increase the numbers of women coaches in youth sports. It matters because today's generation of mothers is rich with athletic experience and talent; many women want to coach, but are discour-aged from doing so. It matters because what adults do in youth sports is linked to gender divisions of labor in other realms; an "unfinished feminist revolution" in work and family life is further reinforced by such a skewed male dominance in youth sports coaching. It matters because, as preparation for the world they will inhabit as adults, boys need to see and experience the full range of women's leadership and physical abilities. It matters because women coaches can be an inspiration to today's girls, giving them a vision of what they can do when they are adults. And it matters because including larger numbers of women is an important part of broadening the field for men coaches, making it a safe place for emergence of a more nurturing style of male coach, which will surely be a benefit for all of our kids.

Source: Okun, Rob. *Voice Male: The Untold Story of the Pro-Feminist Men's Movement.* Northampton, MA: Interlink Books, 2014.

THE FAMILY AND MEDICAL LEAVE ACT'S BENEFITS TO WORKING PARENTS, 2008

In 2008 the Bush administration proposed a number of changes to the 1993 Family and Medical Leave Act (FMLA), a landmark law that guaranteed millions of American workers—both men and women—the right to take up to 12 weeks of unpaid leave each year to address health issues and other crises that they or immediate family members were facing, without losing their jobs or their health insurance. The law's inclusion of men as eligible for leave was seen as a particular victory for working women, given traditional societal assumptions about family caregiving duties.

When congressional hearings were called to weigh potential changes to the FMLA, one of the people who testified was Debra Ness, president of the National Partnership for Women and Families (NPWF), an organization she described as "a non-profit, non-partisan advocacy group dedicated to promoting fairness in the workplace, access to quality health care, and policies that help workers in the United States meet the dual responsibilities of work and family." She told the subcommittee on workforce protections that the Bush administration proposals would weaken the FMLA, and after touting the law's various benefits—including its expansion to include eligible military families—she urged Congress to instead use the FMLA as a stepping stone toward passing a law that would guarantee paid family and medical leave to working men and women. Her testimony, delivered on April 10, 2008, is excerpted below.

On November 17, 2008, the Bush administration approved most of the changes to the FMLA regulations that Ness had criticized. "There are a few pieces of good news in the [new] regulations, but their overall effect will be to make it harder for workers to take the leave they need," asserted the NPWF.

I am especially pleased to be here today because this year marks the 15th anniversary of the FMLA. Its passage was a watershed moment for government support of working families in the United States. The law guarantees eligible workers up to twelve weeks of unpaid leave each year to care for immediate family members or to address serious personal health concerns. By making job-protected leave available to all eligible workers, and requiring that health insurance continue through the leave, the law has enabled both women and men to meet their responsibilities for their families without sacrificing their jobs and long-term economic stability. The law also helps combat gender discrimination and pernicious stereotypes about gender roles because both male and female workers can take FMLA leave. The law helps to ensure that women are not penalized or unfairly denied job opportunities simply because of assumptions about their family care giving responsibilities. . . .

Many of us in the room today were instrumental in the long fight to pass the FMLA. We braved an unrelenting stream of attacks from businesses that claimed the law would be the end of them. Fifteen years later, the law is well established and businesses have flourished. It is important to remember that lesson when we talk about expanding the FMLA and creating a way to include wage replacement while workers are on leave. We will undoubtedly hear that the same scare tactics and predictions that the sky will fall again. It did not fall when we passed the FMLA, and it will not fall if we make this basic family support available and accessible to more workers. In fact, as we explain in more detail below, the strongest economies in the world are in countries that provide paid family leave to all workers. The FMLA is good for families, and it is good for business. Expanding it will make it even more so.

It is an exceptionally sweet anniversary for supporters of the FMLA because this year also marks the first time the law has been expanded since its inception. Now under the FMLA, military families will be able to take up to 26 weeks of leave to help care for their soldiers injured in combat. These families have sacrificed so much for our country, and we are very pleased that the expansion of the FMLA will help them access a necessary support—leave to care for a wounded soldier. Additionally, military family members will be able to use FMLA leave to help them cope with the deployment of a close relative. . . .

I. The FMLA is Working Well

Since 1993, workers have used the FMLA approximately 100 million times to take the unpaid time off that they need to care for themselves or their families. This includes employees from all walks of life. Twenty seven percent of leave-takers earn less than 30,000/year; 51% of leave-takers earn between $30,000 and $74,999/year; and 22% of leave-takers earn $75,000/year or more. A significant number of leave-takers are men (42%), who use the FMLA for both their own serious illness (58%) and to care for seriously ill family members (42%). When taken, leave is usually quite short: the median length is just 10 days.

Workers overwhelmingly support the FMLA. In 2006, DOL issued a Request for Information about the FMLA and received thousands of comments from individual workers concerning how incredibly important the FMLA is in their lives. Indeed, DOL observed that it could have "written an entire report" based solely on the individual stories supplied by workers. Some of the stories included by DOL in its report illustrate why the FMLA is so important:

> As a cancer survivor myself, I cannot imagine how much more difficult those days of treatments and frequent doctor appointments would've been without FMLA. I did my best to be at work as much as possible, but chemotherapy and radiation not only

sap the body of energy, but also take hours every day and every week in treatment rooms.

FMLA has tremendously helped my family. I have a child born w/[asthma], allergies & other medical issues. And, there are times I'm out of work for days. [I]f I didn't have FMLA I would have been fired [a long] time ago. I've been able to maintain my employment and keep my household from having to need assistance from the commonwealth.

The FMLA has also been accepted and welcomed by employers. Data from the most recent national research on it, conducted by the U.S. Department of Labor, show that the vast majority of employers in this country report that complying with the FMLA has a positive or neutral effect on productivity (83 percent), profitability (90 percent), growth (90 percent), and employee morale (90 percent). The Act benefits employers in numerous ways, most notably the savings derived from retaining trained employees, from productive workers on the job, and from a positive work environment.

The Department of Labor agrees that the FMLA is working well. According to its 2007 Report:

> [The] Department is pleased to observe that, in the vast majority of cases, the FMLA is working as intended. For example, the FMLA has succeeded in allowing working parents to take leave for the birth or adoption of a child, and in allowing employees to care for family members with serious health conditions. The FMLA also appears to work well when employees require block or foreseeable intermittent leave because of their own truly serious health condition. Absent the protections of the FMLA, many of these workers might not otherwise be permitted to be absent from their jobs when they need to be.

Of course, we recognize that the FMLA is only working well for those employees who can access its protections. In the rest of my statement, I will discuss where we should expand the law to cover more employees. At the same time, we should also look at how we need to fix the law—a good example of that is making sure that flight attendants are covered under the FMLA, and there is a bill to make that happen currently pending in Congress.

II. The Department of Labor's Proposed Regulations

In February, the Department issued new proposed regulations for the FMLA. Taken as a whole, the proposed changes are cause for concern for workers. The proposed changes upset the careful balance struck by the FMLA between the needs of employers and workers to favor the employers. If these regulations are enacted, workers will find that they must give more notice, more information, have more medical examinations, and respond to employer requirements in shorter time frames. Employers, on the other hand, would have more time to respond to employees' request for FMLA leave and more ways to delay or deny FMLA leave.

These proposed changes that could make it harder for workers are almost entirely based on anecdotal information from employers. DOL has not conducted any rigorous analysis or surveys of how the law is working since 2000. We believe that lacking such data, DOL should not be making wide-ranging policy changes. Furthermore, in the proposed regulations, DOL has provided for limited additional education for employees to learn about these changes and the FMLA in general. We already know that many employees do not take FMLA leave because they are simply unaware that they have the right to do so. These proposed regulatory changes may make it even more difficult for employees, including those who know about the FMLA, to take their FMLA leave. Thus, DOL should be proposing a major mandatory FMLA education campaign for workers and employers to accompany any changes it makes. . . .

Among the proposed changes that DOL did put forward, the ones about which we are most concerned are the following:

- *Making it More Difficult to Use Paid Leave While on FMLA Leave*
  Being unable to afford to take unpaid leave is the most common reason that workers who qualify for and need FMLA leave do not take it. Currently, workers are relatively free to use their earned paid leave (vacation time and personal time) while on FMLA leave so they are able to be paid while on FMLA leave. Under the proposed regulations, in order to use that earned vacation or personal time while on FMLA leave, workers will have to meet the employer's rules for using vacation or personal time. Many employers require advance notice for using vacation leave, require that it be used in day-long increments, or refuse to allow vacation leave during certain times of the year. Because of these employer policies, this change would make it more difficult for workers to use their accrued paid time off while on FMLA leave. Many workers may not be able to take the FMLA leave they need because they cannot afford to miss a paycheck.
- *Increased Requirements for Workers Seeking Leave*
  If enacted, the proposed regulations will shorten the time in which employees must give notice of their need for leave, increase the amount of information they must give their employers, require them to follow certain employer practices for notification, and increase the number of medical re-certifications and fitness for duty certifications employees must produce. Employees who fail to meet these new standards may find their FMLA leave delayed or denied. Meanwhile, the proposed regulations extend the time employers have to respond to employee requests for leave.
- *Increased Direct Contact between the Employer and the Employee's Health Care Provider*
  Currently, if an employer wants to clarify information on a worker's FMLA medical certificate or authenticate the information, the employer has to follow a two-step process. First, the employer has to obtain the employee's permission to talk to her doctor and then the employer has to have a medical professional

talk directly with the worker's doctor. Under the proposed rule, to clarify information on the medical certification, an employer could contact an employee's health care provider after obtaining a medical release from the employee; there would not longer be a requirement that the employer use a health care provider to make this contact. If the employee refuses to allow the employer access to the health care provider, FMLA leave could be delayed or denied.

If the employer wants to check that the health care provider listed on the certificate actually saw the employee and filled out the certificate, under the proposed rules the employer could contact the health care provider directly, without getting the employee's permission.

Employees, especially those with serious health conditions that carry social stigma, are very concerned that employers will now have more direct access to their health information.

III. Expanding the Number of Employees Covered by the FMLA

Rather than working to limit employees' access to family and medical leave, we should be examining how we can make FMLA a reality for more employees. Currently, close to 40% of workers in the United States work for employers with less than 50 employees and thus are not covered by the minimal protections the FMLA provides. Analysis by the National Partnership shows that reducing the employer-size threshold to 25 workers would extend FMLA protections to approximately 13 million more workers. This would reduce the percentage of employees not covered by the FMLA from 40% of the workforce to 29%. . . .

It is also important to cover more employees by removing the requirements that limit employees from being eligible for FMLA leave because they have not been on the job long enough. FMLA leave is a basic labor standard. With very few exceptions, we do not allow other labor standards, such as minimum wage or basic workplace safety standards, to be accessed only by employees who have been on the job for a certain length of time. . . . Removing job tenure requirements would give part-time workers or workers employed at more than one job access to FMLA leave and ensure they are better equipped to meet critical family responsibilities without risking their jobs.

IV. Expanding the Family Members Covered by the Family and Medical Leave Act

Families in the United States are not "one size fits all," and the FMLA needs to be expanded to recognize this reality. For example, several states have extended the protections of their state family and medical leave laws to domestic partners; Maine did so just last year. Ideally, the federal FMLA should be extended to all domestic partners. Furthermore, as families are more spread apart geographically than ever before and caregiving requirements are increasing as the population ages, extended family members like grandparents, siblings, adult children, and parents-in-law are either needing care or stepping forward to take care of family members in need. Currently, the FMLA does not recognize these relationships for the purposes of caregiving, leaving these caregivers without access to FMLA leave when they desperately need it. I am glad to report that the new military leave provisions of the FMLA accommodate this dynamic and extend FMLA leave to qualifying "next of kin" rather than simply the family members currently covered in the FMLA. To truly support working families, we need for this expansion to apply to more than just military families.

V. Paid Sick Days—The Next Minimum Labor Standard?

FMLA coverage for illnesses is limited to serious, longer-term illnesses and the effects of long-term chronic conditions. The statute is predicated on the belief that workers have access to sick time off in order to deal with illnesses that do not meet the FMLA standard of "serious" and for routine medical visits for themselves and their families. However, in reality, many workers do not have sick time and even those covered by the FMLA may not have job-protected sick time or sick time that they may use to care for a family member. In order to address this issue, we urge Congress to pass the Healthy Families Act, a law that guarantees seven paid sick days a year for full-time workers and a pro-rated amount for part-time workers employed in businesses with 15 or more workers. . . .

VI. Paid Family and Medical Leave

Politicians and lawmakers often speak passionately about building a nation that values families, and the FMLA was a monumental step toward this goal. But it was only a first step. Millions of Americans cannot afford to take advantage of the protections it affords. We strongly support expanding the FMLA to make it more accessible to all working families and to make paid family and medical leave an option for working families who simply cannot afford to take the unpaid leave the FMLA provides.

Without some form of wage replacement, the FMLA's promise of job-protected leave is a chimera for too many women and men. In fact, 78% of employees who qualified for FMLA leave and needed to take the leave did not because they could not afford to go without a paycheck. More than one-third (34%) of the men and women who take FMLA receive no pay during leave, and another large share of the population have a very limited amount of paid leave available to them.

Two months ago, we received a story from a woman in Colorado that illustrates how devastating the lack of wages while on leave can be:

> I needed to take FMLA when I was pregnant. My job didn't offer paid leave when I gave birth to my daughter. Because of FMLA I was guaranteed time off when I was put on bed rest. Because it was unpaid I had to work from my bed and go back to work before my daughter was ready for me to go back. Financially I needed to go back to work. My daughter was 4 weeks old and on oxygen. I had to make special arrangements for a family friend to watch her instead of the childcare facility because of her age and special needs.

When a personal or family medical crisis strikes, workers frequently have no choice but to take unpaid leave or leave their jobs. As a result, for many workers, the birth of a child or an illness in the family forces them into a cycle of economic distress. Twenty-five percent of all poverty spells begin with the birth of a child, according to The David and Lucile Packard Foundation.

The lack of paid family and medical leave hits low-income workers hardest; almost three in four low-income employees who take family and medical leave receive no pay, compared to between one in three and one in four middle- and upper-income employees. In addition, low-income workers, as well as their children and family members, are more likely to be in poor health, in large part because many lack health insurance and are not eligible for coverage under Medicaid and SCHIP.

Providing paid family and medical leave helps ensure workers can perform essential caretaking responsibilities for newborns and newly-adopted children. Parents who are financially able to take leave are able to give new babies the critical care they need in the early weeks of life, laying a strong foundation for later development. Paid family and medical leave may even reduce health care costs. Studies have shown that when parents are able to be involved in their children's health care, children recover faster.

Paid family and medical leave will also help the exponentially growing number of workers who are caring for older family members. Thirty-five percent of workers, both women and men, report they have cared for an older relative in the past year. Roughly half of Americans 65 years of age and older participate in the labor force. Many require time away from work to care for their own health or the health of a family member.

A national paid family and medical leave program will help businesses. Studies show that the cost of losing an employee (advertising for, interviewing and training a replacement) is often far greater than the cost of providing short-term leave to retain existing employees. The average cost of turnover is 25% of an employee's total compensation. When businesses take care of their workers, they are better able to retain them, and when workers have the security of paid family leave, they experience increased commitment, productivity, and morale, and their employers reap the benefits of lower turnover and training costs. Finally, establishing a national paid family and medical leave program will help small business owners because it will allow them to offer a benefit that they could not afford to provide on their own. This will help level the playing field with larger businesses, making it easier for small businesses to compete for the best workers.

As described below, only a handful of states offer paid family and medical leave programs for workers in their states. . . .

The public strongly supports paid family and medical leave. This fall, the National Partnership released national polling data that shows consistent support for paid family and medical leave. Respondents were asked whether they would support a plan in which workers and employers pay a dollar each every week for paid family and medical leave. 76% of the total sample were supportive. Hispanics and African

Americans were even more strongly supportive—86% and 84% respectively. Neither gender nor age affected support for the proposal: 73% of men and 78% of women supported it as did, as noted above, a large majority of respondents of all ages.

A. States Leading the Way

Realizing the importance of paid family and medical leave, state programs are starting to provide it. Already, the six states with temporary disability programs (California, Hawaii, New Jersey, New York, Rhode Island and Puerto Rico) provide wage replacement for women during the period of disability due to pregnancy.

California

In 2004, California became the first state to provide wage replacement while a worker is on family leave. The most comprehensive of its kind, the law has given more than 13 million California workers (nearly one-tenth our country's workforce) partial income replacement (roughly 55% of wages) while they care for a new child or seriously ill family member. Premiums for the program are paid entirely by workers and are incorporated into the state's temporary disability fund. Critically, the wage replacement program covers all California workers who pay into the system; it is not limited to those who are covered by the federal or state family medical leave act. Thus, the program reaches workers who may need it the most—those who are not covered because they work for small businesses or do not have a long tenure at their current job. Studies of workers using the wage replacement offered by the law show that 88% do so to care for a new baby and 12% do so to take care of another family member.

Washington State

In May of 2007, Washington State became the second state in the country to enact a paid parental leave program. Washington's program will provide $250.00 per week for five weeks to new parents who are staying home with their child. Although not as expansive as California's, Washington's program also covers more workers than the FMLA and provides job-protected leave for employees who work in establishments with over 25 employees.

New Jersey

This week, New Jersey passed a paid family and medical leave program. New Jersey expanded its existing temporary disability insurance program to add six weeks of paid family leave, providing two-thirds of a worker's salary while they are on leave, and making it available to all workers in the state.

Wage Replacement or Income Insurance Campaigns in Other States

More states are engaging in efforts to provide the necessary income for workers to be able to take the leave the need. In the past year there have been active campaigns to make family and medical leave affordable by guaranteeing some wage replacement in New York, Illinois, and Oregon. Additionally, Massachusetts, Pennsylvania, Arizona and Texas all introduced bills to create paid family and medical leave.

VII. Where We Stand Internationally

The United States stands alone among industrialized nations in its complete lack of a national program to ensure that workers are financially able to take leave when they have a new baby or need to care for an ill family member or recover from an illness. A Harvard/McGill study of 173 nations found that 169 guarantee paid leave to women in connection with childbirth, and 66 ensure that fathers can take paid paternity leave. The United States is the only industrialized country without paid family leave, and guarantees no paid leave at all for mothers. It is in the company of just three other nations: Liberia, Papua New Guinea, and Swaziland.

VIII. Conclusion

It is time—past time—we join the rest of the world and make sure our families do not have to risk their financial health when they do what all of us agree is the right thing—take care of a family member who needs them. Now is the time to put family values to work by protecting the FMLA from burdensome regulations that could make it harder for workers to utilize it, and by expanding it to cover more workers and help those who urgently need paid leave.

Source: Ness, Debra. "Testimony. Subcommittee on Workforce Protections, Hearing on the Family and Medical Leave Act, April 10, 2008." 110th Congress, 2nd session, Committee on Education and Labor. Serial No. 110-86. Washington, DC: Government Printing Office, 2008, pp. 49–59.

SOCIOLOGIST MICHAEL KIMMEL EXAMINES THE WORLD OF "GUYLAND," 2008

As American girls and women have made cultural and economic inroads into areas of American life that were once the domains of men, they have increasingly come to regard themselves as fully equal with men, with agency to build whatever lives they want for themselves, resisting the desires of a culture that still remains paternalistic and sexist in many respects. The evolving attitudes, challenges, and opportunities of today's girls and women have been widely discussed and dissected, but the impact of evolving gender roles on American boys and men has been less extensively studied, at least historically. In recent years, however, a growing body of scholarship has been devoted to exploring American men and the ways they have responded to the women's rights movement, both positively (increased sharing in domestic chores and child-rearing responsibilities) and negatively (misogynistic attitudes and language). One of the most prominent of these scholars is sociologist and author Michael Kimmel (1951–), founder and director of the Center for the Study of Men and Masculinities at Stony Brook University. Following is an excerpt from his 2008 book Guyland: The Perilous World Where Boys Become Men, *a work that focuses on the social and cultural currents that many modern teen boys navigate on their passage into adulthood.*

Just Who Are These Guys?

The guys who populate Guyland are mostly white, middle-class kids; they are college-bound, in college, or have recently graduated; they're unmarried. They live communally with other guys, in dorms, apartments, or fraternities. Or they live with their parents (even after college). Their jobs, if they have them, are modest, low-paying, low-prestige ones in the service sector or entry-level corporate jobs that leave them with plenty of time to party. They're good kids, by and large. They blend into the crowd, drift with the tide, and often pass unnoticed through the lecture halls and multistory dorms of America's large college campuses.

Of course, there are many young people of this age group who are highly motivated, focused, with a clear vision and direction in their lives. Their stories of resilience and motivation will provide a telling rejoinder to many of the dominant patterns of Guyland. There are also just as many who immediately move back home after college, directionless, with a liberal arts BA that qualifies them for nothing more than a dead-end job making lattes or folding jeans. So while a few of them might jump right into a career or graduate school immediately after college, many more simply drift for a while, comforting themselves with the assurances that they have plenty of time to settle down later, after they've had their fun.

In some respects, Guyland can be defined by what guys do for fun. It's the "boyhood" side of the continuum they're so reluctant to leave. It's drinking, sex, and video games. It's watching sports, reading about sports, listening to sports on the radio. It's television—cartoons, reality shows, music videos, shoot-em-up movies, sports, and porn—pizza, and beer. It's all the behavior that makes the real grownups in their lives roll their eyes and wonder, "When will he *grow up*?!"

There are some parts of Guyland that are quite positive. The advancing age of marriage, for example, benefits both women and men, who have more time to explore career opportunities, not to mention establishing their identities, before committing to home and family. And much of what qualifies as fun in Guyland is relatively harmless. Guys grow out of a lot of the sophomoric humor—if not after their "sophomore" year, then at least by their mid-twenties.

Yet, there is a disturbing undercurrent to much of it as well. Teenage boys spend countless hours blowing up the galaxy, graphically splattering their computer screens in violent video games. College guys post pornography everywhere in their dorm rooms; indeed, pornographic pictures are among the most popular screen savers on male college students' computers. In fraternities and dorms on virtually every campus, plenty of guys are getting drunk almost every night, prowling for women with whom they can hook up, and chalking it all up to harmless fun. White suburban boys don do-rags and gangsta tattoos appropriating inner-city

African-American styles to be cool. Homophobia is ubiquitous; indeed, "that's so gay" is probably the most frequently used put-down in middle schools, high schools, and college today. And sometimes gay-baiting takes an ugly turn and becomes gay-bashing.

All the while, these young people are listening to shock jocks on the radio, laughing at cable-rated T&A on the current generation's spinoffs of "The Man Show" and watching Spike TV, the "man's network," guffawing to sophomoric body-fluid humor of college circuit comedians who make Beavis and Butt-head sound quaint. They're laughing at clueless henpecked husbands on TV sitcoms; snorting derisively at guys who say the wrong thing on beer ads; snickering at duded-up metrosexuals prancing around major metropolitan centers drinking Cosmos and imported vodka. Unapologetically "politically incorrect" magazines, radio hosts, and television shows abound, filled with macho bluster and bikini-clad women bouncing on trampolines. And the soundtrack in these new boys' clubhouses, the sonic wallpaper in every dorm room and every shared apartment, is some of the angriest music ever made. Nearly four out of every five gangsta rap CDs are bought by suburban white guys. It is not just the "boys in the hood" who are a "menace to society." It's the boys in the "burbs."

Occasionally, the news from Guyland is shocking—and sometimes even criminal. There are guys who are drinking themselves into oblivion on campus on any given night of the week, organizing parties where they spike women's drinks with Rohypnol (the date rape drug), or just try to ply them with alcohol to make them more compliant—and then videotaping their conquests. These are the guys who are devising elaborately sadomasochistic hazing rituals for high-school athletic teams, collegiate fraternities, or military squads.

It is true, of course, that white guys do not have a monopoly on appalling behavior. There are plenty of young black and Latino boys who are equally desperate to prove their manhood, to test themselves before the watchful evaluative eyes of other guys. But only among white boys do the negative dynamics of Guyland seem to play themselves out so invisibly. Often, when there's news of young black boys behaving badly, the media takes on a "what can you expect?" attitude, failing to recognize that expecting such behavior from black men is just plain racism. But every time white boys hit the headlines, regardless of how frequently, there is an element of shock, a collective, "How could this happen? He came from such a good family!" Perhaps not identifying the parallel criminal behavior among white guys adds an additional cultural element to the equation: identification. Middle-class white families see the perpetrators as "our guys." We know them, we are them, they cannot be like that.

Though Guyland is not exclusively white, neither is it an equal opportunity venture. Guyland rests on a bed of middle-class entitlement, a privileged sense that you are special, that the world is there for you to take. Upwardly mobile minorities feel the same tugs between claiming their rightful share of good times and delaying adult responsibilities that the more privileged white guys feel. But it often works itself out differently for them. Because of the needs and expectations of their families, they tend to opt for a more traditional trajectory. Indeed, many minority youths have begun to move into those slots designated for the ambitious and motivated, just at the moment that those slots are being abandoned by white guys having fun.

Some think they're fulfilling the American Dream, yet most feel as if they're wearing another man's clothes. Take Carlos, the son of illegal immigrants, who worked in the central California fields, harvesting artichokes and Brussels sprouts. Carlos is their success story, a track star and good student, who got recruited to several colleges and landed a scholarship to USC. But now he feels torn between the pressure from his family "to be the first in everything"—the first college grad, the first doctor—and from his friends in his hometown of Gilroy to hang out with them over the summer.

Or Eric, who just graduated from Morehouse College in Atlanta. He says he's "out of step" with his other African-American friends; he is highly motivated and serious, eschews hip-hop, and always knew he wanted to get married, start a family, and get a good job. Heavily recruited out of college, he's already a regional manager for Coca-Cola in Atlanta and dating a senior at Spelman. They plan to marry next June. "Too many of my friends think gangsta is the way to go," he says, nodding at a table nearby of college guys sporting the latest do-rags and bling. "But in my family, being a man meant stepping up and being responsible. That was what being a Morehouse Man meant to me. I can live with that."

And while the American college campus is Guyland Central, guys who don't go to college have ample opportunities—in the military, in police stations and firehouses, on every construction site and in every factory, in every neighborhood bar—for the intimately crude male bonding that characterizes Guyland's standard operating procedure. Sure, some working-class guys cannot afford to prolong their adolescence; their family needs them, and their grownup income, too badly. With no college degree to fall back on, and parents who are not financially able or willing to support a prolonged adolescence, they don't have the safety net that makes Guyland possible. But they find other ways, symbolic or real, at work or at play, to hold onto their glory days—or they become so resentful they seethe with jealous rage at the privileged few who seem able to delay responsibility indefinitely.

Greg, for example, never made it to college. He didn't regret it at the time, but now he wonders. The son and grandson of steel workers near Bethlehem, Pennsylvania, Greg knew he'd end up at Beth Steel also—except the steel plant closed and suddenly all those jobs disappeared. Even if he could go to college now, it's too expensive, and besides, he needs to save for a new car so he can move out of his parents' house. In the past two years he's worked at a gas station, Home Depot, a minimart convenience store, and as a groundskeeper at a local university. "I'm trying, honest, I really am," he says, with a certain resigned sadness already creeping into his 24-year-old eyes. "But there is just no way an honest white guy can make a living in this economy—not with these Bush fat cats and all the illegals."

Rather than embracing Guyland as a way of life, working-class guys instead seem to inhabit Guyland at their local sports bar, on the factory shop floor, and in the bowling league or military unit. Yet the same sense of entitlement, the same outraged response to the waning of privilege, is clear. One Brooklyn bar near my house has been home to generations of firefighters and their pals. There's an easy ambience about the place, the comfort of younger and older guys (all white) sharing a beer and shooting the breeze. Until I happen to ask one guy about female firefighters. The atmosphere turns menacing, and a defensive anger spills out of the guys near me. "Those b**ches have taken over," says Patrick.

> They're everywhere. You know that ad "it's everywhere you want to be." That's like women. *They're* everywhere *they* want to be! There's nowhere you can go anymore—factories, beer joints, military, even the goddamned firehouse! [Raucous agreement all around.] We working guys are just f****d.

The camaraderie of working-class guys long celebrated in American history and romanticized in Hollywood films—the playful bonding of the locker room, the sacrificial love of the foxhole, the courageous tenacity of the firehouse or police station—has a darker side. Homophobic harassment of the new guys, racial slurs, and seething sexism often lie alongside the casual banter of the band of brothers, and this is true in both the working-class bar and the university coffee house.

And although my focus is American guys, Guyland is not exclusively American terrain. Both Britain and Australia have begun to examine "Laddism"—the anomic, free-floating, unattached and often boorish behavior of young males. "Lads" are Guys with British accents—consuming the same media, engaging in the same sorts of behaviors, and lubricating their activities with the same alcohol. In Italy, they're called *bamboccioni,* or "*mammoni,*" or Mama's boys. Half of all Italian men between 25 and 34 live with their parents. In France, they're called "*Tanguys*" after the French film with that title about their lifestyle.

Guyland revolves almost exclusively around other guys. It is a social space as well as a time zone—a pure, homosocial Eden, uncorrupted by the sober responsibilities of adulthood. The motto of Guyland is simple: "Bros Before Hos" (Long "o" in both Bro and Ho.) Just about every guy knows this—knows that his "brothers" are his real soul mates, his real life-partners. To them he swears allegiance and will take their secrets to his grave. And guys do not live in Guyland all the time. They take temporary vacations—when they are alone with their girlfriends or even a female friend, or when they are with their parents, teachers, or coaches.

Girls in Guyland—Babes in Boyland

What about girls? Guys love girls—all that homosociality might become suspect if they didn't! It's *women* they can't stand. Guyland is the more grownup version of the clubhouse on *The Little Rascals*—the "He-Man Woman Haters Club." Women demand responsibility and respectability, the antitheses of Guyland. Girls are fun and sexy, even friends, as long as they respect the centrality of guys' commitment to the band of brothers. And when girls are allowed in, they have to play by guy rules—or they don't get to play at all.

Girls contend daily with Guyland—the constant stream of pornographic humor in college dorms or libraries, or at countless work stations in offices across the country; the constant pressure to shape their bodies into idealized hyper-Barbies. Guyland sets the terms under which girls try to claim their own agency, develop their own senses of self. Guyland sets the terms of friendship, of sexual activity, of who is "in" and who is decidedly "out." Girls can even *be* guys—if they know something about sports (but not too much), enjoy casual banter about sex (but not too actively), and dress and act in ways that are pleasantly unthreatening to boys' fragile sense of masculinity.

Some of the girls have mastered the slouching look, the indifferent affect, the contemptuous attitude, the swaggering posture, the foul language, and the aggressive behaviors of guys. Since Guyland is often the only game in town, who can blame them if they indulge in a little—or a lot—of what I call "guyification"? Observe a group of college-age women. It's likely they're wearing jeans, T-shirts, oversized sweatshirts, running shoes or sandals—guywear. If not, they'll be wearing thong underwear, skimpy mini T-shirts that leave their midriffs bare, and supertight pants, leggings, or miniskirts. And for which gender are they getting all Barbied up? (Here's a quiz: Which gender invented the thong and presents it as the latest fashion accessory for women?) And listen as they call each other "guys" all the time, even when no actual guys are around. It's become the generic term for "person."

Some girls have parlayed their post-feminist assertiveness into "girl power," or *grrrl* power. A few think that they can achieve equality by imitating guys' behaviors—by running circles around them on the athletic field or matching them drink for drink or sexual hookup for hookup. But it's a cruel distortion of those ideals of early feminist liberation when female assertiveness is redefined as the willingness to hike up your sweater and reveal your breasts for a roving camera in a "Girls Gone Wild" video. And sexual equality is hardly achieved when she is willing to perform oral sex on his entire group of friends.

And most girls also know the motto "Bros Before Hos." A girl senses that she is less than, not a bro, and that underneath all his syrupy flattering is the condescension and contempt one naturally has for a ho. Girls also know the joke about the difference between a b**ch and a sl*t (their only two choices in Guyland): "A b**ch will sleep with everyone but you." Girls live in Guyland, but they do not define it. They contend with it and make their peace with it, each in their own way.

Source: Kimmel, Michael. *Guyland: The Perilous World Where Boys Become Men.* New York: HarperCollins, 2008, pp. 8–15.

Chapter 8: 2008–Present: The Fight to Restore Women's Rights

Democrat Barack Obama served two terms, from January 2009 to January 2017, as president of the United States. He was first elected in 2008, following George W. Bush, and he was reelected in 2012. One of his administration's top policy priorities was helping women succeed, because as Obama himself said, when women succeed, America succeeds.[1] Obama's stance reflected some realities of U.S. society that would have stunned Americans of earlier generations. Women were now the majority of college graduates. They were also a growing proportion of the labor force. And they were primary or co-primary wage earners in two-thirds of American families. In spite of women's essential contributions to the economic and cultural vitality of the nation, however, Obama argued that our society still did not sufficiently value women or ensure that they were treated equitably. He supported numerous policies that trained women for better-paying jobs and that provided support for them in the workplace and in their homes. He also prioritized policies and legislation to provide women and girls greater protection from violence at home and at school, to give them opportunities in educational subjects historically closed off to them, and to encourage leadership positions for women in the government.

Shortly after taking office, Obama began to take action in regard to these priorities. The first act he signed after taking office was the Lilly Ledbetter[2] Fair Pay Act, which extended the statute of limitations on reporting sex discrimination in the workforce. Upon signing this act, President Obama stated, "It is fitting that with the very first bill I sign . . . we are upholding one of this nation's first principles: that we are all created equal and each deserve a chance to pursue our own version of happiness."

Throughout his eight years in office, Obama launched initiatives that monitored the gender gap in wages. In 2010, for instance, he established the National Equal Pay Enforcement Task Force to support executive agencies tasked with monitoring equal pay enforcement. In April 2014, to celebrate Equal Pay Day, he signed two executive actions to recognize the full equality of women and increase equity for

---

1. Obama's commitment to women's economic equality resulted in a gender gap in the ballot box. In both of his elections, he won a much higher proportion of women's votes than his opponents (i.e., a 14% gap in 2008 and a 20% gap in 2012).

2. Lilly Ledbetter was a supervisor at a Goodyear Tire and Rubber who filed a sex discrimination claim after discovering that her salary was 40 percent lower than the lowest-paid male supervisor at the company. Ledbetter won the case and won 3.5 million dollars for her losses. The decision was overturned in 2007 due to its ambiguous language.

all in the workplace. The first of these orders prohibited federal contractors from discriminating against employees who discuss their compensation. The second was a presidential memorandum instructing the Secretary of Labor to propose a new regulation requiring federal contractors to submit summary data on compensation paid to their employees, including by race and gender (Obama White House Archives 2016).

Another significant action that Obama took early in his first term in office was the creation of the White House Council on Women and Girls. The purpose of the council was to ensure that all federal agencies "take into account the needs of women and girls in the policies they draft, the programs they create, [and] the legislation they support," and in signing the executive order, Obama emphasized that "the purpose of our government is to ensure that in America, all things are still possible for all people."

In 2016, Obama convened a White House summit entitled the United State of Women. The summit was designed as a vehicle to summarize the issues the administration considered of great importance, had taken action on, and wanted to identify as ongoing challenges that the next president would have to address. The summit was hosted by the White House, along with the U.S. Department of State, the U.S. Department of Labor, and the Aspen Institute. The summit's theme was "Today We Change Tomorrow," and it was dedicated to discussing a number of topics, including economic empowerment, equal pay for equal work, women's health and education, and violence against women

Gender Gap in Pay

The United States has had an Equal Pay Act since 1963. In spite of this, a significant gender gap in pay still exists. This is caused, in part, by gender segregation in the workforce. Women are concentrated in lower-paying and lower-status jobs. While this may be due in some way to women's choices to select these jobs, research has shown that there are structural constraints and discrimination at play that also act to keep women from reaching full pay parity. One solution to this problem would be to set pay schedules for women in line with "male-dominated jobs" that are of comparable value. This proposal has long been opposed by the national Chamber of Commerce and other business-related lobbying groups. Federal law now states that "employers may not pay unequal wages to men and women who perform jobs that require substantially equal skill, effort and responsibility, and that are performed under similar working conditions within the same establishment."

Obama supported the Paycheck Fairness Act, which was introduced into the House and Senate in 2014. The act was designed to update and strengthen the Equal Pay Act in important ways, including providing for more efficient solutions to the pay gap, instituting a systematic program for the collection of data on wages, preventing retaliation by employers against employees who file complaints of sex discrimination in wages, and allowing workers to file class action suits. The act failed to gain passage in the Republican-controlled Congress (National Women's Law Center 2014).

In January 2016, Obama proposed a new rule that would require businesses with 100 or more employees to report pay data by gender, race, and ethnicity. Having these data would help the federal government to monitor and enforce laws pertaining to equal opportunity.

Combating Violence against Women

Addressing the continuing prevalence of violence directed at women was another priority of the Obama administration. Obama's vice president, Joe Biden, had actually written the original Violence Against Women Act, the landmark legislation passed by Congress and signed into law by President Clinton in 1994. Passage of the original act increased public awareness of this issue and was followed by a decline in annual rates of domestic violence. But it still occurs. Obama and Biden applauded when Congress reauthorized the Violence Against Women Act in 2013. They initiated a public awareness campaign, "It's On Us," to encourage all Americans to commit themselves to become part of the solution in stamping out gender-based violence. They also created a task force to investigate the high incidence of sexual assault on college campuses. Obama stated the rationale for this as follows: "An estimated one in five women has been sexually assaulted during her college years— one in five. Of those assaults, only 12 percent are reported, and of those reported assaults, only a fraction of the offenders are punished" (Somanader 2014).

The Obama administration also grappled with the problem of sexual assault in the U.S. military, an enduring issue despite the fact that women fulfill a wide array of essential roles in the nation's defense (including serving in ground combat capacities as of 2015). The Pentagon first systematically collected data on the prevalence of sexual assault (i.e., rape, sexual assault, forcible sodomy, aggravated sexual contact, abusive sexual contact, and attempts to commit these offenses) in 2006 and has continued doing so since then. According to the results of the surveys, the number of sexual assaults appears to be declining. There were 14,900 reported sexual assaults in 2016, the lowest recorded by the survey since it was first conducted. The survey estimated 26,000 sexual assaults in 2012 and 20,300 in 2014. Men as well as women experience sexual assault. In fact, until recently, more men than women had been victimized. Prior to the repeal of "Don't Ask, Don't Tell" in 2011, male-on-male rape victims could actually be discharged for having engaged in homosexual conduct.

Victims of sexual assault in the military are reluctant to report the assault for several reasons; one is fear of retaliation, and another is shame. In 2016, Senator Claire McCaskill of Missouri and Senator Joni Ernst of Iowa sponsored the Military Retaliation Prevention Act, which is aimed at ending retaliation for reporting sexual assault. In some cases, the person to whom the victim reports may be an assailant.

In 2017, a shocking example of disrespect and sexual harassment of women in the U.S. military by current and former Marines once again came under intense scrutiny. A private Facebook group called Marines United, which had more than 30,000 male members, was caught sharing thousands of nude photos of women (many of whom were current or former members of the military) on Facebook without their consent. Observers of the Marine Corps culture have found it to be extremely misogynistic, which may account for the fact that it has the smallest proportion of women among its ranks as well as the highest rate of sexual assault (Keller 2017).

The U.S. military opened an inquiry, and senior lawmakers on Capitol Hill have denounced the violations. Marine Corps general Robert Neller, in his testimony before the Senate, included the following comments:

> To the men in our Corps, serving today and those whom no longer wear the uniform, you're still Marines. I need you to ask yourselves, how much more do the females of our Corps have to do to be accepted? Was it enough when Major Megan McClung was killed by an IED in Ramadi? Or Captain Jennifer Harris killed when her helicopter was shot down while she was flying blood from Baghdad to Fallujah Surgical? Or Corporals Jennifer Parcell and Hallie Ann Sharat and Ramona Valdez all killed by the hands of our enemies? What is it going to take for you to accept these Marines as Marines? I'm committed to making this right and I need all Marines equally committed. We all have to commit to getting rid of this perversion to our culture. Enough is enough. (Gajanan 2017).

Health Care Reform: The Affordable Care Act

The Affordable Care Act (ACA), though not often branded as a gendered policy, has had enormous implications for women. Before the passage of the ACA, also commonly known as "Obamacare," insurance companies could—and often did—charge women different premiums than men for the same coverage. As of January 1, 2014, the ACA prohibits this gender discrimination. The ACA has increased coverage for millions of women and helped millions more remain healthy with improved access to preventive services such as mammograms, Pap smears, contraception, domestic violence screening, and other vital health services for no out-of-pocket cost. The ACA has also been instrumental in providing maternity benefits. The ACA requires insurance plans to cover maternity-related preventive services, which help increase the likelihood of a healthy and safe delivery (Jarrett 2015).

The Fatherhood Initiative

In June 2010, President Obama announced a new program designed to inform men about parenting and to help them become more engaged as fathers. Acknowledging that the federal government can't force men to participate in the lives of their children (other than state laws requiring men to pay child support), Obama proposed community programs that would provide job training, parenting skills classes, and domestic violence prevention. He also spoke about a special initiative to help men who were transitioning from incarceration to meet their child support obligations and to successfully reenter society. "The President's Fatherhood Pledge is an effort to encourage individuals, especially fathers, to be involved in the lives of their children, and to be positive role models and mentors for the children in their lives and communities" (https://www.fatherhood.gov/pledge).

Presidential Election of 2016

In 2016, Hillary Rodham Clinton, a two-term U.S. senator from New York (2001 to 2009) and former secretary of state under Obama (from 2009 to 2013), earned the Democratic nomination for president. Clinton's campaign focused on raising middle-class incomes, expanding women's rights, instituting campaign finance reform, and improving the Affordable Care Act. Clinton explicitly endorsed equal pay for equal work (a major feminist issue), the right to same-sex marriage, and providing undocumented immigrants with a path to citizenship.

Clinton was widely expected to win the election against Republican nominee Donald J. Trump, a television celebrity and business executive who had no previous political experience. In fact, Clinton did win nearly three million more popular votes than Trump, but Trump won the election because he garnered more electoral votes. Clinton is the first woman to win the popular vote in an election for U.S. president. On January 21, 2017, the day after Trump's inauguration, over 2.6 million people around the world (including an estimated 500,000 in the nation's capital) participated in the Women's March, which emphasized support for the positions that Hillary Clinton, and Barack Obama before her, had promoted on women's issues.

The American public hasn't always been comfortable with the idea of having a woman president. The Gallup Organization began to ask Americans this question in 1937. That year, Gallup asked a sample of 1,500 adults if they would vote for a woman for president if she were qualified "in every other respect." Sixty-four percent of the respondents said they would not support a woman for president even if she were qualified. Gallup continued the poll but changed the wording slightly in 1945. The new question was, "If the party whose candidate you most often support nominated a woman for president of the United States, would you vote for her if she seemed the best qualified for the job?" More than half of the respondents said they would not vote for a woman candidate even under the circumstances mentioned. Data from opinion polls show a gradual increase in support starting in the 1950s and 1960s. During the 1970s, public support for a woman president increased, such that by 1978, nearly three-quarters of the population said they would vote for a woman candidate if the party they supported nominated her. By 2015, nearly all Americans (95 percent) said they would vote for a qualified woman candidate if their party nominated one (Vavreck 2015). Given this level of willingness to vote for a woman candidate for president, along with Hillary

Clinton's success in winning the popular vote, it is reasonable to expect that there will be a woman president before the middle of the 21st century.

References

Gajanan, Mahita. "What the Head of the U.S. Marines Said to Female Marines after the Naked Photo Scandal." *Time*, March 14, 2017. http://time.com/4701509/robert-neller -marine-nude-photo.

Jarrett, Valerie. "Great Strides for Women's Health Under the Affordable Care Act." White House, President Barack Obama. January 19, 2015. https://obamawhitehouse.archives .gov/blog/2015/01/09/great-strides-women-s-health-under-affordable-care-act.

Keller, Jared. "The Rise and Fall (and Rise) of 'Marines United'." Task and Purpose, 2017. http://taskandpurpose.com/rise-fall-rise-marines-united.

Morelli, Caitlin. "Women's Issues in the Obama Era: Expanding Equality and Social Opportunity Under the Obama Administration." *Inquiries*, vol. 7, no. 2 (2015). http://www .inquiriesjournal.com/articles/992/3/womens-issues-in-the-obama-era-expanding -equality-and-social-opportunity-under-the-obama-administration.

National Women's Law Center. "How the Paycheck Fairness Act Will Strengthen the Equal Pay Act." 2014. https://nwlc.org/resources/how-paycheck-fairness-act-will-strengthen -equal-pay-act.

Obama White House Archives, "This Is Why Today Is Equal Pay Day," April 12, 2016. https://obamawhitehouse.archives.gov/blog/2016/04/12/why-today-equal-pay-day.

Somanader, Tanya. "President Obama Launches the "It's On Us" Campaign to End Sexual Assault on Campus." White House blog, September 19, 2014. https:// obamawhitehouse.archives.gov/blog/2014/09/19/president-obama-launches-its-us -campaign-end-sexual-assault-campus.

Vavreck, Lynn. "Changing View on a Female President." *New York Times* blog, June 19, 2015. https://www.nytimes.com/2015/06/20/upshot/changing-views-on-a-female -president.html.

THE BUSH ADMINISTRATION MINIMIZES WAGE DISPARITIES BETWEEN MEN AND WOMEN, 2009

One of the most common criticisms leveled against American workplaces by women's rights advocates is that they consistently pay women less than men, even for the same or comparable jobs. In the waning days of the George W. Bush administration, though, the Department of Labor released a study written for the department by the CONSAD Research Corporation that found that the so-called wage gap was much smaller than usually characterized by equal pay advocates. This study determined that much of the wage gap between men and women stemmed from the fact that women were more likely to work part-time, prioritize good benefits over higher pay in making employment choices, and leave the labor force to care for children or elderly parents. In a foreword to the study (reprinted below), Deputy Assistant Secretary for Labor Charles James Sr. wrote that the study indicated that "the raw wage gap should not be used as the basis to justify corrective action. . . . There may be nothing to correct." Equal pay advocates, however, noted that even though the CONSAD report downplayed the severity of wage inequality in American workplaces, it still found, even after controlling for the above-mentioned gender variables in employment circumstances, an adjusted gender wage gap of between 4.8 and 7.1 percent.

During the past three decades, women have made notable gains in the workplace and in pay equity, including increased labor force participation, substantial gains in educational attainment, employment growth in higher-paying occupations, and significant gains in real earnings.

In 1970, about 43 percent of women aged 16 and older were in the labor force; by 2007, over 59 percent were in labor force.

In 1970, only 17.9 percent of women aged 25 and older had gone to college; by 2000, almost half had gone to college; and by 2006 one-third of the women in the labor force held a college degree.

In 2007, women accounted for 51 percent of all workers in the high-paying management, professional, and related occupations. They outnumbered men in such occupations as financial managers, human resource managers, education administrators, medical and health services managers, and accountants and auditors.

In 1970, the median usual weekly earnings for women working full-time was only 62.1 percent of those for men; by 2007, the raw wage gap had shrunk from 37.9 percent to just 21.5 percent.

However, despite these gains the raw wage gap continues to be used in misleading ways to advance public policy agendas without fully explaining the reasons behind the gap. The purpose of this report is to identify the reasons that explain the wage gap in order to more fully inform policymakers and the public.

The following report prepared by CONSAD Research Corporation presents the results of a detailed statistical analysis of the attributes that contribute to the wage gap and a synopsis of the economic research that has been conducted on the issue. The major findings are:

There are observable differences in the attributes of men and women that account for most of the wage gap. Statistical analysis that includes those variables has produced results that collectively account for between 65.1 and 76.4 percent of a raw gender wage gap of 20.4 percent, and thereby leave an adjusted gender wage gap that is between 4.8 and 7.1 percent. These variables include:

> A greater percentage of women than men tend to work part-time. Part-time work tends to pay less than full-time work.
>
> A greater percentage of women than men tend to leave the labor force for child-birth, child care and elder care. Some of the wage gap is explained by the percentage of women who were not in the labor force during previous years, the age of women, and the number of children in the home.
>
> Women, especially working mothers, tend to value "family friendly" workplace policies more than men. Some of the wage gap is explained by industry and occupation, particularly, the percentage of women who work in the industry and occupation.

Research also suggests that differences not incorporated into the model due to data limitations may account for part of the remaining gap. Specifically, CONSAD's model and much of the literature, including the Bureau of Labor Statistics *Highlights of Women's Earnings*, focus on wages rather than total compensation. Research indicates that women may value non-wage benefits more than men do, and as a result prefer to take a greater portion of their compensation in the form of health insurance and other fringe benefits.

In principle, more of the raw wage gap could be explained by including some additional variables within a single comprehensive analysis that considers all of the factors simultaneously; however, such an analysis is not feasible to conduct with available data bases. Factors, such as work experience and job tenure, require data that describe the behavior of individual workers over extended time periods. The longitudinal data bases that contain such information include too few workers, however, to support adequate analysis of factors like occupation and industry. Cross-sectional data bases that include enough workers to enable analysis of factors like occupation and industry do not collect data on individual workers over long enough periods to support adequate analysis of factors like work experience and job tenure.

Although additional research in this area is clearly needed, this study leads to the unambiguous conclusion that the differences in the compensation of men and women are the result of a multitude of factors and that the raw wage gap should not be used as the basis to justify corrective action. Indeed, there may be nothing to correct. The differences in raw wages may be almost entirely the result of the individual choices being made by both male and female workers.

Charles E. James, Sr.
Deputy Assistant Secretary for
Federal Contract Compliance

Source: James, Charles E., Sr. "Foreword." In *An Analysis of Reasons for Disparity in Wages Between Men and Women.* U.S. Department of Labor, January 2009.

PARTISAN DIFFERENCES OVER THE LILLY LEDBETTER FAIR PAY RESTORATION ACT, 2009

In 2007 the U.S. Supreme Court issued a 5–4 decision in Ledbetter v. Goodyear Tire and Rubber Company *that greatly restricted the time period for filing complaints of employment discrimination in the realm of wages and other compensation. In essence, it stated that workers had only 180 days to file wage-discrimination lawsuits, even if the discrimination dated back years or decades. Civil rights and women's rights organizations condemned the decision, arguing that it meant that if employers kept their wage discrimination—whether based on gender, race, sexual orientation, religion, or another factor—effectively hidden from view for a long enough period of time, they wouldn't ever have to suffer the consequences for violating the Civil Rights Act of 1964, which explicitly bans such discrimination.*

Congressional Democrats promptly responded to the Ledbetter v. Goodyear *decision by introducing a bill called the Lilly Ledbetter Fair Pay Act that would greatly expand the time period during which employees could file lawsuits alleging wage discrimination. But although the bill was passed in the Democrat-controlled House, it was derailed in April 2008 by Senate Republicans who argued that it would lead to frivolous lawsuits and unfairly punish management teams that might have had nothing to do with past wage discrimination. But on January 8, 2009, Democrats, armed with majorities in both houses of Congress, reintroduced the act. The following are representative arguments made by most members of the two parties when the Ledbetter Act was reintroduced. The first excerpt is from a statement by Senator Patrick Leahy (D-VT), while the second is an excerpt from a Senate floor speech delivered by Senate minority leader Mitch McConnell (R-KY).*

Ultimately, Leahy and his Democratic colleagues prevailed on the Ledbetter bill. After being introduced in the 111th Congress by Senator Barbara Mikulski (D-MD), the Lilly Ledbetter Fair Pay Act passed the Senate by a 61–36 vote on January 22, 2009, with five Republicans crossing the party line to join with the unanimously supportive Democratic caucus. It passed the House five days later on a largely partisan 250–177 vote, as only three GOP members voted for it and only five Democrats voted against it. On January 29, 2009, Barack Obama made the bill the first legislation he signed into law as America's 44th president.

Statement of Senator Patrick Leahy

I am pleased to join Senators Mikulski, Kennedy, Snowe and others in introducing the Lilly Ledbetter Fair Pay Restoration Act of 2009. This legislation is long overdue and I am pleased that the Majority Leader will try again to move this legislation in the opening days of this new Congress. The Supreme Court's divided decision in *Ledbetter v. Goodyear Tire* struck a severe blow to the rights of working families across our country. More than 40 years ago, Congress acted to protect women and others against discrimination in the workplace. In the 21st century, equal pay for equal work should be a given in this country. Unfortunately, the reality is still far from this basic principle. American women still earn only 77 cents for every dollar earned by a male counterpart. That decreases to 62 cents on the dollar for African-American women and just 53 cents on the dollar for Hispanic-American women.

For nearly twenty years, Ms. Ledbetter was a manager at a Goodyear factory in Gadsden, Alabama. After decades of service, she learned through an anonymous note that her employer had been discriminating against her for years. She was the only woman among 16 employees at her management level, yet Ms. Ledbetter was paid between 15 and 40 percent less than all of her male colleagues, including several who had significantly less seniority. After filing a complaint with the Equal Employment Opportunity Commission, a Federal jury found that Ms. Ledbetter was owed almost $225,000 in back pay. However, five members of the Supreme Court overturned her jury verdict because she had filed her lawsuit more than 180 days after her employer's original discriminatory act.

I was honored to invite Ms. Ledbetter to testify at a Judiciary Committee Hearing I chaired in September to examine how the Supreme Court's recent decisions have affected the lives of ordinary Americans. Ms. Ledbetter's case is but one example of how the Supreme Court has dramatically misinterpreted the intent of Congress and offered a liability shield to corporate wrong-doers.

This decision is yet another example of the Supreme Court's increasing willingness to overturn juries who hear the factual evidence and decide cases. A recent study revealed that in employment discrimination cases, Federal Courts of Appeal are five times more likely to overturn an employee's favorable trial verdict against an employer than they are to overturn a verdict in favor of the corporation. That is a startling disparity for those of us who expect employees and employers to be treated fairly by the judges sitting on our appellate courts.

In the 110th Congress, the House passed the bipartisan Lilly Ledbetter Fair Pay Act by a vote of 225–199. In the Senate, despite the support of 57 Senators who urged its consideration, the majority of Republican Senators objected to even proceeding to consideration of this bipartisan measure. One Republican Senator who supported the filibuster introduced an alternative bill, claiming to offer a solution for victims of pay discrimination. In reality, that partisan alternative proposal would fail to correct the injustice created by the Ledbetter decision. At the Judiciary Committee hearing in September, Ms. Ledbetter confirmed that the alternative bill would not have remedied her case, but instead would have imposed additional burdens and increased the costs of her litigation.

Congress passed Title VII of the Civil Rights Act to protect employees against discrimination with respect to compensation because of an individual's race, color, religion, sex or national origin—however the Supreme Court's cramped interpretation of this important law contradicts Congress's intent to ensure equal pay for equal work.

This Supreme Court decision goes against both the spirit and clear intent of Title VII of the Civil Rights Act, and sends the message to employers that wage discrimination cannot be punished as long as it is kept under wraps. At a time when one third of private sector employers have rules prohibiting employees from discussing their pay with each other, the Court's decision ignores a reality of the workplace—pay discrimination is often intentionally concealed by employers.

Equal pay is not just a women's issue, it is a family issue. With a record 70.2 million women in the workforce, wage discrimination continues to hurt the majority of American families. As a working mother, the discrimination inflicted on Ms. Ledbetter affected her entire family and continues to affect her retirement benefits. As the economy continues to worsen, many Americans are struggling to put food on the table and money in their retirement funds. It is regrettable that recent decisions handed down by the Supreme Court and Federal appellate courts have contributed to the financial struggles of so many women and their families. In the next weeks, I hope we can act to overturn the wrongly-decided Ledbetter decision to prevent the devastating consequences of pay discrimination.

Remarks of Senator Mitch McConnell

Let me say to my good friend the majority leader [Democratic Senator Harry Reid of Nevada], I intend to vote for cloture on the motion to proceed [with the Ledbetter bill]. He and I have had a number of constructive conversations privately, and he has reiterated again today publicly that we are going to make an effort to get the Senate back to operating the way it used to, which is that bills are amendable. So I have said to my colleagues and I would say to my good friend from Nevada that I trust you and believe you that we are going to get on the Ledbetter bill, we are going to have amendments and have votes and then dispose of the legislation in the normal way.

With regard to the substance of that particular measure, despite the gross distortions voters heard about this legislation in the runup to the November elections, the Ledbetter bill as written is neither about women nor fairness, and it is not about whether pay discrimination should be illegal. Pay discrimination is illegal, and it has been since 1963. Rather, this bill is about how long the statute of limitations on pay discrimination suits should be.

Last night, Republicans began to outline a proposal for addressing this question in a way that is fair for everyone. Senator Hutchison's bill strikes the right balance. It says the clock should not run out on someone who has been discriminated against until he or she discovers the alleged discrimination. This way, the focus is where it should be, on the injured party.

The Ledbetter legislation unfairly targets business owners, who may or may not have discriminated against a man or a woman, on the basis of pay years or even decades ago. Its primary beneficiaries are lawyers, who want to squeeze a major settlement out of every company that fears the expense or the publicity of going to court. This bill is unfair to business owners who in many cases will no longer have the evidence they would need to mount a convincing defense, and it is unfair to the millions of American workers who are worried about losing their jobs in the current economic downturn. Job creators have enough to worry about at the moment. Adding the threat of never-ending lawsuits is a new burden the Federal Government should not even be considering at this particular time.

No right-thinking American would defend discrimination of any kind in the workplace or anywhere else. And it is unfair to the public to suggest that those who oppose this bill endorse discrimination. It degrades our public discourse and it degrades the legislative process.

Many of us oppose this bill as written because it will paralyze businesses and add an even greater strain on workers than they currently face. We support a business climate that creates the conditions for success, not a climate that harasses the millions of men and women in this country who support themselves, their families, and their workers by owning and operating small businesses.

Republicans have a better proposal and other good ideas to help American workers. I believe we need to get on the Ledbetter bill, as I said a few minutes ago, and have an open debate about it so the American people can hear Republican alternatives and the Senate has an opportunity to vote on more than what our good friends on the other side have offered.

Sources: Leahy, Patrick. "Leahy Presses for Early Action on Fair Pay Bill." Press Release, Janu`ary 9, 2009. Available online at https://www.leahy.senate.gov/press/leahy-presses-for-early-action-on-fair-pay-bill.

McConnell, Mitch. "Lilly Ledbetter Fair Pay Act." *Congressional Record*, 155, no. 9 (January 15, 2009). Washington, DC: Government Printing Office, 2009, pp. S402–S403.

A CONSERVATIVE ECONOMIST DISMISSES THE EXISTENCE OF A MEANINGFUL GENDER PAY GAP, 2010

In 2010 Diana Furchtgott-Roth (1958), a prominent conservative economist, appeared before Congress to testify at a special hearing on the alleged gender pay gap victimizing women, including mothers, in business. In her testimony, Furchtgott-Roth asserted that concerns about the gender pay gap, long identified as a key factor in keeping women from achieving full equality in the workplace and limiting their life choices, were greatly overblown. She indicated that women and men simply have different priorities when choosing careers and employment options, with women much more likely than men to take lower-paying but more "family friendly" work.

Ms. Chairwoman, members of the Committee, I am honored to be invited to testify before your Committee today on the subject of the pay gap between men and women. I have followed and written about this and related issues for many years. . . .

Currently I am a senior fellow at Hudson Institute. From February 2003 until April 2005 I was chief economist at the U.S. Department of Labor. From 2001 until 2003 I served at the Council of Economic Advisers as chief of staff and special adviser. Previously, I was a resident fellow at the American Enterprise Institute.

I have served as deputy executive secretary of the Domestic Policy Council under President George H. W. Bush and as an economist on the staff of the Council of Economic Advisers under President Reagan.

The most current figures indicate that women have nearly closed the formerly wide divisions that separated men and women in terms of economic and social status.

Over the past three decades, the average wage gap decreased steadily. However, average wage gaps do not represent the compensation of women compared to men in specific jobs, because they average all full-time men and women in the population, rather than comparing men and women in the same jobs with the same experience. Data from the U.S. Department of Labor's Bureau of Labor Statistics that women earned 80 cents for every dollar that men earned in 2008 and in 2009, using full-time median weekly earnings, ignore fundamental differences between jobs, experience, and hours worked.

If we compare wages of men and women who work 40 hours a week, without accounting for any differences in jobs, training, or time in the labor force, Labor Department data show the gender wage ratio increases to 86 percent. Marriage and children explain some of the wage gap, because many mothers value flexible schedules. In 2009 single women working full-time earned 95% of men's earnings, but married women earned 76%, even before accounting for differences in education, jobs, and experience.

When the wage gap is analyzed by individual occupations, jobs and employee characteristics, regional labor markets, job titles, job responsibility, and experience; then the wage gap shrinks even more. When these differences are considered, many studies show that men and women make about the same. For instance, a 2009 study by the economics consulting firm CONSAD Research Corporation, prepared for the Labor Department, shows that women make around 94% of what men make. The remaining six cents are due to unexplained variables, one of which might be discrimination. . . .

Dozens of studies on the gender wage gap that attempt to measure "discrimination" have been published in academic journals in the past couple of decades. Unlike the Bureau of Labor Statistics, which uses simple mathematical tools to calculate the wage ratio, these studies use an econometric technique called regression analysis to measure contributing effects of all factors that could plausibly explain the wage gap. The residual that cannot be explained by any of the included variables is frequently termed as "discrimination." However, it has been found that an increase in the number of explanatory variables significantly reduces the residual portion attributable to "discrimination." Many of these studies suffer from a problem called omitted variable bias, which means that they fail to include enough explanatory variables to truly account for all, or even most, of the factors that plausibly affect wages. A quantitative analysis of studies that reported sex discrimination, conducted by University of Florida professor Henry Tosi and engineer Steven W. Einbender of Electronic Data Systems, found that of the 11 studies showing discrimination, 10 used fewer than 4 explanatory variables. On the other hand, only 3 out of the 10 studies that did not report discrimination used less than 4 explanatory variables.

Similarly, Professor Marianne Bertrand of the University of Chicago and Professor Kevin Hallock of Cornell University found an insignificant difference in the pay of male and female top corporate executives when factoring in the size of the firm, company position, age, seniority, and tenure. When accounting for detailed manager occupation, the female–male wage ratio rises from 56 percent to 87 percent and, when accounting for age and tenure, the wage ratio jumps from 56 percent to 95 percent.

Moreover, studies on the pay gap largely ignore the fringe benefits given to workers that account for approximately one-third of total compensation. Professor Helen Levy of the University of Michigan found in her study that the adjusted own-employer health coverage gap, 0.088, was only half as large as the pay gap, 0.25. Thus, data show smaller gender wage gaps when using both health insurance and wages than wages alone.

Indeed, the rate at which the wage gap is closing has slowed down in recent years, but this is understandable if we take into account the various other factors that are consistent with the slowdown. For one, fertility rates of female college graduates have increased substantially. Professor Qingyan Shang of the University at Buffalo and Professor Bruce Weinberg of Ohio State University conducted a study that analyzed fertility data between 1940 and 2006. The results showed an increase in fertility among highly educated female college graduates of all ages since 2000, indicating that women are increasingly opting for family over career. Thus, motherhood is a major factor behind the slowdown and the pay gap all-together.

Official labor statistics indicate a higher gender wage ratio for women without any children than for women with children. Thus, mothers tend to have lower wages than women without children. This is widely known as the "mother's penalty," and some argue that it exists because of discrimination. However, various empirical findings prove that it is rather a matter of productivity and preference, than discrimination.

In a study that addresses the notion of how the majority of parenting responsibilities fall on the mother rather than the father, the AAUW writes that "women's personal choices are similarly fraught with inequities." This statement suggests that what people choose for themselves is not right for them. They are referring to the problem of the "social construct" of gender roles, but it can be argued that this is not entirely about "nurture" but also about "nature." After birth, it is the mothers who need time off to rest and recover. Even if the social construct of gender roles were eliminated, it still would not stop the need for women to take work leave, while men continue working in their respective professions. Consequently, it is unclear how laws would help us change such gender roles.

Mothers often choose to work fewer hours and do flexible jobs in order to spend more time with their children, and it is highly unlikely that mothers perceive childcare as a burden. Professor Elizabeth Fox-Genovese writes from her research that "even highly successful women frequently want to spend much more time with their young children than the sixty-hour weeks required by the corporate fast tracks will permit." Having done a thorough study on the extent to which non-discriminatory factors explain the wage gaps, Professor June O'Neill and Professor Dave O'Neill of the City University of New York, argue that the gender pay gap arises from women's choices on "the amount of time and energy devoted to her career, as reflected in years of work, experience, utilization of part-time work, and other workplace and job characteristics."

Professor Paula England of Stanford University also comes to similar conclusions. She explains that mothers tend to choose "mother-friendly" jobs in which flexibility is traded off for higher earnings, promotion prospects and on-the-job training. Another study by Professor Lalith Munasinghe, Professor Alice Henriques, and Tania Reif of Barnard College, Columbia University and Citigroup respectively finds that women, compared to men, are less likely to invest in learning job-specific skills, and are much less likely to select jobs with "back-loaded" compensation, because they know that they are likely to face more job separations.

In her book, *What Children Need*, Professor Jane Waldfogel of Columbia University writes that there is a positive correlation between the number of children and the pay gap. Her analysis of the importance of family status in determining the pay gap using cohorts from national longitudinal surveys found that mothers earned much less than non-mothers and men. She found that the 20 percentage point increase in the wage ratio from 64 percent to 84 percent during the 1980s was averaged from a higher increase in wages of non-mothers and a lower increase in wages of mothers. Mothers' wages had only grown from 60 percent to 75 percent, while the wages of childless women had risen sharply from 72 percent of men's pay to 95 percent.

Consistent with her findings are those of Professors Claudia Goldin and Lawrence Katz of Harvard University and Professor Marianne Bertrand of the University of Chicago, which report that the presence of children was the major reason behind career interruptions and fewer working hours of the female MBA graduates they studied. Their study found that although all MBA graduates entered the job market with the same amount of compensation, their pay gap started rising steadily over the years because of the difference in MBA training, working hours and career interruptions.

The home page of the Yale Law Women Web site, the site for female law students at Yale Law School, reads "In the aftermath of the recent global financial crisis, YLW believes that the focus on family friendly firm policies and policies designed for the retention of women remains more important and pressing than ever." Friendly firm policies are those that allow children to be combined with a professional career.

In addition to a desire for flexibility within full-time work, the Labor Department reports that 31 percent of women chose to work part-time in 2009. (Another 5 percent reported that they worked part-time because they could not find full-time work.) Labor Department data show that in 2009 single women working full-time earned about 95 percent of men's earnings, but married women earned 76 percent of what married men earned. Married women with children between the ages of 6–17 earned 70 percent of men with children of the same age.

Childbearing may be the reason for some differences in preferences between men and women, but experimental psychology proves that women's preferences are different than men's even regardless of the presence of children. Professor Rachel Croson of the University of Texas at Dallas and Professor Uri Gneezy of the University of California, San Diego conducted a thorough review of experimental studies on behavior and found that women and men have significant differences in preferences when it comes to risk-taking, social preferences and competition. Lab results reported that women are more risk-averse, less competitive and are more sensitive to subtle social cues than men; leading them to choose professions with less risk-taking, fewer degrees of competition, and careers that are deemed socially appropriate for them. This behavior translates into lower pay and slower advancement within their chosen professions, a phenomenon that is allegedly called the "pink ghetto." Taking into consideration such evidence, it becomes clear just how simplistic the argument for discrimination theory really is.

In the book *Women Don't Ask*, Professor Linda Babcock of Carnegie-Mellon University and writer Sara Laschever argue that women avoid competitive negotiation situations, leading them to receive lower wages and fewer concessions. They based their argument on a variety of evidence, including a laboratory study where the participants were promised to be paid between three and ten dollars for their participation. Once the participants finished, the experimenter thanked them and said, "Here's $3. Is $3 OK?" The findings reported that nine times as many men requested for more money than women. Similar findings have been reported at the workplace. Professor Lisa Baron of the University of California, Irvine found that only 7 percent of the women in her study negotiated their salary offer, as opposed to 57 percent of men.

With all these elements working against the unexplained pay gap, it is simply irrational to argue that it exists because of "persistent discrimination." It also shows how government intervention targeted towards discrimination will not be effective. However, supporters of the discrimination theory have kept pushing bills like the Pay Check Fairness Act, which have a higher potential of harming women than helping them. For example, in order to escape the heavy guidelines set by the Pay Check Fairness Act, employers may actually find it easier to hire males than females.

Proponents of wage guidelines, such as the National Committee on Pay Equity, approvingly cite examples of areas where pay equity has been used, but fail to acknowledge major problems with the practice. One example cited occurred in Hawaii in 1995, where nurses, mostly female, were given a sum of $11,500 in their annual raises to equate their salaries to those of adult correction workers, who were mostly male. Another example cited was in Oregon, where female clerical specialists were deemed underpaid by $7,000 annually in comparison to male senior sewer workers. In both cases, working conditions were not taken into account.

Working conditions in prisons and sewers are far more dangerous and unpleasant than conditions in hospitals and offices. Most people, given a choice of working in an office or sewer at the same salary, would choose the office. So, to allocate workers into sewers and prisons, one must offer them higher pay.

Many organizations like the American Association of University Women (AAUW) and the National Organization for Women (NOW) are quick to falsely attribute the unexplained portion of the pay gap to discrimination. These organizations believe discrimination plagues the American workplace, and their argument is not surprising given that their work begins with the weight of their preconceived notions on the gender wage gap. The AAUW study "Behind the Pay Gap" shows that even when all various factors normally associated with pay have been included in the computation, the wage gap persists, which the study's authors then attribute to gender discrimination. But that claim is a rather narrow and simplistic interpretation of the gender pay gap for it ignores the complexity of the issue at hand.

In earlier decades, when the pay gap was larger, many blamed discrimination. As the years went by and the narrowing gaps in pay rates reflected increasing similarity in the characteristics of workers in terms of jobs, educational attainment and level of experience, as the 2009 GAO report shows, it became clear that the American workplace is rather meritocratic. Yet the allegations of discrimination continued, even though, under current law, it is possible for workers to sue employers if they feel discriminated against. Today American women have the same opportunities as men in the workplace; they simply make different choices. Thus, there is a clear path for women to achieve what they want.

Similar to the case of the "Gender Wage Gap," the concept of the "Glass Ceiling" has made its way into popular belief as a fact not requiring further questioning. Coined in the 1980s by the *Wall Street Journal*, this catchy phrase is defined as an "invisible but impenetrable barrier between women and the executive suite." Proponents of the theory, such as the Glass Ceiling Commission, imply that women are systematically excluded from career advancement opportunities to higher level management and leadership roles. Their reports point to the underrepresentation of women at top corporate positions as evidence of the existence of the "glass ceiling." However, underrepresentation alone is a rather weak argument to assert such a theory, for if we look at the issue as a whole and not just the numbers, we find very different reasons behind the statistics.

When the Glass Ceiling Commission released its ominous report in 1995, stating that only 5 percent of senior managers at Fortune 1000 and Fortune 500 service companies were women, it completely ignored the qualified labor pool in its assessment. Instead, it compared that number to the entire labor force. The numbers used and the theory would have made sense if the Commission had used the number of working men and women who have an MBA with at least twenty-five years of work experience in order to calculate the percentages of men and women who are represented in top corporate jobs. It is surprising why the number was not correctly adjusted despite the researchers' study into "preparedness" of women and minorities to rise to top corporate positions. And although the study supported the pipeline theory, the report's authors were quick to argue that there are barriers within the pipeline.

The pipeline theory holds that one needs to be "in the pipeline" long enough to gain the necessary experience and skills before qualifying for top executive jobs. It is not difficult to realize that very few women entered the pipeline a couple of decades ago: only few graduated with professional degrees and even fewer remained in the workforce long enough to garner necessary experience, which explains why there is a dearth of women executives today. . . .

[T]oday, less than 25 percent of those qualified for executive jobs are women, even assuming that all female MBA recipients have been active in their business careers since graduation. In 2008, about 45 percent of Master's degrees in business were awarded to women, so we can expect the pipeline to balance out only after 2030, provided that all women graduates with master's degrees in business remain active in their business careers. Thus, critics who seem appalled by the system's unequal gender distribution of top managerial and executive positions must consider these statistics before jumping to conclusions.

The Glass Ceiling Commission report also noted that "certain functional areas are more likely than others to lead to the top. The 'right' areas are most likely to be line functions such as marketing and production or critical control functions such as accounting and finance." The report also cited studies that concluded that there are certain factors that are very important in climbing the corporate ladder, such as broad and varied experience in the core areas of business; access to information, particularly through networks and mentoring; company seniority; initial job assignment; high job mobility; education; organizational savvy; long hours and hard work; and career planning. As discussed in the previous section, women have different preferences, are more likely to work part-time and also tend to take more career breaks, leading them to end up with less experience than men, shorter hours, and more interruptions in their career. Such factors that become "barriers" to upward mobility at work are the same reasons behind the gender wage gap.

Women in management have been attaining increasingly similar levels of education and work characteristics as men, but significant differences still remain. The GAO's report on women in management showed that for most industries in 2000, female managers had less education, were younger, were more likely to work part-time, and were less likely to be married than men in management.

The GAO also found that in 2000, half of the ten industries studied had no statistically significant difference between the percent of management positions filled by women and the percent of all industry positions filled by women. In the industries where the difference was significant, namely, educational services; retail trade, finance, insurance and real estate, hospitals and medical services, and professional medical services; the majority of management positions were filled by women, except in retail trade. By 2009, women made up the majority of higher-level jobs in public administration, financial managing, accounting and auditing, insurance underwriting, and health and medicine managing. This encouraging evidence highlights women's achievements in the workplace, and casts further doubt on discrimination theory.

Although individual cases of discrimination still take place, there is no evidence that discrimination is systematic and persistent. The Korn/Ferry executive search firm reported in July that, by 2007, women were represented on corporate boards in 85 percent of the Fortune 1000 companies, compared with 78 percent in 2001, 53 percent in 1988 and 11 percent in 1973. This growth is notable for women, and there is no reason to believe that it has stalled.

The danger is not that progress for women in slowing, but that Congress will overreact to false discrimination claims and pass legislation that will slow the growth of jobs in America for both men and women. . . .

Source: Furchtgott-Roth, Diana. "Testimony on the Gender Pay Gap: New Evidence on the Gender Pay Gap for Women and Mothers in Management." Hearing before the Joint Economic Committee, 111th Congress, 2nd Session, S. Hrg. 111-789, September 28, 2010. Washington, DC: Government Printing Office, 2011, pp. 119–135.

A BOSTON COLLEGE STUDY TAKES STOCK OF "THE NEW DAD," 2010

The Boston College Center for Work and Family is a research and advocacy organization focused on helping companies, communities, and families find a mutually beneficial balance between family and work responsibilities. To that end, the Center has focused a great deal of attention on the changing role of fathers in American society. Since 2010 the Center has published seven reports on the attitudes and behaviors of contemporary fathers, including their efforts to find an appropriate balance between their work responsibilities and their obligations as husbands and fathers. Following is an excerpt from the first of these reports, The New Dad: Exploring Fatherhood within a Career Context.

The Research Results

Our analysis of the interview data we collected showed a shift in new father attitudes and behaviors that is consistent with the research findings highlighted in the earlier sections Changing Generational Values and Changing Role of Men. The men in our study were clearly re-thinking and re-defining traditional gender based roles. They were very happy in their roles as fathers and doing their best to spend time with their children and be good fathers. Their own fathers worked full-time while their mothers for the most part stayed home and cared for them, at least while they were young children. The new dads in our study were working hard to better share both the childcare and home care duties with their spouses.

In many cases the men were not prepared for how much work it can be to take care of a young child. They choose to spend this time with their children, often at the expense of personal activities they previously enjoyed. Often their priorities changed to focus more on family and less on work. In some cases they adjusted their ambitions for professional advancement and career to take into account their new responsibilities and joys. As these new fathers in our study adjusted to this new child in their lives, there were many impacts that we observed. We have laid out our research findings to highlight the important impacts that becoming a new father has on the fathers themselves, on their marriages, on their work, and on their careers.

The Personal Impact of Fatherhood

Definition of "A Good Father"

One of the key issues we hoped to explore through the study was "What is the meaning of fatherhood today and does it differ from the traditional or stereotypical views that were held of fathers in days gone by (e.g. father as breadwinner, father as disciplinarian, etc.)?" From our interviews it became clear that the father as a primary (not sole) breadwinner was still an integral component of these fathers' identities. However, other equally important themes emerged in our interviews as well (i.e. being a good provider but . . .). As one of the fathers, Alex, put it, "I think being a good father—it's hard. A little bit less though just putting food on the table, and more raising the child, being involved in their life, being a good role model for them, and encouraging them, providing emotional support."

A good deal of the emphasis was placed on the emotional aspects of being a father. Words and phrases such as listening, understanding, compassion, being a role model, less a disciplinarian, more a friend all emerged in our discussion. It was clear that providing emotional support was just as important as financial support. As Tom, an Organization Development Director of an insurance company summed it up:

> "I think [being a father] means a lot of things. It means love. It means demonstrating your love for someone and a commitment to them at all costs. So supporting them, nurturing them, being there, and I think not only as a father, but as a friend, as a guide, as a mentor."

The theme of "being there, being present, spending time, being accessible" was oft repeated. "To be very participatory, to take an active interest, to spend time just being in the same room together" was the way one of the dads described it. William, a sales executive for a technology startup, expressed a similar sentiment in his response:

> "Obviously being a good provider is important to me. Knowing [my son] has what he needs, his being safe is important to me. I think just enjoying life is a generic way of saying it. 'You want to go outside? Let's go outside. I don't care if it's raining or snowing out, let's go outside. You want to hang out with the dogs? Let's hang out with the dogs.' It's not on my terms, this is our time together."

Role Models for Fatherhood

Through one of the first questions in our discussions we delved into the personal and career histories of the participants, focusing on how they developed their sense of career and paternal identity. Not surprisingly, most of the participants focused on their parents and most often their fathers, as their primary role model.

Evan, a computer analyst for a large investment company stressed the critical role his father had played in helping him to define what it meant to be a good father/parent:

> "He's the president of a small business. We were always sort of around that, whether coming in to help out in his office, doing little tasks, or I worked there when I was in high school. He had a very strong influence on how I think about the mix of work and family and why I find it important not to work so many hours now. He was always home at reasonable hours . . . he would balance doing that kind of thing at work with coming home and doing yard work with us, house projects. That's the one thing I got from him, he was always tearing something apart and I'm starting to do that."

Another participant, Peter, age 29, echoed this sentiment when he said "I think seeing my father's approach to [work–family] gave me a fairly balanced outlook on the way I actually approached it as well."

The lack of a father's presence or the lack of a positive example in some cases led those men to also develop ideals of fatherhood, but in reaction to their lack of a personal role model. Dan, who is in the military but who was attending an MBA program on a full-time basis at the time we met, describes his experiences in this way:

> "My family life growing up, that's a separate interview altogether. I came from a family that, you know, my dad and mom divorced at a very early age. My dad was always working. I don't think that shaped my views on the whole balance stuff . . . my two siblings and I both stayed with my mom and my dad was kind of in the fringes. Later on he came back into our life. . . . Back to the original question, I don't think that directly affected how I see my role as a father, but I guess in very general terms you always try to improve upon the experiences you had which isn't to say that my dad wasn't a good father. But there are definitely some things I would like to do differently.
>   INT: Any particular example?
>   Just level of engagement I guess, you know, to get more involved in my son's activities as he grows up. Probably more than my dad did. I think the way I would like to participate in [my son's] development is different too. I think my dad just always kind of set the line in the sand and if you strayed outside of the acceptable, those boundaries, he was there to provide some incentives to get back on the right path. And you know, I think I'd like to have a little bit more of a give and take interaction, kind of a mentorship role with my son."

In addition to their father's role modeling, participants also learned a great deal by observing how their parents interacted and shared responsibilities for child rearing and domestic tasks. Rob, a director of a non-profit economic development agency, had perhaps the most conspicuously "shared care" arrangement with his wife, a full-time teacher and Ivy League–educated lawyer. Rob spoke about the example his parents had set for him in this respect:

> "My parents—my father is a Buddhist minister, and my mother is a public school teacher. She taught elementary school. The way the Buddhist Temples are kind of structured there is that—it is a pretty loose kind of work day. A lot of my father's actual work occurred in the evenings and weekends. Funerals, services, meetings, stuff like that, so during the day, he had a little bit more flexibility.
>
> So growing up, my father was the one cooking us breakfast, taking us to school, picking us up from school—watching us. Mom would come in after she got off from her work day. And then, mom helped out from there. So I would say now at least, in terms of kind of seeing the sharing of the workload? I would say I got a lot from that.
>
> INT: And did you view that as a model for you?
>
> I saw that as more of the norm—I mean, I didn't know any different, right? And you know, just as being the kids of the Buddhist minister, it could be pretty rough in terms of demands of my parents, so we were pretty much raised by a bunch of people who were very active in the church. So you know, baby-sitting. Or sleeping over [at] their houses—during services they'd watch us. So, it was very much a communal kind of upbringing."

In addition to parental influence, meanings of good fathering and fatherhood also seemed to be shaped by making comparisons with friends. Lew, a 45-year-old scientist in our study, stated, "I would say in between your own childhood and seeing other people raise their children, that's probably the two things that influence how we're raising our child the most."

Other participants echoed a similar sentiment about watching how their peers were raising their children and drawing lessons from these observations. In Craig's case, he tried to emulate the example of some close family friends. "I have some really close friends I look up to. I just look at the ways they live their lives as families and workers." In other cases, such examples can serve as "what I don't want to do" as was the case for Evan. He and his wife had decided she would stop working when the baby was born, and watching the experiences of friends in a dual career couple reinforced that the decision Evan and his wife made was the right one for them. As Evan stated, "I have friends who have 3 month old babies and they drop them off at daycare. I can't even imagine doing that."

Anticipation of Becoming a Father

Perhaps not surprisingly, many of the men were not sure what to expect when they became fathers. For example, two of our study participants, Craig and Sam, stated:

> "I envisioned that it would be difficult and that I would have trouble wanting to find the time to be a parent. . . . I had no understanding of the emotional bond genetically that occurs when you have a baby. . . . I think it's very hard for a man especially to really understand what's going to happen." [Craig, entrepreneur]

> "I knew I would probably like it. But the negative side of it was, 'Oh my gosh, I'm going to be responsible for this kid for 18 years! [gasp]'" [Sam, account executive]

This lack of understanding and inability to grasp what to expect changed very quickly when their babies were born. The fathers we spoke with were profoundly impacted by the birth of their children and expressed nearly universally positive reactions to that event. Some typical reactions to becoming a father included:

> "Just elation. Just absolute elation. Seeing a beautiful baby boy come out of what was an unbelievably difficult delivery was like a gift. It was like a blessing." [Sam]
> "It hit me in a way that nothing else ever has. . . . It was just absolutely overwhelming in a positive way." [Paul]
> ". . . it was the first time in my life I ever cried from happiness . . . it was a very new sensation for me to be that happy." [Josh]

In addition, there were a number of participants who also experienced fear and anxiety at the same time in regards to the daunting responsibility of caring for and raising their child. Dan admitted feeling absolutely terrified.

> "Absolute terror, yeah. It was overwhelming. I think it kind of made me experience feelings that I didn't know were even out there."

As Lew pointed out, the responsibility can be overwhelming.

> "You don't quite know what's coming. And you feel kind of a responsibility drops like a piano in a carton on your shoulders. It's frightening. It's exciting but scary. Mostly scary right at first."

Best Aspects of Being a Father

Since the participants now had an average of nearly 18 months' experience as a father, we asked them to reflect on what they liked best about fatherhood. Their responses focused primarily on the feeling of being a "real" family for the first time, the close emotional bonds they felt with their new child, and having the opportunity to watch their child develop. Somewhat surprisingly, even the heightened sense of responsibility was mentioned as one of the positive outcomes of being a new father.

Among the best aspects, about half of our participants talked about building a loving relationship with another human being. It's clear from the comments that their children's smiles have a remarkable impact on the new dads, and the tenderness they feel towards their children comes through clearly in their words.

> "One of the best parts of being a Dad is sharing those moments, and having a relationship with him that, admittedly, my wife says, 'I don't have that relationship.' And knowing that it's a unique kind of a relationship that you're nurturing, you're building, and you're spending the time with him to do that." [William]

"There are moments where you are going to pick him up. And, he sees you and just gets that huge smile on. You know those moments of him giggling and falling asleep on your shoulder. Those things just are priceless. Nothing can beat that." [Jesse]

"It's almost indescribable because being a father right now doesn't mean anything other than just spending time with your child and, I mean it's, it's a weird thing because you didn't think you'd be able to love another human being like this. But I love being a father so much more than I thought I would and I can't say exactly why except that spending time with my daughter . . . the highlight of my day is in the morning when I hear her start to wake up and I can just go in there and pick her up. And how do you, how do you define that other than [love]." [Josh]

The new fathers in our study were also very excited about the opportunity to watch and assist in another person's growth.

"I mean I love just being with them and playing with them. You know, you watch them smile and laugh, seeing them figure out things on their own and wondering how they figured it out." [Matt]

"She is only five months old but she already recognizes me when I walk in and gives me a smile and is happy to see me. You [have a] feeling like you have really accomplished something and you've produced something that is a contributing member of society someday. . . . I've been working on teaching her how to sit up on her own and when she actually does sit up on her own a little bit without toppling right over—that's a great feeling." [Richard]

They talked about the joy and happiness they feel and the ability to share that joy with others. As Anthony shared in his interview:

"The joy of when they wake up, when they smile at you and when they grab your hand and every single second being with them is just fun and enjoyable. Even when they're sad or they're mad at you for whatever reason, you're not giving them what they want to eat or something or it's just it's always something new with them. And everything's a discovery. And, everything's an adventure that it's just fun to even just sit back and watch them play. That aspect of it is fantastic."

Many of our participants also felt that one of the best aspects of being a father is being responsible for another living person and influencing what they become. As Sam commented, "I think the best aspect of being a father is, just . . . knowing that I am responsible now for another human being. His well-being, entirely—he's completely dependent on us." Or as Corey said, "It's a huge responsibility, but it's also something that I take a lot of pride in. I really want to be a good father. And following that goal I try and be a better [person than] I might otherwise be."

Several of the new fathers relished the thought of starting a family and bringing someone new into the world. A few talked about enjoying the day-to-day activities, time spent playing with their child, and some were looking forward to a time with even more possibilities for interaction. In addition, there were a number of instances of self-discovery that our participants felt were important. As Tim stated,

> "It's challenging at times. It brings insight. You find yourself having to actually think about things you had done automatically for years. And you ask yourself 'do I want my children emulating this?'"

Don summarized the change that had taken place in his life:

> "It puts life in perspective. How important is money, is career, is vacation? There's more to life than [these things]. There are lots of opportunities, learning opportunities for myself about my own temperament, my own desires and interests. There's a self discovery benefit."

Challenges of Fatherhood

Of course there are many trying aspects of fatherhood as well. We asked our participants what they like least about being a father. Some of the expected subjects came up such as changing diapers, preparing meals, being "tested" by a 2 year old, dealing with a crying child, and the cost of child care. Quite a few of the participants raised the issue of simply being tired and that being a father was more work than they expected.

> "Gosh, so it's a lot more work than I ever imagined. The lack of control is phenomenally frustrating because you just don't know what night you will get a full night sleep." [Don]
> "Probably the lack of free time and the late nights, you know the middle of the night stuff. I think my wife and I share that middle of the night [a lot]. It's just tough." [Ben]

This extra work and fatigue can cause some strain on a marriage.

> "I think it's also sometimes the responsibility, if you like it or not. Sometimes crying in the middle of the night, and having to take care of her, or having to—something comes up, and I have to cancel an appointment, because I need to take her to an appointment. I think just priorities have changed. So if my priorities or my business haven't changed, or aren't flexible, then it's sometimes difficult negotiations with myself or with my wife on what I should be doing." [Charles]

This new responsibility, this new commitment of time and energy leads to the concerns mentioned most often by our study participants—less personal time, little uninterrupted time and less time for other pursuits. As William commented:

> "Sometimes I wish I had time to myself. Sometimes I will kind of close my office door and say, 'Okay, this is Dad time.' I need time just to sit down and veg out in front of the Internet, or whatever it is. You know, grab a beer, and watch a football game, or—I do miss some of that. I miss the ability of being able to pick up a project and doing that project."

And finally, a few participants said that the aspect they liked least about being a father was having to miss important parts of their kids' lives. As Keith summarized, "A least favorite aspect of being a father is I've got to leave and go to work every day."

Changes Resulting from Becoming a Father

We explored with our new fathers the ways in which becoming a father had changed them. Most, called fatherhood a life-changing event but it did not necessarily change all of the men we spoke with dramatically. Perhaps not surprisingly, due to the lack of time for personal pursuits, one of the common themes was best expressed by Lew who simply replied half-kiddingly, "I'm definitely more boring."

Most described the changes that they had experienced in their own lives in compelling ways. For these men, becoming a father was a growing and maturing experience that left them with a higher level of patience and empathy for others. As Grant, a sales manager stated, "I think as a manager I've definitely lightened up because I understand now that having a family and trying to get stuff done, work, family, all that stuff—there's only so much time in a day." Mark agreed, saying that he is "more patient and understanding of others." Matt also echoed this, saying, "I think I've always been a patient person but I think I'm more patient, more understanding with people in general."

Another effect of fatherhood seems to have been an increase in focus and clarity in priorities. One father put it very succinctly: "I'm more focused on those two priorities, work and family." Another father, Tom said:

> "I look back to being in Boston when he was born. We kind of were just floating and saying oh, we'll figure things out. And I think it really hit home. Okay, we got someone who is depending on us that we need to support. We need to come up with a longer term plan. We need to get closer to family that can help us out with some of the care giving from time-to-time. We need to establish ourselves in a place that we're comfortable with. It's less crowded; it's more conducive to a family. So I think it changed my outlook on life considerably. And that it's no longer just about me. . . ."

The other thing that fathers emphasized was the way that fatherhood had increased the meaning in their lives, their sense of purpose. Patrick, a financial analyst from Boston, reflected:

> "I feel like I have a real purpose, not that I was a zero before but I never really, with my job, felt like I was making a difference I guess. I know that sounds extreme—but I feel like I have a purpose now. I know that sounds kind of deep, I guess."

Marriage and Family Impact

It is clear that becoming a father has had a significant impact on our study participants. They have altered their lives to adjust to their major new responsibility as well as a significant new interpersonal relationship with a child. The large majority of our study participants have working spouses (28 of 33), and most of these work full-time. The median hours worked per week for the majority of spouses who did work is 40 and the range is from 10 hours to more than 60 hours/week. In this section we will explore the approaches that the partners take to navigate these major new responsibilities for child care and household responsibilities on top of their full-time jobs.

Sharing Care Giving

One of the key questions we wanted to explore with study participants was how these new fathers and their spouses shared care-giving responsibilities. Most fathers said that they were striving to achieve a 50/50 split in terms of responsibilities for care giving. Where they fell short, they stated that they were working to address this. Particularly those with very young children spoke of the fact that their wives' leave of absences coupled with breast feeding made it difficult for the care giving to be 50/50. But as the children aged and the wives returned to work, most participants suggested that an equal share of co-parenting was the goal. When asked to rate themselves as a care-giver on a scale of 1–5 (1 being not at all involved and 5 being very involved), the participants rated themselves a 4.16 out of 5 on average.

Although there was some hedging on the question including frequent, half-joking references to, "Do you mean compared to my wife?" the general senti-ment was simply put by Mark, a consultant, whose reply was, "We try to be close to 50/50 in terms of responsibilities. We generally alternate pretty evenly on all of that stuff."

When asked for greater specificity, most of the men described in greater detail the ways they divided up the care giving responsibilities with their wives in order to accommodate each spouse's work schedule. Charles, a real estate broker, described how the duties were negotiated to fit each spouse's schedule.

> "In the mornings . . . my wife has to go [in] earlier than I do. So I take care of the morning shift of getting [my daughter] dressed, feeding her breakfast and taking her to day care . . . until about 5:30, and that's when my wife picks her up."

John, a 36 year old IT manager, described a similar pattern, reminding us that the schedule was not fixed and was subject to adjustments as needed:

> "It's a lot of give and take. In the morning I wake her up, get her dressed and I get her out the door. [My wife] picks her up, she takes care of her while she's cooking, and when I get home we feed her together, sit down as a family for dinner as much as possible. Then she takes care of her while I do the dishes and then we play for a while. I put her to bed."

On average the fathers stated that they believed they spent 3.3 hours per work-day with their children and in care giving activities. This is consistent with (but somewhat exceeds) the findings in recent studies, that suggest the average time fathers spend with their children has doubled over the last three decades to about 3 hours per work day (Galinsky, Aumann, Kerstin, & Bond, 2008). One caution in reflecting on these findings is that we did not seek or obtain validation of these time estimates using other tracking methodologies or by asking the participants' spouses for their estimates.

The Stay-at-Home Father Option

As previously mentioned, both spouses work in most U.S. couples with children under the age of 18. In those cases where there is one spouse at home full-time, 97% of the time, that person is female. In spite of the many changes we have discussed in women's work roles and changing family structures, very few fathers are choosing to stay at home full-time to raise their children. This reminds us of an old *New Yorker* cartoon which depicts a husband and wife walking together as the husband comments, "Of course I want to have kids, Claire— just not all the time."

The participants in our study seemed to reflect this reality of the US workforce. While the question at times elicited a smile from the participants, most suggested that they had at least considered the option of being a stay-at-home father. However, only 2 of 33 participants had considered this a realistic possibility. For most, family finances were the major stumbling block. Perhaps the fact that we targeted dual career couples with both spouses working full-time, meant that for many of these couples both incomes were needed to sustain their standard of living. When asked about this option, Patrick, who is a financial analyst for a major insurance company stated clearly "I never considered that, no. Would I like to? Sure. It just wasn't financially feasible. There was no way."

. . .

Career Impact

In this final section of the research findings, we examine the perceived career impact that becoming a father has had on our participants. It was clear that becoming a father had a significant impact on them personally. We wanted to know how this impact carried over to their career expectations and realities.

While a number of fathers suggested that their career aspirations had not changed dramatically, the general sentiment seemed to be that the participants had altered their view of what constituted success. Some were just coming to grips with the possibility of lower levels of career progression when viewed through a traditional career development perspective (i.e. career success as determined by organizational level achieved). As one father stated, "The title is somewhat important to me which I am sort of having a problem with right now, trying to work that out. Am I going to be okay not being a VP of something in five years? I'm sort of dealing with that right now and I haven't come to any conclusions." But more of the fathers were clear that they were prepared to either lower their expectations or at least, accept a lower rung on the ladder as long as they were happy in their personal lives. As two of our participants stated:

"I'm not so ambitious. I could keep moving up . . . but I know that will come with other requirements as well. I'm happy where I am now. I don't want the pendulum to swing back in the other direction where it was before, where it's going to encroach on my ability to spend quality time with my family." [Tom, age 34]

"When my first child was born, I was working at the law firm and there's always an aspiration of becoming partner and the expectation of having to bring in the business, do a lot of travel. . . . With my new job and the second child, if I was never to advance a whole lot career wise, I'd be happy because the work is good, the money is good and you know, the family is happy." [Matt, age 37]

A few of the fathers mentioned that a heightened sense of "doing work that mattered" as well as finding the right balance that resulted from becoming a father. As one stated, "I think if anything, it's just strengthened my focus on wanting to do meaningful work that allows me to have balance. If anything, I might want to consider scaling back on my hours in the future."

Source: Harrington, Brad, Fred Van Deusen, and Jamie Ladge. *The New Dad: Exploring Fatherhood within a Career Context.* Boston: Boston College Center for Work & Family, 2010, pp. 12–19, 25–26. Available online at http://www.bc.edu/content /dam/files/centers/cwf/pdf/BCCWF_Fatherhood_Study_The_New_Dad1.pdf. Used by permission of Boston College Center for Work & Family.

THE DEPARTMENT OF LABOR EXAMINES PAY GAP MYTHS, 2012

On June 5, 2012, a Republican filibuster in the Senate derailed a bill known as the Paycheck Fairness Act, which had been widely supported by Democrats, who framed it as a regulatory tool to close persistent gender-based wage gaps in American business. The 2012 bill was actually the latest iteration of legislation that had been presented to Congress on numerous occasions since 1997. But as with earlier versions of the bill, the GOP complained that the 2012 version of the Paycheck Fairness Act would stunt business growth. Moreover, conservative critics charged that the bill was a solution in search of a problem since the wage gap between men and women, although once a legitimate concern, had largely become a myth.

Two days after the Republican filibuster, however, Pamela Coukos, a senior program adviser in the Obama administration's Department of Labor, published an essay on the agency's official blog that flatly insisted that gender-based differences in wages remained a real and persistent problem in American society. Even Coukos, though, acknowledged that gender discrimination was only a partial factor in the raw wage gap between men and women.

Surely it can't be true. President Kennedy signed the Equal Pay Act in 1963. The very next year Congress passed Title VII of the Civil Rights Act of 1964, which banned sex discrimination at work. Yet nearly fifty years later, women still make less than men.

We live today in a world where women run Fortune 500 companies, sit on the Supreme Court, and push back the frontiers of knowledge. We live during a time when more young women than men hold bachelor's degrees, and when women make up almost half of all new law school graduates. Given all our progress, there must be some explanation behind the fact that women still lag behind men when it comes to pay equity.

Earlier this week, the Paycheck Fairness Act failed to advance in the Senate, triggering a new round of conversation about the pay gap and what the numbers really mean. Research shows that even though equal pay for women is a legal right, it is not yet a reality. Despite the evidence, myths that women's choices or other legitimate factors are the "real" cause of the pay gap persist. So does confusion about how to measure the gap and what figures to use. That's why today, we are going to bust a few myths.

MYTH: Saying women only earn 77 cents on the dollar is a huge exaggeration—the "real" pay gap is much smaller than that (if it even exists).

REALITY: The size of the pay gap depends on how you measure it. The most common estimate is based on differences in annual earnings (currently about 23 cents difference per dollar). Another approach uses weekly earnings data (closer to an 18- or 19-cent difference). Analyzing the weekly figures can be more precise in certain ways, like accounting for work hours that vary over the course of the year, and less accurate in others, like certain forms of compensation that don't get paid as weekly wages. No matter which number you start with, the differences in pay for women and men really add up. According to one analysis by the Department of Labor's Chief Economist, a typical 25-year-old woman working full time would have already earned $5,000 less over the course of her working career than a typical 25-year old man. If that earnings gap is not corrected, by age 65, she will have lost hundreds of thousands of dollars over her working lifetime. We also know that women earn less than men in every state and region of the country, and that once you factor in race, the pay gap for women of color is even larger.

MYTH: There is no such thing as the gender pay gap—legitimate differences between men and women cause the gap in pay, not discrimination.

REALITY: Decades of research shows a gender gap in pay even after factors like the kind of work performed and qualifications (education and experience) are taken into account. These studies consistently conclude that discrimination is the best explanation of the remaining difference in pay. Economists generally attribute about 40% of the pay gap to discrimination—making about 60% explained by differences between workers or their jobs. However, even the "explained" differences between men and women might be more complicated. For example: If high school girls are discouraged from taking the math and science classes that lead to high-paying STEM jobs, shouldn't we in some way count that as a lost equal earnings opportunity? As one commentator put it recently, "I don't think that simply saying we have 9 cents of discrimination and then 14 cents of life choices is very satisfying." In other words, no matter how you slice the data, pay discrimination is a real and persistent problem that continues to shortchange American women and their families.

MYTH: But the pay gap is not my problem. Once you account for the jobs that require specialized skills or education it goes away.

REALITY: The pay gap for women with advanced degrees, corporate positions, and high paying, high skill jobs is just as real as the gap for workers overall. In a recent study of newly trained doctors, even after considering the effects of specialty, practice setting, work hours and other factors, the gender pay gap was nearly $17,000 in 2008. Catalyst reviewed 2011 government data showing a gender pay gap for women lawyers, and that data confirms that the gap exists for a range of professional and technical occupations. In fact, according to a study by the Institute for Women's Policy Research that used information from the Bureau of Labor Statistics, women earn less than men even within the same occupations. Despite differences in the types of jobs women and men typically perform, women earn less than men in male dominated occupations (such as managers, software developers and CEOs) and in those jobs commonly filled by women (like teachers, nurses and receptionists). In a recent review of 2010 Census data, Bloomberg found only one of 285 major occupations where women's median pay was higher than that of men—personal care and service workers. Because the data showed a particularly large pay gap in the financial sector, Bloomberg suggested that for women on Wall Street, shining shoes was the best way to earn more than the men.

MYTH: Women are responsible for the pay gap because they seek out flexible jobs or choose to work fewer hours. Putting family above work is why women earn less.

REALITY: Putting aside whether it's right to ask women (or men) to sacrifice financially in order to work and have a family, those kinds of choices aren't enough to explain away the gender pay gap. The gender gap in pay exists for women working full time. Taking time off for children also doesn't explain gaps at the start of a career. And although researchers have addressed various ways that work hours or schedule might or might not explain some portion of the wage gap, there may be a "motherhood penalty." This is based on nothing more than the expectation that mothers will work less. Researchers have found that merely the status of being a mother can lead to perceptions of lowered competence and commitment and lower salary offers.

MYTH: We don't need to do anything, the gender pay gap will eventually go away by itself.

REALITY: It has been nearly fifty years since Congress mandated equal pay for women, and we still have a pay gap. There is evidence that our initial progress in closing the gap has slowed. We can't sit back and wait decades more. Just this year the Department of Labor launched an app challenge, working to give women the tools they need to know their worth. My office continues to increase its enforcement of requirements that federal contractors pay workers without discriminating on the basis of race or gender. And we are teaming up with other members of the National Equal Pay Task Force to ensure a coordinated federal response to equal pay enforcement. You can read more about our work on equal pay here.

The pay gap isn't a myth, it's a reality—and it's our job to fix it.

Source: Coukos, Pamela. "Myth Busting the Pay Gap." U.S. Department of Labor Blog, June 7, 2012. Available online at https://blog.dol.gov/2012/06/07/myth-busting-the-pay-gap.

A FATHER CONSIDERS GENDER STEREOTYPES IN PRESCHOOL, 2012

Although many observers believe that there has been a dramatic upsurge since the 1990s in acceptance of men and women pursuing careers and shouldering domestic chores traditionally associated with the opposite gender, American culture is still saturated with messages that enforce traditional gender stereotypes. In the following short essay published in 2012 in Montessori Life, *father John Carl relates how these stereotypes are evident even in preschool celebrations of Mother's Day and Father's Day.*

As a parent, sociologist, and educator, I often seem to see the world differently from others. While some see a public policy debate as a football game between winners and losers, I see it as a vital way to create a good society. While some see education as a means to an end, I see it as a goal in and of itself. Some see gender equality growing in society because of the obvious changes in women's roles. However, I question this perception of increasing equality, as gender roles appear to me to remain strongly tied to traditional practices.

My youngest daughter attended an excellent preschool program. It was widely known for its open atmosphere, its racial and ethnic diversity and its fair-minded attitude toward teaching young children. At this bastion of equality gender differences still existed. Each year on Mother's Day the children held a Mother's Day Tea Party at which they sang to their mothers a song of love and tenderness. The event ended with the children presenting their mothers with a longstemmed rose and a kiss on the cheek, reciting, "In all the world, there is no other to take the place of my dear mother."

Contrast this with Father's Day. For that holiday, the school held a hot dog cookout on the playground. The fathers did the cooking and played with their children. For the presentation, the children sang a ditty called "Roadkill Charlie," a fun little song about a man who cooks and serves dead opossum. While singing the song, the children tossed hand-painted T-shirts with "DAD" on them to their fathers.

When I suggested to the director of the school that fathers might prefer a touching poem and/or song in lieu of an invitation to eat roadkill, she laughed, saying, "Dads don't want that. Mommies are special." This progressive, well-intentioned person was unknowingly reinforcing gender stereotypes. Such are the ills of thinking of gender differences in the United States. You find yourself often raising points of view that others don't seem to be able to see.

Gender and sex are not the same thing. Gender is defined as the personal traits and position in society connected with being a male or female. For instance, wearing high heels is associated with the female gender, while wearing combat boots is associated with the male gender. Gender is different from sex because sex refers strictly to the biological makeup of a male or a female. Clearly boys and girls have different biology, but that does not necessarily mean that biology creates personality. The simple correlations of boys to aggression and girls to verbal expression are not the whole story. Correlation is not cause, though it may be tempting to think that these simple correlations support the idea that gender-based behavior emanates from biological sex (Kennelly Merz & Lorber, 2001). As a sociologist, I would suggest that a more important factor than biology is socialization.

I am not a house husband, but I do my share of cooking, shopping, and chores around the house. When my daughter was born, I was in graduate school, so I spent a lot of time bathing, feeding, and caring for her. At one point, my father suggested that I was "doing too much with her." He said, "She's a girl, and fathers need to be careful about that kind of stuff." I can only surmise that he feared she might develop some nontraditional ideas about gender because her father was so involved. Personally, I hoped she would become nontraditional in her understanding of gender roles.

Source: Carl, John. "Gender Versus Sex: What's the Difference?" *Montessori Life* 24, no. 1, Spring 2012. Copyright © 2012 by the American Montessori Society. All rights reserved. Used by permission.

EVIDENCE OF GENDER BIAS AMONG MALE AND FEMALE SCIENCE FACULTY MEMBERS, 2012

In 2012 researchers at Yale University published the results of a major study that found that science faculty at American research universities seeking to fill laboratory manager positions commonly (if unconsciously) gave preferential treatment to male college graduates over equally qualified women applicants. The researchers found that this gender bias existed among female faculty members just as much as male faculty members. Moreover, they found that faculty gave male students higher starting salaries and higher levels of mentoring than equally qualified female students. The study, excerpted below, triggered a firestorm of controversy in the scientific community, with critics saying that the study's research was fundamentally flawed and supporters asserting that it showed that faculty bias was an underappreciated obstacle to increased participation of women in STEM (science, technology, engineering, and math) fields.

Discussion

The present study is unique in investigating subtle gender bias on the part of faculty in the biological and physical sciences. It therefore informs the debate on possible causes of the gender disparity in academic science by providing unique experimental evidence that science faculty of both genders exhibit bias against female undergraduates. As a controlled experiment, it fills a critical gap in the existing literature, which consisted only of experiments in other domains (with undergraduate students as participants) and correlational data that could not conclusively rule out the influence of other variables.

Our results revealed that both male and female faculty judged a female student to be less competent and less worthy of being hired than an identical male student, and also offered her a smaller starting salary and less career mentoring. Although the differences in ratings may be perceived as modest, the effect sizes were all moderate to large ($d = 0.60 - 0.75$). Thus, the current results suggest that subtle gender bias is important to address because it could translate into large real-world disadvantages in the judgment and treatment of female science students. Moreover, our mediation findings shed light on the processes responsible for this bias, suggesting that the female student was less likely to be hired than the male student because she was perceived as less competent. Additionally, moderation results indicated that faculty participants' preexisting subtle bias against women undermined their perceptions and treatment of the female (but not the male) student, further suggesting that chronic subtle biases may harm women within academic science. Use of a randomized controlled design and established practices from audit study methodology support the ecological validity and educational implications of our findings (*SI Materials and Methods*).

It is noteworthy that female faculty members were just as likely as their male colleagues to favor the male student. The fact that faculty members' bias was independent of their gender, scientific discipline, age, and tenure status suggests that it is likely unintentional, generated from widespread cultural stereotypes rather than a conscious intention to harm women. Additionally, the fact that faculty participants reported liking the female more than the male student further underscores the point that our results likely do not reflect faculty members' overt hostility toward women. Instead, despite expressing warmth toward emerging female scientists, faculty members of both genders appear to be affected by enduring cultural stereotypes about women's lack of science competence that translate into biases in student evaluation and mentoring.

Our careful selection of expert participants revealed gender discrimination among existing science faculty members who interact with students on a regular basis (*SI Materials and Methods: Subjects and Recruitment Strategy*). This method allowed for a high degree of ecological validity and generalizability relative to an approach using nonexpert participants, such as other undergraduates or lay people unfamiliar with laboratory manager job requirements and academic science mentoring (i.e., the participants in much psychological research on gender discrimination). The results presented here reinforce those of Stenpries, Anders, and Ritzke, the only other experiment we know of that recruited faculty participants. Because this previous experiment also indicated bias within academic science, its results raised serious concerns about the potential for faculty bias within the biological and physical sciences, casting further doubt on assertions (based on correlational data) that such biases do not exist. In the Steinpreis et al. experiment, psychologists were more likely to hire a psychology faculty job applicant when the applicant's curriculum vitae was assigned a male (rather than female) name. This previous work invited a study that would extend the finding to faculty in the biological and physical sciences and to reactions to undergraduates, whose competence was not already fairly established by accomplishments associated with the advanced career status of the faculty target group of the previous study. By providing this unique investigation of faculty bias against female students in biological and physical sciences, the present study extends past work to a critical early career stage, and to fields where women's underrepresentation remains stark.

Indeed, our findings raise concerns about the extent to which negative predoctoral experiences may shape women's subsequent decisions about persistence and career specialization. Following conventions established in classic experimental studies to create enough ambiguity to leave room for potentially biased responses, the student applicants in the present research were described as qualified to succeed in academic science (i.e., having coauthored a publication after obtaining 2 years of research experience), but not irrefutably excellent. As such, they represented a majority of aspiring scientists, and were precisely the type of students most affected by faculty judgments and mentoring (see *SI Materials and Methods* for more discussion). Our results raise the possibility that not only do such women encounter biased judgments of their competence and hireability, but also receive less faculty encouragement and financial rewards than identical male counterparts. Because most students depend on feedback from their environments to calibrate their own worth, faculty's assessments of students' competence likely contribute to students' self-efficacy and goal setting as scientists, which may influence decisions much later in their careers. Likewise, inasmuch as the advice and mentoring that students receive affect their ambitions and choices, it is significant that the faculty in this study were less inclined to mentor women than men. This finding raises the possibility that women may opt out of academic science careers in part because of diminished competence judgments, rewards, and mentoring received in the early years of the careers. In sum, the predoctoral years represent a window during which students' experiences of faculty bias or encouragement are particularly likely to shape their persistence in academic science. Thus, the present study not only fills an important gap in the research literature, but also has critical implications for pressing social and educational issues associated with the gender disparity in science.

If women's decisions to leave science fields when or before they reach the faculty level are influenced by unequal treatment by undergraduate advisors, then existing efforts to create more flexible work settings or increase women's identification with science may not fully alleviate a critical underlying problem. Our results suggest that academic policies and mentoring interventions targeting undergraduate advisors could contribute to reducing the gender disparity. Future research should evaluate the efficacy of educating faculty and students about the existence and impact of bias within academia, an approach that has reduced racial bias among students. Educational efforts might address research on factors that attenuate gender bias in real-world settings, such as increasing women's self-monitoring. Our results also point to the importance of establishing objective, transparent student evaluation and admissions criteria to guard against observers' tendency to unintentionally use different standards when assessing women relative to men. Without such actions, faculty bias against female undergraduates may continue to undermine meritocratic advancement, to the detriment of research and education.

Conclusions

The dearth of women within academic science reflects a significant wasted opportunity to benefit from the capabilities of our best potential scientists, whether male or female. Although women have begun to enter some science fields in greater numbers, their mere increased presence is not evidence of the absence of bias. Rather, some women may persist in academic science despite the damaging effects of unintended gender bias on the part of faculty. Similarly, it is not yet possible to conclude that the preferences for other fields and lifestyle choices that lead many women to leave academic science (even after obtaining advanced degrees) are not themselves influenced by experiences of bias, at least to some degree. To the extent that faculty gender bias impedes women's full participation in science, it may undercut not only academic meritocracy, but also the expansion of the scientific workforce needed for the next decade's advancement of national competitiveness.

Source: Moss-Racusin, Corinne A., et al. "Science Faculty's Subtle Gender Biases Favor Male Students." *Proceedings of the National Academy of the Sciences* 109, no. 41 (October 9, 2012): 16476–16477. Used by permission of PNAS.

A WORLD OF CEO MOMS AND TROPHY HUSBANDS, 2012

Journalist and author Carol Hymowitz is a recognized authority on executive management issues in the American business world. She has held prominent editorial roles with prestigious news organizations such as the Wall Street Journal, Forbes Woman, *and*

Bloomberg News. *In addition to her research and commentary on general management and workplace issues and business trends, Hymowitz has devoted a good deal of attention to working women and their experiences in the executive suites of America's leading companies and industries. In 2012 she wrote the following essay for* Bloomberg Businessweek *on the growing number of marriages in which wives work as high-profile, high-powered executives while their husbands stay at home.*

Among the 80 or so customers crammed into Bare Escentuals, it's easy to spot Leslie Blodgett. It's not merely her six-inch platform heels and bright magenta-and-blue dress that set her apart in the Thousand Oaks (Calif.) mall boutique, but her confidence. To the woman concerned she's too old for shimmery eye shadow, Blodgett swoops in and encourages her to wear whatever she wants. With a deft sweep of a brush, she demonstrates a new shade of blush on another customer's cheek. And when she isn't helping anyone, she pivots on her heels for admirers gushing about her dress, made by the breakout designer Erdem.

Blodgett, 49, has spent the past 18 years nurturing Bare Escentuals from a startup into a global cosmetics empire. She sold the company for $1.7 billion to Shiseido in March 2010 but still pitches products in stores around the world and chats incessantly with customers online. Scores of fans post daily messages on Blodgett's Facebook page, confessing details about their personal lives and offering opinions on her additive-free makeup. She only wishes her 19-year-old son, Trent, were in touch with her as frequently as he is with her husband, Keith. In 1995, at 38, Keith quit making television commercials to raise Trent, freeing up Leslie to build her business. She'd do it all again, but she's jealous of her husband's relationship with her son. Trent, a college sophomore, texts his father almost every day; he often goes a week without texting her.

"Once I knew my role was providing for the family, I took that very seriously. But there was envy knowing I wasn't there for our son during the day," says Blodgett. "Keith does everything at home—the cooking, repairs, finances, vacation planning—and I could work long hours and travel a lot, knowing he took such good care of Trent. I love my work, but I would have liked to have a little more balance or even understand what that means."

Blodgett's lament is becoming more familiar as a generation of female breadwinners look back on the sacrifices—some little, some profound—required to have the careers they wanted. Like hundreds of thousands of women who have advanced into management roles in the past two decades—and, in particular, the hundreds who've become senior corporate officers—she figured out early what every man with a corner office has long known: To make it to the top, you need a wife. If that wife happens to be a husband, and increasingly it is, so be it.

When Carly Fiorina became Hewlett-Packard's first female chief executive officer, the existence of her househusband, Frank Fiorina, who had retired early from AT&T to support her career, was a mini-sensation; now this arrangement isn't at all unusual. Seven of the 18 women who are currently CEOs of Fortune 500 companies—including Xerox's Ursula Burns, PepsiCo's Indra Nooyi, and Well-Point's Angela Braly—have, or at some point have had, a stay-at-home husband.

So do scores of female CEOs of smaller companies and women in other senior executive jobs. Others, like IBM's new CEO, Ginni Rometty, have spouses who dialed back their careers to become their powerful wives' chief domestic officers.

This role reversal is occurring more and more as women edge past men at work. Women now fill a majority of jobs in the U.S., including 51.4 percent of managerial and professional positions, according to U.S. Census Bureau data. Some 23 percent of wives now out-earn their husbands, according to a 2010 study by the Pew Research Center. And this earnings trend is more dramatic among younger people. Women 30 and under make more money, on average, than their male counterparts in all but three of the largest cities in the U.S.

During the recent recession, three men lost their jobs for every woman. Many unemployed fathers, casualties of layoffs in manufacturing and finance, have ended up caring for their children full-time while their wives are the primary wage earners. The number of men in the U.S. who regularly care for children under age five increased to 32 percent in 2010 from 19 percent in 1988, according to Census figures. Among those fathers with preschool-age children, one in five served as the main caregiver.

Even as the trend becomes more widespread, stigmas persist. At-home dads are sometimes perceived as freeloaders, even if they've lost jobs. Or they're considered frivolous kept men—gentlemen who golf. The househusbands of highly successful women, after all, live in luxurious homes, take nice vacations, and can afford nannies and housekeepers, which many employ at least part-time. In reaction, at-home dads have launched a spate of support groups and daddy blogs to defend themselves.

"Men are suddenly seeing what it's been like for women throughout history," says Linda R. Hirshman, a lawyer and the author of *Get to Work*, a book that challenges at-home moms to secure paying jobs and insist that their husbands do at least half the housework. Caring for children all day and doing housework is tiring, unappreciated work that few are cut out for—and it leaves men and women alike feeling isolated and diminished.

There's some good news about the at-home dads trend. "By going against the grain, men get to stretch their parenting abilities and women can advance," notes Stephanie Coontz, a family studies professor at Evergreen State College in Olympia, Wash., and author of *Marriage: a History*. And yet the trend underscores something else: When jobs are scarce or one partner is aiming high, a two-career partnership is next to impossible. "Top power jobs are so time-consuming and difficult, you can't have two spouses doing them and maintain a marriage and family," says Coontz. This explains why, even as women make up more of the workforce, they're still a small minority (14 percent, according to New York–based Catalyst) in senior executive jobs. When they reach the always-on, all-consuming executive level, "it's still women who more often put family ahead of their careers," says Ken Matos, a senior director at Families and Work Institute in New York. It may explain, too, why bookstore shelves and e-book catalogs are jammed with self-help books for ambitious women, of which *I'd Rather Be in*

Charge, by former Ogilvy-Mather Worldwide CEO Charlotte Beers, is merely the latest. Some, such as Hirshman's top-selling *Get to Work*, recommend that women "marry down"—find husbands who won't mind staying at home—or wed older men who are ready to retire as their careers take off. What's indisputable is that couples increasingly are negotiating whose career will take precedence before they start a family.

"Your wife's career is about to soar, and you need to get out of her way." That's what Ken Gladden says his boss told him shortly before his wife, Dawn Lepore, was named the first female CIO at Charles Schwab in 1994. He was a vice-president at Schwab in computer systems. Lepore's promotion meant she'd become his top boss. "I married above my station," Gladden jokes.

Gladden moved to a job at Visa. When their son, Andrew, was born four years later in 1998, Gladden quit working altogether. He and Lepore had tried for years to have a child and didn't want him raised by a nanny. Being a full-time dad wasn't the biggest adjustment Gladden made for Lepore's career. That came later, when Seattle-based drugstore.com recruited Lepore to become its CEO in 2004.

Gladden had lived in the San Francisco Bay Area for 25 years and wasn't keen to move to a city where it rains a lot and he didn't know anyone. He rejected Lepore's suggestion that she commute between Seattle and San Francisco, and after some long discussions he agreed to relocate—on the condition that they kept their Bay Area home. They still return for holidays and some vacations. "To do what I'm doing, you've got to be able to say 'my wife's the breadwinner, the more powerful one,' and be O.K. with that. But you also need your own interests," says Gladden, who has used his computing skills to launch a home-based business developing software for schools.

The couple's five-bedroom Seattle home overlooks Lake Washington. Gladden, 63, is chief administrator of it and their children, who now are 9 and 13. While they're in school, he works on his software. From 3 p.m. until bedtime, he carpools to and from sports and music lessons, warms up dinners prepared by a part-time housekeeper, and supervises homework. Lepore, 57, is often out of town. She oversaw the sale of drugstore.com to Walgreens last year, for $429 million. As CEO, she was rarely home before 8 or 9 p.m. and traveled several days a week. Now, as a consultant to several startups and a director at EBay, she still travels frequently. If Gladden envies anything, it's the ease with which his wife can walk into a room filled with well-known executives like Bill Gates and "go right up to them and start talking. I don't feel like I can participate," he says.

Lepore wishes her "biggest supporter" would get more recognition for everything he does at home. When an executive recently told her "having an at-home husband makes it easy for you to be a CEO," she responded, "no, not easy. He makes it possible." Lepore advises younger women to "choose your spouse carefully. If you want a top job, you need a husband who isn't self-involved and will support your success," even if you go further than him. There are tradeoffs, she warns: "I've missed so much with my kids—school plays, recitals, just seeing them every day."

For Lepore and Gladden, the role reversal paid off, and, as one of the few couples willing to go public about their domestic arrangement, they're a rare source of inspiration for those who are still figuring it out. Like Gladden, Matt Schneider, 36, is an at-home dad. A former technology company manager and then a sixth grade teacher, he cares for his sons Max and Sam, 6 and 3, while his wife, Priyanka, also 36, puts in 10-hour days as chief operating officer at a Manhattan real estate management startup. He feels "privileged," he says, to be with his sons full-time "and see them change every day," while allowing that child care and housework can be mind-numbing. He uses every minute of the 2½ hours each weekday when Sam is in preschool to expand the NYC DADS Group he co-founded, 450 members strong. Members meet for play dates with their kids, discuss parenting, and stand up for at-home dads. "We're still portrayed as bumbling idiots," Schneider says. He rails against a prejudice that moms would do a better job—if only they were there. "Everyone is learning from scratch how to change diapers and toilet-train," he says, "and there's no reason to think this is woman's work."

Schneider and his wife, who met as undergraduates at University of Pennsylvania's Wharton School of Business, decided before they wed that she'd have the big career and he'd be the primary parent. "It's her name on the paycheck, and sure, we've thought about the precariousness of having just one breadwinner. But she wouldn't earn what she does if I wasn't doing what I do," he says. Which is not to say that he doesn't wonder "whether I can get back to a career when I want to and build on what I've done before."

At-home moms have snubbed him at arts and crafts classes and on playgrounds. "Men, even those of us pushing strollers, are perceived as dangerous," Schneider says. He was rejected when he wanted to join an at-home neighborhood moms' group, which prompted him to blog more about the similarities among moms and dads. "I've met moms *and* dads who are happy to give a screaming kid a candy bar to get him to settle down, and moms *and* dads who show up at play dates with containers filled with organic fruit," he says. "The differences aren't gender-specific."

It's no different for gay couples. Brad Kleinerman and Flint Gehre have taken turns being at-home dads for their three sons, now 19, 18, and 10. When their sons—biological siblings they adopted through the Los Angeles County foster care system—were young, Kleinerman and Gehre relied first on a weekday nanny and then a live-in one while both worked full-time. Kleinerman, 50, was an executive in human resources at Walt Disney and NASA. Gehre, 46, was a teacher and then director of global learning and communications at Disney. Five years ago, they decided they no longer wanted to outsource parenting. "We always wanted to have dinner together as a family, but by the time we got home, the nanny had fed our kids," says Gehre. "Our kids were at pivotal ages—the two oldest about to go to high school and the youngest to first grade. We wanted to be the ones instilling our values and be there when they needed help with homework or had to get to a doctor."

In 2007 the couple moved from Los Angeles to Avon, Conn., where they were able to get married legally and find better schools for their kids. Kleinerman became the full-time dad and Gehre kept his Disney job, working partly from home and traveling frequently to Los Angeles. A year later they switched: Gehre quit Disney to parent full-time and Kleinerman found a new job as a human resources director at Cigna Healthcare. Gehre says he's never felt discriminated against as a gay dad or a stay-at-home dad. "No one has ever said to me, 'Why would you stay home with the kids?' Where we're discriminated is when we pay taxes. We don't qualify for the marriage deduction, we have to file as single people," he says. If he has one regret about being at home, it's the lack of adult conversation and stimulation: "I worked in a very high-intensity atmosphere with very intelligent and hard-driving people, and that keeps you sharp." Any dullness doesn't make Gehre doubt his decision. Having consciously chosen to have a family, he and Kleinerman felt they had not only to provide the essentials, but also to be present.

Is there an alternate universe where both parents can pursue careers without outsourcing child care? The five Nordic countries—Iceland, Norway, Sweden, Finland, and Denmark—are noted leaders in keeping moms, in particular, on the job. "These countries have made it possible to have a better division of labor both at work and at home through policies that both encourage the participation of women in the labor force and men in their families," says Saadia Zahidi, co-author of the World Economic Forum's *Global Gender Gap Report*. The policies Zahidi refers to include mandatory paternal leave in combination with maternity leave; generous, federally mandated parental leave benefits; gender-neutral tax incentives; and post-maternity reentry programs.

There were no such programs or precedents for Jennifer Granholm and Dan Mulhern. When the two met at Harvard Law School, she grilled him about what he expected from a wife. Mulhern accepted that Granholm would never be a homemaker like his mother, but he never expected her to run for political office. "When I was young," he says, "I thought *I'd* be the governor"—not married to the governor. Granholm was governor of Michigan from 2003 through 2010, and her election forced Mulhern to walk away from the Detroit-based consulting business he founded, which had numerous contracts with state-licensed health insurance companies, municipalities, and school districts. Once that happened, he felt "in a backroom somewhere" and in a marriage that was "a lot more give than take."

Mulhern understood that his wife faced "extraordinary pressure" during her two terms, including a $1.7 billion budget deficit and the bankruptcies of General Motors and Chrysler. She had limited time for their three children, who were 6, 11, and 14 when she was elected, and even less for him. "I didn't want to say, 'hey, you missed my birthday' or 'you haven't even noticed what happened with the kids,' but I sometimes felt resentful," he says.

Mulhern says he complained to his wife that they spent 95 percent of the little time they had together talking about her work. He missed the attention she used to give him but felt humiliated asking for it. He gradually changed his expectations. He stopped waiting for Granholm to call him in the middle of the day to share what had happened at meetings they'd spent time talking about the prior evening. And he realized he couldn't recreate for her all the memorable or awkward moments he had with their children—like the time he found his daughter and her high school friends in the outdoor shower, "ostensibly with their clothes on. I had to call all the parents and tell them, as a courtesy, 'I want you to know this happened at the Governor's mansion,'" he says. "While my wife was battling the Republican head of the State Senate, I had a teenage daughter who was a more formidable opponent."

When Granholm left office and was asked "what's next?," she said, "it's Dan's turn." As a former governor, though, she's the one with more obvious opportunities. Later this month, Granholm launches a daily political commentary show on Current TV. She's also teaching at the University of California at Berkeley, where Dan has a part-time gig thanks to his wife.

"The employment opportunities that come my way—and my salary potential—aren't what my wife's are now," says Mulhern. He plans to continue to teach, write, and do some consulting, while also taking care of their 14-year-old son. "Someone has to be focused on him every day," he says.

The experiences and reflections of powerful women and their at-home husbands could lead to changes at work so that neither women nor men have to sacrifice their careers or families. "There's no reason women should feel guilty about achieving great success, but there should be a way for success to include professional and personal happiness for everyone," says *Get to Work* author Hirshman. "If you have to kill yourself at work, that's bad for everyone."

Kathleen Christensen agrees. As program director at the Alfred P. Sloan Foundation, she has focused on work and family issues and says we're back to the 1950s, only "instead of Jane at home, it's John. But it's still one person doing 100 percent of work outside the home and the other doing 100 percent at home." Just as we saw the Feminine Mystique in the 1960s among frustrated housewives, Christensen predicts, "we may see the Masculine Mystique in 2020." The children of couples who have reversed roles know the stakes better than anyone. One morning last year, when Dawn Lepore was packing for a business trip to New York, her nine-year-old daughter burst into tears. "I don't want you to travel so much," Elizabeth told her mother. Lepore hugged her, called her school, and said her daughter would be staying home that morning. Then she rescheduled her flight until much later that day. "There have been times when what Elizabeth wants most is a mom who stays home and bakes cookies," she says.

Lepore is sometimes concerned that her children won't be ambitious because they've often heard her complain about how exhausted she is after work. But they're much closer to their father than kids whose dads work full-time, and they have a different perspective about men's and women's potential. When a friend of her daughter's said that fathers go to offices every day, Lepore recalls, "Elizabeth replied, 'Don't be silly, dads are at home.'"

Source: Hymowitz, Carol. "Behind Every Great Woman: The Rise of the CEO Mom Has Created a New Kind of Trophy Husband." *Bloomberg Businessweek,* January 5, 2012. Available online at https://www.bloomberg.com/news/articles/2012-01-04/behind-every-great-woman.

NANCY PELOSI DECLARES THAT "WHEN WOMEN SUCCEED, AMERICA SUCCEEDS," 2013

In 2013 the Center for American Progress, a progressive policy institute based in Washington, DC, announced a new initiative called Fair Shot dedicated to supporting women in leadership roles, protecting women's health, and advancing policies to improve women's economic opportunities and security. As part of the rollout of that initiative, Democratic House minority leader Nancy Pelosi (1940–) of California delivered a speech called "When Women Succeed, America Succeeds" in which she traced the progress of the women's rights movement from the Seneca Falls Convention of 1848 to the present day and discussed major policy issues of importance to working women.

. . . And so, it was 165 years ago, 165 years ago. Imagine the courage it took for those women to go to Seneca Falls and do what they did there, to even leave home without their husband's permission, or father's, or whoever it was. To go to Seneca Falls, and to paraphrase what our founders said in the [Declaration of Independence] of the United States: they said the truths that are self-evident, that every man and woman, that men and women were created equal and that we must go forward in recognition of that.

I'm very honored—I mean, self-promotion is a terrible thing, but somebody has to do it, right? I'm very honored—I want you to go into this mode yourselves, know your power, do your thing—I'm going to be inducted into the Hall of Fame at Seneca Falls on October 12th.

[Laughter and Cheering]

I'm very excited about that. Because of it, when they said that every man and woman—"such it is now the necessity for women to demand equal station to which," they, it said, "we are entitled." And that's what this is about.

How could it be 165 years later we are still fighting this fight? Well, in that tradition we've come together to prioritize a women's economic agenda, an agenda—"When Women Succeed, America Succeeds: An Economic Agenda for Women and their Families." I think it fits comfortably with what CAP is doing, with what our sisters in the Senate are doing, what labor unions and others around the country are doing, in keeping with what Planned Parenthood is doing in terms of health—with Stephanie and them always listening, full agenda there. With our friends in labor, SEIU, Mary Kay Henry [Henry is president of the two-million-member Service Employees International Union-SEIU]. . . . Thank you all.

When we brought together lots of groups, a large number of women, leaders of women's groups and said: "if we were to prioritize and just narrow in on just a few things that make a difference, what would they be?" And it came down to— and again, we did this under the leadership of Congresswoman Rosa DeLauro, who's been a relentless champion on this subject, relentless is sort of a mild word for it. . . .

And Congresswoman Donna Edwards, Chair of the Women's Caucus who's been very much a part, and Doris Matsui, and the rest. We really had diversity in our decision-making and unanimity—almost unanimously concluded that we had to have three components, just talking this, we're not talking about every issue, we're just talking about workplace and home. Paycheck fairness, and that involves raising the minimum wage to a living wage, and we must get that done. It affects our whole country, it affects our families, and it affects our women. And we passed Lilly Ledbetter—the first bill the President signed. And let's thank our President, I know Valerie Jarrett was here this morning giving a call to arms and we're so fortunate to have her there and the President in the White House because the agenda of CAP [Center for American Progress] about making progress for our country, is the President's agenda. So we're fortunate he's there to pass that, sign that bill, but we didn't get paycheck fairness and we cannot rest until we do. Lilly Ledbetter is important in terms of recourse that women have when discriminated against, but paycheck fairness sets a place where it is the law of the land.

So, paycheck fairness, of course we have our bills, our bill to do just that. Paycheck fairness and raising the minimum wage. So, thank you, SEIU, for your leadership on the minimum wage issue.

Second point is paid leave. Now many of us, well you're all too young, but some of us were there for the—I'm not doing this by age, I just meant by involvement at the time when we passed the Family and Medical Leave Act. It was the first bill that President, it was an early bill that President Clinton signed and [Former Congresswoman] Pat Schroeder, [Former Senator] Chris Dodd deserves a tremendous [amount] of credit. But anyway, and many of you in this room, but we had that on the desk, the President signed it. One hundred million families have taken advantage of the Family and Medical Leave [Act]; it's a great thing—it ain't paid, by and large.

So we must have paid leave and we have legislation to do it—the Healthy Families Act—to do that. That I think fits comfortably in what you are talking about here. Paid leave—I'm telling you that we've, we've had for this, I'll go to the third point. The third point is . . . quality, affordable child care to unleash the power of women and families in our workforce. When we forge to get these three things done, the third one is more like a crusade, a cultural crusade—we have to change people's minds. This was on President Nixon's desk in the '70s and the Pat Buchanans of the world and others culturally talked him into not signing the bill. And here we are 40 years later. And we must get this done. It's absolutely essential that women can have peace—and fathers, moms and dads can have peace of mind in the workplace, security that their children are taken care of.

Now, we started in Seneca Falls. Those women came out, they fought forever to get the power, the right to vote. When the bill finally, when the Amendment was finally approved, the newspapers said: "women given the right to vote." I don't think so. Women fought for, women worked for, women insisted, women would not take no for an answer, women worked for and achieved the right to vote.

Now, fast forward a couple—decades, almost a hundred years from Seneca, not a hundred but decades, a long time from Seneca Falls to—but that's not where it all began. That's where it was all declared. OK. Fast forward to World War II, women in the workplace, Rosie the Riveter, all of that, women out of the house. This is revolutionary. So there's the idea that women are going to be in the workplace. Higher education of women, women in the professions, all of that. But what's the missing link? No child care. No child care. So whether it's women in executive positions, or women in entry level, whatever it is, across the board economically, culturally, in every way there is a very big missing link about how we train people, how we pay them, how we enable them to organize. Right, Mary Kay? How we just value work. Whether it's minimum wage and paycheck fairness. Whether it's paid leave, or whether it's valuing work that these people do so that other women, as we say in San Francisco: "children learning, parents earning." And we thank the President for having universal child care, which is a step, not everything, but is an important step to help with that sense of security.

OK. So that's what our agenda is, those three things. Of course, the liberation of health, the health care bill—no longer will being a woman be a preexisting medical condition. No longer will women be discriminated against in premiums because, you know, they've had babies and all of the rest. By the way, when I came to Congress and I ran when I was 46, elected when I was 47, they said: "I came to Congress late in life." And I thought: "late in whose life?"

[Laughter]

"I just got out of the House." My kids are 47 right now, I think of them as babies. But in any event, whenever it's your turn to go out there, it's the right time. So don't let anybody characterize that as late in life and by the way, that takes me to the next point, women in leadership, which is a part of this. If we want to have women coming into politics and government earlier, we have to make our own environment. Whether it's in the economy we have to make our own environment with what we talked about and what you have on your agenda today, to make our economy. Children are cared for, workers rewarded, time is there if people are sick but in politics I promise you this: if you reduce the role of money in politics and increase the level of civility in the political debate, you will elect many more women to public office, and minorities, and young people, but many more women.

So if we—we're very proud, when I came to Congress there were 20, equally, practically divided between Democrats and Republicans. We've increased our number up to 60, it's 100 all together—isn't that Senate beautiful with their numbers and thanks to EMILY's List and all of the groups that helped with that. But that isn't enough, this is incremental, we're tired of it. Kick open the door, change the environment in which all of these decisions are made in how women can succeed and thrive and do the job. Because nothing is more wholesome to the politics and the government of our country than the increased participation of women.

So, that just touches on some, you think I've, I could talk all day about this, and you think I probably will. We look forward to working with you, to continuing this. I've been all over the country since we announced, I think we've had 13 events. From—I'd say Boston, but it was Beverly, Massachusetts—down south, across the east coast, west coast, Albuquerque, Chicago, everything in between. Members have had hundreds of events on different pieces of this. Again, it reconciles very beautifully with leadership and the affordable health care because that is about life, liberty, and the pursuit of happiness. A healthier life, the liberty to pursue your happiness. The freedom not to be job locked. You could choose—you can be self-employed as an artist, as a photographer, and whatever. You could start your own business, you could change jobs and follow your passion, not your [health insurance] policy. And that's very important for women as well. . . . And so many women have come to me before the Affordable Care Act and said: "I have a business, I have a coffee shop, I make brownies, I am inventing the newest widget, but I have to have another job to have, to get health care benefits because my small company can't afford to give them to me." Imagine.

So, we have to, this is a great thing. It's transformative for our country. Transformative for women. Just close with this one little story: in New Haven we had one of our breakout events with Rosa DeLauro, of course in the lead, most enthusiastically in front, one of the witnesses, one of the persons who bore testimony to what we were doing was a woman who drove the bus, a school bus. And she said that, that's it, it's so sad, she told us her troubles of getting a job and minimum wage and you know, all that stuff. But, she said, I want to tell you about my job. I drive a bus, I pick up kids to take them to school. I see moms practically in tears, putting their children on a bus, knowing that their children are not well, but they can't keep them home because they can't stay home with them because they don't have paid sick leave. And so they have to send their child to school sick because they can't afford to be docked a day of pay. Now, it relates to pay, it relates to paid leave. And so these not so well kids are getting on the bus, some of them throwing up, others of them just not feeling well. That's just not right, this is the United States of America, the greatest country that ever existed in the history of the world and we can't have a mom stay home to take care of a sick child because somebody's going to have a bigger bottom line because they don't have paid leave?

Well, you got to, you got to make sure that, that happens so I thank you all for the role that you are playing in all of that. Our House Democratic women will—I think it's tomorrow that we're meeting with them again to put out, we want the men to be doing it too and when they see how women turn out for women, women helping women, they're shocked. It's absolutely essential. It can happen. We're not going to rest until it does. And it wouldn't happen without all of you. So thank you for your leadership.

Source: Pelosi, Nancy. "Pelosi Remarks on 'When Women Succeed, America Succeeds' Agenda at Center for American Progress," September 18, 2013. Available online at https://pelosi.house.gov/news/press-releases/pelosi-remarks-on-when -women-succeed-america-succeeds-agenda-at-center-for.

PRESIDENT OBAMA DECLARES THAT "IT'S ON US" TO STOP VIOLENCE AGAINST WOMEN, 2014

Sexism and outright misogyny are widely recognized as significant obstacles to full gender equality in American society. They make it more difficult for girls and women to pursue educational and career interests, especially in areas that have traditionally been dominated by men. And in many cases, these misogynistic attitudes have been cited as a key contributor to the problem of sexual assault and other forms of violence against women in the United States. Some experts, in fact, have asserted that incidents of rape and other forms of sexual assault against women have reached epidemic levels in America.

Many lawmakers, organizations, and public figures have rallied to speak out against misogyny in American culture and to combat sexual assault in all its forms—including on college campuses, where some studies have indicated that as many as one in five female students are victims of sexual assault. One such effort was the "It's On Us" education campaign, launched in 2014 by President Barack Obama (1961–) and the White House Council on Women and Girls to raise awareness of sexual assault on campus and urge young men and women to be more proactive in promoting campus environments that are safe for all students. The following are Obama's remarks from the formal unveiling of the campaign on September 19, 2014.

THE PRESIDENT: Welcome to the White House, everybody. And thank you to Joe Biden not just for the introduction, not just for being a great Vice President—but for decades, since long before he was in his current office, Joe has brought unmatched passion to this cause. He has. (Applause.)

And at a time when domestic violence was all too often seen as a private matter, Joe was out there saying that this was unacceptable. Thanks to him and so many others, last week we were able to commemorate the 20th anniversary of the law Joe wrote, a law that transformed the way we handle domestic abuse in this country—the Violence Against Women Act.

And we're here to talk today about an issue that is a priority for me, and that's ending campus sexual assault. I want to thank all of you who are participating. I particularly want to thank Lilly for her wonderful presentation and grace. I want to thank her parents for being here. As a father of two daughters, I on the one hand am enraged about what has happened; on the other hand, am empowered to see such an incredible young woman be so strong and do so well. And we're going to be thrilled watching all of the great things she is going to be doing in her life. So we're really proud of her.

I want to thank the White House Council on Women and Girls. Good Job. Valerie, thank you. (Applause.) I want to thank our White House Adviser on Violence Against Women—the work that you do every day partnering with others to prevent the outrage, the crime of sexual violence.

We've got some outstanding lawmakers with us. Senator Claire McCaskill is right here from the great state of Missouri, who I love. (Applause.) And we've got Dick Blumenthal from the great state of Connecticut, as well as Congresswoman Susan Davis. So thank you so much, I'm thrilled to have you guys here. (Applause.)

I also want to thank other members of Congress who are here and have worked on this issue so hard for so long. A lot of the people in this room have been on the front lines in fighting sexual assault for a long time. And along with Lilly, I want to thank all the survivors who are here today, and so many others around the country. (Applause.) Lilly I'm sure took strength from a community of people—some who came before, some who were peers—who were able to summon the courage to speak out about the darkest moment of their lives. They endure pain and the fear that too often isolates victims of sexual assault. So when they give voice to their own experiences, they're giving voice to countless others—women and men, girls and boys—who still suffer in silence.

So to the survivors who are leading the fight against sexual assault on campuses, your efforts have helped to start a movement. I know that, as Lilly described, there are times where the fight feels lonely, and it feels as if you're dredging up stuff that you'd rather put behind you. But we're here to say, today, it's not on you. This is not your fight alone. This is on all of us, every one of us, to fight campus sexual assault. You are not alone, and we have your back, and we are going to organize campus by campus, city by city, state by state. This entire country is going to make sure that we understand what this is about, and that we're going to put a stop to it.

And this is a new school year. We've been working on campus sexual assault for several years, but the issue of violence against women is now in the news every day. We started to I think get a better picture about what domestic violence is all about. People are talking about it. Victims are realizing they're not alone. Brave people have come forward, they're opening up about their own experiences.

And so we think today's event is all that more relevant, all that more important for us to say that campus sexual assault is no longer something we as a nation can turn away from and say that's not our problem. This is a problem that matters to all of us.

An estimated one in five women has been sexually assaulted during her college years—one in five. Of those assaults, only 12 percent are reported, and of those reported assaults, only a fraction of the offenders are punished. And while these assaults overwhelmingly happen to women, we know that men are assaulted, too. Men get raped. They're even less likely to talk about it. We know that sexual assault can happen to anyone, no matter their race, their economic status, sexual orientation, gender identity—and LGBT victims can feel even more isolated, feel even more alone.

For anybody whose once-normal, everyday life was suddenly shattered by an act of sexual violence, the trauma, the terror can shadow you long after one horrible attack. It lingers when you don't know where to go or who to turn to. It's there when you're forced to sit in the same class or stay in the same dorm with the person who raped you; when people are more suspicious of what you were wearing or what you were drinking, as if it's your fault, not the fault of the person who assaulted you. It's a haunting presence when the very people entrusted with your welfare fail to protect you.

Students work hard to get into college. I know—I'm watching Malia right now, she's a junior. She's got a lot of homework. And parents can do everything they can to support their kids' dreams of getting a good education. When they finally make it onto campus, only to be assaulted, that's not just a nightmare for them and their families; it's not just an affront to everything they've worked so hard to achieve—it is an affront to our basic humanity. It insults our most basic values as individuals and families, and as a nation. We are a nation that values liberty and equality and justice. And we're a people who believe every child deserves an education that allows them to fulfill their God-given potential, free from fear of intimidation or violence. And we owe it to our children to live up to those values. So my administration is trying to do our part.

First of all, three years ago, we sent guidance to every school district, every college, every university that receives federal funding, and we clarified their legal obligations to prevent and respond to sexual assault. And we reminded them that sexual violence isn't just a crime, it is a civil rights violation. And I want to acknowledge Secretary of Education Arne Duncan for his department's work in holding schools accountable and making sure that they stand up for students.

Number two, in January, I created a White House task force to prevent—a Task Force to Protect Students from Sexual Assault. Their job is to work with colleges and universities on better ways to prevent and respond to assaults, to lift up best practices. And we held conversations with thousands of people—survivors, parents, student groups, faculty, law enforcement, advocates, academics. In April, the task force released the first report, recommending a number of best practices for colleges and universities to keep our kids safe. And these are tested, and they are common-sense measures like campus surveys to figure out the scope of the problem, giving survivors a safe place to go and a trusted person to talk to, training school officials in how to handle trauma. Because when you read some of the accounts, you think, what were they thinking? You just get a sense of too many people in charge dropping the ball, fumbling something that should be taken with the most—the utmost seriousness and the utmost care.

Number three, we're stepping up enforcement efforts and increasing the transparency of our efforts. So we're reviewing existing laws to make sure they're adequate. And we're going to keep on working with educational institutions across the country to help them appropriately respond to these crimes.

So that's what we have been doing, but there's always more that we can do. And today, we're taking a step and joining with people across the country to change our culture and help prevent sexual assault from happening. Because that's where prevention—that's what prevention is going to require—we've got to have a fundamental shift in our culture.

As far as we've come, the fact is that from sports leagues to pop culture to politics, our society still does not sufficiently value women. We still don't condemn sexual assault as loudly as we should. We make excuses. We look the other way. The message that sends can have a chilling effect on our young women.

And I've said before, when women succeed, America succeeds—let me be clear, that's not just true in America. If you look internationally, countries that oppress their women are countries that do badly. Countries that empower their women are countries that thrive.

And so this is something that requires us to shift how we think about these issues. One letter from a young woman really brought this point home. Katherine Morrison, a young student from Youngstown, Ohio, she wrote, "How are we supposed to succeed when so many of our voices are being stifled? How can we succeed when our society says that as a woman, it's your fault if you are at a party or walked home alone. How can we succeed when people look at women and say 'you should have known better,' or 'boys will be boys'?"

And Katherine is absolutely right. Women make up half this country; half its workforce; more than half of our college students. They are not going to succeed the way they should unless they are treated as true equals, and are supported and respected. And unless women are allowed to fulfill their full potential, America will not reach its full potential. So we've got to change.

This is not just the work of survivors, it's not just the work of activists. It's not just the work of college administrators. It's the responsibility of the soccer coach, and the captain of the basketball team, and the football players. And it's on fraternities and sororities, and it's on the editor of the school paper, and the drum major in the band. And it's on the English department and the engineering department, and it's on the high schools and the elementary schools, and it's on teachers, and it's on counselors, and it's on mentors, and it's on ministers.

It's on celebrities, and sports leagues, and the media, to set a better example. It's on parents and grandparents and older brothers and sisters to sit down young people and talk about this issue. (Applause.)

And it's not just on the parents of young women to caution them. It is on the parents of young men to teach them respect for women. (Applause.) And it's on grown men to set an example and be clear about what it means to be a man.

It is on all of us to reject the quiet tolerance of sexual assault and to refuse to accept what's unacceptable. And we especially need our young men to show women the respect they deserve, and to recognize sexual assault, and to do their part to stop it. Because most young men on college campuses are not perpetrators. But the rest—we can't generalize across the board. But the rest of us can help stop those who think in these terms and shut stuff down. And that's not always easy to do with all the social pressures to stay quiet or go along; you don't want to be the guy who's stopping another friend from taking a woman home even if it looks like she doesn't or can't consent. Maybe you hear something in the locker room that makes you feel uncomfortable, or see something at a party that you know isn't right, but you're not sure whether you should stand up, not sure it's okay to intervene.

And I think Joe said it well—the truth is, it's not just okay to intervene, it is your responsibility. It is your responsibility to speak your mind. It is your responsibility to tell your buddy when he's messing up. It is your responsibility to set the right tone when you're talking about women, even when women aren't around—maybe especially when they're not around.

And it's not just men who should intervene. Women should also speak up when something doesn't look right, even if the men don't like it. It's all of us taking responsibility. Everybody has a role to play.

And in fact, we're here with Generation Progress to launch, appropriately enough, a campaign called "It's On Us." The idea is to fundamentally shift the way we think about sexual assault. So we're inviting colleges and universities to join us in saying, we are not tolerating this anymore—not on our campuses, not in our community, not in this country. And the campaign is building on the momentum that's already being generated by college campuses by the incredible young people around the country who have stepped up and are leading the way. I couldn't be prouder of them.

And we're also joined by some great partners in this effort—including the Office of Women's Health, the college sports community, media platforms. We've got universities who have signed up, including, by the way, our military academies, who are represented here today. So the goal is to hold ourselves and each other accountable, and to look out for those who don't consent and can't consent. And anybody can be a part of this campaign.

So the first step on this is to go to ItsOnUs.org—that's ItsOnUs.org. Take a pledge to help keep women and men safe from sexual assault. It's a promise not to be a bystander to the problem, but to be part of the solution. I took the pledge. Joe took the pledge. You can take the pledge. You can share it on social media, you can encourage others to join us.

And this campaign is just part of a broader effort, but it's a critical part, because even as we continue to enforce our laws and work with colleges to improve their responses, and to make sure that survivors are taken care of, it won't be enough unless we change the culture that allows assault to happen in the first place.

And I'm confident we can. I'm confident because of incredible young people like Lilly who speak out for change and empower other survivors. They inspire me to keep fighting. I'm assuming they inspire you as well. And this is a personal priority not just as a President, obviously, not just as a husband and a father of two extraordinary girls, but as an American who believes that our nation's success depends on how we value and defend the rights of women and girls.

So I'm asking all of you, join us in this campaign. Commit to being part of the solution. Help make sure our schools are safe havens where everybody, men and women, can pursue their dreams and fulfill their potential.

Source: Obama, Barack. "Remarks by the President at 'It's On Us' Campaign Rollout." September 19, 2014. White House Press Office. Available online at https://obamawhitehouse.archives.gov/the-press-office/2014/09/19/remarks-president-its-us-campaign-rollout.

STEADY GAINS FOR WOMEN IN EDUCATION AND THE WORKFORCE, 2014

During the early 2010s advocates for gender equality at home and at work were heartened by a variety of studies indicating that despite persistent inequities in some areas of American society, women were making meaningful gains in educational attainment, professional advancement, and earnings. In 2014 the Obama administration's Council of Economic Advisers published a report (excerpted below) summarizing many of these developments.

Executive Summary

Over the past forty years, women have made substantial gains in the workforce and economy, but in 2014, far more can still be done to expand economic opportunities for women. While female labor force participation rose through the 1970s and 1980s, it began to stall in the 1990s. Yet women have continued to make gains in earning educational credentials—today young women are more likely than young men to be college graduates or have a graduate degree. These improvements have important implications for American families. On average, women's earnings account for more than 40 percent of married parents' income, up from less than a third 40 years ago. And women are the primary breadwinner for nearly 30 percent of dual-earning couples.

Despite this progress, a gender wage gap persists: on average, full-time year-round female workers earn 78 cents for every dollar earned by their male counterparts. This gap is even more pronounced among women of color. While the wage gap reflects a variety of causes, there are gaps across the income distribution, within occupations, and are seen even when men and women are working side-by-side performing similar tasks. Additionally, women are still more likely to work in low-wage occupations and are more likely than men to earn the minimum wage.

The Administration has supported numerous policies to help ensure equal pay for equal work and help workers better balance their work and family obligations. For example, the President's proposal to raise the minimum wage would help shrink the gender wage gap by nearly 5 percent. Expanding the EITC for childless workers and extending the 2009 expansions to the EITC and CTC would likewise benefit millions of women. And workplace policies such as paid leave and workplace flexibility can help workers maintain a connection to the labor force as they balance their work and family demands.

Female Labor Force Participation Increased Between 1948 and 2000; Most of the Recent Decline is Due to the Aging Population and Cyclical Effects

Of the total decrease in labor force participation since 2007:

- *Half is due to the aging population,*
- *One-sixth is due to cyclical factors in line with historical patterns following a recession, and*
- *One-third is due to other factors, such as trends that pre-date the recession and the unique severity of the Great Recession.*

Postsecondary Attainment Has Risen Among Men and Women; Women Now Complete College and Graduate School at Higher Rates Than Men

Women's college going has surpassed men's in recent decades and has continued to increase.

- *Women are more likely to go to college and graduate school and more likely to graduate from when they go.*
- *In 2013, 25–34 year old women were 21 percent more likely than men to be college graduates and 48 percent more likely to have completed graduate school.*

Women Are Increasingly Attending Professional Degree Programs

Women now account for almost half of students in JD, MBA, and MD programs, up from less than 10 percent in the 1960s.

Occupational Segregation Has Fallen: Female College Graduates are Increasingly Employed in Traditionally Male-Dominated Occupations

Women have increasingly entered previously male-dominated occupations.

- *College-educated young women are now as likely to be employed as doctors, dentists, lawyers, professors, managers and scientists as traditionally female-dominated occupations such as teachers, nurses, librarians, secretaries, or social workers.*
- *Although the share of male-dominated occupations has fallen since 1970, the share of occupations in which women are at least 80 percent of all workers has remained relatively constant.*

Over the Past Four Decades, Women's Earnings Have Tracked Per Capita GDP More Closely Than Men's

- *Since 1970, men's real median earnings have slightly fallen 1.3 percent, from $35,709 in 1970 to $35,228 in 2013 (in 2013 dollars).*
- *Women's real median earnings have risen faster and more closely tracked GDP growth, nearly doubling since 1970. In 2013 women's real median earnings were $22,063, up from $11,976 in 1970. As a result, women's share of household earnings has risen.*

Women Are Increasingly Primary Breadwinners in Dual-Earner Couples

Women earn more than men in 16 percent of all married couples and 29 percent of married couples where both spouses work. These shares have nearly doubled since 1981.

Since the 1970s, Real Earnings Have Increased for Both Married and Single Mothers

Typical income was $84,916 for married parents in 2013.

- *Median income among married parents increased 2.8 percent between 2012 and 2013.*
- *Median income among single mothers increased 1.1 percent between 2012 and 2013, and stood at $26,148 in 2013.*
- *While married mothers' earnings accounted for less than a third of family income in 1974, they have accounted for more than 40 percent since 2010.*

Women Have Gained 4.2 Million Jobs Over the Last 55 Months of Private-Sector Job Growth

Women's employment is less cyclical than men's:

- *Women lost 2.7 million jobs between December 2007 and February 2010, compared to 6.1 million lost among men.*
- *Since February 2010, women and men have recouped 4.2 and 6.1 million private sector jobs, respectively.*
- *The share of private sector workers who are women rose from 46.9 percent prior to the recession to 47.9 percent this past September.*

Women's Unemployment Has Fallen From 9.0 Percent in 2010 to 6.0 Percent

Broader measures of labor underutilization show the same general pattern as the headline unemployment rate.

- *The fraction of female workers either discouraged from looking for work or unemployed averaged 6.7 percent over the past 12 months, down from a 12-month moving average peak of 9.2 percent in 2011.*
- *The fraction unemployed, discouraged, or conditionally available for work averaged 8.2 percent, down from 11.2 percent in 2010.*

Over the Past Year, the Labor Market was about 65–75 Percent Recovered for Women on Average

Paralleling trends for the labor market as a whole, among women, unemployment rates have fallen across demographic groups and by measures of labor underutilization, but the recovery remains incomplete.

On Average, Full-Time, Year-Round Women Workers Make 78 Percent of What Men Earn; The Gender Pay Gap Is Greater Among Women of Color

Despite gains over the past half century, a gender pay gap still exists. For every dollar earned for full-time, year-round, non-Hispanic white men, in 2013:

- *Non-Hispanic black women earned 64 cents.*
- *Hispanic women earned 56 cents.*

Men and Women Have Similar Earnings After Completing Professional School, but Men's Earnings Grow Substantially More Thereafter

The gender wage gap is particularly high among those with advanced degrees and it grows throughout women's lifetimes.

- *Men and women with professional degrees have similar earnings in their 20s. The earnings gap widens over time, so that by their late 30s, men earn approximately 50% more than women.*

Women of Color, Particularly Hispanic Women, Are Less Likely to Have Access to Paid Leave and Flexible Work Arrangements

Less than half of Hispanic women have access to paid leave, compared to just under 60 percent of non-Hispanic women. Hispanic and black women are also less likely than non-Hispanic white women to have access to unpaid leave or flexible work arrangements.

Administration Proposals to Increase the Minimum Wage and Expand the EITC Would Help Millions of African-American and Hispanic Women

- *Black and Hispanic women account for 6 and 7 percent of the labor force, respectively, and:*
- *9 and 12 percent of workers who would benefit from increasing the minimum wage,*
- *7 and 9 percent of workers who would benefit from expanding the EITC for childless workers, and*
- *10 and 16 percent of workers who would benefit from extending the EITC and CTC expansions.*

Source: Council of Economic Advisers. "Women's Participation in Education and the Workforce," 2014. Available online at https://obamawhitehouse.archives.gov /the-press-office/2014/10/31/white-house-report-women-s-participation -education-and-workforce.

PRESIDENT OBAMA DISCUSSES THE PERSISTENCE OF GENDER DISCRIMINATION, 2014

In mid-2014 Democratic president Barack Obama (1961–) held a town hall event in Minneapolis, Minnesota, in which he fielded a question from a woman who related her own story of being subjected to gender-based wage discrimination during her years of employment with a Fortune 500 corporation. Obama's response, reprinted below, focused in large part on how gender-based wage inequities hinder women both at work and at home.

Q. Hi, my name is Erin. I just left a corporation in Minnesota, a Fortune 500 corporation, where I had my 4-year degree, my male counterpart did not, and he was making $3 more an hour than I was. My question for you is, what are we going to do about it so as I grow up and other women grow up, we are not experiencing the wage gap anymore?

The President. Well, I've got all kinds of opinions on this. [*Laughter*]

First of all—I told this story at the Working Families Summit—my mom was a single mom. She worked, went to school, raised two kids with the help of my grandparents. And I remember what it was like for her. Coming home, she's dead tired, she's trying to fix a healthy meal for me and my sister, which meant there were only really like five things in the rotation because she didn't have time to be practicing with a whole bunch of stuff. And sometimes, because you're a kid, you're stupid, so you're all like, I don't want to eat that again. And she's like, really? What did you make? Eat your food.

But I remember the struggles that she would go through when she did finally get her advanced degree, got a job, and she'd experience on-the-job discrimination because of her gender.

My grandmother, she was Rosie the Riveter. She—when my grandfather went to fight in World War II, part of Patton's army, she stayed home because my mom was born at—in Kansas, at Fort Leavenworth, and my grandmother worked at a bomber assembly line. And she was whip smart. I mean, she—in another era, she would have ended up running a company. But at the time, she didn't even get her college degree—worked as a secretary. She was smart enough that she worked her way up to be a vice president at the local bank where she—where we lived, which is why sometimes, when I watch *Mad Men*, there's Peggy and Joan, the two women there, I'm always rooting for them because that—I imagine them—that's what it was like for my grandmother, kind of working her way up.

But she, as smart as she was, she got to a certain point, and then she stopped advancing. And then she would train guys how to do the job, and they would end up being her boss. And it happened three or four times.

So this is something that I care a lot about not just because of my past, but also because of my future. I've got two daughters. The idea that they would not be paid the same or not have the same opportunities as somebody's sons is infuriating. And even if you're not a dad, those of you who have partners, spouses—men—this is not a women's issue. Because if they're not getting paid, that means they're not bringing home as much money, which means your family budget is tighter. So this is a family issue and not a gender issue.

So what can we do? First bill I signed was something called the Lilly Ledbetter Act, that allowed folks to sue if they found out that they had been discriminated against, like you found out. Back then, Lilly Ledbetter, this wonderful woman, she had been paid less than her male counterparts for the same job for over a decade. When she finally finds out, she sues, and the Supreme Court says, well, the statute of limitations has run out; you can't sue for all of that backpay. She says, well, I just found out—well, that doesn't matter. So we've reversed that law, allowing people to sue based on when you find out.

Most recently what I did was, we made it against the law, at least for Federal contractors, to retaliate against employees for sharing job—or salary information. Because part of the problem—part of the reason that it's hard to enforce equal pay for equal work is, most employers don't let you talk, or discourage talk, about what everybody else is getting paid. And what we've said is, women have a right to know what the guy sitting next to them who's doing the exact same job is getting paid. So that's something we were able to do.

But ultimately, we're going to need Congress to act. There have been repeated efforts at us—by us to get what we call the "Paycheck Fairness Act" through Congress, and Republicans have blocked it. Some have denied that it's a problem. What they've said is, you know what, women make different choices. That explains the wage gap. That's the reason that women on average make 77 cents to every dollar that a man earns, is because they're making different choices.

Well, first of all, that's not true in your case, because you were doing the same job. You didn't make a different choice; you just were getting paid less. But let's even unpack this whole idea of making different choices. What they're really saying is, because women have to bear children, so—and a company doesn't give them enough maternity leave or doesn't give them enough flexibility, that they should be punished.

And our whole point is that this is a family issue and that if we structure the workplace to actually be family friendly, which everybody always talks about, but we don't always actually practice, then women won't have to make different choices. Then if they're pregnant and have a child, it's expected that they're going to have some time off. By the way, the dads should too. They should have some flexibility in the workplace. They should be able to take care of a sick kid without getting docked for pay.

And there are some wonderful companies who are doing this. And as I said before, it turns out that when companies adopt family-friendly policies their productivity goes up, they have lower turnover, which makes sense. You—look, if you have a family emergency and you go to your boss and you say, "Can I have a week off? I've got to take care of a sick child or dad," or, "Can I leave early this afternoon because my kid is in a school play and I really think this is important?," and they say, "Of course, nothing is more important than family," how hard are you going to work for that person when you get back on the job? You're going to feel invested in them. You're going to say to yourself, man, these folks care about me, which means I care about you. And if I have to take some extra time on a weekend, or I've got to do some work late at night when I'm not under an emergency situation, I'm going to do that.

So this makes good business sense. But the problem is, is that we haven't done enough to encourage these new models. And this is part of the reason why we did this family summit—we wanted to lift this stuff up, show companies that are doing the right thing, encourage others to adopt the same practices, and maybe get some legislation that incentivizes better policies.

In the meantime, though, if you're doing the same job, you should make the same pay, period, full stop. That should be a basic rule. That shouldn't be subject to confusion.

Source: Obama, Barack. "Remarks at a Town Hall Meeting and a Question-and-Answer Session in Minneapolis, Minnesota," June 26, 2014. Office of the Federal Register, Compilation of Presidential Documents. DCPD-201400493. Washington, DC: Government Printing Office, 2014.

NEERA TANDEN DISCUSSES "WOMEN'S CHANGING ROLE IN THE WORKPLACE," 2014

Neera Tanden (1970–) is a prominent authority on public policy in Democratic Party circles and the president of the Center for American Progress, an influential and progressive policy research and advocacy organization based in Washington, DC. On May 20, 2014, she appeared before a special congressional roundtable discussion on "Economic Security for Working Women" and delivered the following statement on changing gender roles in American workplaces, the challenges that working women still face, and the need to place women at the "center of [America's] policy agenda."

If we want a thriving economy that works for all Americans, strengthens our businesses, and makes our Nation more competitive on the global stage, we have to start with a clear understanding of today's workplace and the changing workforce. The reality is that workplaces—and the people who work in them—are changing. Fifty years after groundbreaking laws like the Equal Pay Act helped usher in a new era of opportunity for women in the workplace, more women are working than ever before.

While it used to be rare for mothers to work outside the home, today, women make up nearly half the workforce. But this demographic shift has enormous implications for how our workplaces operate and for our overall economic growth. More than 6 in 10 women are breadwinners or co-breadwinners for their families, yet women, on average, continue to earn less than their male counterparts. This gap is even larger for women of color, who are more likely to be stuck in minimum-wage jobs.

Our workplace culture and national policy have been slow to adapt. Even in two-parent households, women are often the primary caregivers in their families, with the main responsibility for providing, coordinating, or securing care. And although there are clearly some employers who have adopted progressive policies, too many women—and men—continue to work in environments without the protections they need to balance work and family responsibilities or ensure that they are paid fairly for their work.

If we want real economic progress, we need policies that respond to the everyday challenges facing the diverse group of women who are part of today's economy, particularly those women who too often get ignored.

Why women's work matters to our economic well-being

Women's rapid entry into the workplace during the last three decades of the 20th century transformed our country and its labor force. Between 1970 and 2000, the percentage of women who work rose from 43.3 percent to 59.9 percent. Before the Great Recession, more than three-quarters of women worked 35 hours or more per week. And today, the majority of employed women work full-time.

Because more women are working, women's income has become a lynchpin of our Nation's economic success. Today, two-thirds of mothers are breadwinners or co-breadwinners, up from slightly more than a quarter of mothers in 1967.

But women's paychecks don't just contribute to their families' bottom lines. They are also vital for America's economic growth.

Continuing women's economic progress

Over the past four decades, women have made huge economic gains. But those gains were unequal. While some women have broken into typically male-dominated professions, 43.6 percent of women still work in just 20 types of typically low-paying jobs, such as secretary, nurse, teacher, and salesperson, among others.

Low- and middle-wage, young, and less-educated workers in particular lack access to benefits that help balance work and family life. Employers too often view paid leave or sick days as perks for higher-paid workers: The lowest quarter of wage earners are nearly three times less likely to have access to paid family and medical leave than those in the top quarter.

Women of color are also more likely to lack benefits such as paid leave. Women of color are just as likely to work as white women, but twice as likely to work in a low-wage sector or the service industry in jobs that don't offer these middle-class benefits. This is especially concerning given the additional demographic change that is inevitable in the coming decades.

Women of color will make up 53 percent of the female population by 2050. Hispanic women will lead this growth, increasing from a share of 16.7 percent of the female population in 2015 to 25.7 percent in 2050.

And unequal policy will continue to produce unequal economic gains. It's bad for families, for labor, and for the economy. But policy can—and should—change to react to changing demographics.

Federal policies that benefit working women and families

There are a number of public policy solutions that can make an immediate dif-ference in the lives of working women. At the Federal level, mandating paid sick days, paid family and medical leave, and a more flexible workplace, and strength-ening pay equity legislation could empower women to meet their full potential.

Since nearly two-thirds of minimum-wage workers and 70 percent of tipped minimum-wage workers are women, making the minimum wage a living wage would help close the pay gap and lift millions of Americans out of poverty.

Fostering the policies that allow women to be full participants in today's work-force will boost businesses' bottom lines and ensure America's competitiveness in the global economy.

Among the public policy solutions that would empower women to meet their full potential are:

- Paid sick days, as proposed in the Healthy Families Act, and paid family and medical leave insurance, as proposed in the Family and Medical Insurance Leave Act, or FAMILY Act.
- Pay equity, as proposed in the Paycheck Fairness Act.
- High-quality, affordable early childhood education and universal pre-K.
- A higher minimum wage and tipped minimum wage.

[. . .]

Pay equity

Today, women make up nearly half of the American workforce. Women graduate from college at higher rates than men. More women are serving in Congress than ever before. Yet for millions of American women, no amount of hard work will bring pay equity with their male peers.

Women, on average, still take home 77 cents for every dollar earned by a man. The average American woman makes $11,084 less than her male counterpart per year. If women working full-time, year round were paid the same for their work as comparable men, we would cut the poverty rate for working women and their families in half.

And for women of color, the disparity is even greater. Women of color are twice as likely as white, non-Hispanic women to live in poverty. And the wage gap is more like a gulf. For every dollar a man makes, white women make 77 cents, African-American women take home 64 cents, and Hispanic women take home 55 cents on the dollar.

These differences among women can be attributed to a variety of economic fac-tors, including occupational segregation and higher rates of unemployment among women of color, which lead to longer gaps in work histories. Wage disparities—even compared to men of color—depress lifetime earnings of women of color even more than those of white women.

When women are shortchanged over the course of a lifetime, the dollars and cents add up. Over the course of a 35-year career, a woman with a college degree will make an average of $1.2 million less than a man with the same level of education.

Since the Equal Pay Act was signed 50 years ago, we have made significant progress. Back then, women were paid just 59 cents for every dollar earned by men. Legislation has narrowed the pay gap, but didn't close it. The Lilly Ledbetter Fair Pay Act, the first bill that Barack Obama signed as President, was another important step toward making women full, equal participants in the workforce.

But if a woman doesn't know she is underpaid, she can't take action to close the gap. The Paycheck Fairness Act, sponsored by Sen. Barbara Mikulski (D-MD), would enable the Department of Labor to gather better information about wage differences. The Paycheck Fairness Act would protect employees from retaliation for discussing their salaries. And it would empower women to negotiate for equal pay and create strong incentives for employers to obey the laws already in place.

Making sure women receive equal pay for equal work increases their lifetime earnings and strengthens our economy in the process. The Institute for Women's Policy Research found that if women had received pay equal to their male counterparts in 2012, the U.S. economy would have produced $447.6 billion in additional income—similar to the economic output of the entire State of Virginia.

[. . .]

The minimum wage becomes a living wage

We should raise the Federal minimum wage to $10.10 per hour. Currently, a full-time worker making the minimum wage earns just $15,080 per year. For a family of three, that is $4,000 below the Federal poverty line. Raising the minimum wage to $10.10 would increase yearly earnings to $19,777. It would directly raise the wages of 16.5 million American workers and would lift almost 1 million Americans out of poverty.

Nearly two-thirds of minimum-wage workers are women, so raising the minimum wage, as proposed by Sen. Harkin, would give 15.4 million women a raise and help close the pay gap. These workers are not just teenagers. Nearly 90 percent of minimum-wage workers are 20 years old or older, and the average minimum-wage worker is 35 years old.

Seventy percent of tipped restaurant workers are women, so raising the tipped minimum wage would also strengthen women's prospects. While the Federal minimum wage is $7.25 per hour, the minimum for workers who receive tips is just $2.13. Tips are supposed to make up the difference. Yet servers are twice as likely to use food stamps as is the rest of the U.S. workforce, and three times as likely to live in poverty.

The number of female minimum-wage workers has also increased markedly since the beginning of the Great Recession. In 2007, there were almost 1.2 million female minimum-wage workers—nearly double the number of male minimum-wage workers. But the number of women making minimum wage had doubled by 2012.

And while the number of workers earning minimum wage increased for all racial and ethnic groups of women from 2007 to 2012, the share of Latina women at minimum wage tripled, and the share of African-American and Asian women more than doubled.

We're already seeing businesses, such as the Gap, Costco, and Whole Foods, adopt the attitude that a fair wage is good for corporate profits and reputations. Raising the wages of frontline workers helps minimize employee turnover, encourage hard work, and increase employee productivity, commitment, and loyalty. Cities, counties, and States have also adopted measures to raise the incomes of their lowest paid workers because they know that if workers can earn a living wage, it will help grow their local economies. More than half of the States that raised the minimum wage during periods of high unemployment saw their unemployment decrease over the next 12 months.

And increasing the minimum wage has positive implications for the Federal budget as well. CAP recently published research showing that a $10.10 minimum wage would reduce spending on the Supplemental Nutrition Assistance Program by $46 billion over the next decade.

The business case

Successful businesses already see a competitive advantage when they ensure workers with families are happy and successful. Policies that support working women and families lead to more productive employees. They also help business attract and retain top-notch talent, paying dividends in the long term. But there are immediate savings for businesses with family friendly benefits as well.

Studies showed companies that are flexible—that allow adjustable work schedules or telework, for example—improved employee retention and recruitment, as well as revenue generation and client satisfaction. Employees said their ability to prioritize both career and family influenced their choice to remain with the company. This translates into real and immediate savings for businesses. While replacing a worker can cost up to 20 percent of that worker's salary, policies such as earned sick days or flexible options can be implemented at little to no net cost.

But the companies that will excel in tomorrow's economy won't just be focused on retaining female employees; they'll be interested in cultivating the next generation of female leaders and executives. That will mean more than adopting flexible schedules and worker-friendly policies. It will mean changing the culture from the factory floor to the board room to allow talented, dedicated women to advance and succeed. It will mean combating workplace discrimination of every kind. It will mean encouraging mentor relationships that pair successful women with future leaders in their organizations. And it will mean including women in the decisionmaking process, so their voices are heard and their concerns are considered.

After all, when women have a place at the table, they can advocate for the very worker-friendly policies that boost morale along with the bottom line.

Conclusion

Public policies that help women also strengthen our families, our workplaces, our economy, and our Nation. It's time to put women at the center of the policy agenda. Every Member of Congress must work together to demonstrate, with a proactive policy agenda, that government is committed to our families.

Families are changing. Our workforce is changing. The way we live is changing. And our economic success hinges on recognizing those changes and committing to public policy that improves the lives and livelihood of working families.

Source: Tanden, Neera. "Women's Changing Role in the Workplace: How Gender Demographics Should Inform Public Policy." Economic Security for Working Women: A Roundtable Discussion. Hearing on the Committee of Health, Education, Labor, and Pensions. 113th Congress, 2nd Session, S. Hrg. 113-837, May 20, 2014. Washington, DC: Government Printing Office, 2017, pp. 6–13.

REMARKS BY PRESIDENT OBAMA AT A WORKING MOTHERS TOWN HALL, 2015

On April 15, 2015, President Barack Obama (1961–) appeared at a town hall event in Charlotte, North Carolina, that was specifically focused on the challenges faced by working mothers both at home and in their jobs. During the event, which the Obama White House organized in conjunction with two prominent blogs dedicated to women's issues, Obama answered several questions from attendees about the gender wage gap, child care challenges, and the continued underrepresentation of women—and especially women of color— in so-called STEM fields (careers in science, technology, engineering, and mathematics).

. . . I want to thank Dianna [Jolly, a Mecklenburg County social worker], for the introduction. I'm actually here because Dianna sent me a letter, and I wanted to reply in person. (Laughter.) And I want to thank Lisa and everybody who helped put this together.

Let me just read an excerpt of what Dianna wrote me: "As part of the middle class, I know how it feels to work hard every day, and even with a college education and a full-time job find it harder and harder to make ends meet." Now, I think it's fair to say that what Dianna said is true for so many people here in North Carolina and all across the country.

It's the kind of letter that I would get all the time from folks who ask for one thing—that in America, their hard work and their sense of responsibility is rewarded with the chance to get ahead. And I know it's on the minds of working moms every day—(baby cries)—yes it is, and you, too. (Laughter.) (Baby cries)— There, yes, I know. (Laughter.)

And because a lot of working moms use BlogHer and SheKnows to talk about these issues, we've decided to partner with them for this town hall. So I'm going to keep my remarks brief at the front end so we can spend most of the time having a conversation.

Now, thanks, in part, to some of the decisions that we made early on in the worst financial crisis since the Great Depression—right when I came into office—we've made real progress. Our businesses have created more than 12 million new jobs over the past five years. The unemployment rate has fallen from 10 percent right when I was coming into office to 5.5 percent.

More kids are graduating from high school. More kids are attending college. More people are able to save more money at the pump because our energy production has gone up. Our clean energy production has gone up. More Americans know the security of health care because of this thing called the Affordable Care Act, aka, Obamacare. (Applause.)

And so the recovery reaches more Americans every single day. And the question we now face is, are we going to accept an economy in which, going forward, just a few folks are doing exceptionally well, or, are we going to have an economy where everybody who's willing to work hard is able to get ahead?

And that's what I've been calling middle-class economics. The idea that in this country, we do best when everybody is getting a fair shot, and everybody is doing their fair share, and everybody is playing by the same set of rules. And that's what has driven my policies ever since I became President. A lot of my policies have been specifically focused on working moms, because I believe that when women succeed here in America then the whole country succeeds. I'm a firm believer in that. (Applause.)

Now, part of middle-class economics means helping working families feel more economically secure in this global, technologically driven, constantly changing economy. Which is why my budget puts forward proposals to lower the taxes for working families who are trying to pay for things like child care and college and retirement.

In today's economy, having both parents in the workforce is an economic reality for many families. But in 31 states, including North Carolina, high-quality child care costs are higher than a year of tuition at a state university. Average cost here in North Carolina, $16,000 for child care. And that's why my plan would make it much more affordable for every working and middle-class family with young children.

In today's economy, higher education has never been more important—or more expensive. And that's why I want to bring down the cost of community college for responsible students—all the way down to zero—(applause)—so that they know that if they are doing well in high school they can get that higher education they need for a job.

In today's economy, women still hold most of the low-paying jobs—jobs that often demand the hardest work. And that's why we've successfully worked with states, and cities, and companies to raise their workers' wages without having to wait for Congress—which, although Alma and David Price are on board on this, for some reason we've got a whole bunch of members of Congress who don't get it when it comes to raising wages. And I know there are workers here in Charlotte and across the country that are organizing for higher wages. It's time that we stood alongside them and made it happen. America deserves a raise. (Applause.)

Now, it is significant that today is Tax Day. (Laughter.) If you haven't filed, you—(laughter.) But the reason I mentioned all the policies that I just talked about is that overall when you put my policies together in the budget, I want to cut taxes for more than 5 million middle-class families who need help paying for child care. (Applause.) I want to cut taxes for more than 8 million families of students who need help paying for college. (Applause.) I want to cut taxes to help 30 million workers save for retirement. I want to cut taxes for 13 million low-wage workers the same way that I fought to expand tax cuts like the child tax credit and the earned income tax credit—and we've been able to implement those.

So all told, my plan would cut taxes for 44 million working and middle-class families. That's who our tax code should benefit—working Americans who are out there struggling every day, doing the right thing, supporting their families and trying to get a leg up in this new economy.

Now, it is a good thing that Republicans in Washington have started to talk about wages and incomes and the middle class. It's better late than never, and so I'm encouraged. Unfortunately, the policies they're putting forward don't answer the mail—they don't speak to the issues that ordinary families are facing.

I'll just give you a couple examples. Their tax plan would give the average millionaire and billionaire a $50,000 tax cut. That's about what the average middle-class worker makes in an entire year. They're also pushing a new $270 billion tax cut for the very wealthiest of the wealthiest. It would affect about 5,000 families all across America; it would cost $270 billion. Here in North Carolina, it would benefit precisely 120 households.

AUDIENCE: Ooooh—

THE PRESIDENT: For $270 billion, which is the cost approximately of the tax breaks I'm giving to 44 million people, it would benefit a little over 5,000 people.

So their plan would cut taxes for the top one-tenth of 1 percent and let taxes go up on 25 million working families and students. And my view is we don't need tax cuts for millionaires and billionaires. I don't need a tax cut. We're already doing well. (Applause.) We've been blessed by this country and the opportunities it offers, and now what we have to focus on is making sure everybody has opportunity and making sure middle-class families have tax cuts, and a young family that just had their first child and are still struggling to get by, that they get a little bit of relief, a little bit of a break. Those are the folks who need help. That's what middle-class economics is all about, and that's what I'm going to be fighting for. (Applause.)

But I'm going to stop talking because I promised I would be short. (Laughter.) And one of the things that I'm going to want to do is not just do the talking but I also want to do some listening. And what I'm really interested in is hearing from all of you about what are you facing in your lives. How do you think government policy would be helpful? What do you think folks in Congress, the President, mayors, governors, what do you think would actually make a difference in the lives of middle-class families? And because we've got some powerful, hardworking women around here—(applause)—I also want to specifically hear from the women in terms of what you think would make a different as well.

So with that, I'm going to take my seat right here. (Laughter.)

MS. STONE: Thank you, Mr. President. I'm going to be selfish and kick off with the first question. But then we are going to hand over a few questions to you all. And when the time comes for you, just raise your hand and a mic wrangler will magically appear and hold it for you.

I'd like to cover off on something that happened yesterday: Equal Pay Day in the United States. The Paycheck Fairness Act has failed I believe now four times in Congress. I know you've been a proponent of it. I heard from a user of SheKnows.com yesterday, Lily Onate (ph)—she works one-and-a-half jobs to be the single supporter of her son. She's making just enough that she cannot afford to get sick, but she also cannot achieve certain benefits. She's trying to save for college. And more than anything, she is very disappointed to learn she is making less than men 10 years younger than she is on the job. Women make 78 cents on the dollar unless they're women of color, in which [case] they make significantly less.

Why is the Paycheck Fairness Act failing? And does someone dispute the existence of the pay difference?

THE PRESIDENT: The reason we haven't gotten it done is because Republicans in Congress have blocked it. And some of them do dispute that it's a problem. I mean, many say it's a woman's choice that is resulting in women getting paid less than men; lifestyle decisions, and they'd rather stay at home, or they'd rather work part time, or what have you.

Now, understand that the whole point of equal pay is people doing the same job and getting paid less. That's the problem. The Paycheck Fairness Act would say not that women should get paid more or the same if they're doing less work; it's saying they should get paid the same for doing the same work.

Now, this should be a no-brainer. There are some things that are conceptually complicated. (Laughter.) There are other things that are pretty simple. If you've got two people doing the same job, they should get paid the same.

And this is personal for me, because I think a lot of people are aware, I was raised by a single mom who worked, went to school, got her advanced degree, and helped raise me and my sister. And we also got help from my grandparents, and actually the main breadwinner in our entire family was my grandmother. And she's a great story. Grew up in Kansas—my grandfather went to fight in World War II in Europe. When he came back he got benefits of the GI Bill, but she was Rosie the Riveter. She was working back home on an assembly line. And she didn't get, unfortunately, benefits the way we set up the Post-9/11 GI Bill, where spouses and family members can get help, as well.

So she never got a college education. But she was smarter than my grandfather— I apologize, Gramps—(laughter)—but I think everybody who knew her understood that. She got a job as a secretary, worked her way up, became the vice president of a bank, but then hit the glass ceiling, and for the next 20 years, kept on training younger men who came up and would end up going ahead of her, including the presidents of the banks.

And that was pretty typical at that time. The question is, why is it still typical now. I've got two daughters. I expect them to be treated the same as somebody else's sons when it comes to their opportunities on the job.

So what we did when I came into office, we passed something called the Lilly Ledbetter Act, named after—(applause)—a good friend of mine, Lilly Ledbetter, who had worked for years and found out long into her work that she had been getting paid all these years less than men, substantially. She brought suit. They said, well, it's too late to file suit because you should have filed suit right when it started happening. She said, I just found out. They said, it doesn't matter. So we changed that law to allow somebody like Lilly, when they find out, to finally be able to go ahead and file suit.

What we also did then is I signed what's called an executive order that said if you want to be a federal contractor with us then you've got to allow your employees to share compensation data. Because a lot of companies discourage or even penalize employees for telling each other what they're getting paid, in part, because they don't want everybody finding out that maybe the men are getting paid more than the women for doing the same job. So we said you want to work for the federal government, you can't do that.

But we still need to get this Paycheck Fairness Act passed. And it really is just a matter of convincing a number of Republicans to recognize that they've got daughters, too, they've got spouses, and at a time when the majority of families have both spouses working, or if you've got a single parent—that's most likely to be a single mom—working, this is an economic issue. It's a family issue. It's not just a women's issue. Families are going to be better off.

Let me tell you, now, Michelle would point out First Ladies get paid nothing. (Laughter.) So there's clearly not equal pay in the White House when it comes to her and me. But before we were in the White House, I wanted to make sure Michelle got paid as much as she could. (Laughter.) I want a big paycheck for Michelle. (Laughter.) That wasn't a women's issue. If she had a bigger paycheck, that made us able to pay the bills. (Applause.) Why would I want my spouse or my daughter discriminated against? That doesn't make any sense.

[Question and answer session, including question from moderator Stone]

. . . MS. STONE: Mr. President, you were just talking about some of the nation's leading wealthy and also a little bit of corporate responsibility. I want to ask you about the private enterprise and their role.

I am visiting beautiful North Carolina today from Silicon Valley, where for the past year, unfortunately, it seems the Valley has become a poster child for the challenges women are having penetrating the leadership of some of our best technology companies. Women are lacking in venture capital firms. We're not running as many companies. We're not in the leadership pipeline. We're not in the engineering product groups in the same number. In fact, we are not getting as many STEM-related majors as we used to.

So when I think about some of the responsibilities you're saying the government has, I would ask you what is the economic risk, either in Silicon Valley or here in the entire American economy, competitively, to having fewer women empowered in both leadership positions at home and in corporate America? What are we giving up in the economy? Product benefits? Insight?

THE PRESIDENT: Well, let me use a sports analogy since I'm in North Carolina. There's some pretty good basketball here in North Carolina. (Applause.)

MS. STONE: And perhaps I'm off base.

THE PRESIDENT: No—oh. Did everybody catch that—off base? (Laughter.) You wouldn't field a team with just half the players, right? You wouldn't go in the game and the other side has got 12 players and you decide, well, we'll just have six. You'd want all the team, the entire team to be available for you to win. And the same is true for the country.

You mentioned, for example, engineers. We have a shortage of engineers in this country. We need more. But the fact of the matter is, is that because of how we structured STEM education—that's science, technology, engineering, and math—the way we structure it, oftentimes girls get discouraged early from going into those fields. And we know, actually, from experiments and data, and what happens in the classroom, that some of it's just making little changes in terms of how things are taught so that girls feel more empowered and more engaged in those fields. They've got just as much talent as the boys do.

And that, unfortunately, is still true in a lot of our economy. There are certain things that we don't encourage our daughters to do. They start making choices because they don't see representation of themselves in certain fields.

Really interesting story: My Chief Technology Officer, Megan Smith, who came over from Google, she told me that when *CSI* came on—now, I've got to admit, I don't watch that very often. I mean, I just don't watch—no offense to *CSI*—I just don't see it. It seems like a really popular show. But apparently, there was a woman—or women—who were involved in forensics, in the show. A lot of the show is about finding hair fiber or something, and then you solve a big crime. And once this show came on, the number of young women going into the field skyrocketed. Because all it took was a girl saying, oh, I didn't know I could be that. I didn't know I could do that.

So we as a society have to do better—public sector, private sector. We're putting a lot of emphasis on STEM education specifically for girls. The same is true, by the way, for underrepresented minority groups—African Americans, Latinos are underrepresented in these fields and we've have got to—(applause.) Now that requires us, collectively—parents, community, churches, others—encouraging people into these fields—because these are the fields where we're going to be growing.

But some of it also has to do with companies have to want to make it happen. They've got to be intentional about it. They've got to pay attention to it. And those companies that pay attention to it end up succeeding in recruiting more women, promoting more women, and those companies end up being more successful.

And I'm trying to set an example in the White House right now. The highest level of adviser I have on the White House staff is called an Assistant to the President, and we actually have more women than men right now—I think 13 to 11. (Applause.) But that wasn't always the case, because when I first came in, we had to say, you know what, we got to do better, and how do we make sure that we're promoting talent.

And it's true that companies can make a big difference. I'm going to give two examples of how companies can make a difference—slightly different issue, but it shows the power companies have. When we started this minimum wage campaign, one of the places I went to was Costco, because not only did they pay their workers minimum wage, they paid them a living wage, and they provided them health care benefits. And they were a hugely profitable company, and we wanted to show that could be done. And then suddenly you had other companies like Gap announce that they were going to raise wages on their employees. And then, most recently, Walmart came in. And once Walmart is paying people more, then you know that something is happening, right? (Laughter.)

So you can change attitudes and culture through a corporate example. One of the issues that's important to a lot of families is the issue of paid leave. There are 40 million–plus Americans who are working and don't have sick leave. They don't have sick leave. They get sick, there's nothing they can do. Either they go to work sick or they lose their job, potentially, or at least they lose a paycheck. And family leave is still unpaid, so a lot of women can't take advantage of it if their child is sick at home.

Well, recently, Microsoft just announced that not only does it make sure that it has strong sick leave and paid leave, but it's actually only going to do business with contractors that do the same thing. (Applause.) So a big company like Microsoft can start influencing some of their subcontractors and suppliers down the chain. That can end up having a huge impact.

So for companies that are brand names and set the standard, for them to show we're doing more to recruit women, promote women, put them in positions of authority, that sends a signal to our daughters, but it also sends a signal to other companies that it's the right thing to do. (Applause.)

Source: Obama, Barack. "Remarks by the President in Working Mothers Town Hall," April 15, 2015. White House Press Office. Available online at https://obamawhitehouse.archives.gov/the-press-office/2015/04/15/remarks-president-working-mothers-town-hall.

A WOMAN ADVERTISING EXECUTIVE DISCUSSES *MAD MEN* AND MODERN-DAY SEXISM, 2015

Mad Men was a television series that ran from 2007 to 2015 on the cable network AMC. It was a period drama that took place at a Manhattan advertising agency at the beginning of the 1960s, when women were primarily relegated to supporting roles as secretaries or typists and when sexism—often descending into outright sexual harassment—was a standard part of the office environment. In the following article published in the New Republic in 2015, Anne K. Ream, who spent many years working in the American advertising industry, discussed the many ways in which the storylines of Mad Men continued to reflect the reality of many working women's lives.

In all its gauzy, gorgeous mid-century modern detail, "Mad Men" is a kind of fun-house mirror held up to the cultural norms of sixties America. *Look how far we've come. Look how cool it was.*

But "Mad Men" is a period piece that very often isn't for women—and I am one of them—who have worked in advertising. Because for every office tableau that seems hopelessly retro—*The typewriters; those African American elevator operators; that three-martini lunch!*—there comes a moment that feels a bit too contemporary. A male account executive bemoaning the "humorless" women who take offense at his inappropriate jokes. The unofficial client meeting that ends up happening at a gentlemen's club. That free-floating sexual innuendo that is just benign enough to ignore, especially when you're the only woman in the room—but not so benign that you're sure you should have.

My own "Mad Men" moments have been many. At the first presentation I made at a General Motors meeting, a dealer in the front row asks if I could move to the left so that the audience could better see the storyboards. When I said yes and shifted, a second dealer called out "Hey, we'd rather see you."

It's amazing how swiftly women in the workplace have to calculate in moments like this. *How much respect will I lose if I say nothing? How much animus will I invite if I say too much? How do I get back to my presentation without missing more than a beat?* My response, as I recall, was some version of what I hoped was an arch, but not too arch, "I'd rather you looked at the boards." Delivered with the requisite smile, of course. So unsurprising—ordinary, even—was this event that when I brought it up not long ago to a male colleague and friend who was in the room that day, his first response was "Oh, that happened for sure." He then noted that he had no memory of it.

It's also telling that even today—over a decade later—I can still remember what I was wearing: A red A-Line skirt, a black turtleneck, and boots. That the memory of my fashion choices exists at all speaks to the self-questioning that women wrestle with after they have been reduced to a stereotype—*was it something I did?*—and the deeply engrained belief that we can change men's responses to us simply by changing our clothes. That memory may also explain my mixed response to "Severance," the first episode of the second half of the final season, when account executive Joan Holloway—in the wake of being harassed by the client—dons black glasses and a high-necked blouse. It's the sort of age-old capitulation that feels both unfortunately necessary and self-defeating.

The male dominated environs of ad agency Sterling Cooper remain less of an anachronism than we might think. According to a 2013 article in *Fast Company*, only 3 percent of agency creative directors are women, even though women control 80 percent of consumer spending. The underrepresentation of women in advertising is contributing to an industry that is too often churning out work that relies on female stereotypes to "gain eyeballs," as a Slate article about 2015's sexist Superbowl ads makes clear.

"Mad Men" creator Matthew Weiner has often stated that two 1960s-era classics—Betty Friedan's *The Feminine Mystique* and Helen Gurley Brown's *Sex and the Single Girl*—have had an outsize influence on the show. "I felt I was presented with the deep conflict that existed in my female characters of the period," Weiner noted in an interview with *The New York Times*. "Obstacles in the career and at home, motherhood, the pill . . . the identity of a woman in our culture was in complete crisis. Now I know that it wasn't just that period."

It's not surprising that Weiner has co-opted the central theme of both of these books—addressing the female crisis of identity—in creating his show's women. What's surprising is that he imposes them on his lead male character, Don Draper.

Like the women around him, Don has constructed a self that closely approximates a particular American ideal. There is something of the perpetual outsider about him. He is in the room but never quite feels of it—perpetually taking a slow drag of his cigarette as he rolls mental tape on all he sees. Don watches women, and he watches the world watching women, but he is well aware that he is also under the watch of the more powerful and privileged men in his milieu. This may explain Don's very real moments of feminist sympathy. It certainly underscores the fact that class, as well as gender, can be a marginalizing force.

To call Don an anti-hero—as many have—is to miss the point. It's more accurate to say that he is a contradiction in terms. He is a vessel for past prejudices who has rare moments of enlightenment. He's a philanderer who gravitates toward strong and independent women. He finds the plan to prostitute Joan in exchange for a prize car account appalling, even though he has sought the company of prostituted women himself.

His response to the sexist banter—usually directed downward at the secretaries—that is the lingua franca of the other men in the Sterling Cooper office is to frown slightly and change the subject or shut down the speaker entirely, as he does with sycophantic account director Peter Campbell: "Advertising is a small world, Pete, and when you malign a girl from the steno pool it gets even smaller. Keep it up and you'll never run this place. You know why? Because no one will like you."

Don is not afraid to advocate for women he respects, as Peggy Olson, the secretary he mentors all the way to her own corner office, recognizes when she says, "The day you saw something in me, my whole life changed." But in earlier seasons he was also not above reducing her success to gendered binaries, praising her for "presenting like a man." He gets it right just often enough to redeem himself with women like Peggy, but not so often that he contributes to any real change.

But Don—as deeply flawed as he is—is one of the most feminist characters on the show, more so, even, than many of the women. Joan suggests to Peggy that she bask in the unwanted attention of the office men ("You're the new girl, and you're not much, so you might as well enjoy it while it lasts"). Talent manager Bobbie Barrett believes that professional power can be gained through sexual power ("Be a woman. It's powerful stuff when done well"). These feel like antecedents to a sort of Beyoncé-style, "work it" feminism that holds that self-objectification isn't really objectification as all. And when Betty Draper tells Don that Sally's life wouldn't be worth living if Sally lost her looks, we are watching a woman who has internalized a form of sexism that social scientists and feminist critics have been alerting us to for years.

Yet if "Mad Men" is gimlet-eyed about the ways that marginalized women can turn on one another, it's not unsympathetic about why this is so. When Joan tells Peggy, who has been left out of an all-male meeting, "You're in their country. Learn to speak the language," she does it with the faintest hint of a shrug. This isn't a woman embracing the state of office affairs. It's a woman coping with a reality she believes she cannot alter.

More than a few "Mad Men" fans have expressed the opinion that the show's representations of workplace harassment go too far. Weiner, addressing recent criticism of the show, notes that women who work in advertising have consistently responded differently to "Mad Men" than the men in the industry do. "Men will say, 'This is outrageous . . . it's too unbelievable' . . . and women will say . . . 'You're nuts. It's still like that.'"

My own sense is that this is less a question of whether what's being represented on the show once happened, or is still happening today—as this National Women's Law Center report makes clear, workplace sexual harassment is indeed alive and well—and more about how differently women and men remember (and not just experience) those events. For a woman on the receiving end of a degrading comment, the memory lingers. For men, such rhetoric is just in the ether: ever present, rarely notable, and easily forgettable.

Still, something feels too obvious by half about the show's last few episodes—as if ideology were driving character, instead of the other way around. The best "Mad Men" episodes have characters saying offensive things that are far more nuanced. The show is at its thought-provoking best when it takes on the sexism that's far less obvious—the "micro-aggressions" that so barely register that they might not be recognized as aggressions at all.

At the beginning of season seven, a drunken and recently demoted Don confides to his former colleague Freddy— an aging freelancer no longer much in demand—that he reports to Peggy, whom Freddy also mentored. "Peggy!" Freddy replies—in wonder, perhaps in anger, and almost certainly in the knowledge that she now has the career he never will. Was it an ageing man's fear of being replaced? A sexist man's surprise that the timid young woman who once reported to him had outpaced him?

The ambiguity of the moment is what makes it so difficult to watch—and more difficult still to name. We don't know what drives Freddy, and in the end it doesn't much matter. Male motive isn't really the issue. The marginalization of women in the workplace is.

My own experience in advertising was in many ways a positive one. I was hired as a copywriter in 1994, after a series of interviews done by six (all white, all male) Leo Burnett executives, four of them who had been at the agency during the tail end of the "Mad Men" era. They were almost always appropriate, if also occasionally paternalistic. Years later, a trifecta of male mentors advocated for my promotions to creative director, senior vice president, and group creative director. Put another way, my experience hews closer to Peggy's than to Joan's. But that 3 percent figure for female creative directors at the agency? It was about right.

What makes the story of Peggy's rise most poignant is that she is beginning and ending the series as the exception, not the rule.

Source: Ream, Anne K. "Don Draper, Feminist." *New Republic,* April 20, 2015. https://newrepublic.com/article/121587/female-ad-exec-says-mad-men-gets-it-right.

THE DEPARTMENT OF DEFENSE OPENS COMBAT POSITIONS TO WOMEN, 2015

On December 3, 2015, U.S. secretary of defense Ash Carter announced that the Pentagon was opening all combat positions in every branch of the nation's armed services to women. The decision, which came nearly three years after the Obama administration specifically instructed the U.S. military to open combat jobs to women in their ranks or provide justification for exemptions, opened approximately 220,000 military jobs to women that had previously been off-limits to them. Carter's announcement had its biggest impact on the Marines and the Army, as the Navy and Air Force had already voluntarily opened almost all of their combat-related jobs to women. As the New York Times *noted, the announcement was a particular "rebuke to the Marine Corps, which has a 93 percent male force dominated by infantry and a culture that still segregates recruits by gender for basic training." The Marines had also been the only military branch to ask for a partial exemption (for certain infantry and armor positions), but Carter turned down the request, explaining, "We are a joint force, and I have decided to make a decision which applies to the entire force." Following is the full text of Carter's historic announcement.*

When I became secretary of defense, I made a commitment to building America's force of the future: the all-volunteer military that will defend our nation for generations to come.

Like our outstanding force of today, our force of the future must continue to benefit from the best people America has to offer. In the 21st century, that requires drawing strength from the broadest possible pool of talent.

This includes women, because they make over—up over 50 percent of the American population. To succeed in our mission of national defense, we cannot afford to cut ourselves off from half the country's talents and skills. We have to take full advantage of every individual who can meet our standards.

The Defense Department has increasingly done this in recent decades, in 1975, for example, opening up the military service academies to women, and in 1993, allowing women to fly fighter jets and serve on combat ships at sea.

About the same time, though, DOD also issued the Direct Ground Combat Definition and Assignment Rule, which still prohibited women from being assigned to units whose primary mission was engaging in direct ground combat.

That rule was in turn rescinded in January 2013, when then-Secretary Panetta directed that all positions be opened to qualified women by January 1st, 2016—that is, less than one month from today—while also giving the secretary of the Army, the secretary of the Navy, the secretary of the Air Force and the commander of U.S. Special Operations Command three years to request any exceptions, which would have to be reviewed first by the chairman of the Joint Chiefs of Staff and then approved by the secretary of defense.

As many of you know, I was deputy secretary of defense at the time. That decision reflected, among other things, the fact that by that time the issue of women in combat per se was no longer a question. It was a reality, because women had seen combat throughout the wars in Iraq and Afghanistan, serving, fighting, and in some cases making the ultimate sacrifice alongside their fellow comrades in arms.

We've made important strides over the last three years since then. We've seen women soldiers graduate from the Army's Ranger School. We have women serving on submarines. And we've up—opened up over 111,000 positions to women across the services.

While that represents real progress, it also means that approximately 10 percent of positions in the military—that is, nearly 220,000—currently remain closed to women, including infantry, armor, reconnaissance, and some special operations units.

Over the last three years, the senior civilian and military leaders across the Army, Navy, Air Force, Marine Corps and Special Operations Command have been studying the integration of women into these positions.

And last month I received their recommendations, as well as the data, studies, and surveys on which they were based, regarding whether any of those remaining positions warrant a continued exemption from being opened to women.

I reviewed these inputs carefully. And today, I'm announcing my decision not to make continued exceptions, that is, to proceed with opening all these remaining occupations and positions to women. There will be no exceptions.

This means that, as long as they qualify and meet the standards, women will now be able to contribute to our mission in ways they could not before.

They'll be allowed to drive tanks, fire mortars, and lead infantry soldiers into combat. They'll be able to serve as Army rangers and green berets, Navy SEALS, Marine Corps infantry, Air Force parajumpers and everything else that was previously open only to men.

And even more importantly, our military will be better able to harness the skills and perspectives that talented women have to offer. No exceptions was the recommendation of the secretary of the Army, the secretary of the Air Force, and the secretary of the Navy, as well as the chief of staff of the Army, chief of staff of the Air Force, chief of Naval operations, and the commander of U.S. Special Operations Command.

While the Marine Corps asked for a partial exception in some areas such as infantry, machine gunner, fire support reconnaissance and others, we are a joint force, and I have decided to make a decision which applies to the entire force.

Let me explain how I came to this decision. First, I've been mindful of several key principles throughout this process. One is that mission effectiveness is most important. Defending this country is our primary responsibility, and it cannot be compromised. That means everyone who serves in uniform—men and women alike—has to be able to meet the high standards for whatever job they're in. To be sure fairness is also important, because everyone who's able and willing to serve their country, who can meet those standards, should have the full and equal opportunity to do so. But the important factor in making my decision was to have access to every American who could add strength to the joint force.

Now, more than ever, we cannot afford to have barriers limiting our access to talent. The past three years of extensive studies and reviews leading up to this decision, all of which we're gonna post online, by the way, have led to genuine insights and real progress. Where we found that some standards previously were either outdated or didn't reflect the tasks actually required in combat, important work has been done to ensure each position now has standards that are grounded in real-world operational requirements—both physical and otherwise. So we're positioned to be better at finding not only the most qualified women, but also the qualified men for military specialties.

Another principal is that the careful implementation of integrating women into combat positions would be a key to success—integration. And also that any decision to do so, or not would have to be based on rigorous analysis of factual data. And that's exactly how we've conducted this review.

It's been evidence-based, and iterative. I'm confident the Defense Department can implement this successfully, because throughout our history we've consistently proven ourselves to be a learning organization. Just look at the last decade and a half. We've seen this in war where we adapted to counter insurgency and counter terrorism missions in the wake of 9/11 and in the wars in Iraq and Afghanistan. We've seen it technically, as new capabilities like unmanned systems and cyber capabilities have entered our inventory. And we've also seen it institutionally when we repealed Don't Ask Don't Tell. In every case, our people have mastered change excellently, and they've been able to do so because their leaders have taken care to implement change thoughtfully. Always putting the missions and our people first. We will do the same today.

As we integrate women into the remaining combat positions, we must keep in mind the welfare and total readiness of our entire force. And as we focus on the individual contributions that each service member makes, we also have to remember that in military operations, teams matter. That's why it's important that the services chose to study both individual performance and team performance. And they not only made comparisons to other elite units like NASA, long-duration flight crews, and police SWAT teams, they also worked with our international partners to examine how they have integrated women into ground combat roles.

Again, how we implement this is key. As Chairman Dunford has noted, simply declaring all career fields open is not successful integration. We must not only continue to implement change thoughtfully, but also track and monitor our progress to ensure we're doing it right. Leveraging the skills and strengths of our entire population. All of us have a role to play.

As we proceed with full integration of women into combat roles in a deliberate and methodical manner, I'm directing that seven guidelines be used to steer this implementation.

First, implementation must be pursued with the clear objective of improved force effectiveness. Leaders must emphasize that objective to all service members, men and women alike. Second, leaders must assign tasks and jobs throughout the force based on ability, not gender. Advancement must be based on objective and validated standards.

A good example of this is SOCOM's selection processes which combine objective and substantive criteria in, and I quote, "a whole person concept that includes rigorous physical standards and also strong moral character, leadership skills, mental agility, problem-solving skills, selflessness, maturity and humility."

The third guideline is that for a variety of reasons, equal opportunity likely will not mean equal participation by men and women in all specialties. There must be no quotas or perception thereof. So we will work as a joint force to expertly manage the impacts of what studies may—the studies that have been done suggest may be smaller numbers of women in these fields, the fields that were previously closed.

Fourth, the studies conducted by the services and SOCOM indicate there are physical and other differences on average between men and women. While this cannot be applied to every man or woman, it is real and must be taken into account in implementation. Thus far, we've only seen small numbers of women qualified to meet our high physical standards in some of our most physically demanding combat occupational specialties, and going forward, we shouldn't be surprised if these small numbers are also reflected in areas like recruitment, voluntary assignment, retention and advancement in some of these specific specialties.

Fifth, we'll have to address the fact that some surveys suggest that some service members, both men and women, have a perception that integration would be pursued at the cost of combat effectiveness. Survey data also suggests that women service members emphatically do not want integration to be based on any considerations other than the ability to perform and combat effectiveness. In both cases, based on these surveys, leaders have to be clear that mission effectiveness comes first, and I'm confident that given the strength of our leaders throughout the ranks, over time, these concerns will no longer be an issue.

Sixth, as I noted, both survey data and the judgment of the services leadership strongly indicate that particularly in the specialties that will be opened, the performance of small teams is important, even as individual performance is important.

The seventh guideline has to do with international realities. While we know the United States is a nation committed to using our entire population to the fullest, as are some of our closest friends and allies, we also know that not all nations share this perspective. Our military has long dealt with this reality, notably, over the last 15 years in Iraq and also Afghanistan. And we'll need to be prepared to do so going forward as it bears on the specialties that will be opened by this decision.

With all these factors in mind, Chairman Dunford recommended that if we were to integrate women into combat positions, then implementation should be done in a combined manner by all the services working together. And I agree, and that will be my direction.

Accordingly, I'm directing all the military services to proceed to open all military occupational specialties to women 30 days from today, that is, after a 30-day waiting period required by law, and to provide their updated implementation plans for integrating women into these positions by that date.

Deputy Secretary of Defense Bob Work and Vice Chairman of the Joint Chiefs of Staff Paul—General Paul Selva will work with the services to oversee the short term implementation of this decision, ensure there are no unintended consequences on the joint force, and periodically update me and Chairman Dunford.

Before I conclude, it's important to keep all this in perspective. Implementation won't happen overnight. And while at the end of the day this will make us a better and stronger force, there still will be problems to fix and challenges to overcome. We shouldn't diminish that.

At the same time, we should also remember that the military has long prided itself on being a meritocracy, where those who serve are judged not based on who they are or where they come from, but rather what they have to offer to help defend this country. That's why we have the finest fighting force the world has ever known.

And it's one other way we will strive to ensure that the force of the future remains so long into the future. Today, we take another step toward that continued excellence.

Thank you.

Now, I'll take your questions.

Q: Mr. Secretary, you mentioned that the Marine Corps had asked for a partial exception. The Marine Corps made a very vigorous and detailed case for keeping some combat positions open to men only. In what ways did you find their argument unpersuasive?

SEC. CARTER: I did review the Marine Corps data, surveys, studies, and also the recommendation of the commandant of the Marine Corps at the time, of course who was General Dunford, now our chairman, that certain Marine Corps specialties remain closed to women.

I reviewed that information and I looked at it carefully. I also heard from other leaders of other services who had studied similar issues in their own force, the recommendations of the other service secretaries and service chiefs, and I came to a different conclusion in respect of those specialties in the Marine Corps.

Where I strongly agreed with now Chairman Dunford is two very important points. I noted them in here. The first is that the key here is going to be implementation. And I viewed the—the issues that were raised by all the services, by the way, in varying degrees, and obviously by the Marine Corps, that we needed to take those seriously and address them in implementation. And I believe that the issues raised, including by the Marine Corps, could be addressed successfully in implementation.

And second, that there was great value in having a joint or combined approach to implementation. That's why I have decided to have no exceptions in any service and to have them all working together on implementation.

Q: You said—sorry—just a quick follow-up. You said you came to a different conclusion, obviously. I was asking what about the argument you found lacking?

SEC. CARTER: Because I believe that we could in implementation address the issues that were raised. . . .

Q: Secretary Carter, the three women who made it through the Ranger School, will they now be welcomed into the ranger regiment? Will they become a part of the regiment? Because they weren't until now.

SEC. CARTER: Those—those positions will now be available to women. Once again, just to remind you, you have—people have to qualify for—for positions, positions have to be open and so forth.

So there's a lot that goes into it. But those positions will now be open to them, yes.

Q: And secondly, can we assume that you found the Marine Corps study which concluded that mixed gender units aren't as capable as male units to be flawed?

SEC. CARTER: It—just not definitive, not determinative. There are other issues other than the—those—those studies are reflective of something I spoke of, which is teams do matter and we need to take that into account.

And at the same time, the—the individual's capabilities, and the—the capabilities of the individual to contribute are extremely important. On average, and I said this very directly, men and women will have different physical capabilities. I'm—I—the data show that clearly.

Now, that's on average. So there will be women who can meet the physical requirements of these specialties—even as there are men who cannot meet those requirements.

And so averages tell you something about the need to pay attention to numbers, team dynamics and so forth. But they do not determine whether an individual is qualified to participate in a given unit. . . .

Q:	Mr. Secretary, will the women's desire to enter combat roles or missions be entirely voluntary? Or will there be a time to—where they could, like many of their male counterparts, be required to go into combat missions?
SEC. CARTER:	Absolutely. If you're a service member, you have some choices, but you don't have absolute—absolute choice. People are assigned to missions, tasks, and functions according to need as well as their capabilities. And women will be subject to the same standard and rules that men will. . . .

Source: Carter, Ash. "Department of Defense Press Briefing by Secretary Carter in the Pentagon Briefing Room." December 3, 2015. U.S. Department of Defense. Available online at https://www.defense.gov/News/Transcripts/Transcript-View/Article/632578/department-of-defense-press-briefing-by-secretary-carter-in-the-pentagon-briefi.

SENATOR ERNST EXPRESSES CONCERN ABOUT WOMEN IN GROUND COMBAT POSITIONS, 2016

When the Obama administration announced in December 2015 that all ground combat positions in the U.S. Armed Forces would be opened to women, the public and political reaction was mixed. Most women's rights advocates praised the decision, but many conservative lawmakers and members of the general public expressed profound doubts about the wisdom of such a move. One such critic was Republican senator Joni Ernst of Iowa, a military veteran herself. A long-time member of the Iowa Army National Guard, Ernst had in 2003 commanded 150 soldiers in Kuwait and Iraq. She retired from the National Guard with the rank of lieutenant colonel after 23 years of service. On February 2, 2016, Ernst delivered a formal statement expressing suspicion that the decision to open all combat positions in the U.S. military to women was primarily a "social experiment" rather than an effort to improve America's combat capabilities.

As I have said on numerous occasions, I fully support providing women the opportunity to serve in any military capacity, as long as standards are not lowered and it enhances our combat effectiveness. However, I remain concerned that some within the Administration, and some of my colleagues in Congress, are rushing toward this historical change in policy without much concern for the second and third order effects to our men and women in uniform and our combat capabilities.

In order to ensure women are fully integrated into these previously closed positions, the implementation strategy must be fully developed, and methodically and deliberately implemented, to include having an understanding of second and third order effects to ensure we do not set women, or men, up for failure. These are the men, and will be the women, who meet our enemies in close combat—their lives depend on it.

Over the past few weeks, I have visited Fort Bragg, NC and Marine Corps Base Quantico, Virginia to speak with Soldiers and Marines about this topic. During my trip to Fort Bragg, I sat down with special operations soldiers and paratroopers from the 82nd Airborne Division to discuss gender integration. At Quantico, I had the same open discussion with Marine infantrymen and scout snipers. Both of these groups comprised mostly of mid to senior level NCOs and junior officers—the servicemembers who over the past 14 years of war have met the enemy in close combat—and who will do so again in the future with their female counterparts.

Our discussions began with the understanding that gender integration is the new policy, and now it is time to move forward. Primarily, these young Soldiers and Marines were concerned that gender integration was not being done for the right reasons—to enhance their combat capabilities—and instead as a social experiment. To this point, even as a supporter of gender integration, I share their concern due to the haphazard way this process has been led by some in DoD's civilian leadership. This was especially troubling as we witnessed a distinguished military leader muzzled, inappropriate comments from civilian leadership about our female Marines, and disturbing, unmerited, and unprofessional assertions that our Marine leaders do not value the service of our female Marines.

The other primary concern expressed by these Soldiers and Marines was the implementation strategy, for which I also share their concern. This Congress is being asked to support a policy for which the implementation strategy—which is key to ensuring our military will maintain its combat effectiveness—has not yet been fully developed or revealed. Nor has it taken into account the impacts on women's health, lodging, physiological differences between men and women which could lead to female physical fitness test scores, on average, being lower than their male counterparts, and how that could affect their ability to compete for promotions, schools, and senior command positions.

For example with command positions, most of our Army senior leaders have served in elite units during their time as junior and field grade officers—which is often key to being slotted into command positions from battalion commander and above. GEN Milley is a Special Forces veteran, and others have served in the elite 75th Ranger Regiment like the Army Vice Chief of Staff, LTG John Nicholson—who may be confirmed as the next commander of our troops in Afghanistan, our next potential CENTCOM commander, the 18th Airborne Corps Commander, and division commanders of the 101st and 82nd Airborne Divisions, the 10th Mountain Division, and 3rd Infantry Division.

Also, while there have been three female graduates of Ranger School in the Army, the unfortunate truth is an Infantry officer without a Ranger tab is often looked down upon by their fellow infantrymen, and tab-less Infantry officers are often not as competitive for senior leadership positions.

In the Marine Corps, some of our female Marines have voiced concerns that they anticipate there will be pressure to lower standards if not enough of them are able to qualify to serve in combat positions. Lowering standards for more female participation is against the best military advice of our military leaders, but I agree with these women that the pressure will come—likely from civilian leadership—who have motives other than supporting gender integration to enhance our nation's ability to destroy our enemies on the battlefield.

Female Marines have also voiced that leadership and training will not solve physiological differences between men and women, and some are worried that they will be involuntary assigned to combat MOSs or even assigned to an infantry unit in a support position which would require them to meet the higher physical standards for infantry units.

Furthermore, retention of female Marines and their ability to continue to serve if they are injured while serving in a combat position is an area of concern for some of them. The data is clear—women do get injured at a higher rate than their male counterparts when performing combat arms tasks. Will we allow women to continue to serve in another role or will we medically discharge them if they are injured while serving in a combat position or combat unit? If it becomes commonplace that female combat arms Marines are injured while training, how will that impact unit cohesion, especially for those who will be platoon and company commanders?

After nearly 15 years of war, our country, and many within this Administration, are disconnected from our combat soldiers who have borne the brunt of the battle. These Soldiers and Marines are the best we have. They have taken the majority of the casualties since the founding of our nation and on battlefields from Yorktown, Gettysburg, Iwo Jima, and Normandy—they have made the difference between Americans enjoying life, liberty, and the pursuit of happiness, or being subjugated by foreign powers. Their life is one of mostly suffering and hardship, and they honorably carry that mental and physical burden not only in service, but afterwards as well. We must honor them by ensuring this process moves forward in a thoughtful and methodical way.

Source: Ernst, Joni. "Statement for the Record on Implementation of the Decision to Open All Ground Combat Units to Women." February 2, 2016. Available online at http://www.ernst.senate.gov/public/index.cfm/press-releases?ID=E58515C4 -2722-4DF6-A45E-274DB7C4AF8C.

A WOMAN JOURNALIST DESCRIBES SEXISM AND MISOGYNY IN AMERICAN SPORTS MEDIA, 2016

Julie DiCaro is a Chicago-based sports journalist who became a target of misogynistic Internet trolls for her reporting on the sexual assault investigation into Patrick Kane, a star hockey player for the Chicago Blackhawks. The following is an excerpt from a 2016 essay that DiCaro wrote about the sexism and misogyny that she and other women journalists face—both from sports fans and the sports media industry—when covering sports.

I was never truly aware of sexism until I started working in sports media. In the 13 years I spent as an attorney, I saw and felt a lot of injustice, but it was the kind I recognized: preference based on seniority, office politics or nepotism. It wasn't until I made the move to working full time in sports media that I really felt the soul-crushing, confidence-eroding, rage-inducing injustice of being considered "less" than my colleagues solely because of my gender. Today, I fully register the reality that I am treated differently every day because I am a woman. . . .

Last year, I reported extensively on the Patrick Kane rape investigation. I was repeatedly accused of being biased and reporting only part of the story. Hundreds of men on Twitter demanded I reveal my sources and detail my vetting procedures publicly before they would accept my reporting as accurate. Even when my reports were borne out by later events, I was accused of having an agenda and pushing a narrative. Though I pushed back, demanding to know how I was biased or what facts I was omitting, no one could ever really tell me. While I'd love to believe I was alone in this, women reporting on hot button issues (like Jane McManus on domestic violence in the NFL, and Jessica Luther on sexual assault in college sports) have been subjected to the same questions and accusations.

I've even had my credibility questioned when reporting easily verifiable information, like the World Series schedule or a starting lineup. I am routinely asked "Where did you get this information?" and "Who's your source?" Yet my male co-workers rarely experience these challenges. . . .

Part of the issue for women in sports media is that the industry is even more male-dominated than the rest of media. In part, the public is simply reacting to the lack of trust they see sports media putting in women professionals, who are often relegated to the role of sideline reporters or hosts. . . .

The perceived lack of credibility by female reporters leads to a far uglier problem: online harassment. While a recent Pew study revealed that men are slightly more likely than women to experience online harassment, the harassment experienced by women tends to be disproportionately severe, involving sexual harassment and online stalking. The online harassment women reporters face daily has a distinctly misogynistic bent, using, above all, the reporter's gender, in and of itself, as an insult.

"@JulieDiCaro I feel sorry that you falsely accuse men of doing something they didn't. You are a fat, miserable white c**t" — @masterdon40

"@udpaule: @JulieDiCaro One of the Blackhawks player should beat you to death with their hockey stick like the WHORE you are. C**T"

The message this gendered harassment conveys to women in sports media is clear: You don't belong here by virtue of your gender. You are not credible by virtue of your gender. And for those reasons, you are deserving of violence.

Source: DiCaro, Julie. "Women in Sports Media Face Unrelenting Sexism in Challenges to Their Expertise and Opinions," Women's Media Center, April 30, 2016. http://wmcspeechproject.com/2016/04/30/women-in-sports-media-face-unrelenting-sexism-in-challenges-to-their-expertise-and-opinions/. Used by permission of the Women's Media Center.

MICHELLE OBAMA AND OPRAH WINFREY DISCUSS WOMEN'S EQUALITY, 2016

On June 14, 2016, the Washington Convention Center played host to a "United State of Women Summit" organized by the Obama administration and the Aspen Institute, an international foundation devoted to studying public policy issues and promoting international dialogue. The Summit itself orbited around issues of particular concern to women in America, including economic empowerment and wage equality, changing gender roles, women's health and education issues, political engagement, and violence against women. The day's events also included an extended conversation on "trailblazing the path for a new generation of women" between First Lady Michelle Obama and television personality and media titan Oprah Winfrey. The following is the transcript of their discussion.

MS. WINFREY: Hello.

MRS. OBAMA: We have Oprah Winfrey here. (Applause.)

MS. WINFREY: And our First Lady of the United States. (Applause.)

MRS. OBAMA: Of America.

MS. WINFREY: Of America, not just of women, yes. (Laughter.) So I think that the fact that—I've been watching this being streamed all day, and the fact that there are men here, women here of all ages—young women, maturing women—and all walks of life is a move in the right direction, would you not say?

MRS. OBAMA: Absolutely, absolutely. I'm just proud of all the work that's been done here. So I agree.

MS. WINFREY: Well, I wanted to start with the issue of self-value and self-worth. Because over the years, I've interviewed thousands of people, most of them women, and I would say that the root of every dysfunction I've ever encountered, every problem has been some sense of a lacking of self-value or of self-worth. And I know that we all know that we live in a world where you are constantly being bombarded by images that encourage you to be liked, literally. And it's a lot to live up to. And I wonder, particularly you, who have had to face this as your own woman and as a candidate's wife, the pressure of other people's expectations—and what can you share with our audience here and online that would help us stand more inside ourselves and own that space?

MRS. OBAMA: Very good question. Well, one of the things that I always—I tell my mentees, I tell my daughters is that our first job in life as women, I think, is to get to know ourselves. And I think a lot of times we don't do that. We spend our time pleasing, satisfying, looking out into the world to define who we are—listening to the messages, the images, the limited definitions that people have of who we are. And that's true for women of color for sure. There is a limited box that we are put in, and if we live by that limited definition we miss out on a lot of who we are.

But it takes taking the time to know who you are to be able to deal with the onslaught of negative messages that you're bound to get. So for me, I came into this with a pretty clear sense of myself. And some of that comes with age. Some of that comes with experience. Some of that comes from being fortunate enough to have been raised by a loving mother, strong, focused, and a father who loved me dearly.

So I fortunately came into this situation with a really clear sense of who I was. So when you hear the smack-talking from outside the world, it's easy to sort of brush that off. Because I know who I am. (Applause.)

MS. WINFREY:	But when you came in, there were the world's expectations, there were other expectations. What did you really expect?
MRS. OBAMA:	It's interesting, I really tried not to limit myself by expectations.
MS. WINFREY:	Because nobody grows up thinking "I'm going to be a First Lady."
MRS. OBAMA:	Absolutely not. And as you all know, when Barack was talking about running, I was like, are you crazy? I mean, would you just, like, chill out and do something else with your life? (Laughter.)

So I was working hard to try to get him to do the other thing, so—whatever that was. So, yeah, absolutely, it wasn't something that I could have planned for, could have expected from myself. But one of the things I knew—because people asked all throughout the campaign what are your issues going to be, what are you going to be like as First Lady, and I said, I have to wait until I get there to figure out what that's going to feel like for me. I specifically did not read other First Ladies' books, because I didn't want to be influenced by how they defined the role. I knew that I would have to find this role—(applause)—very uniquely and specifically to me and who I was.

So I came in thinking about who I wanted to be in this position and who I needed to be for my girls, first of all. So you remember, Malia and Sasha were little itty-bitties when we came into office. I mean, it still moves me to tears to think about the first day I put them in the car with their Secret Service agents to go to their first day of school. And I saw them leaving and I thought, what on Earth am I doing to these babies? So I knew right then and there my first job was to make sure they were going to be whole and normal and cared for in the midst of all this craziness. (Applause.) And then I started to understand that if I was going to protect them, I had to, number one, protect myself and protect my time.

So I knew going into this role that I didn't want to waste any time; that any time I spent away from my kids—and I actually took this on even before I became First Lady, even as a lawyer, as a vice president at a hospital. One of the things I realized is that if you do not take control over your time and your life, other people will gobble it up. If you don't prioritize yourself, you constantly start falling lower and lower on your list, your kids fall lower and lower on your list.

MS. WINFREY: So by the time you got here you knew how to do that.

MRS. OBAMA: I knew how to do that.

MS. WINFREY: I think that's one of the number-one issues with women. I never, in all my years of interviewing, have ever heard a man say, you know, I just don't have the time, I just don't, I don't find a way to balance.

MRS. OBAMA: You know why? Because they don't have to balance anything. Sorry. (Laughter and applause.) And I hope that that is changing, but so many men don't have to do it all.

MS. WINFREY: So how did you figure it out? I've read the story—I'm sure many of you have heard the story of early on, you were going to a job interview and you took Sasha with you to interview.

MRS. OBAMA: Oh, yeah.

MS. WINFREY: We never heard, did you get that job?

MRS. OBAMA: I did. I did.

MS. WINFREY: Okay.

MRS. OBAMA: I was the vice president of community outreach for the University of Chicago Hospital. (Applause.) And I got that job because I didn't compromise. Because before getting—working at that job, I was working as an associate dean. I had had Malia, Barack was in the U.S. Senate, so I was basically mothering part time on my own, having—I had a full-time job. So I tried part time—I've talked about this before—I tried part time because I thought, I have to figure this out, I have to be able to pick the kids up, I've got to be able to do all this. So I tried part time. So the only thing I found out from part time was that you just get paid part time. (Applause.) Because I was still doing a full-time job—

MS. WINFREY: Everything, yeah.

MRS. OBAMA: —I was just cramming it all into the few hours that I was there and driving myself crazy. So I had vowed that if I continued to work, that I would never settle for part time. I knew what my time and energy was worth.

So when I went into that—the president's office to interview for that job, I thought, I have a little baby, I don't have babysitting, so here we go, we're all going to go in to see the president because this is who I am. (Laughter.) And I said, and if I take this job, I need flexibility and I need full pay. So if you want me to leave my baby and my kids, then you're going to have to pay me, because I'm going to do the job—that was never a question. I could deliver. But I knew then I wasn't going to sell myself short. And I had the leverage, at the time, to make that decision.

MS. WINFREY: Well, that comes from a sense of—and you said you arrived here knowing who you were. I think that is the journey. That is the journey. And there is a question from FarmFreshGal.

MRS. OBAMA: FarmFreshGal.

MS. WINFREY: She must have her own garden.

MRS. OBAMA: I hope.

MS. WINFREY: Like we do, yes. And FarmFreshGal says, "As a woman leader in the corporate world, I feel like I have to be brave a lot,"—and what you just described was brave—"any advice or tips on bravery?"

MRS. OBAMA: That's a good question. Gosh, I don't know. If I ever—I don't ever view it as bravery.

MS. WINFREY: You didn't think that was brave? Saying, look, I'm going to be paid full time?

MRS. OBAMA: Right.

MS. WINFREY: I think that's brave.

MRS. OBAMA: I just viewed it as I'm not going to be taken advantage of. (Applause.) I am just not going to keep selling myself—

MS. WINFREY: You knew your value.

MRS. OBAMA: Value. That's absolutely right.

MS. WINFREY: You knew your value. I was just saying that to a friend recently.

MRS. OBAMA: And that goes back to knowing who you are. And I think as women and young girls, we have to invest that time in getting to understand who we are and liking who we are. (Applause.) Because I like me. I've liked me for a very long time. (Applause.) So for a long time I've had a very good relationship with myself.

MS. WINFREY: I know.

MRS. OBAMA: And we like—we all like ourselves in here. But you've got to work to get to that place. And if you're going out into the world as a professional and you don't know who you are, you don't know what you want, you don't know how much you're worth, then you have to be brave. And then you have to count on the kindness and goodness of others to bestow that goodness on you when you should be working to get it on your own. Because you deserve it.

MS. WINFREY: Because you know your own value.

MRS. OBAMA: Know your own value. Absolutely. . . .

MS. WINFREY: So how do we get there? You were there. You've loved yourself a long time. What is that process?

MRS. OBAMA: I think it's different for everyone. And I can't say that I've loved myself for a long time, but there was a journey to get there. And some of it starts as a young girl—when you confront your first bully, the first time somebody calls you out—your name, as we would say. The first disappointments and failures that you have, how do you deal with that? What support systems do you set up for yourself?

I always tell young girls, surround yourself with goodness. I learned early on how to get the haters out of my life. (Applause.) You've got to just sort of surround yourself with people who uplift you, who hold you up. And for whatever reason—well, I was lucky I had people like—I had parents who held me up. I had a father that valued me.

MS. WINFREY: I think people who have good parents are—they come into the world with a strength, yes, and an advantage.

MRS. OBAMA: And that was an advantage. But if you don't have that parent—that mother, that father—then you've got to find it. You've got to find those people. Because they're out there. I tell my mentees all of—there is somebody out there who loves you and who is waiting to love you, and you just have to find them. And that means you have to make room for them. And if you're surrounded by a bunch of low-life folks who aren't supporting you, then there is no room for the people who do love you. (Applause.)

MS. WINFREY: You mentioned a moment ago "the haters." How do you handle the haters, particularly in this office, where haters have to be handled politically correctly and with discretion? (Laughter.) And I know so many people are faced with it—we know this about social media—people say just the meanest things, and you're faced in your life with people who can tear you down a lot—the haters, hateration.

MRS. OBAMA: Well, when it comes to social media—there are just times I turn off the world, you know. There are just some times you have to give yourself space to be quiet, which means you've got to set those phones down. You can't be reading all that stuff. I mean, that's like letting somebody just walk up and slap you, you know? (Laughter.) You would never do that. You would never just sit there and go, slap me in the face and I'm good with it. No. So why would you open yourself up to that?

So that's one thing. With social media and—I don't read that stuff. I learned that early in the campaign. I couldn't keep reading stuff about my husband and what people thought and—because I knew who he was. I knew what was going on in our home, in our lives. So I didn't need to read about it from somebody else.

But the other thing that I have found, particularly in this job, that it's—people won't remember what other people say about you, but they will remember what you do. So my strategy—and I've always been like this. When a teacher would come and tell me that I couldn't do something, I would get so much satisfaction proving them wrong. I'd be like, okay, all right, oh, you don't think I'm going to do X, Y and Z, well I'm going to be the best X, Y, Z you can imagine.

So when it came to this role, I just said, you know, let me just be First Lady. Let me wake up every day and work hard to do something of value, and to do it well, and to do something consequential, and to do something that I care about. And then let that speak for itself. . . .

MS. WINFREY: There's a lot of cool men out here. I love the President's speech saying you're looking at a feminist. What can men do leaving here?

MRS. OBAMA: Be better. (Laughter and applause.) Be better at everything. (Applause.) Be better fathers. Good lord, just being good fathers who love your daughters and are providing a solid example of what it means to be a good man in the world, showing them what it feels like to be loved. That is the greatest gift that the men in my life gave to me.

And we've talked about this—the fact that I never experienced abuse at the hands of any man in my life. And that's sad to say that that's a rare reality. So men can be better at that.

Men can be better husbands, which is—be a part of your family's life. Do the dishes. (Applause.) Don't babysit your children. You don't babysit your own children. (Applause.) Be engaged. Don't just think going to work and coming home makes you a man. Being a father, being engaged, all that stuff is important.

Be a better employer. When you are sitting at a seat of power at a table of any kind and you look around you just see you, it's just you and a bunch of men around a table, on a golf course, making deals, and you allow that to happen, and you're okay with that—be better.

MS. WINFREY: Be better.
MRS. OBAMA: Be better.
MS. WINFREY: Be better. (Applause.) I love that.
MRS. OBAMA: Just be better. (Laughter and applause.) I could go on but I'm not. (Laughter.) You get the point, fellas, right? Fellas? (Applause.) What are you going to be?
AUDIENCE MEMBERS: Better!
MRS. OBAMA: There you go.
MS. WINFREY: There you go. (Applause.) So here's the question that comes up over and over and over—we talked a little bit about it—this idea of balance. Is that a false notion for women? Because can we really—are we ever going to have it all? I used to say you can have it all you just can't have it all at one time. Is that a false notion?
MRS. OBAMA: I am always irritated by the "you can have it all" statement. And I grew irritated with that phrase and that expectation the older I got, as you're trying to have it

MS. WINFREY: all. And you're beating yourself up, and feeling less than because you aren't having it all. Because it's a ridiculous aspiration.

MS. WINFREY: Especially if you're looking at everybody else's Facebook page.

MRS. OBAMA: Oh, god, everybody has it all. Everybody is lying. They're lying. (Laughter and applause.) You all need to stop lying. Be real about the fact that—no one gets everything. That was one of the first rules you learned as a little kid. You don't always get your way. Come on, people. You don't always get what you want all the time. And that's true in life.

So what I've told many young people is that you can have it all, but oftentimes it's hard to get it all at the same time.

MS. WINFREY: Yeah, I believe that.

MRS. OBAMA: So it's just a matter of managing expectations. So for me, for example, you know, when your husband is President of the United States and you have children, something has got to give. I've made compromises in my life and my career, but I've also, in exchange, gained a wonderful platform to do some great work. Who would have ever imagined that we would make the inroads we've made on healthy eating and changing the way our kids are fed in school? (Applause.) I can point to so many things that I've had—that I've been able to do. If I want to be heavily involved in my girls' lives that means that sometimes I have to put some things on the back burner to give them what they need.

So it's hard to have it all. But that's where you go back to knowing who you are, and knowing that you're really living through phases. And if you're compromising through one phase of your journey, you're not giving it all up, you're compromising for that phase. There's another phase that's coming up where you might be able to have more of what you thought you wanted. You get to know yourself a little bit more.

So, no, I don't want young women out there to have the expectation that if they're not having it all that somehow they're failing. Life is hard. But life is long if you maintain your health, which is one of the reasons why we talk about health, talk about taking care of yourself. Because you want to get to the next phases in life where you can do more of what you want to do at any given time. . . .

MS. WINFREY: What is the one thing you want us to leave here with? What is the one charge or one offering? What do you want to say?

MRS. OBAMA: It's hard to think of one thing.

MS. WINFREY: Okay, a couple.

MRS. OBAMA: But the work always continues. And by that I mean we're never done. We can never be complacent and think that we've arrived now as women. Because I hear this from young women. Some of you young women who aren't feeling the pains that many of our predecessors have felt—you think, well, there aren't any problems, women's rights, we've got this all figured out, I'm already equal, I'm good—I'm just like, oh, just you wait, you'll feel it.

So the work continues. And for all the young women in this room, all the young men, we can never be complacent. Because we have seen in recent times how quickly things can be taken away if we aren't vigilant, if we don't know our history, if we don't continue the work. (Applause.)

So my hope is that people leave here inspired and ready to do something. Again, remember, it's not what people say about you, it's what you do. So the question is what are you going to do? How are you going to be better? What are you going to change in your office, in your life, in your relationships? What are you going to change in your family dynamic? And how are you going to empower yourself with the knowledge that you need to know what work needs to be done?

We can't afford to be ignorant. We can't afford to be complacent. So we have to continue the work. . . .

Source: Obama, Michelle. "Remarks by the First Lady and Oprah Winfrey in a Conversation at the United State of Women Summit," June 14, 2016. Online by Gerhard Peters and John T. Woolley, the American Presidency Project: http://www.presidency.ucsb.edu/ws/?pid=120902.

STUDY FINDS PERSISTENT GENDER INEQUITIES IN AMERICAN NEWS AND ENTERTAINMENT, 2017

Founded in 2005 by feminist leaders Jane Fonda (1937–), Robin Morgan (1941–), and Gloria Steinem (1934–), the Women's Media Center (WMC) is a progressive nonprofit organization devoted to addressing what it describes as a "crisis" of unequal representation of gender and ethnicity in U.S. media outlets. "We live in a racially and ethnically diverse nation that is 51% female, but the news media itself remains staggeringly limited to a single demographic," according to the WMC. "The media is the single most powerful tool at our disposal; it has the power to educate, effect social change, and determine the political policies and elections that shape our lives. Our work in diversifying the media landscape is critical to the health of our culture and democracy."

As part of its overall mission, the WMC publishes an annual survey of gender representation in major news and entertainment outlets across the United States. The following is the executive summary from its 2017 report. According to a press release, WMC president Julie Burton said that the study results indicate that "men still dominate media across all

platforms—television, newspapers, online, and wires—with change coming only incre-
mentally, and in the case of broadcast news, regressing at the three major networks. Our
research projects on coverage of campus rape and coverage of reproductive rights show that
the gender of the journalist affects how they cover topics and whom they choose as sources.
Women are not equal partners in telling the story, nor are they equal partners in sourcing
and interpreting what and who is important in the story."

Executive summary

Researchers at universities, media think-tanks and media watchers elsewhere have
gauged, empirically, positions women held, work they produced, strides they made
and constraints they faced—across the news, entertainment, online, gaming and
tech industries—since the Women's Media Center's last report.

For its own part, the WMC's annual examination found that, at 20 of the nation's
top news outlets, men produced 62.3 percent of news reports analyzed during a
studied period while women produced 37.7 percent of news reports. That WMC
"Divided 2017" analysis showed hardly any progress since the WMC's previous
"Divided" report, when women produced 37.3 percent of news.

Additionally, in the broadcast news sector alone, work by women anchors, field
reporters and correspondents actually declined, falling to 25.2 percent of reports
in 2016 from 32 percent when the WMC published its 2015 "Divided" report.

Here is a summary of the other key findings in this report:

- The American Society of News Editors stopped requiring newsrooms to
disclose the names of their organizations alongside race and gender personnel data. The change aimed to get more of ASNE's 1,734 member newspapers and online-only news sites to be more forthcoming about who's on
their staffs.
- At least one woman was among the top three editors at 77 percent of respond-
ing ASNE organizations.
- At least one person of color was among the top three editors at 28 percent of
those news organizations.
- Females accounted for more than a third of ASNE newsroom employees
overall, with more employed at online-only sites than at newspapers.
- Men wrote 52 percent of bylined news articles and opinion pieces about
reproductive issues in the nation's 12 most widely circulated newspapers and
news wires. Women penned 37 percent.
- Whites comprised 83.06 percent of the overall workforce among ASNE
respondents.
- Women penned 37 percent of bylined news articles and opinion pieces
about reproductive issues in the nation's 12 most widely circulated newspapers and news wires.
- Men won 84 percent and whites 84 percent of a century's worth of Pulitzer
Prizes. Women won 16 percent; persons of color 16 percent.

- Women earned less—and minority women, substantially less—than men at Dow Jones and its flagship international newspaper, The Wall Street Journal.
- The number of female assistant sports editors at 100 U.S. and Canadian newspapers and websites fell by roughly half between 2012 and 2014—from 17.2 percent of all such editors to 9.8 percent. Men were 91.2 percent.
- TV news saw a record rise in minority female news directors and overall minority workforce—but that sector's employees still are a long way from reflecting the nation's demographic profile.
- The tally of female radio and TV news directors rose to 33.1 percent in 2015, a roughly 2-percentage-point increase from 2014.
- Minorities comprised 17.2 percent of all radio and TV news directors, up from 13.5 percent in 2014 and breaking a record of 15.5 percent, set in 2008.
- Women radio and TV news staffers, overall, made up 44.2 percent of that workforce, up from 42.3 percent in 2014, but were more likely to be working in the smallest markets.
- Among minorities in radio and TV news, only Asians declined in number, falling 0.2 percent since 2014.
- At TV news stations broadcasting in English—where the workforce remained overwhelmingly white—11.4 percent of newsroom staffs were black, up from 11.1 percent previously; 6.7 percent were Latino, up from 5.9 percent; 2.7 percent were Asian, down from 2.9 percent; and 0.4 percent were Native American, up slightly from 0.3 percent.
- Male voices outnumbered female ones 2 to 1 at National Public Radio, whose top stations' boards of directors were 67 percent male.
- White men continued to prevail on Sunday political talk shows, where the hosts were overwhelmingly male.
- Of the top 100–rated radio talk shows, 87 were hosted by men; 13 by women.
- On the 250 top-grossing domestic films of 2015–16, the tally of female directors, writers, producers, executive producers, editors and cinematographers, combined, fell to 17 percent—the same rate as in 1998. Ninety-two percent of those films had no women directors, and 58 percent had no women executive producers.
- On box-office blockbusters of 2013 and 2014, men accounted for 97 percent of film directors; women accounted for 3 percent of film directors.
- When women wrote the screenplay for small-budget, independent projects, they returned to their investors $3.07 for every dollar spent, while small projects with men writers returned $2.34. The ROI was $2.76 per dollar on films with female lead actors but $2.30 for those with male leads; and $2.65 per dollar on films with female producers but $2.35 per dollar on those with male producers.
- Films with diverse casts received the highest median global box office receipts and ROI.

- Men outnumbered women 2 to 1 as film leads in 2014–15.
- Whites outnumbered non-whites roughly 3 to 1 among film lead actors, 4 to 1 among film directors and 7 to 1 among film writers.
- Women directed 11 percent of American films that could vie for 2017 Oscars.
- At the 10 largest U.S.-based international short film festivals, 68 percent of directors were male over the last five years—a period when the number of females directing short films remained unchanged.
- On entertainment shows available on TV or online, those with at least one female executive producer had more female characters.
- The number of women directors of entertainment TV shows rose slightly, but among first-time directors, women and people of color were largely absent.
- The number of female directors on 270 primetime TV network, cable and high-budget series originating and streaming online rose to 16 percent from 14 percent.
- Women comprised roughly a third of the 11,306 speaking characters in film, TV and digital shows.
- 11 percent of speaking characters in a subset of top-grossing films were aged 60 and older. Of that group, 72.8 percent were men—even as aging women are a substantially larger subset of the U.S. population.
- Of the 895 characters regularly slated to appear in primetime TV series on ABC, NBC and CBS in 2016–17, 43 were lesbian, gay, bisexual, transgender or queer, the highest proportion since GLAAD began its count.
- Hollywood's top paid union executive—a man—earned 60 percent more than the highest-paid female union executive.
- Females constituted 30 percent of playwrights and 33 percent of directors for five seasons' worth of Off-Broadway and Off-Off-Broadway shows at 22 theaters.
- For founders of 700 tech start-ups, creating a diverse workforce ranked 7th on their list of 10 top priorities in business.
- The workforce at the top global tech and social media firms remained overwhelmingly white and male—especially in the C-suite—as those firms also cited some incremental progress toward diversifying their workplaces.
- 40 percent of female engineers leave the job within five to eight years, and that problem seemed more acute among women being groomed for the C-suite.
- 30 percent of surveyed female engineers who left the job attributed their decision to a clash between corporate culture and the women's own goals and life outlook.
- The number of female gamers declined between 2015 and 2016 but has risen overall since 2002.
- Women were protagonists in seven out of 76 showcased games at a major annual expo.

- When it came to perceived sexism against female candidates during Election 2016, polled voters rated social media the No. 1 and cable TV the No. 2 offenders.
- More students enrolled in non-journalism courses; and fewer college journalism and communications professors had backgrounds in journalism.
- Journalism and communications professors, overall, were more likely to be female and not tenured.

Especially at TV networks, women report less of the news—even less than in previous years.

A Women's Media Center report, examining who provides coverage for 20 top news outlets, shows that female journalists continue to report less of the news than do male journalists.

The study, which monitored news outlets for three months of 2016, found that the disparity exists in traditional newspapers, online news, wire services and television news, but is especially glaring in TV news. At ABC, CBS and NBC combined, men report three times as much of the news as women do. In that broadcast sector, work by women field reporters and correspondents has actually declined, falling to 25.2 percent of reports in 2016 from 32 percent when the Women's Media Center published its 2015 "Divided" report.

That analysis aids the WMC's efforts to help level the playing field for women in not only the news business, but also other media platforms.

Overall, at those 20 outlets, men produce 62.3 percent of the analyzed reports while women produce 37.7 percent, roughly the same amount as the 37.3 percent documented in WMC's previous yearly report.

"It's deeply disheartening to see the regression in evening broadcast news at the three major networks," says WMC President Julie Burton. "Who tells the story is as important as what the story is. Our research continues to show that, overwhelmingly, it is men who are telling the story."

"Divided" analyzed bylines, on-camera correspondent appearances and TV producer credits on 24,117 pieces of content produced from Sept. 1, 2016 through Nov. 30, 2016 by those broadcast networks' news divisions; the online news sites of CNN, Fox News, Huffington Post and The Daily Beast; and 10 of the nation's most widely circulated newspapers. They are: Chicago Sun-Times, Los Angeles Times; New York Daily News, New York Post, San Jose Mercury News, The Denver Post, The New York Times, The Wall Street Journal, The Washington Post and USA Today.

WMC's researchers also found that "PBS NewsHour"—where award-winning journalist Gwen Ifill's death in November 2016 left Judy Woodruff the lone member of what had been an all-female anchoring duo—again leads evening news broadcasts in producing the work of female news correspondents. There, men produce 55.0 percent of the news and women, 45.0 percent.

Conversely, ABC News comes in last among the four studied broadcast news operations. For each story with a female correspondent, there are four stories by a male correspondent.

In newspapers, since WMC's last and this current report, The New York Times has done the most to narrow the gap between female- and male-produced journalism. The widest gender gap is at the New York Daily News.

Compared to the other sectors, women garner more bylines—46.1 percent of all bylines—at the four online news sites, combined. Men receive 53.9 percent of bylines. Online news sites, however, are more reliant on freelancers who have less work stability and whose per-article fees are comparatively low. Also, some of those news sites also publish the work of unpaid contributors, some of whom are not journalists.

Best byline counts for women at newspapers are at the San Jose Mercury News, then The Washington Post

None of the print outlets achieve gender parity although The San Jose Mercury News and The Washington Post have the narrowest gap.

In descending order, here are the overall byline percentages at newspapers:

- New York Daily News: 76.0 percent men; 24.0 percent women, down from 30.6 percent.
- USA Today: 69.9 percent men; 30.1 percent women, down from 33 percent.
- The Denver Post: 65.7 percent men; 34.3 percent women, up from 31.7 percent.
- The Wall Street Journal: 65.7 percent men; 34.3 percent women, down from 39.2 percent.
- New York Post: 63.6 percent men; 36.4 percent women, down from 37.2 percent.
- The New York Times: 61.0 percent men; 39.0 percent women, up from 32.3 percent.
- Chicago Sun-Times: 59.8 percent men; 40.2 percent women, down from 54.2.
- Los Angeles Times: 59.8 percent men; 40.2 percent women, which is largely unchanged.
- The Washington Post, 57.5 percent men; 42.5 percent women, up from 39.8 percent.
- San Jose Mercury News, 55.7 percent men; 44.3 percent women, up from 41.0 percent.

Of four major TV newscasts, females fared best at PBS

In descending order, as a proportion of on-camera and producer credits:

- "ABC World News": 88.2 percent men; 11.8 percent women, down from 29.7 percent.
- "CBS Evening News": 67.8 percent men; 32.2 percent women, up from 29.1 percent.

- "NBC Nightly News": 67.7 percent men; 32.3 percent women, down from 43.1 percent.
- "PBS NewsHour": 55.0 percent men; 45 percent women, up from 44.1 percent.

Reuters still leads wire competitor Associated Press in female bylines

Of the two main traditional news wires, supplying news to subscriber newsrooms throughout the world, Reuters again has a higher proportionate tally of female bylines.

At both services, slightly more than one-third of bylines go to women:

- Reuters: 61.1 percent men; 38.9 percent women, down from 41.3 percent.
- Associated Press: 64.6 percent men; 35.4 percent women, down from 35.6 percent.

Fox News' online site outpaced four other digital portals

In descending order, as a proportion of online bylines:

- The Daily Beast: 61.7 percent men; 38.3 percent women, up from 31.2 percent.
- CNN: 54.6 percent men; 45.4 percent women, up from 43.1 percent.
- The Huffington Post: 50.8 percent men; 49.2 percent women, down from 53 percent.
- Fox News: 50.1 percent men; 49.9 percent women, up from 39.7 percent.

On the news beat. . . .

More than half of 2016's women's bylines are on lifestyle, health and education news. (A disproportionate number of lifestyle articles are written by columnists, who, the researchers wrote, help skew that tally toward women.)

Conversely, men produce most stories on sports, weather and crime and justice. Topics, in descending order:

- Sports: 88.6 percent men; 11.4 percent women, up from 10 percent.
- Weather: 71.8 percent men; 28.2 percent women, down from 30 percent.
- Crime and justice: 68.5 percent men; 31.5 percent women, down from 32.5 percent.
- Religion: 67.2 percent men; 32.8 percent women, down from 49.6 percent.
- U.S. politics: 66.1 percent men; 33.9 percent women, down from 34.7 percent.
- Tech: 63.1 percent men; 36.9 percent women, down from 37.7 percent.
- Domestic issues: 63.0 percent men; 37.0 percent women.

- World Politics: 62.7 percent men; 37.3 percent women, up from 34.9 percent.
- Culture: 62.4 percent men; 37.6 percent women, down from 42.2 percent.
- Business and economics: 60.3 percent men; 39.7 percent women, up from 37.7 percent.
- Entertainment: 60.1 percent men; 39.9 percent women, down from 41.3 percent.
- Social issues: 56.3 percent men; 43.7 percent women.
- Science: 50.6 percent men; 49.4 percent women, up from 35.2 percent.
- Health: 49.5 percent men; 50.5 percent women, up from 49.3 percent.
- Education: 46.4 percent men; 53.6 percent women, roughly the same as last year's 54.6 percent.
- Lifestyle news and commentary: 43.2 percent men; 56.8 percent women, up from 49.6 percent.

Source: Women's Media Center (WMC). *The Status of Women in the U.S. Media 2017.* WMC, 2017, pp. 4–8. http://wmc.3cdn.net/10c550d19ef9f3688f_mlbres2jd.pdf. Used by permission of the Women's Media Center.

PRESIDENT TRUMP SPEAKS IN SUPPORT OF WOMEN'S EMPOWERMENT, 2017

Stung by charges that the Trump administration was insensitive to women's health, education, career, and child care issues, and that the president himself did not respect women or their capabilities, the Trump White House and its supporters (including his wife Melania and daughter Ivanka) spent the opening months of Trump's opening months in office highlighting policies, practices, and administration appointments that they said showed his deep concern for women's empowerment, both inside the workplace and out. One of the vehicles for conveying this message was a Women's Empowerment Panel hosted at the White House in late March 2017. The following are Trump's opening remarks at this event.

Thank you very much. What an amazing audience this is. So many young faces that represent the future of leadership in our country. So true. Melania and I are deeply honored to join you. And, Melania, thank you for being here.

So as you know, Melania is a very highly accomplished woman and really an inspiration to so many. And she is doing some great job. In fact, I shouldn't say this, but her poll numbers went through the roof last week. What was that all about? Through the roof. She has to give us the secret, Mike, right? Anyway, I appreciate it very much.

My Cabinet is full of really incredible women leaders. Administrator Linda McMahon, who has been a friend of mine for a long time—long time. She's done an incredible job in business, by the way. Administrator Seema Verma, Secretary Betsy DeVos, and, of course, my good friend from South Carolina who is a very tough competitor, I want to tell you—Nikki Haley, Ambassador. She is doing fantastically well. And we're also joined, of course, by Florida Attorney General, highly respected, Pam Bondi. So I want to thank you, Pam. Thank you.

Elaine Chao, our Secretary of Transportation, who's a real expert. She was Secretary of Labor, but she said, I really wanted to be Secretary of Transportation. That's a real expertise, and she's doing incredibly. She would have been here, but she's celebrating the 50th anniversary of the Department of Transportation right now as we speak. And we're going to work on infrastructure and we're going to put up one of the big and great infrastructure bills of all time. We're going to get our infrastructure fixed in our country, and we're going to rebuild our country, and that's what we need. Lots of jobs, also.

And I want to thank Ford—you saw their big announcement yesterday. And so many others are announcing tremendous numbers of jobs. They're not leaving our country anymore, folks. They're not leaving; they're staying and they're building right here.

So we really have these incredibly strong and dedicated leaders, and they're with me and they're with us. And I'm very happy about it. And I want to thank you as being representative, very much, of our group. Thank you all very much. Thank you.

And I'm so proud that the White House and our administration is filled with so many women of such incredible talent. This week, as we conclude Women's History Month, we honor a great woman of American history. Since the very beginning, women have driven—and I mean each generation of Americans—toward a more free and more prosperous future.

Among these patriots are women like the legendary Abigail Adams—right?—who, during the founding, urged her husband to remember the rights of women. She was very much a pioneer in that way.

We've been blessed with courageous heroes like Harriet Tubman, who escaped slavery—and went on to deliver hundreds of others to freedom, first on the Underground Railroad, and then as a spy for the Union Army. She was very, very courageous, believe me.

And we've had leaders like Susan B. Anthony—have you heard of Susan B. Anthony?—I'm shocked that you've heard of her—who dreamed of a much more equal and fair future, an America where women themselves, as she said, "helped to make laws and elect the lawmakers." And that's what's happening more and more. Tough competition out there, I want to tell you.

From the untamed frontiers of the Western Plains to the skyscrapers of Manhattan, American women in every generation have shown extraordinary grit, courage, and devotion. Our present generation stands on the shoulders of these titans—and that's what they were and are—titans. Only by enlisting the full potential of women in our society will we be truly able to—you have not heard this expression before—make America great again. It's a good expression.

Thank you. Thank you, everybody. Thank you. It's been a lot of fun. And we didn't get that one from Madison Avenue, right?

My administration will work every day to ensure that our economy is a place where women can work, succeed, and thrive like never before. That includes fighting to make sure that all mothers and all families have access to affordable childcare.

We want every daughter in America to grow up in a country where she can believe in herself, believe in her future, and follow her heart and realize her dreams.

And we want a country that celebrates family, that celebrates community, and that creates a safe and loving home for every child—every child. That's what we want.

Earlier this year, I met with a remarkable group of leaders. They were women entrepreneurs from all across the country. They started their businesses from absolutely nothing, and today have grown them into successful enterprises that employ hundreds—and in certain cases, even thousands—of people. Just think of what our country could achieve if we unleashed the power of women entrepreneurs nationwide. Think of that.

So, as a man, I stand before you as President. But if I weren't President, I wouldn't be happy to hear that statement. That would be a very scary statement to me because there's no way we can compete with you. So I would not be happy. Just wouldn't be happy.

One of the business owners I met, Lisa Phillips, used to be homeless. She now is the owner of an event-planning company, and she trains homeless youth in Baltimore for good-paying jobs. Lisa had a message for all of us. As she put it, "This is a country of chances . . . if you're willing to work hard, you'll get the chance." And she means it, and she's become very successful. She's terrific.

Lisa is right—but we have to fight to ensure that more people have the chance to succeed. To do that, we must believe in each other, and we must dare to dream of a better, brighter, and more prosperous future for all of our citizens. We have no choice. That's what we have to do.

And to be honest, whether you're a woman or whether you're a man, you have that same dream: You want to be able to dream. You just have a big advantage over us. You know why? Right there. There's a lot of truth to that, Mike, right?

That's what I want for each and every one, and each and every one of our daughters and our granddaughters. And I know, together, we will get there. I want every young person in the audience today, and watching from home—and they're all over the place; those cameras are all over—to know that the future truly belongs to you. We are Americans, and we will not stop until we have achieved our dreams.

I want to thank you very much for being here. It's my great honor, I will tell you, to be here. In fact, Melania said, this is something I just have to be at. She feels so strongly about it. She feels so strongly about it.

So thank you, God bless you, and God bless America. Thank you very much. Thank you.

Source: Trump, Donald. "Remarks by President Trump at Women's Empowerment Panel." March 29, 2017. White House, Office of the First Lady. Available online at https://www.whitehouse.gov/the-press-office/2017/03/29/remarks-president-trump-womens-empowerment-panel.

DEMOCRATIC SENATORS URGE PRESIDENT TRUMP TO "REVERSE COURSE ON ANTI-WOMEN'S AGENDA," 2017

The 2016 presidential election between Republican nominee Donald Trump and Democratic nominee Hillary Clinton was one of the most bitter and contentious elections in American history. Not only did the election take place at a time when political polarization—fueled in no small part by the ascendance of ideologically rigid news media—seemed to be reaching ever higher levels, the contest also was marked by incidents of blatant misogyny and bitter recriminations about gender roles and expectations in American society. Critics of Clinton's campaign on both the left and right alleged that her election campaign spent too much time trying to convince voters to support her just because she was a woman. But while Clinton and her supporters rejected that charge, her gender was indisputably a recurring element of campaign coverage. This was especially true because Trump cultivated a dominant, hyper-masculine persona on the campaign trail, even after revelations of lewd and sexist statements and actions from his past were revealed. "Trump's slogan 'make America great again' seemed to invoke a return to a never-never land of white male supremacy where coal was an awesome fuel, blue-collar manufacturing jobs were what they had been in 1956, women belonged in the home, and the needs of white men were paramount," asserted feminist writer Rebecca Solnit in the London Review of Books. *"After the election, many on the left joined in the chorus, assuring us that Clinton lost because she hadn't paid enough attention to the so-called white working class, which, given that she wasn't being berated for ignoring women, seemed to be a euphemism for 'white men.' These men were more responsible than any group for Trump's victory (63 percent of them voted for him; 31 percent for Clinton). . . . I've always had the impression—from TV, movies, newspapers, sport, books, my education, my personal life, and my knowledge of who owns most things and holds government office at every level in my country—that white men get a lot of attention already."*

These tensions did not ease after Trump's inauguration on January 20, 2017. One day after he was sworn in as the nation's 45th president, more than two million Americans participated in a massive Women's March at cities across the country to urge resistance against a Trump administration that was characterized as hostile to women's rights. These assertions that Trump and the conservative Republican leadership controlling Congress posed significant threats to women's rights and gender equality continued to be echoed through the first few months of Trump's presidency, as this May 2, 2017, letter from 31 Democratic senators to President Trump makes clear.

Mr. President,

On Saturday, January 21, 2017, women, men, and families across this country and around the globe marched for fairness and equity for all people in historic numbers. Fears of attacks on women's health and the fundamental rights so many women value led to this historic march. Sadly, just 100 days into your administration, many of those fears have already become reality. We ask that you listen to the millions of people who have urged you to support women's rights and cease these despicable attacks.

During the relatively short time since your inauguration, women and their families have been under a constant and unprecedented attack. While women have succeeded in fighting back against key aspects of your agenda thus far, there is no question that your leadership threatens to roll back decades of progress on women's health and rights, as you have taken even standard Republican policies to a new and devastating extreme. As Members of Congress committed to advancing health and economic security, we find it especially unacceptable that your administration has prioritized the following actions:

- "Defunding" Planned Parenthood: Even though you have acknowledged the critical role of Planned Parenthood health centers in providing access to basic health care, your administration has caved to the most extreme anti-women's health special interests by supporting "defunding" Planned Parenthood. While your Administration's recent efforts to defund Planned Parenthood within the disastrous Trumpcare legislation failed, should you succeed, countless women who rely on Medicaid will be blocked from seeking health care from the provider of their choice, which is often the only safety net provider available where they live.
- Repealing the Affordable Care Act: Your administration continues to support repeated attempts to advance the Trumpcare bill, or the American Health Care Act (AHCA). This legislation would devastate our health system and rip coverage away from 24 million people. Those lucky enough to maintain coverage would be forced to pay more for less, as premiums and deductibles climb while benefits decline. The most recent version of AHCA includes provisions that would harm women and their families by gutting maternity care and allowing insurers to charge more for plans that include services women rely on.
- Global Gag Rule: Your administration reinstated and dramatically expanded a version of the harmful global gag rule, targeting non-U.S. organizations that work on any U.S.-funded global health program, including HIV/AIDS prevention and treatment, maternal and child health, and Zika programs. These groups are now banned from all global health funding from the U.S. government if they also happen to provide counseling, referrals, or services for safe and legal abortion—even with their own funding. This historic action will be catastrophic for communities abroad, especially those relying on U.S. funding to address HIV/AIDS, maternal health care, and the fight against Zika, which also protects women and families here at home.
- Eliminating U.S. Funding to United Nations Population Fund (UNFPA): Your administration followed up on the devastating impact of the widening of the global gag rule by eliminating all U.S. funding to UNFPA, one of the most wide-reaching and vital sources of contraceptive and child and maternal health services in the world. UNFPA works in more than 150 countries to facilitate safe births, protect girls from child marriage and female genital mutilation, and provide access to voluntary contraception for women and men. In more than 100 of these countries, USAID does not operate a family planning program, rendering UNFPA's presence even more crucial. UNFPA operates internationally in refugee camps to combat maternal mortality by

providing critical health services that are otherwise unavailable to women and their infant children.

- Appointments that Jeopardize Women's Health: The recent confirmation of your Attorney General and Secretary of Health and Human Services are the most high-profile examples of you working to stock the government with anti-choice voices committed to rolling back the protections women have fought hard for over recent decades. With a historically high amount of vacancies still persistent across the government, we fear that additional appointments will be made that could further erode women's health and rights.

- Nominating a Supreme Court Justice who has harmed women's health: You repeatedly promised to nominate someone to the U.S. Supreme Court who would support overturning *Roe v. Wade*. Throughout the confirmation process, there was no indication that now-Justice Neil Gorsuch failed to meet that promise. Throughout his judicial career, Justice Gorsuch has demonstrated he does not prioritize the rights of women to make their own choices or have access to the care they need. Justice Gorsuch didn't just agree with the Tenth Circuit's ruling in the case of *Hobby Lobby v. Burwell*—he thought the ruling should have gone further. His confirmation—achievable only after your allies in the Senate changed longstanding rules to put him on the bench with only a majority, party-line vote—comes at a time when 70 percent of Americans support a woman's constitutionally-protected right to choose.

- Attacks on Title X Family Planning Providers: You signed a resolution behind closed doors that eliminated important protections in Title X, the nation's family planning program, after Vice President Pence was brought in to cast two tiebreaking votes to advance this harmful legislation in the Senate. The protections you eliminated clarified that health centers could not be prohibited from serving people under Title X for arbitrary or politically-motivated reasons that are unrelated to their ability to provide high-quality care. This resolution threatens access to birth control for four million people who depend on Title X.

- Budget Priorities: Though we have not yet seen your full budget priorities for fiscal year (FY) 2018, your proposal for the remainder of FY 2017 would gut the Teen Pregnancy Prevention Program, a cost effective sex education program for young people that has been proven to reduce sexual risk behaviors and has helped reduce teen pregnancy to a national historic low. In yet another clear sign that your administration de-prioritizes the promotion of women and girls, it has also been reported that your FY18 budget will not only eliminate the ambassador-at-large for Global Women's Issues at the State Department, but will also completely eliminate funding for the Office of Global Women's Issues.

You ran on the idea of promoting economic security for Americans. Your actions to erode reproductive rights completely undermine that promise as reproductive rights are a key part of economic security for women and their families. The ongoing threat your administration poses to reproductive rights and economic security has motivated women and men nationwide. People across the country are turning out in record numbers at town halls, calling their members of Congress, and engaging in the legislative process like never before. Your administration can no longer ignore this groundswell. It should instead begin to listen to the voices of communities nationwide.

If your administration began to listen to the people it represents, you would reverse your harmful agenda and start to prioritize women's access to health care, employment opportunities, and education domestically and around the world. We call on your Administration to do just that, and put the lives of women and working families ahead of ideological and partisan attacks.

Source: U.S. Senate, Office of Senator Maria Cantwell. Letter to President Trump, May 5, 2017. Available online at https://www.cantwell.senate.gov/news/press-releases/cantwell-murray-and-senate-dems-call-on-president-trump-to-reverse-course-on-anti-womens-agenda_.

Index

About the Editor

CONSTANCE L. SHEHAN, PHD, is a professor of sociology and women's studies at the University of Florida She received her PhD in sociology from the Pennsylvania State University. Dr. Shehan's primary areas of expertise are gender, families, and employment. Much of her published work focuses on women's work inside and outside the family. She has published numerous journal articles as well as several books, including the *Wiley Blackwell Encyclopedia of Family Studies* (2016); *The Family Issues Reader* (2016); *Gendering the Body*, with Sara Crawley and Lara Foley (2007); *Marriage and Families: Reflections of a Gendered Society* (1997 and 2003); and *Through the Eyes of a Child: Re-Visioning Children as Active Agents of Family Life* (1999). She is also editor of the *Journal of Family Issues*, published by Sage. She is a Fellow of the National Council on Family Relations, an interdisciplinary and international association of family researchers, educators, and policy makers.